"And the rooks still go home to roost at Apley,
and just when you think you've counted the last one,
another party of stragglers appears in the dusk."
(Cyril Lee, Worfield Parish Magazine November 1935)

Geoff Stephens shearing in 2014

MARGERY THE MUSTARD MAKER

Tales from in and around Worfield

Jane Smith

ISBN: 978-0-9573505-5-7
JS Books WV6 7UE

CONTENTS

ILLUSTRATIONS

ACKNOWLEDGEMENTS

Ingrid Millington encouraged me to put pen to paper more than ten years ago when she suggested that I write a piece for the Parish Magazine on Worfield's history. That single piece became a 1,000 word article each month, a good discipline but a tough one, and there were months when I wished that I hadn't agreed to it. Thanks are due to Ingrid and also to the editor of the magazine, Sarah Millington, who has invariably had to wait for each article.

Many people have contributed to this book, either by writing their own stories or by giving me valuable information. Without this generous sharing of information, Worfield's history would be the poorer.

Ralph Collingwood, Paul Walshe and the late Cicely Taylor, have worked with me each week for nearly ten years, translating Worfield's Manor Court Rolls from Medieval Latin to English. They have helped me build up my linguistic skills and to understand what is written in a wider historical context. I never cease to be amazed at their knowledge. We carry on the work of the late Dr. Sylvia Watts, a teacher of Medieval Latin par excellence, and hope that she would be pleased with our efforts.

Proof reading such a lengthy book is a hard task and I am so grateful to Margaret King and Sandra Barber for finding and correcting my errors.

Finally, it would be remiss of me not to acknowledge the help of my faithful companion, Winnie, without which the book would have been completed much sooner.

INTRODUCTION

This book is a compilation of the articles written for Worfield Parish Magazine with some additions. With no obvious link between most of these short stories, a topographical approach seemed the most logical but some articles covered the whole parish, and others seemed to be better dealt with chronologically. Try as I might, I found no one way of organising the material in a uniform way for which I apologise.

Contrary to popular belief, The Wheel of Worfield or The Wheel of Worvill, as it used to be known, does not denote that it is in Worfield village. Rather confusingly, The Wheel is actually in Wyken (which may have been pronounced Wicken), while Worfield village is tucked away to the north. Why this tiny village was the focus for such a huge parish I have no idea. Reputedly the second largest parish in the country, most of those who live within its boundaries would struggle to draw a map of its extent.

Worfield is an odd name. Open land on the Worfe, is one suggested derivation with the name Worfe being derived from the Old English Worig meaning wandering. However, there is a town in Germany called Worfelden and the derivation I favour is that the Saxon settlers simply named Worfield after their home in Germany. Worfelden apparently comes from ur meaning moist and feld meaning field, which describes Worfield's situation perfectly. But why Worfield and not Urfield you might ask? The explanation may lie in the common practice of prefixing a word beginning with a vowel with a 'w'. In medieval times, Oldington was often written Woldington, and we still hear the usage in the Black Country dialect pronunciation of home as 'wum'. I believe that the river name was then a shortened form of Worfield, that is the River Worfe.

The settlement pattern of the parish was probably well established before 1066, as was a system of local government based on Hundreds. William the Conqueror replaced this with the manorial system based on Lords of the Manor enforcing the law of the land on the King's behalf. For the King's entertainment, large areas of the country were designated Royal Forests, one of which, the Forest of Morfe, included Worfield south of the River Worfe. Strict regulations were applied within the Forest with harsh and cruel penalties for those who broke the law. The system of agriculture across the Manor of Worfield based on three common fields and common or waste, gradually gave way to enclosed fields and by the beginning of the nineteenth century, all the open common land had disappeared. There was no longer room for the small tenant farmer with a few cattle or sheep, and by the twentieth century, machinery had replaced the agricultural workers on whom output had previously depended. Transport has had a big effect on the parish with three major roads separating areas on either side of the road. Particularly isolated in this way has been the area to the west of the A442 Bridgnorth to Telford Road which contains the villages of Newton, Oldington and Ewdness.

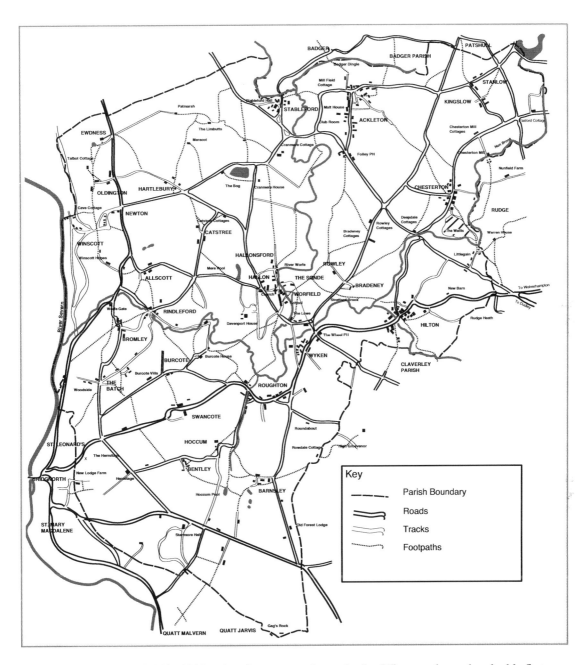

The Parish of Worfield in 1933, taken from a map drawn by Joy Wigram who took a double first at Cambridge and taught at Worfield school 1932-3. The map was a silver wedding gift to the Revd. & Mrs Lunt who gave it to the Parochial Church Council. For many years the map hung in the Old Club Room and at the time of writing is in the Church.

A RURAL PARISH

FARMING

Man has been moulding the natural landscape of Worfield since he first arrived in the parish. Some of these changes have left marks in the landscape still visible on the ground while others can be identified only by aerial photography. Clearance of natural woodland, enclosures, and improvements in agricultural practices during the agricultural revolution have all played their part in creating the modern farming systems we have today.

Initially, Worfield may have been a place of temporary rather than permanent residence but by Saxon times it consisted of small clusters of houses surrounded by three open fields (known as common fields) and common land or waste. Crops were grown on the common fields which were divided into strips and livestock were grazed on the commons and the aftermath in the common fields after the harvest had been taken. The system of agriculture was seemingly unchangeable, laid down in local statutes known as the Customs of the Manor which dictated ownership of land and farming practices. Yet certainly from the fourteenth century, for which we have the manor court rolls, strips in the common fields were being exchanged with those of their neighbours to provide a more easily managed unit which could be enclosed. Common land was also being enclosed as early as the fourteenth century. In 1368, for example, permission was granted to enclose parts of Stanlowe Common.[1]

Permitted enclosures, sometimes called crofts, are mentioned from the fourteenth century, such as that of Robert Faber, in 1345, who surrendered a workshop with a croft in Roughton.[2] Large areas of land were enclosed, 30 acres, in the case of Richard Bradney of Hilton who, in 1677, asked the Lord of the Manor, William Whitmore, for permission to enclose.[3] Permission was granted on the understanding that Whitmore had the game and fishing rights. To ensure Whitmore's pursuit of game was not hindered, Richard Bradney had to install wickets and gates. A year later there was another request to enclose a further 30 acres of the common field of Hilton followed by a request to enclose part of Cranmore Field.

Not all encroachments were legal, of course. Littlegain was a squatter hamlet and Newton and Winscott had several squatters in the seventeenth century who built cottages on the waste. In 1653, John Rowley of Newton was fined for not adhering to a statute requiring every new cottage to have four acres of land attached to it.[4]

One way or another, the commons and the common fields shrank in size so that by the late seventeenth century, perhaps as early as the Commonwealth time of 1648-1660, farmers were building up their holdings as the old three-field system of agriculture became less dominant.

---

[1] *Shropshire Archives*, P314/W/1/1/68

[2] *Shropshire Archives*, P314/W/1/1/25

[3] *Shropshire Archives*, 5586/1/317

[4] *Shropshire Archives*, 5586/1/310

In the eighteenth century, Worfield farmers embraced the changes in farming practices recommended by innovators Robert Bakewell and Turnip Townshend and landlords began to incorporate these new principles of farming in tenancy agreements.[5] New crops, such as turnips, clover, rape, and potatoes prompted battles for tithes leaving wonderfully detailed accounts, not just of the farming systems themselves but the characters involved.[6]

By the early part of the nineteenth century, all the commons in Worfield parish had been enclosed, the end of a process which began, as we have seen, in the fourteenth century. In 1591, when Queen Elizabeth leased the Forest Of Morfe to Francis Bromley, Francis Wolryche and Edward Bromley for 21 years, the inhabitants of Bridgnorth were so aggrieved that after three years the lords of the manor, Edward Nevill, Lord Bergavenny and John Talbot of Grafton Worcestershire, had to insist that all quarrels and suits must come to an end.[7] At the turn of the nineteenth century we have no record of the reaction of those who lost their rights on the commons of Worfield. A mark, perhaps, of how tenants' power had been reduced since the sixteenth century.

One of the consequences of the cultivation of the commons was to ban the sowing of hemp, flax (except for the first year) and rape on new ground. Until now, linen and the coarser fabric produced from hemp, had been a nice source of income for farmers. As Plymley wrote, "There is a small plot of land called the Hemp Yard, attached to almost every farmhouse and to the best sorts of cottages.[8] When it is ready "the hemp is pulled and immediately spread on grassland where it lies for about a month or six weeks. The more rain there is, the sooner it is ready." It was then dried in the sun and dressed by breaking the woody part from the skin with a wooden or metal breaker sometimes known as a tutor. The tow-dresser prepared the thread for spinning before it was whitened and sent to a weaver.

Eating habits had changed in the eighteenth century with wheat flour replacing rye, and a less welcome addition; sugar. Plymley tried to get people to stop eating sugar, thereby reducing the demand for a product which was one of the chief causes of slavery. A tireless worker in the abolition of slavery, Plymley spent sixteen years making Shropshire people aware of the problem and encouraging them to support the cause. The boroughs of Bridgnorth and Much Wenlock were Plymley's greatest success as they regularly petitioned parliament to abolish slavery.

The farm as an identifiable unit is a relatively recent concept and until the collapse of the common field system, 'fields' referred almost exclusively to those for the common use of a township not an individual field. Water meadows were the exception. By the eighteenth century, houses with named fields change hands and gradually both house and fields are

---

[5] *ShropshireArchives*, 5586/1/214

[6]*Stafford Archives*, D30/5/56, B/C/5/1746/106-23

[7] *Shropshire Archives*, 5586/2/1/191

[8] Joseph Plymley, *General View of the Agriculture of Shropshire*, London, 1813

identifiable as a unit or farm such as Folley Farm, mentioned in the Surveyors' Accounts of 1832.[9] [10]

The Apley Estate began to extend its land holding in the west of the parish from the late seventeenth century, and the Davenport Estate from the early eighteenth century, taking in Catstree, Hallon, Cranmere, Worfield, Wyken and Rowley. Other estates incorporated land in Kingslow, Stanmore, Stableford, Hilton, and Ackleton. New relationships arose within the manor, that of tenant and landlord. The latter, as we have seen were able to dictate the terms of occupancy.

Farming is, however, subject not just to the vagaries of the weather but also to changes in the political climate. The high farming period around the turn of the nineteenth century which gave rise to many of the beautiful Georgian farm houses and farm buildings in the parish, soon gave way to a period of economic depression and in 1845 the rates of the parish were reduced "on account of the long depressed state of agriculture".[11] At the end of the nineteenth century there was such a bad depression that many farmers went bankrupt including Thomas Meredith of Rowley Farm.

Meredith had farmed at Rowley for twenty-one years when he became bankrupt in 1899. Apart from the 340 acres at Rowley he also farmed Bradeney and Lea Farms. When he got into difficulties he gave up the tenancies of the latter farms but kept Rowley. Meredith had been a good farmer and the reason for his demise was a series of dry summers and low prices.[12] Poor Mr. Meredith had used his own money as well as that from his friends, and his wife, to try to keep his business afloat. Meredith was not alone in his suffering and it was clear that a national crisis called for a national solution. Discussions were held amongst farmers across the country about the need to set up a farmers' union. Local feeling can be gauged by the fact that 2,500 people attended such a meeting in Bridgnorth in 1892. It was unanimously agreed that an agricultural union should be formed, and W. J. Dodgson, the brother of Charles Dodgson (Lewis Carroll), land agent for Lord Boyne, was to act as secretary and chairman of the local group. In 1908, the National Farmers' Union was formed.[13]

The twentieth century saw the unravelling of the smaller estates after the First World War and an increase in the number of farmer-owned farms. Inevitably there were economic ups and downs but taking the century as a whole, mechanisation and the use of chemicals led to an increase in agricultural output. Our ancestors up to the nineteenth century used oxen, horses, and people to carry out the work on the land. What they would make of today's machinery one cannot imagine. The whole landscape of Worfield has been transformed from when our story began in the fourteenth century. Gone are the wattle hurdles which separated fields, replaced

[9] *Shropshire Archives,* 1066

[10] *Shropshire Archives,* P314/N/1/2

[11] *Shropshire Archives,* Vestry Minutes, P314/C/1/2

[12] *Wellington Journal,* 7 October 1899, p. 6

[13] *Ludlow Advertiser,* 24 December 1892, p. 8

by pig netting and barbed wire, and gone, too, are most of the people who used to work the land, replaced by machinery.

The good news, of course, is that Worfield is still predominantly a rural landscape, with most of the land in the hands of the same families for more than one generation. Post Brexit there will no doubt be new directions farmers are encouraged to take, and once more farmers will adapt their practices as political and market forces dictate.

THE WOOL TRADE

Washing sheep. Location unknown. Postmarked Newport 1905

Sheep have always played a big part in the economy of Worfield. Today profits derive almost entirely from meat, with wool being almost an inconvenience but in former times it was exactly the opposite; wool was the significant cash crop.

Wool was an export of national importance even in the eleventh century. It was big business for those who produced it, the merchants who sold it and the king who benefitted hugely from it. In 1297, the Barons stated that the value of wool in England amounted to half the value of the country and in the fourteenth century, King Edward III ordered that the Lord Chancellor should be seated on a woolsack in Parliament as a reminder of the debt the country owed to this humble animal.[14] The profitability of wool endured for centuries making many people and parishes wealthy. In this, Worfield was no exception.

---

[14] Eileen Power, *The Wool Trade in Medieval History*, Oxford University Press 1941, p. 18

Between 1238 and 1250 there was pasturage within the manor for 18 oxen, 3 boars, 12 cows, 12 sows and their litters, and 500 sheep.[15] By 1495 Worfield farmers were grazing 1,700 sheep in the Forest of Morfe alone and fast forward to 1792, there was so much sheep muck on the Worfield part of Morfe Common that an order was put out that only those who had common grazing rights could gather it. Others found collecting or receiving the dung would be prosecuted.[16] [17] [18]

Worfield sheep prior to the agricultural revolution were probably Ryelands which produced high quality, short staple wool for which there was great demand. Bridgnorth was the likely destination for some Worfield wool to be sold but we also have a tantalising glimpse of merchants coming to the parish to buy wool. In 1350, William of Merydene brought a case in Worfield's court against Mathew of Aldaword & Alice his wife for withholding 6 stones of wool price 6s and other products "which the said Alice it is said had kept and freely transferred to herself as she pleased".[19]

Shearing would be weather- dependent, as it is today, but the aim would be to shear in June. Great care was taken since this would be the biggest harvest of the year providing much-needed cash. To ensure a fleece which was free from sand and dirt the sheep were washed before shearing. This no longer happens but it certainly did in living memory. I remember Derek Rowley telling me that the sheep at Chesterton were washed in the Stratford Brook. Apologies for the quality of the photograph of sheep washing but I could find none better.

The hand-shearing which followed must have been an arduous job. Mechanised shearing is hard enough but hand shearing must have been incredibly tough. It is said that skilled shearers in the seventeenth century could shear 80 to 90 sheep in a day. I imagine that these animals

[15] R. W. Eyton, *Antiquities of Shropshire*, Vol. 3, p. 106ff

[16] *The National Archives*, E32/149

[17] *Shropshire Archives*, 3614/1/176

[18] The Forest of Morfe covered the parish of Worfield south of the River Worfe, and provided common grazing for the permitted townships. Each owner of a yardland (about sixty acres) had the right to graze 100 sheep, 12 cows and 2 horses and in 1495 the number of sheep per person was as follows:
- BURCOTE. John Hichekoks & his mother 100, John Baker 60, Richard Billyngesley 80
- BROMLEY. John Broke & his mother 100, Thomas Valance 80
- BURCOT MEYNE. John Townysende 60, Thomas Robyns 60
- BARNELEY. Roger Baret 80
- ROUGHTON. Thomas Broke & his mother 60, Roger Hille 60, John Matthew 100, John Walker & William his son 200
- WYKEN. Roger Bokenall 160, William Sadelee 60, Richard Barker the Flecher 80, Thomas Walker 60
- SWANCOTE. Jeynkyn Jannys 100, Richard Jannys his son 80, Thomas Felton 60
- HOCCOME. John Willot 60, William Hoccom 60

[19] *Shropshire Archives*, P314/W/1/1/26-32

would have been much smaller and wouldn't have carried the weight of fleece they do today but even so, that is quite an achievement. The fleeces would be wrapped, or wound, as it was called, the job being done carefully to hide the kempy or hairy wool which would reduce its price.

If the wool was to be woven into cloth it would go through a number of processes before it was finished. If it was dyed in might be dyed either "in the wool," after it had been spun or after it was woven. We can identify the dyers through their surnames; not just Dyer but Day, Heuster and possibly Hore. We can't always pinpoint where they worked but Catstree was the place to take your wool to be dyed in 1335 as Richard Ingellbrond had been given permission to build a dye works there.[20]

The wool was spun usually by women with drop spindles. Evidence has been left in the parish in the form of found artefacts. The spindle whorl shown below is a nice reuse of an item,

Spindle Whorl found in Worfield Parish. Ref. No. HESH-1517A7, www.finds.org.uk.
Image Courtesy of the Portable Antiquities Scheme

having previously been a lead seal on a papal document.

Weavers or Webbers wove the cloth in their homes. Alice Webbe was recorded in the court rolls of 1345 and William Webbe in 1396.[21] [22] Between 1562 and 1612 the baptismal records show the following weavers:

- 1562 John Taylor at The Riddings

---

[20]*Shropshire Archives*, P314/W/1/1/19

[21]*Shropshire Archives*, P314/W/1/1/25

[22]*Shropshire Archives*, P314/W/1/1/196-201

- 1567 William Webbe, Chesterton
- 1589 Thomas Webbe of Chesterton
- 1571 Richard Allen at The Lowe
- 1572 Roger Stockall at The Lowe
- 1573 Richard Teverell at Roughton
- 1577 Thomas Wyllot at The Lowe & later at The Sonde
- 1582 William Hoggins of Astrell
- 1586 William Crodgington of Oldington & later of Newton
- 1594 Humphrey Picke of Chesterton, later of Hilton
- 1612 Dan Rowley of Woldington

After the cloth was woven it would have been fulled to remove dirt and tighten the weave. Before water-powered hammers were used to full the cloth it was feet that did the job. The cloth was soaked in a vat of urine and walked, hence the name Walker for this occupation. It must have been an incredibly unpleasant job but was very lucrative and the Walker families of Worfield became very wealthy. By the fourteenth century, fuller's earth had replaced urine, and a system of wooden hammers driven by a water mill had replaced the feet of the people walking the cloth. There were fulling mills at Rindleford, Burcote, Worfield, and Rowley, an old mill at Wyken and an attempt to build one at Ewyke (north of Rowley). In 1369 the Lady of the Manor gave Roger of Kyngeslowe permission to build a fulling mill on waste ground at Crauston.[23] This mill, now known as Chesterton Mill was to prove one of the most successful in the parish, still being in use as a fulling mill when Gilbert Talbot died in 1606/1607 leaving the mill to Sharrington Talbot.[24]

The finishing touch to the cloth was given by shearman. The nap was raised by teasels mounted on a bar across the cloth and the shearmen would trim the threads to give a smooth finish. Finally the cloth was laid out in a field, tied to tenterhooks, and left to dry. In 1610 there is a reference to a washing place in Chemsill Field called Barker's Holde also known as Tenter's Field.[25] At Rindleford there was a field shown on the 1839 Field Names Map called Tenters Field (shown below).

Some of the cloth produced was no doubt made into clothes locally. Again, using the occupations of the fathers given in the baptismal records, the following were tailors between 1562 and 1612:

- 1565 William Weaver at Worfield
- 1568 William Bradney at Worfield
- 1571 Richard Haslewood at Oldington, later at Newton
- 1574 Hewgh Howle at Hilton
- 1577 Hugh Barney at Rindlefort

---

[23]*Shropshire Archives*, P314/W/1/1/25

[24]*Shropshire Archives*, 5586/1/264

[25]*Shropshire Archives*, 5586/1/268

- 1583 John Habberley at the Lowe
- 1588 John Thomas of Chesterton
- 1590 Jerome Warter of Hallon
- 1592 Richard Dun of Worfield
- 1595 William Millens at Hilton
- 1603 Francis Willcox at The Sonde
- 1603 John Barrett of Worfield

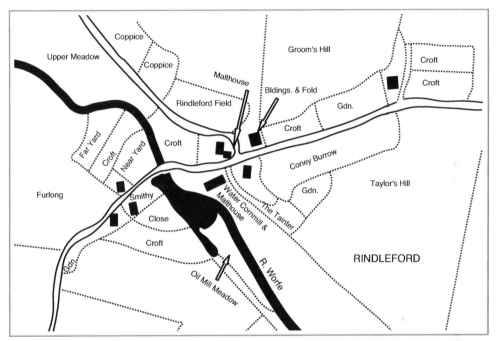

Map of Rindleford drawn from the 1839 Field Names map showing the location of the Tainter or Tenter

There was another group who were essential to the wool trade, the merchants. Cloth not needed locally, or for which one could get a better price outside the area, was sent down the River Severn to Bristol. On the return journey up the Severn the boats or trows carried wine, fish and fruit. The merchants made (and often lost) fortunes in exporting their wares and the risks they took gave them the name, " merchant venturers". Piracy was a constant problem adding to the natural dangers of sailing south to the Mediterranean and as far north as Norway and Iceland. The thought of the wealth these merchants could make must have allayed their fears.

Bristol merchants in the fifteenth century included William Rowley junior, who died in Bordeaux in 1478 and who had entrusted to John Chester the ship and goods for which he was responsible. The following year, William's uncle, William Rowley senior, died in the Netherlands and Thomas Rowley died in Bristol around the same time. The widows of merchants

9

continued their husbands' businesses, and Joanna, the widow of William Rowley senior, was no exception. She received sugar from Lisbon in 1479, and the following year oil and wax from Lisbon and woad and wine from Spain.[26] It would be lovely to say that these Rowleys came from Worfield but sadly I haven't got that proof.

The parish registers reveal the following Worfield merchants in the late sixteenth and early seventeenth centuries.

- 1580 Richard Sonde, merchant, from London
- 1604 William Rowley, clothier, from Rowley
- 1607 Francis Rowley, merchant venturer

Medieval Cloth Seal 1400-1700. Seals such as these identified the manufacturer, certified quality and provided a means of collecting taxes. Ref. no. HESH-8328B8, www.finds.org.uk). Image Courtesy of the Portable Antiquities Scheme

Wool brought many people into the parish, not least the Barker family of Hallon who were most likely bercarii or shepherds. William Barker rented a messuage and virgate of land in Rowley to Thomas Clerke of Staffordshire, woolman, in 1463/4, for twelve years, and Humphrey Lloyd, a draper of Salop, took a messuage & half a virgate of land in Stapulford in 1457 for a similar length of time.[27] [28] William Beech was another incomer; a merchant of the Staple of Calais who had settled in Barnsley with his wife Alice of Catstree by 1613.[29]

Sheep still play an important part in the economy of Worfield today and are a reminder of the contribution the golden fleeces of their predecessors made to the foundations of the parish.

---

[26] E. M. Carus-Wilson, *Medieval Merchant Venturers,* Methuen & Co, 1954, p. 92

[27] *Shropshire Archives,* P314/W/1/1/324

[28] *Shropshire Archives,* P314/W/1/1/312

[29] Shropshire Archives, *Parsons' Map of the Forest of Morfe,* 4296/1

MARGERY THE MUSTARDMAKER

Cooking for me is one of life's pleasures whereas dining out is not. Frankly I have had enough of the disappointment of afternoon tea with small cakes covered in some very odd-tasting goo, and the equally uninspiring evening meals with tasteless vegetables. Once, when I was living in Yorkshire, myself and a group of friends saved up our pennies and went to a Michelin-starred restaurant. It was a very forgettable experience which simply didn't cut the mustard. Which brings us very neatly to the subject of this article.

Growing up in the 1950s, mustard was always Coleman's, a powder which had to be mixed with a little water or milk, to make a soft paste. One of the children was usually told to make it and simple as it is to do now, then it seemed to be very difficult. Too much liquid and it would be runny, too little stirring and it was lumpy. It was made freshly on Sunday and reappeared on Monday, Tuesday and Wednesday, by which time it had turned an unpleasant dark yellow colour and had a skin on top through which one had to fight to get to the more fluid paste beneath. The general rule in our household was that food would not be wasted. The exception, as father would remind us each week, was mustard left on the plate, from which Mr Coleman made his money. Mother's view was that the mustard in the pot was not going in the same direction as that on the plate until absolutely necessary. Why no-one thought of putting a cover on the mustard pot I have no idea.

The other mustard I remember which we always bought ready made, was Dijon Mustard (made from brown mustard seed), and it wasn't until the 1980s that I became aware of Wholegrain Mustard which again came in jars. In fact, given the raw ingredients, mustard is really easy to make. For wholegrain mustard, take 2oz white mustard seeds, 1oz of black mustard seeds and soak in 60 ml of lukewarm water; just enough water to cover the seeds. After a few hours drain off any surplus water, stir in 4 fluid ounces of vinegar and a chopped shallot. If the mustard is to be kept it should be put in sterilised jars and sealed. Mustard making is a matter of blending different flavours and getting the texture to your liking. Lemon/lime, for fragrance, herbs and chillies for a spicy mustard, for example, and for a smoother mustard grind the mixture.

Mustard is a very easy plant to grow, not least because of its habit of self seeding. There are three mustards, all of the Brassica family. The white, or yellow, mustard is Sinapsis Alba, also known as Brassica Alba and Brassica Hirta. Sinapsis Alba was probably introduced into this country by the Romans as was black mustard, Brassica Nigra.

Rosamond Man and Robin Weir in their book "The Compleat Mustard," suggest that until the early Tudors, mustard and other herbs were grown as part of the monastic tradition. "That mustard was important can be seen from the fact that there was a 'mustardarius' - someone in charge of growing and distributing the mustard."[30]

The first town to be noted for its mustard making was Tewkesbury. In 1535, it is believed that mustard balls wrapped in gold leaf were presented to Henry VIII when he visited the

---

[30] Rosamond Man and Robin Weir, *The Compleat Mustard*, p. 17, Constable & Co, 1988

town. Women gathered the mustard seed which was then crushed and sieved to make a flour.
The exact recipe has been lost but the mustard was mixed with herbs such as horseradish,
formed into balls, and dried. When required for use you sliced off what you needed and
steeped it in water, milk, or vinegar, making a thick paste.

In 1602, Sir Hugh Plat noted that in Venice mustard seed was ground as finely as wheat
flour, and in 1720 the idea was taken up by Mrs Clements of Durham using locally grown
mustard. Soon she was selling her mustard powder all over the country and other companies
began milling mustard, notably, Keen and Company of London which was eventually taken

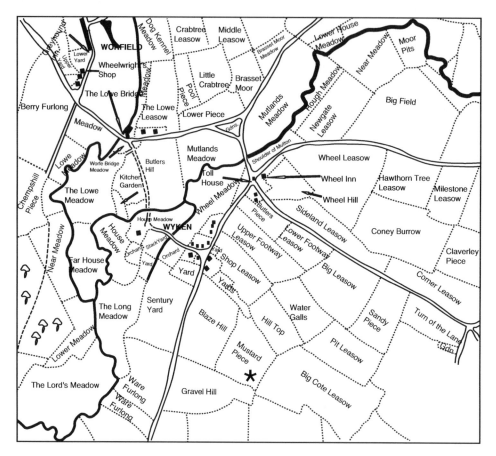

Mustard Piece shown on the Field Names Map of 1839

over by Coleman's. The Durham mustard factory passed into history and in 1814, Jeremiah
Coleman acquired a flour mill and began milling locally grown mustard. Over the years the
recipe has changed. Coleman's used to use both white and black mustard seeds but the for the
last thirty years no black mustard seeds have been used in Coleman's powder. This may explain
why I find the resultant mustard very bland and tasteless, lacking the kick I remember from my

younger days. I thought I was losing my taste but it's a relief to find the company has changed its formula.

A different approach to mustard production was that of William Taylor of Newport Pagnell who, in 1830, developed a method for making a mustard paste which would keep in jars. Salt was the preservative and the sealed stoneware jars ensured that the mustard kept perfectly, even in damp conditions.[31]

Between 1352 and 1437, mustard makers are mentioned in the court rolls of Worfield. There is Margery the Mustardmaker of Wyken in 1352, Margaret the Mustardmaker, John Mustardmon, and T. Elcokes of Worfield, mustardmaker, in 1367 and Elie Mustardmaker of Worfield in 1397 & 1437.[32][33][34][35] No references to mustard makers have been found after that date but that doesn't mean they weren't there just that there is no record of them yet found in the court rolls. The field name "Mustard Piece," survives in Wyken into the nineteenth century, as shown on the 1839 Field Names map so we can be sure it was grown there. It is likely that the mustard was made into balls, as in Tewkesbury, and it is also possible that there was a connection with the monastic tradition. Wyken was owned by the Dean and Chapter of Lichfield who had a fulling mill and a parsonage there. The vicarage in Worfield village next to the Rectory was referred to as the new vicarage in 1617 so perhaps the parsonage in Wyken was its predecessor. Might there also have been a brethren of monks at Wyken as well?[36] We can't be sure, but mustard may reinforce the theory that this was the case.

[31] Laura Mason and Catherine Brown, *The Taste of Britain*, Harper Press, 2006

[32] *Shropshire Archives*, P314/W/1/1/34

[33] *Shropshire Archives*, P314/W/1/1/74

[34] *Shropshire Archives*, P314/W/1/1/202

[35] *Shropshire Archives*, P314/W/1/1/287

[36] John Randall, *Worfield and its Townships*, J. Randall, 1887, p. 26

ALL IN A DAY'S WORK
BARBARA BOLLAND'S STORY

For this piece of history we venture across the parish boundary into Pattingham, to New Buildings Farm, where Barbara Bolland worked alongside her husband Dennis and his three brothers, Tim, Jack and Albert, who was always known as 'Nibble.' It is a fascinating glimpse into farm work when manual labour was the order of the day. While mechanisation has helped to increase farm output it has been at the expense of the cohesiveness of rural communities as George Ewart Evans recorded in oral histories of rural Suffolk in the 1950s.[37]

Barbara Bolland feeding the hens. Image courtesy of Karen Whitehouse

Barbara Ray was born in Pattingham village in 1931 and married Dennis Bolland in 1958 moving to New Buildings Farm, Pattingham. Apart from the odd holiday, she spent the whole

---

[37] George Ewart Evans, *Ask the Fellows who Cut the Hay,* Faber & Faber, 1956

of her life within a few miles of where she was born. Barbara loved to talk about life on the farm and it was in 2012 that I sat down and listened as she shared her memories.

"I didn't get involved in the ploughing. We had a tractor to do the ploughing but side hoeing with horses carried on until 1962 or 1963. Side hoeing cleared the weeds. Hand hoeing to thin out the crops was an essential job before precision drilling came in and was a job where you could earn good money, Three of us would hoe twenty acres, mind you your back ached so you earned your money.

Barbara Bolland pitching the corn up to the thrashing box. Image courtesy of Karen Whitehouse

When it came to harvesting we had a reaper and binder. The binder would tie the corn bundles in the middle and then we had to stook them in fours and leave them to dry. If it rained or they were blown over, we had to stook them again. You could do the job two or three times before you got the crop inside. When it rained you got soaked. You couldn't afford waterproofs and the clothes you wore just held the water. It was horrible to work like that. When the sheaves were dry you pitched them onto the wagon with your pikel, took the wagon back to the yard and put them in a rick. You started at the corner and laid one on top of

15

another at right angles so you got a square corner. As the rick got higher it became impossible to pitch the sheaves up to the top in one go. Someone had to stand halfway up, receive the corn and then pitch it to the top. No prizes for guessing who did that job. You couldn't move in the hole and your arms ached so much. I can feel the pain now.

By September the harvest should have been in and it wasn't thrashed until the winter. By this time the rats might have had a merry time with it, making nests in the ricks. One year you could see the top of the rick moving, there were so many rats. My job was cutting bonds. I had to cut the strings round the middle of the shoffs (sheaves) and put them in the machine. I was terrified of the rats. I think if one had come up in the corn I would have gone straight down the drum. The thrashing box didn't belong to the farm, it was owned by the Laws from Clive Road who went from farm to farm.

From the right, Jack Bolland, Dennis Bolland and Albert Bolland aka "Nibble." Date: 1936, when Dennis Bolland was aged five. Image courtesy of Karen Whitehouse

My husband and his brothers were all expected to work on the farm. The photograph shows three of the boys going down the field to take kale to the cattle. It was so tall when it was growing that you could shelter under it. The children were at school in Pattingham, three

16

quarters of a mile away and they had to run home in the lunch hour to do their work and then run back to school for afternoon lessons. Can you imagine children of that age doing that today?

Potatoes were an important crop which were hand-planted. Myself and another woman used to hold the seed tray between us and use our feet to measure the distance between the potatoes. And so we went on all day working as a pair, planting two rows at a time. Your back ached and your legs ached, but there is no easy job on a farm. When the potatoes were harvested the tractor dug them and scattered them over quite an area. We picked them by hand and put them in hessian sacks. If potatoes were to be stored in bulk they were put in clamps in the field; ridges of potatoes covered in soil.

At peak times such as harvest we needed extra labour. Men came from the village to do various jobs, stooking corn, picking peas and potatoes, and bringing in the hay. When we had transport, we collected people from Wolverhampton.

We milked fifty or sixty cows and you remember the cold. When the water froze it was bad; it took so long to get the work done. I remember one Sunday morning when the frost froze the tractor tyres. We had filled the tyres with water to provide ballast and we had to light a fire in a bucket to thaw them out.

In spite of all the hard times I wish it was all back as it was. You can't believe how it has all ended up. Farming isn't farming today, it is a factory."

Acknowledgement
Barbara Bolland died in 2016 and thanks are due to Barbara's daughter, Karen Whitehouse, for permitting the inclusion of this article and for supplying the photographs.

THE EARLY YEARS OF FARM MACHINERY

Machinery was a blessing beyond our imagination today, yet in the early days, as these photographs show, there was still a great deal of manual input. The ricks were all built by hand, as we have seen in Barbara Bolland's story, and the machinery itself looks heavy and complicated. There was a long way to go before we would get to the sophisticated equipment used on farms today.

Sibell Corbett harrowing a field at Stableford at the beginning of the twentieth century. Images of Stableford Farm are courtesy of Val and Peter Williams

Above: The hard work of building ricks. Below: William Herbert Chester at Rowley Farm. Images Courtesy of John Chester.

Above: Unloading sacks at Stableford Farm at the beginning of the twentieth century. Sibell Corbett on the cart. Below Wyken Farm early twentieth century. B. Hallam was the farmer at the time so perhaps he is in the foreground, and Anna or Kate Morrison on the horse.

Above: Thrashing Box at Rowley Farm. Circa 1930s. Below: Tractor & drawn Combine 1940s or early 1950s. Images Courtesy of John Chester.

MEDIEVAL TIMES

WORFIELD IN 1327

1327 is significant in the history of Worfield as it is from this date that many documents have survived which give us a picture of what life was like at the time. Before this we have to piece the story together from a few documents, place names, archaeological finds and landscape evidence. After this date we can begin to familiarise ourselves with Worfield's inhabitants and the minutiae of their lives and to build up a social history of the Manor of Worfield. Nationally, more important matters were at stake.

Edward II had become King in 1307 at the age of 20 on his father's death. He inherited a kingdom impoverished not least by Edward I's extravagant castle building in Wales. A man of skill and fine judgment was needed to hold the country together but sadly Edward lacked both. He played at being King and although his wife Isabella, the daughter of the King of France, was both beautiful and intelligent, Edward's head had already been turned by a young Frenchman called Piers Gaveston. The aristocracy (to say nothing of the Queen) were outraged by the couple's behaviour. Gaveston was executed to solve the problem but his place as the King's favourite was taken in 1320 by the equally unsuitable Hugh Despenser. Just a year later, Despenser embroiled the King in a power struggle with the Marcher Lords which would eventually cost the King his throne and possibly his life.

The Marcher Lords were an influential group of lords living in the Welsh Marches who had the task of maintaining peace in Wales and preventing Welsh incursions into England. Worfield's Lord of the Manor at this time was John, Lord Hastings, one of the Marcher Lords. In 1321, forced by Despenser into open rebellion against the King, the Marcher Lords mustered their armies. Initially, fortune favoured the rebels who pushed the King back to London but then the tables turned and the Lords were pushed back west of the River Severn. Edward's troops tried to take control of the River crossing at Worcester but Roger Mortimer held it. The King's army then went on to Bridgnorth, and here they succeeded in taking the bridge. The royal army's success was short-lived, however. Mortimer's troops with their local knowledge surprised the royal army at night and retook the crossing. The bridge at Bridgnorth and most of the town were burnt and losses amongst the royal soldiers were heavy. It would have been impossible for Worfield people to be unaware of what was happening with the noise of the skirmishes and the smell of the burning town carrying across the countryside. In addition, some Worfield people would have been taking part in the battles, either on Mortimer's side or on the King's.

The royal army moved on to Shrewsbury and it was here that the tables turned once again, as support for Mortimer faded away, and the King's men took Shrewsbury town. Realising by January 1322 that they were not going to win, and believing the promise that they would be pardoned and their lives spared, Roger Mortimer of Wigmore and his uncle of the same name from Chirk came to Shrewsbury Castle. They had been deceived and both Mortimers were taken in chains to the Tower of London to serve life sentences. Roger Mortimer of Chirk died in the Tower in 1326 but Roger Mortimer of Wigmore escaped and fled to France; helped, it is thought, by Queen Isabella. Edward's reaction was to take revenge on those even remotely involved in the rebellion. All Frenchmen in London were imprisoned and Roger's family and household were punished severely. With Mortimer in exile there was no restraint on Hugh Despenser, and Isabella recognised that there would be dire consequences for the country if this situation continued. For her son's sake, if nothing else, she had to take action.

On the pretext of going on a diplomatic mission, Isabella went to France and allied herself with Mortimer. Until this point Roger and Isabella had been faithful to their spouses but now they became lovers. Perhaps this made them even more resolved to sort out the problem of what to do with Isabella's husband. The plan was an audacious and dangerous one; to take control of the country. Roger Mortimer mortgaged his lands in France in exchange for troops and in September 1326, Isabella, Roger Mortimer, and a small number of Flemish troops, landed in Suffolk. As they marched eastwards others joined them. In contrast, the King found few followers and was forced to flee from London to the Welsh borders to find support from Welsh tenants. It was not to be. Edward was captured and taken to Kenilworth Castle where, in January 1327, he abdicated.

Two questions now arose: what to do with Edward II, and how to deal with the succession, as Prince Edward was only fourteen. Edward II was taken to Berkeley Castle, the home of Thomas Berkeley, to be held prisoner there. (Three hundred years later, a descendant of Thomas Berkeley, also called Thomas Berkeley, would live at Eudenas on the western side of Worfield.) Officially Edward II died in September 1327 but questions remained and rumours abounded. Had the King died or had he been smuggled out of the castle alive and was living elsewhere? If he had died, was this from natural causes or had he been murdered? Ian Mortimer makes a case for suggesting that Edward II did not die in September 1327 but was taken elsewhere to live out the rest of his life.[38] Prince Edward succeeded his father as King in January 1327 and was crowned the following month, but because of his age he was King in name only, with Isabella acting as regent, and Mortimer co-regent from 1327 to 1330.

In contrast to the national turmoil which culminated in the accession of Edward III, life in Worfield in 1327was much more tranquil. From the Manor Court Rolls we get a picture of everyday life; who was contravening the local statutes, who was getting married, who had died, what property was changing hands, who was brewing and baking etc.

For each year there were two types of court held on behalf of the Lord of the Manor before his steward or substeward. Small Courts (later called Leet Courts), were held every three weeks, and a Great Court or View of Frankpledge (later called Courts Baron) were held every six months. Twelve of the tenants of the Manor were sworn as jurors and all tenants of property were expected to attend the courts unless they paid to be exempt. The business of the small courts was adherence to the local ordinances known as the customs of the manor. Matters such as property transfers, death payments (heriots), legal cases or pleas, recognition of coming of age and marriage licences as well as marital transgressions or adultery were brought before the Small Court. At the View of Frankpledge, each township (or group of townships) presented any strays which had come into the manor, petty crimes such as thefts and burglaries and anything which was contra to the efficient running of the manor. Bridges had to be maintained,

[38] Ian Mortimer, *The Greatest Traitor: The Life of Sir Roger Mortimer 1st Earl of March*, Pimlico 2004

roads kept free of obstructions, and ditches had to be cleaned. After the townships had presented, the tasters presented those who had baked and brewed. Thus were food standards maintained.

Because they were written on parchment and rolled up for storage, most of the court rolls are remarkably well preserved. However because the language is Medieval Latin and the handwriting idiosyncratic, they aren't easy to read. Many of the scribes were not from the area either, and the spelling of place names, always variable and phonetic, is sometimes very odd indeed.

This is a translation of the Worfield Manor Court Roll of 1327.[39]

View of the Great Court of Worfeld held on 5 May 1327.
The 12 jurors: Stephen Henry, Alexander of Alvescote, Roger of Eudenas, William Jones, Roger the Walker, Richard Forester of Roughton, Roger of Swancote, Thomas of Catstre, William Wermod, Thomas Nicholls of Bradeney, John Gerbode.

- Mabil of Barndeleye who held of the lord there half a messuage and half a virgate of land has died and given to the lord for heriot are 3 oxen, 3 pigs and a 6th part of a sow price 3s 6d and a 6th part of [illegible] 3d. And John of Barndeleye came and took the tenements from the lord and gives to the lord 16s for ingress according to the custom of the manor. Pledge Stephen son of Henry

- Robert of Bradeney who held of the lord half a messuage here and half a virgate of land has died [torn] and in the name of heriot 1 heifer price half a mark and Thomas of Bradeney came as next of kin and took [torn] and gives to the lord for ingress 20s according to the custom of the manor. Pledge Thomas of Ewyke

- John Henry who held of the lord one toft and half a virgate of land in Roughton has died and nothing falls to the lord in the name of heriot [torn] and here came Henry son of the aforesaid John and claimed the land in the right of Alice his mother who was the wife of the aforesaid John. And on this came William the Beadle and Matilda his wife and claimed part of the said land to wit the toft, Horscroft, Depedale, and Wodendale [field names] by the feoffment of the aforesaid John 24 years past. And 12 jurors said that the aforesaid tenements were recovered here by a licence to recover and they don't know by what right William held the land therefore to investigate the rolls for all the half virgate of land at this side of the next court

- Sibill daughter of Roger the shepherd of Neuton surrendered into the hands of the lord half a messuage and one nook of land with appurtenances to the use of Robert Kene and the said Robert gives to the lord for ingress 6s 8d to hold according to the custom of the manor. Pledge Roger of Ewdenas, Thomas of Kattestre.

- William of Shareshul gives here to William Wermode one virgate of land with a messuage in Hale for the term of 20 years and the said William Wermode gives to the lord for ingress 6s 8d to hold according to the custom of the manor pledge Thomas of Kattestre

---

[39] *Shropshire Archives,* P314/W/1/1/1

- Stephen son of Henry of Hulton surrendered into the hands of the lord 1 nook of land bought from Adam atte Walle to the use of Stephen his son and he gave to the lord for ingress 3s 4d to hold according to the custom of the manor. Pledge Stephen his father
- Henry at Felde surrendered into the hands of the lord half a nook of land in the Hale to the use of Roger his son and the said Roger gives to the lord for ingress 5s to hold according to the custom . Pledge: Henry his father and William Macy
- Agnes daughter of Matilda at Yate of Roughton gives to the lord 12d for a licence to marry. Pledge Richard the Forester
- William Huncbachane gives to the lord 12d for his crop sown on the land of John the Chamburleyn of Hale. Pledge William Macy
- Alice the daughter of Robert the Mercer gives the lord 12d to marry by her will. Pledge Robert the Mercer

  [The View of Frankpledge]

- ACLINTON all is well
- OLDINTON all is well
- EUDENAS, KATTESTRE all is well
- ROULOWE, ASTURHUL, BRADENEYE, SONDE, EWYK all is well
- NEUTON all is well
- HULTON all is well
- STANLOWE & KYNGESLOWE all is well
- BROMLEY all is well
- WYKE presents that Nicholas Knokel (2d) baked and sold against the assize. John Dun (2d) baked without a licence. The wife (2d) of Nicholas Knokel is an itinerant retailer of ale
- ALVESCOTE, WYNNESCOTE. Blood flowed between Roger the Baker and William the Walker to the cost of William (6d). Pledge Thomas Bryde. Also they present John Garbode of Worfeld by the reeve for digging stone in the woods of Soudley without a licence and the said John was attached to respond to the lord etc. Also they present that the aforesaid person pastured pigs and animals on the pasture of the lord in the same wood and other places on the common here because he has no land in the demesne therefore it is ordered the bailiff take the aforesaid animals
- CHESTERTON presents that Reginald de Walton (3d) did not come. Present Reginald Hospicer (6d) for an agreement
- STAPULFORD presents Agnes at Forde for a brothel in a cottage she held of the lord in the manor 6d. Pledge Robert at Broke
- BURCOTE, BURCOTE, RYNDELFORD & BARNEDLEY present that John Haukyn extended into the lord's land for no reason within the manor and in the name of his parents is distrained for this to the next court
- HALE presents that cottars entered the woods of the lord and took old wood and greenwood and gorse and heather therefore attached etc. Also they present that Stephen the Kynge (3d) is a baker and Roger (2d) Nelde similarly

- WORFELD presents that blood flowed between John Hichekoc and Walter atte Sonde to the cost of the said John (3d) therefore in mercy. Pledge William Ingebrond. Also the hue and cry was raised between Christiana of Penne and Emma at Sonde to the cost of Emma (3d). Pledge John Hichekoc. Also blood flowed between Amicia of Northale and Margaret daughter of Robert of Houndeslowe to the cost of Amicia (2d). Pledge William Ingebrond. Also blood flowed between the aforesaid Amicia (2d) and Agnes (2d) Alote to the cost of both of them therefore in mercy. Pledge against William Ingebrond. Also Matilda (6d) Bonde for a tavern and Agnes (6d) Dovy similarly. Also for the hue and cry between Isabella Bryd and Alice the Deye to the cost of the said Alice (6d). Pledge the villages

- The ale tasters present that William the Palmer (6d) brewed 4 times, John atte Sonde (1d) once, Stephen in the Boure (2d) once, Thomas of the Hill of Stapelford (2d) once, Agnes Gitten of Stapelford (3d) twice, Nicholas Jones of Aclinton (2d) once, Thomas the Freeman of Aclinton (2d) once, Robert ate Heath of Aclinton (2d) once, Robert Elkince of Aclinton (2d) once, John of Stanlowe (2d) once, William Edith of Kynggeslowe (2d) once, William of Stanlowe of Chesterton (2d) once, Alice Briddes of Hulton (2d) once, Thomas Bryd (2d) once, Robert Williames of Bradeney (2d) once, William of Roulowe (2d) once, Elena Hawote of Wykin (6d) 3, Petronella of Wykin (1d) once, Edith Haukence of Roughton (3d) three, Nicholas Knokel (1d) twice, Amicia the Breuster (4d) four, Rose of Asterhull (4d) three, Margaret Nelde (3d) twice, Matilda of Castel (2d) twice, Thomas Poynant (2d) once, John Inge (2d) twice, Alex of Catstre (2d) twice, Roger of Cattestre (4d) twice, Roger of Eudenas (2d) once, Robert Faber of Roughton (1d) once, Richard Forester (1d) once, Thomas of Hockombe (4d) twice and sold against the assize and are in mercy

- Inquiry between Stephen Smyth and he has a day at the next court. He has part of a house after the death of Margery and corn and other chattels which he administered and gave rent for part according to custom

- Margery the wife of William Edith of Kyngeslowe gives to the lord 12d for consideration of the court what title she has after the death of her husband of the tenements that were granted to her son Thomas of Ewyke pledge William Wermod. And it is considered by the whole court that all that he held after the death of her husband should not be obstructed after the grant aforesaid

- Edith Haukyn plaintiff of Walter Haukyn that in her house he beat and injured her. And the aforesaid Walter was not able to contradict Edith and Walter is in mercy (2d). Pledge Henry at Pyrie

- The bailiff presents that Thomas (2d) the son of Christopher trespassed in the woods of the lord therefore in mercy. Pledge the bailiff. Presents that William Maweson (2d) similarly pledge of the bailiff. Presents that Thomas (2d) the son of Felicia similarly pledge of the bailiff.

- William son of Roger of Bromley sought one moor at Ryndelford which his father held of the said Lord John of Hastings therefore the rolls are to be scrutinised this side of the next court

- William Forester and Stephen Adam sought two parts of one messuage at Bromley which Thomas the Younger of the same held therefore the aforesaid Thomas was summoned to respond to the aforesaid William and Stephen
- The 12 jurors the reeve and the beadle with others of the manor have a day to view the wood at Soudley and the damage and trespass here to be scrutinised at the next court

[Small Court}

Court of Worfeld held on Friday next after the Feast of the Nativity of St John the Baptist 1327

- Edward son of William the Forester who held of the lord one nook of land in Bromley has died. On this came William his father and gives to the lord 3s 4d for ingress to the said nook of land with appurtenances to hold according to the custom of the manor. Pledge Robert atte Broke
- The same William surrendered into the hands of the lord the aforesaid nook of land to the use of Alice his daughter to hold according to the custom of the manor and she gives to the lord 3s. Pledge Richard Forester
- John of Bardeley claimed 2 selions in Barndeley of which Mabil of Barndeley his mother died seized etc. and Thomas the son of Roger of Barndeley claimed the said selions after the death of his father and the said selions are to remain in the hands of the lord until the next court
- Robert of Asterhull came in court and took from the lord one messuage and one virgate of land with appurtenances in Asterhul to hold to himself, his heirs and assigns according to the custom of the manor and he gives the lord for ingress 26s 8d pledges John Stanlowe & Walter Pattch.
- Alice Hatheway gave to the lord for fornication 18d
- Stephen at Asterne elsewhere took from the lord one piece of land at the castle and now takes one piece containing 6 feet from each part of the increase and rendering for this increase 8d per annum and encloses between the house and the ditch and he gives to the lord for ingress 6d
- William Macy was removed from the office of beadle and Thomas Wynter elected in his place and sworn
- Accounted for the mansion which Stephen Smyth has by virtue of his office a vacant right in 4 acres of land in Bromley which John Wem held which the aforesaid John and his father have a day at the next court by pre-arrangement to show his right
- An inquiry held by the oaths of William of Kynggeslowe, Reginald Agneys, Roger the Walkere, Stephen Henry of Hulton, Henry at Pyrye, Roger of Alvescote, Alexander of Alvescote, William Gille, Thomas son of Thomas of Hocombe, Walter at Nashe, Thomas of the Hul, Richard the Forester, Thomas of Cattestre, Thomas Nicholes, John Gerbode, Walter Heyne, John of Brandeley, Roger Howe, Thomas the Younger, Thomas Hugynes, John of Stanlowe, Roger Lovesticke, Robert Luyce, Thomas Bryd who are tenants of John of Bichppaton [Bishpetone now Bishton]and Alice his wife tenants of the lord in the manor of Worfeld how and in what manner saying by their oaths that the aforesaid Alice held by right and heredity according to the custom of the manor to wit one messuage and half a virgate of

land in the domain of the manor situated in Routon, Horscroft, one messuage in Hale, one parcel of meadow in Swancote, three parcels of land, that is, Wodundale, Depundale and Wildecote Rudynge. They say that the aforesaid Alice died 26 years ago and that the aforesaid John held all the aforesaid tenements in his life who died at Easter last past without any reclamation. And they say that they understand that the aforesaid tenements were freehold and are of the demesne of the manor and by custom of primogeniture he held the land and the title of the tenements in the demesne after the death and continuing by a fine thence made. Therefore they understand that the said John was permitted to hold the tenements for the whole of his life charged freely. They say that John in his life demised to William the Beadle and Matilda his wife Horscroft, Wodundale, Depundale but for what term they don't know and the aforesaid John always did services due to the lord during his life and because the aforesaid John moved out of the manor with any goods he had within the manor the lord has nothing for heriot. And on this came Henry son of the aforesaid John and Alice and claimed the aforesaid tenements in his own right according to the custom of the manor and therefore the aforesaid tenements were taken into the hands of the lord until etc. And the aforesaid Henry sought the aforesaid tenements to himself freely and as to the parcel of meadow in the Hale and Wildecote Rudinge in Swancote he has a day at the next court to make a fine etc. And the reeve meanwhile is charged with conserving and answering concerning the profits of Horscroft, Wodundale and Depundale which are to remain in the hands of the lord. And therefore it is ordered that the bailiff summon and make known to the aforesaid William and Matilda his wife to come to the next court to render in the plea aforesaid and to show both to the lord and the aforesaid Henry if they have unjustly detained the aforesaid tenements

MARRIAGE

Marriages in the fourteenth century required a licence, not from the church but from the lord of the manor. The cost seems to have been variable, based I suppose on the ability to pay, but it was always cheaper to marry someone within the manor than someone outside it. The licence itself may seem odd to us today because the name of the husband was not necessarily stated.

1327[40]

- Agnes daughter of Matilda atte Yate of Roughton gave to the lord 12d for a licence to marry. Pledge Richard the Forester
- Alice the daughter of Robert the Mercer gave the lord 12d to marry by her will. Pledge Robert the Mercer

1329[41]

- Thomas of Burcote came into court and gave to the lord 12d for a licence to have Agnes his daughter marry whoever she wishes
- William Massy gave to the lord 2s for a licence to marry Margery his daughter to whoever she wishes pledge Thomas the reeve

A marriage was often arranged by the parents of the bride and groom. Firstly, a financial arrangement was agreed. The bride-to-be was expected to bring goods and cash, her dowry, to the marriage, and in return would be given rights in the groom's lands. Betrothal could take place at the age of seven and marriage when the bride was twelve and the bridegroom fourteen.

In 1328 a case was brought to the manor court concerning the rights of a woman not to be married against her will.[42] Robert of Asterhull had made plans for his daughter Margaret to marry Roger of Swancote's son, Thomas. Robert applied for a licence to transfer his property to Margaret and since Thomas, her chosen husband-to-be, was already in possession of his father's property, Roger applied for a marriage licence for his son to marry Margaret. There were however three stumbling blocks. Firstly, it was doubted that Thomas had ownership of his father's property; secondly, Margaret was under twelve, and finally Margaret had never wanted to marry Thomas. Margaret's mother came to court in support of her daughter and the court ruling was that no woman should be married against their will, whether under age or not. One can only imagine how Robert of Asterhull might have reacted to this public humiliation.

---

[40] *Shropshire Archives,* P314/W/1/1/1

[41] *Shropshire Archives,* P314/W/1/1/10

[42] *Shropshire Archives,* P314/W/1/1/7

Margaret was put in the custody of the bailiff, presumably because there were doubts as to how her father might treat her, but even the bailiff couldn't secure Margaret's safety. With 'force of arms' the aggrieved Roger of Swancote came with Thomas of Cattestre and other 'malefactors' and kidnapped Margaret. Fortunately, Margaret survived the ordeal and married the man of her choice, Thomas Ewyk's son, Richard.

The timetable of the Asterhull marriage was as follows:
- 29 October 1328 previous marriage arrangements annulled. Margaret is free to marry Richard Ewyke. Thomas gives 33s 4d for his son, Richard, to marry Margaret
- 4 March 1329 Margaret of Asterhull pays for a licence to marry
- December 1329 Robert of Asterhull surrenders to the use of Richard Ewyke one messuage and a virgate of land with appurtenances

Where the couple married we don't know. They may have been married in the church porch at Worfield Church, as was the norm for a church wedding, or simply outside the church door if there was no porch at that time. The wedding would be followed by mass in the church and then afterwards by a wedding breakfast. Civil ceremonies were as legitimate as church weddings, and 'ceremony' might be putting it too strongly. The couple just had to agree to marry each other and provided they weren't related that was fine.

Leaving the emotional compatibility of the couple to one side, since we know nothing of it, the marriage of Margaret Asterhull and Richard Ewyke was a perfect match. Richard brought money into the marriage and Margaret brought property. As he was not the eldest son, Richard would not inherit his father's property but Margaret Asterhull's father gave her a house (a messuage) and land, from which he might make a living. Technically, Margaret was given property by her father but the gift was actually handed over to her husband at the time of the marriage. While she was married, Margaret's land at Asterhull would be administered by her husband but he couldn't dispose of his wife's property without her permission and confirmation by examination that there had been no coercion. The custom of the manor provided a widow with at least a life interest in her husband's property giving her somewhere to live and an income. When Robert Asterhull died, his wife Rose had an annuity from his tenements of four quarters of rye and half a quarter of barley, paid for her life, four times a year.[4]

Margaret's refusal to adhere to the arranged betrothal caused a violent backlash from the men of both families but one cannot fail to note that it was Margaret and her mother who won the day.

THE BLACK DEATH

As I write this, in April 2020, the whole of the UK as well as a large part of the rest of the world is in lockdown due to Covid-19. UK residents are allowed out once a day for exercise and all non-essential businesses are shut, as are pubs, restaurants and leisure centres. It is a funny old time and one can't help wonder how we are going to get out of this dangerous situation. Of all the pandemics there have been, the one we are most likely to think of is the Black Death. Before Coronavirus arrived we might have dismissed a pandemic as being irrelevant in the modern world but a new threat has caused us to think again.

It was in 1348 that the Black Death arrived at various ports in England. In June of that year the Black Death came to the port of Bristol, a major shipping city of 10,000 people. Contemporary accounts speak of almost the whole of the city's population being wiped out. The disease travelled fast across the country and while we might have hoped that Worfield would have escaped, the parish was not so fortunate. Exactly when the disease arrived here and by what means it was brought, whether up the Severn or over land, we don't know. No documentary evidence has survived for Worfield in 1348, indicative perhaps of the fact that there was something which had upset the normal routine of life. Similarly, the clerk of the July 1349 Manor Court is not our usual man. His writing is scarcely legible, and his spelling of place names suggests he may have come from elsewhere. What has happened to our usual scribe, whose phraseology and hand we have become accustomed to?

Between 1327 and 1348, the average number of deaths recorded annually in the court rolls of Worfield was three. In 1349 the clerk recorded the following deaths: John Hartola, John Matheu, John Richards, John Bullok, Robert at Broke, Thomas of Stanlowe, Roger of Ewyk, John of Stanlowe, Stephen of Stanlowe, Thomas of Stanlowe, William Bisschop, William Huche, Stephen Anneys, Roger Walker of Hulton, Thomas Brette, Thomas at Yate the reeve, John Turner, Reginald of Bradeney, Richard of Wyghomere, John of Forster, William Toward, Reginald Toward, Matilda Gille, William son of Alan son of Simon, Thomas son of Roger Heanis, Robert Gille, William Heynes, Roger Richardes, Edith Kynges & William her son, John Hugges, William of Walton, Robert Hugges, Thomas Cattestre, Thomas of Hull, Robert at Forde, William son of Thomas Wilkes, William Marcor, Henry of Felde, Alice at Tounsende of Alvescote, Roger of Swancote, William the son of Thomas Annesone, Reginald Colet, the daughter of Thomas the Hore, Walter the Newe, Roger of Barndeley, Alice Lawen and Reginald of Kingslowe.[43] In total this was over fifty people of the middle class and above. This was by no means the total number of Worfield's population who died. There would have been servants and day labourers and their wives and children, and even people passing through the parish; for them we have no names. We can't be sure that all of the fifty died in 1348 or 1349, since the purpose of the record is to ensure the heriots or death payments are collected, nor

---

[43]*Shropshire Archives*, P314/W/1/1/26-32

that they all died from the Black Death but with such an abnormally high figure the "pestilence," as it was known, must have been the key factor.

We do not know how long the disease lasted in Worfield, but no deaths are recorded in January and March 1350 and only one, Robert Janekyns, in December 1350, so perhaps by this time the disease had done its worst. The death rate as the disease swept through Europe was between a third and half of the population, sometimes more. It is estimated that London lost 60% of its population.

In Worfield, villages were depleted and houses left empty. Property and land were taken over by next of kin where possible, whilst under-age children were made wards of guardians who managed their land until they could inherit. Agnes, the daughter of Roger Deakin, came and took from the lord a house and land in Hilton which Thomas Percs would hold as her guardian until she is of full age.[44] Survivors must have struggled to work the land and some lost the battle. In 1356, Peter Tandy came in court and surrendered one messuage and half a virgate of land [30 acres perhaps] "ruined and in decay" in Chesterton to the use of John Stevenes.[45] Even in 1370 we still find property being occupied for the first time in fifty years.

The Lady of the Manor meanwhile, was fighting to maintain her authority here in Worfield. The customs and services of the Manor laid down the rights and obligations of its tenants which, at this time, many tenants were not meeting. One such duty was to mow and make the hay in the Lady's meadow. In 1356, for example, the townships of Kyngeslowe & Stanlowe failed to provide two men at hay making and Chesterton and Hilton failed to provide ten men at this time.[46]

Another manorial obligation if you had property was to attend the manor court. The frequency with which it was held, every three weeks, ensured that breaches of local law could be quickly remedied and the system worked because the tenants respected the law. After 1349 cases such as the following were common. In 1357, John Millward accused John Stroubrugge of trespass and the court bailed the defendant to attend at a future court. He was bailed by the reeve by one pot but the reeve himself failed to attend.[47]

Whether Worfield's tenants were deliberately flouting the authority of the manorial system, or whether they were just struggling to survive is a moot point. It is a fact that they were many more defaults of suit of court and transfers of land outside the court, as well as failures to maintain bridges and keep ditches scoured.[48] Eighteen men and one woman illegally put their livestock into the Lady's meadow, usually an ox or a couple of cows, but Roger Barker turned thirty sheep in there.[49] Did the tenants see an opportunity for change? If so, they were to be

---

[44] *Shropshire Archives*, P314/W/1/1/26-32

[45] *Shropshire Archives*, P314/W/1/1/39

[46] *Shropshire Archives*, P314/W/1/1/36

[47] *Shropshire Archives*, P314/W/1/1/40

[48] *Shropshire Archives*, P314/W/1/1/39

[49] *Shropshire Archives*, P314/W/1/1/43

disappointed. The Lady came down hard on her tenants by imposing heavy penalties for infringement of customs.

- 1350 Every tenant shall enclose their hayes. [50]
- 1353-1354 It is ordered by the steward that the brewers of ale do not sell the dearest gallon of good and fitting ale for three halfpennies more & regrators per gallon 1d. And anyone selling dearer is to forfeit the ale to the lord. The ale tasters are answerable for that sold dearer paying to the lord 120s. 1353-1354.[51]
- 1355 It is ordered that all regrators and brewers do not sell unless with a measure sealed and examined by the steward under a pain for each offence of 6s 8d. And bakers that they do not bake unless they make an oath to well and faithfully serve strangers and all others under the aforesaid pain 1355.[52]
- 1355-1356 It is ordered by the agreement of the whole manor that there will be no disturbance of another's common pasture under pain of 20s.[53]

Worfield Manor survived intact perhaps because there was no obvious alternative or perhaps because there was no consensus of opposition. Indeed, inasmuch as a number of the tenants seemed to be "agin the government," they were even more at odds with each other. The only option was to stick with the manorial system for good or ill. The pestilence left behind decimated villages and land uncultivated for many years and the fear of its return must have been a constant presence.

[50] *Shropshire Archives,* P314/W/1/1/33

[51] *Shropshire Archives,* P314/W/1/1/35

[52] *Shropshire Archives,* P314/W/1/1/37

[53] *Shropshire Archives,* P314/W/1/1/38

ROADS & TRACKS

FOOTPATHS

On October 5 2018, a number of walkers did a 9 mile walk within the Parish to raise funds in aid of the illumination of the Church spire which, when lit, can be seen for miles around. It was a pleasure to join in with such a worthy cause. It was also great fun, and nice to walk with people I haven't seen for a long time. Some weathered the journey better than others as knees and legs began to ache towards the end but I have to say I was amused to see Des Plain finishing the walk looking as though he could have done the distance all over again and I am sure he could. Some of those who took part had never walked these paths and for the first time they were able to enjoy the landscape at a leisurely pace instead of from inside a speeding car.

I walked for a while with John Thornley from Hilton whose wife, Jennifer, looked after my children at Worfield Playgroup. John entertained me as we walked from Worfield to Burcote with tales of fishing for trout on the Worfe. This is a delightful stretch of the river, not far from the nineteenth century iron wheel which once powered a pump to raise water up the hill to Davenport House.

Claire Evitt had the original idea and together with her team did an excellent job of organising the event. Some serious clearance work was needed before the walk could take place. Brambles & overgrown hedges had made some of the paths impassable, while other paths were planted across with gay abandon. Wading through shoulder-high maize and other similarly tall crops is not fun. There is a legal obligation to have paths passable throughout the year and I wish it was respected by all farmers. The culprits presumably don't walk the paths themselves or they wouldn't do it.

I have wanted to write about footpaths for a long time but the enormity of the subject put me off. It was only when Val Edwards presented me with a pile of papers relating to rights of way in the parish in the 1950s and 1960s that I felt I had to knuckle down and write. I have deposited this material with Shropshire Archives so that they are in the public domain. The papers are a reminder of how hard people have worked to preserve these rights of way. We might mourn the fact that so many have disappeared or become roads but we must use those that are left so they are kept open.

It was in 1949 that the National Parks and Access to the Countryside Act gave the County Councils' Highway Authorities responsibility for rights of way. Their immediate task was to identify what were understood to be public paths and to plot them on a map. Thereafter no-one could summarily close them, even if they were hardly ever used. Any closure or even diversion could only be carried out by following strict procedures and closure was only permitted if a path was not needed for public use. Lewis Silkin, a name familiar to those who have walked along the Silkin Way in Telford, was the Minister of Town and Country Planning, and the man behind the 1949 Act. In Worfield it was the Parish Council, under the chairmanship of Sidney Knowles, which had the task of deciding which footpaths should close.

Even before the 1949 Act there had been 'discussions' between Worfield and government departments regarding paths across RAF Stanmore. Under the Requisitioned Land and War

Works Acts of 1945 & 1948, the Ministry of Transport proposed closing the footpath connecting cottages at Bentley & Hoccum Pools belonging to Mrs. Evans and a bridle path going through and near to the RAF station. Worfield Parish council objected. The Hon. E. S. Hamilton Russell worried that one of his properties, Stanmore Cottage would have no roadway to it at all.

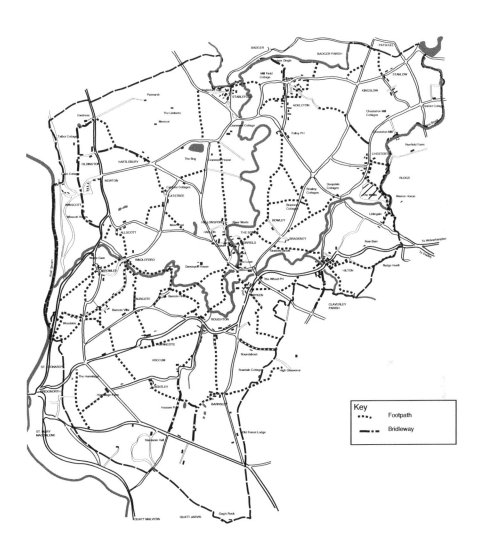

Footpaths & bridleways in the Parish of Worfield in 2021 superimposed on a map drawn by Joy Wigram in 1933

Mrs. R. C. H. Evans also objected strongly and wrote to the Commons, Open Spaces and Footpath Preservation Society in London as follows. 'In our view it is entirely unreasonable for the Air Ministry to acquire the site of this footpath, fence it in and then expect the adjoining owner to grant facilities for the construction of a further foot road or bridle road over her property.' Furthermore, the closure of the footpath would cut off the two cottages at Hoccum Pool & access from Hoccum Farm to the Stourbridge Road. Eventually even the Ministry of Transport succumbed to the force of Mrs Evans and it is through her efforts that we still have the bridleway alongside Stanmore Country Park and the right of way to Hoccum Pool and Barnsley. The cottages at Hoccum Pool are now gone but the path remains.

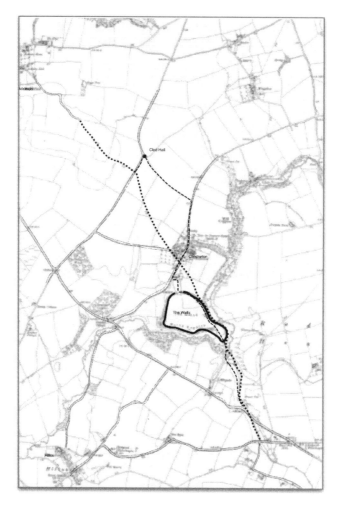

The original purpose of a right of way can be lost when it is rerouted as can be seen on the above map. The old route (dotted line) followed a straight diagonal line between the two villages and beyond whereas the new route (dashed line) takes a detour so making it hard to see the path's purpose. The footpaths are superimposed on the 1921 OS map

The task of the Parish Council in 1950 was to determine which of the rights of way shown on a map supplied by the County Council were in use and which were private paths as opposed to public rights of way. It was a big job, as you can imagine, and a difficult one because not all farmers liked having a right of way across their land. Some farmers had taken matters into their own hands by blocking paths to prevent access ('nailed up for years' in one case), and allowing bridges to fall into disrepair. The path from Deepdale to Bradeney, for example, was blocked by barbed wire as was the footbridge in Worfield. Diligently the council examined the evidence and asked awkward questions, such as why a farm building had been erected across a footpath, why another path had been diverted, and why others had been ploughed across. Some of the offenders were on the Parish Council which must have made the Chairman's job particularly difficult but fortunately the objections recorded were submitted to the County Council for them to sort out. Every five years until 1979 the rights of way had to be reviewed but it has not altogether stopped the blocking up of paths some which had been in use for centuries. The track from Hilton to the B4176 was deemed never to have been a public right of way when it was closed in the 1980s. Similarly we can no longer walk from Newton to the ferry point on the Severn which was once a significant public thoroughfare.

Made by the feet of our ancestors and the animals and carts which traversed the landscape, footpaths are a significant legacy from the past with which we can directly connect. Inconvenient they may sometimes be to the owner of the land they cross but many of these paths have existed for centuries and we should think very carefully before we change them in any way. Once they have gone, another piece of historical evidence, as important as any document, is gone for ever.

DROVING

In 2011 Colin Brown and Ron Summers led a walk from Wyken via High Grosvenor and Dallicott to Hilton which focussed on drovers' roads.

We started our walk from the Village Hall (formerly the Recreation Room), walking along the road to Worfield, turning left before the bridge at The Lowe and going towards Wyken. Taking our lives in our hands, we crossed the A454 at Wyken and just to the right of the last house, next to the former shop, went up a footpath towards the edge of the parish. After crossing the golf course we were in a green lane and could begin to see what ancient tracks would have looked like. The track was wide enough to take one or even two carts side by side and was bounded by earth banks or stone walls surmounted by a hedge, usually of hazel or quickthorn, both good for containing livestock. We walked until we were on top of a ridge near to High Grosvenor from which one could take in a spectacular view towards the Wrekin and then followed a green lane along the ridge, possibly part of a long-distance drovers' road. Some of these routes date from Neolithic times, others will be more recent. Within living memory, the main way of getting livestock to their destination was to walk them along roads which are now so fast you wouldn't dare to walk along them yourself, let alone with livestock.

Cattle and sheep were not only moved to and from markets, they were often moved long distances to make up for losses through disease. In the thirteenth century, 600 head of sheep were delivered to Worfield to restock the flocks. One wonders where they came from, and which routes they followed.[54]

There is plenty of evidence in the court rolls of livestock being driven to local grazing which was available at certain times of the year in the common fields, in meadows or on commons. There was always pressure on grazing, especially following enclosures, and there was often overstocking or animals were put into the common fields before the harvest had been gathered. There were also constant arguments about the boundaries of commons. In the following example, the parish of Rudge was protecting Rudge Heath from incursions by the inhabitants of Claverley, Shipley and Worfield. Thomas Whitmore of Ludstone was one of the chief culprits, certain that he had the right to graze his stock on Rudge Heath. At an inquiry in 1730-1732 he said his rights were supported by documentary evidence. He "believed that Rudge liberty went to the Rill," and, "had in his Custody as many writeings concerning Rudge Estate as would fill a Large Kettle that was then in his kitchin standing by em, which would hold 2 pails full at the least in his Judgment."[55]

There was a pool on Rudge Heath in which sheep from neighbouring parishes could be washed and left for two or three days to dry, so they could be sheared, but apart from that there were no grazing rights on the Common.

---

[54] *A History of the County of Shropshire*, Vol. 4 pp. 26-71

[55] *Shropshire Archives*, 330/14

One of the witnesses was John Mason whose father had leased Rudge Warren. Around 1707 he was asked by Mr Cresswell to drive Whitmore's sheep off Rudge Common. There were other offenders and other protectors of the common. A Mr. Mason warned Foxall from Hilton who once drove his sheep on the common that he would complain to Cresswell and Foxall did not return, About 1710 or 1711, Thomason of Sutton began to drive his sheep but a sister of Mason's was sent by her father to beat the shepherd boy who was looking after them. Thomason thought the retribution unnecessarily harsh and spoke to Mason who said he would have done exactly the same so Thomason took the matter no further.

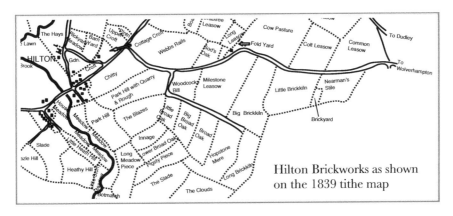

Hilton Brickworks as shown
on the 1839 tithe map

George Smith, another witness, " sais he was borne at a place call'd Tutors-Hill in the parish of Pattingham and is now 68 years of age, and said that about the time William Wood first set up his Brick killn in the way to Hilton which to the best of his Remembrance is now neare 20 years ago he for some time had work't at the said Brickilln and very often in that time as he was passing early in a morning to his work he us'd to meet one Thomas Green an old man who then liv'd by the Heathside within Clarely liberty driveing his sheep in a morning and observing he usually drove them up to the Gravelly way and no farther, he often asking him why he went with them thither and no farther, his answer was he durst not go farther with them for feare of mischief or to that effect.

He sais farther that in this present Mr Whitmore's father's time and neare 20 years ago he was often times sent for, to come to Ludson and to bring his netts and forretts with him to help Mr Whitmore to take some Rabbitts which lay under some stacks of Corne he had by his House at Ludson and he particularly remembers one time as Mr Whitmore sate by him being brought thither came in a chaise to see him take up the Rabbitts, one Pratt who was then Mr Whitmores sheppard came to his Master and they falling into discourses together about theire sheep he heard Pratt tell him that he had much ado to keep some of his sheep from straying towards Rudge Heath when Mr Whitmore seemingly angry tould him he must not suffer them to goe any more that way at which Prat said they shou'd not any more if he cou'd help it, farther that about this time it was much talkt about in the neighbourhood that there was some misunderstanding between Mr Creswell and Mr Whitmore about Mr Whitmore's sheep and it was said as that some Bonds or agreement were entred into about it, but whether it was so or not he knows no more than common discourse." Pratt had no easy job in containing Whitmore's sheep as there were rarely less than eight hundred of them, according to a witness.

Rights to grazing on commons were sought after and fiercely protected as this inquiry shows but the value of this account is in the witness statements. We can hear the way people speak, picture Mr Whitmore arriving in his carriage to watch the ferrets at work, and sympathise with poor Mr Pratt as he tries to control a flock of eight hundred sheep. We learn of the punishment meted out to offenders such that even Mr Whitmore advised his shepherd to avoid confrontation and find that Mr. Wood set up his brickyard in Hilton around 1711. The witnesses often include comments which have nothing to do with the matter in hand such as the following: "Mr. Dalley, under instruction from Mr. Caswell, told Mr. Knock that if he did not keep Pattingham Church he would come and knock his house down." As a piece of social history the Rudge Heath inquiry is a sheer delight.

Bricks found in Hilton Brickyards 2015

HUNTING, SHOOTING AND FISHING

HUNTING

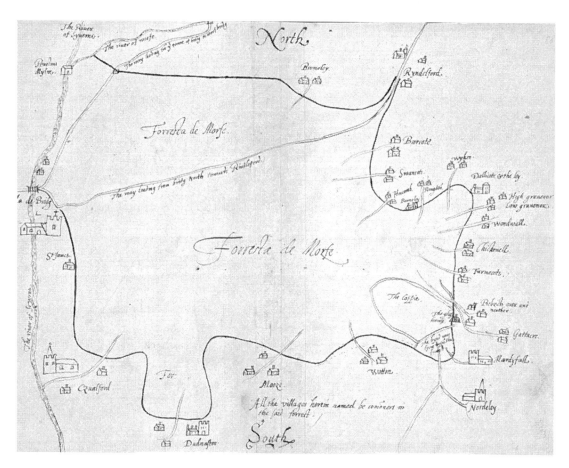

Forest of Morfe 1595. Pencil and ink drawing on paper (British Library)

The Forest of Morfe was a royal hunting ground which in medieval times stretched from Kinver in the east to Bridgnorth in the west and included the southern part of the parish of Worfield up to the River Worfe. Strict rules were put in place to preserve the hunting ground for the King or Queen which included restrictions on grazing, lopping of greenery, felling of trees, and, of course, hunting by local men.

44

The Talbot .
Source: *Rees's Cyclopædia* or *Universal Dictionary of the Arts and Sciences* edited by the Revd. Abraham Rees. (1743-1825)

This silver vervel found in the Worfield area would have been attached to a hawk's leg. It is inscribed John Talbot and appropriately shows a Talbot dog. Image courtesy of the Portable Antiquities Scheme. Reference: HESH-3A6AE5. Estimated date 1601-1654

We have no record of the monarchs of England hunting in the Morfe Forest but assuming that they did, we can imagine the pageantry of the occasion in which both horse and rider were attired in their finest regalia. The landscape of the Morfe Forest was not that of dense woodland as one might deduce from the word, 'forest', but open parkland well suited to a fast chase with greyhounds. Weary from the chase the deer would either be killed by the hounds or shot with a strongbow. In Edward III's reign (1328-1377) a number of licences were granted for small acreages of land to be enclosed which must have made a chase more difficult, but poachers managed to enjoy their hunting nonetheless.[56] We can see from the few fragments of Forest court records which have survived, that illegal hunting was not uncommon.[57]

- 1490 William Gravenor, Humphrey Lee and five others were charged with chasing and driving deer.
- 1492 Roger & Thomas Blike formerly of Alveley killed a deer at the Castle of Bowwe
- 1492 Humphrey Wolrich kept a brache [scenting hound] which has distressed 20 fawns. He was told many times by officers in the King's name to put the said brache away. He also keeps a grey bitch which struck a deer

[56] *National Archives,* E32/149

[57] *National Archives,* DL 39/1/26

- 1492 Edward Grey, Robert Gatacre of Gatacre hunted hares many times in the said Forest and some times cast of their hounds at the Broad Moor hunting all the Forest ...and sometimes kill a deer. Daily they hunt the hares so that the king's deer have no rest
- 1492 There are so many cattle & pigs in the forest that the deer stand in despair
- 1492 A deer was killed at the Broad Moor by someone unknown
- 1492 Thomas Underhill of Bridgnorth, Richard Caldecote of Brugge kept a ferret and destroyed the conies in the Forest of Morfe
- 1492 Thomas Cresset & others came to the Forest of Shirlett with bows and arrows and greyhounds & killed two fawns
- 1494 Humphrey Gatacre hunted on St Katherine's day with his greyhounds
- 1494 Richard Jordan & John Foxall hunted
- 1496 Edward Grey & Robert Gatacre killed a doe in the forest of Claverley, and bare it to the Hall of Gatacre and there disposed of it to their pleasure.
- 1496 4 hunted with greyhounds in Round Hill to the disturbance of the King's game

In the early years of the seventeenth century large areas of the Forest of Morfe were leased to local landowners and by the early nineteenth century the whole of the Forest had been enclosed. As there were no more deer to be hunted another quarry had to be sought; foxes

Whether fox hunting was initially to control their numbers or simply an opportunity to have a good gallop is debatable. By 1908, when the following pictures were taken, it was the Albrighton Hunt which was hunting across Worfield parish. Originally a sport for those wealthy enough to have their own hounds, and land to hunt over, by the nineteenth century fox hunting had become organised into a more public sport, funded by subscription. Local estate owners might become masters of the hunt, as befitted their status, but farmers, business people, and anyone who chose, was welcome to follow as long as they paid their dues. Notable local Masters of Foxhounds were Thomas Boycott of Rudge (1825), who was followed by Walter Gifford of Chillington. It was Gifford who built new kennels at Albrighton from which the hunt derived its name.[58] Captain James Foster of Apley, was joint Master in 1887 and Col. C. E. Goulburn of Somerford Hall, Brewood, a relation by marriage to Captain James Foster, in 1903. The Goulburns later ran the Apley Estate and lived at Ewdness.

The speed of the chase and the challenge of jumping fences were obvious attractions of hunting but riding to hounds also gave social standing. Property for sale was advertised with the benefit of being in a particular hunt and the Albrighton was quite prestigious. Industrialists in Wolverhampton, such as Sir Alfred Hickman, colliery owner and ironmaster, might have built his wealth from grime, but once a week (three times if he had the time), he could ride to hounds, enjoy the fresh air of the countryside and rub shoulders with his equals or betters in society. Status within the hunting fraternity depended partly on money ie the quality of one's horse, but also on how good a horseman/woman one was.

One of those in Worfield who hunted was Eve Collis. Eve and her husband John had moved to Hayes Bank, Stableford, in the late 1930s after they had married. The house had a loose box

---

[58] *Staffordshire Advertiser,* 8 November 1930, p. 11

so that was good enough for Eve who loved her horses. Born Eve Pepperell Bent, her parents lived in Calcutta so she spent most of her childhood with her grandfather, Sam Loveridge, in Bilbrook, Staffordshire. Sam Loveridge was Master of the Albrighton Hounds for forty years, so Eve must have grown up with hunting in her blood. As an adult, she rejoined her parents in India where she rode in steeplechases against men. She was quite a woman. One hunt follower recalled that she would regularly canter from the back of the field shouting, "Out of the way, I can't stop." This was very unlikely, because when she did get to the front, she pulled up without any trouble at all.

Albrighton Hunt meeting at Davenport House c1908

No sooner had the fox-hunting season ended in late spring, than otter hunting began. The Hawkstone Otter Hounds (HOH) covered a huge area of Wales and the Borders, including Worfield. Otter hunting dates back to the fourteenth century although it was only in the nineteenth century that the sport grew in popularity. Hounds were bred specifically for otter hunting, but less than a century later there were calls for otter hunting to be banned in the UK. Ostensibly the reason for killing otters was to protect fish stocks but actually, as with fox-hunting, otter hunting probably had more to do with the fact that one could walk across countryside otherwise out of bounds, meet friends, and have a good day out. It is perhaps surprising to us today how many did follow otter hounds. In 1860, there were about forty followers on horseback and a hundred and fifty on foot when the HOH met at Davenport House. An otter was found near Worfield Mill and caught near Stableford, being the first otter to be killed on the Worfe for more than twenty years. In this instance it was not the hounds who killed the otter, but the unfortunate animal was trapped by a net which had been strung across the Worfe; not quite sporting behaviour, methinks![59] In 1879, hounds met at Rindleford and again caught their quarry at Stableford.[60] The last date I have found for an otter hunt was 1939 when the Hawkstone pack met at Apley Gates.[61] An otter was followed up the Worfe to Worfield where they lost him, for which I can imagine every reader is saying, "thank goodness for that!"

The Albrighton Hunt Meet at the Wheel in 1908

---

[59] *Shrewsbury Chronicle*, 21 April 1860, p. 2

[60] *Eddowes Journal & General Advertiser for Shropshire & the Principality of Wales*, 9 April 1879, p. 6

[61] *Birmingham Post*, 6 May 1939, p. 14

Hunting hares is another ancient sport with hares being hunted down by scent or sight hounds. There were two packs of scent hounds hunting in Worfield in the nineteenth century; the Wheatland Beagles, kennelled in Bridgnorth, and a pack of harriers kept by John Jasper of Stableford. [62] Descended from the Talbot and St. Hubert hound, harriers are mid-way in height between beagles and foxhounds.

Sight hound coursing was another popular sport in the nineteenth century. Beaters would drive a hare to the coursing field and one greyhound competed against another to see how many times it could turn the animal. A slipper ensured that the two greyhounds had their leads slipped at the same time. Apley prided itself on staging the best coursing event in the country and at an annual event in 1864, there were seventy participants and a good number of hares.[63] The Davenport Estate was not to be outdone but in 1858 there were very few hares. Sensibly the animals had decided to stay away from the party.[64] In 1860, however, eleven hares were killed.[65] Fox terriers were also used in coursing and in 1888 a private coursing event was held at the Wheel.[66]

Further Reference: John Randall, *Old Sports and Sportsmen*, Madeley, 1873

Acknowledgment
Information about Eve and John Collis was kindly provided by their daughter, Marietta King.

[62] *Bridgnorth Journal*, 9 December 1893, p. 8

[63] *Eddowes Journal*, 20 September, 1843, p. 2

[64] *Bridgnorth Journal*, 23 January 1864, p. 4

[65] *Wellington Journal*, 6 March 1858, p. 3

[66] *Bridgnorth Journal*, 14 January, 1888, p. 5

SHOOTING

The first record found to date of game birds being caught within the parish is in 1365 when William Bullokes gives 6d to the Lady of the Manor for permission to raise a cockshutt.[67] Cockshutt is a common enough name in Shropshire but the 1839 Field Names Map shows only two cockshutt names within Worfield parish; Cockshutt Coppice and Cockshutt in Bromley. Perhaps this was the location for Mr Bullokes' Cockshutt. The only doubt I have about this is whether that would have been permitted as Bromley was within the Forest of Morfe.

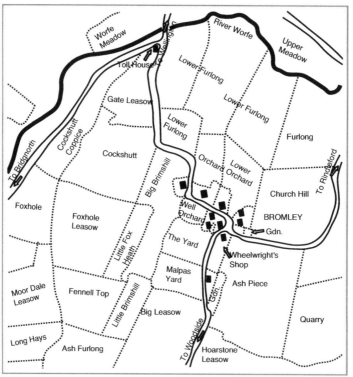

Cockshutt & Cockshutt Coppice in Bromley

Wherever Mr Bullokes' cockshutt was, Woodcock were the quarry, and the birds were netted rather than shot. Alongside the coppice in which the birds lived, an open area was used to trap them as they came out at dusk. These nocturnal birds lie low in the daytime, only flying up when you are almost about to put your foot on them, frightening both you and the poor bird to death. The dog which was bred to flush out woodcock, and from which it derives its name, was

---

[67] *Shropshire Archives*, P314/W/1/1/54

the Cocker Spaniel but whether dogs were used to drive the birds into the nets of a cockshutt we don't know. Unsurprisingly, we have no record of the workings of the Bromley cockshutt.

It was not, however, the Cocker Spaniel which was the gundog of choice at Davenport House at the beginning of the twentieth century but the Flat Coated Retriever. The shooting tenant of Davenport at that time was Henry Reginald Cooke whose devotion to the breed was legendary.[68] In 1881, Cooke had set up his Riverside Kennels at Riverside near Nantwich, and spared no expense in breeding and buying the best of the breed. This was both a good and a bad thing. Flat Coats became standardised but Cooke's dominance of trials and shows inflated prices and inhibited other breeders. In 1908 Cooke turned down an offer of 260 guineas (about £30,000 in today's money) for one of his dogs, an example of the huge prices these dogs could command. However, the tide was beginning to turn ever so slightly in favour of the Labrador.[69]

It was in 1903 that the Labrador was recognised by the Kennel Club as a definite and distinct breed and it soon began to make its mark in field trials. The battle for supremacy between the Flat Coat and the Labrador had begun. In 1909 and 1910, the International Gundog League's Retriever Society held field trials at Davenport.[70] In 1909, Cooke had success with one of his Riverside Flat Coated Retrievers and in 1910 the battle of the retrievers was repeated at Stanmore. The shooters were W. J. Knox, W. Marchant, G. Whitmore, H. Bath, R. E. Birch, Sir Henry Grey, Colonel Wakeman and Major Amphlett. The retrievers worked on partridges and hares and the result must have been a great disappointment to Mr Cooke, with three out of the four prizes going to Labradors.[71] [72]The demise of the Flat Coated Retriever was nigh but in spite of reduced interest in the breed, Reginald Cooke remained its staunch advocate until his death in 1951 at Dalicote.

Meanwhile at Apley in 1902, Mr Sharpe had taken over as head gamekeeper, presiding over kennels containing Curly Coated Retrievers, Flat Coated Retrievers, and Springer Spaniels. Gradually the Labrador's supremacy ensured that all were replaced except Springers; the gamekeeper's dog. For an all-round dog, the Springer could not be surpassed. In 1928, Mr Sharpe's son, Norman, took over from his father and on his retirement wrote an excellent book on his reminiscences of life at Apley before the Second World War.[73]

Game Records for the Davenport Estate from 1925-1930 were deposited in Dudley Archives by Douglas Hawthorne who farmed at Catstree. Whether Hawthorne was the tenant of the shoot or whether this was a local syndicate, I don't know. Reared birds; partridges, pheasants,

[68] *The Field*, 4 September 1909, p. 50

[69] David Tomlinson, *Flat Coated Retrievers: the Edwardian Gentleman's Choice*, The Field, June 19, 2018

[70] *The Scotsman*, 9 October 1909, p. 7

[71] *The Scotsman*, 12 October 1910, p. 12

[72] *The Field*, 15 October 1910

[73] Norman Sharpe, *Apley Hall, The Golden Years of a Sporting Estate*, Merlin Unwin Books, 2009

and duck, provided most of the sport, with the occasional native birds such as woodcock and snipe getting far too involved for their own good.

Both Apley and Davenport shoots continue today on much more of a commercial basis than when Reginald Cooke was tenant of the Davenport shoot, and I would be very surprised if there was either a Flat or Curly Coated Retriever to be seen. Labradors and Spaniels reign supreme.

Game	1925-1926	1926-1927	1928-1929	1929-1930
Partridge	119	221	78	247
Pheasants	318	541	442	621
Wild Duck	339	342	282	170
Snipe	5	2	2	3
Hares	9	16	6	1
Rabbits	15	46	37	32
Woodcock	5	1	-	1
Tufted Duck	1	-	-	-
Landrail	-	1	-	-
Plovers	-	2	-	-
Otters	2	-	2	2
Number of guns	5-8	4-10	4-9	4-10

Game Shot on the Davenport Estate 1925-1930[74]

---

[74] *Dudley Archives*, D8/X4/6

POACHING

I swear I was not poaching but walking innocently along a footpath in Burcote Woods in 2019 when I had an uncomfortable reminder of what a flashpoint the humble pheasant can be. I had my new dog with me, a Field Spaniel, and had just, very unwisely, let her off the lead. Suddenly she took off after a pheasant like an Exocet missile and immediately someone shouted aggressively, 'call that dog back.' Of course, my usually obedient dog refused to come back with pheasants in the vicinity, and my confidence was not helped by comments such as, 'you shouldn't have let the dog off the lead if you can't get it back,' and, 'it's a good job the gamekeeper isn't around or he would shoot it.' Fortunately Winnie did return without a pheasant in her mouth which would have gone down very badly. Away we walked, tails definitely between our legs, to a commentary which refused to switch off. Of course I was in the wrong but there was something so violent about this encounter, so aggressive, to use that modern term, abusive, that seemed disproportionate to my 'crime'.

It is a fact that the pursuit of game polarises us into those who exercise their right to shoot or fish, whom we call sportsmen, and those who shoot or fish with no right whom we refer to as poachers. Clashes between poachers and gamekeepers can be dangerous, especially if the poachers carry guns, and in 1945 one such encounter in Worfield made the national newspapers.

On the night of the 2nd January 1945, William Chaplin, aged 79, gamekeeper, of Patmarsh Cottage, heard shots in Apley Woods and decided to investigate with the help of his son, John, aged 52. Armed with sticks, the two went into the woods, and shortly afterwards William Chaplin was shot with a .410 shotgun. John Chaplin gave chase but lost the culprit in the wood. He then roused the occupants of a nearby house and the police were sent for.

The following day, Scotland Yard took over the investigation from the local police. The male suspects were described as follows. The first was aged 35 to 40, thick-set, and 5ft 3in tall. He wore a dark trilby and an overcoat that was rather too long for him and spoke with a local accent. The second, aged about 30, was 5ft 8in tall & slim;. He wore a light coloured mac and a light cap. The third was aged about 35, 5ft 5in tall and thick set. He wore a dark, belted overcoat ,and a scarf around his neck and over his head. The last two had cycles and were seen by a lorry-driver at 1am on the night of the incident. The poachers seemed to have had an intimate knowledge of the woods and a search was made of all the local shops selling ammunition of the type used in the shooting.

On the 13th January, William Henry Harris aged 50 was brought before the magistrates in Bridgnorth and charged with the murder of Chaplin. "About two hundred people, many of them from the rural areas and carrying shopping baskets waited outside the Town Hall to see the accused."[75] Harris was from Tweedale Crescent, Madeley and was known locally as "the Little Man." He worked at Madeley Wood Colliery and had eight children. In his defence

---

[75] *Shields Daily News*, 13 January, 1945 p. 8

Harris said, "All I wish to say is that I had been out drinking. I had six pints and a half, and went home at a quarter past ten. It was a mad spasm and I was struck." Harris said that the gamekeeper had hit him on the face with a stick and in backing away from further blows, he accidentally fired his gun at Chaplin.[76] John Chaplin described how he was separated from his father in the woods and saw him confront a man who had a gun. His father had a stick raised and the man said, "Stand back. No, you don't." The two men were five or six feet apart, said John Chaplin, the gun went off and his father fell to the ground. John Chaplin denied that his father had hit the poacher.[77] On the way home, Harris dumped his overcoat in which were five pheasants. He later burnt the stock of the gun and threw the rest down a mine shaft.

The prosecution said that even if Chaplin had threatened the man with a stick, he was still entitled to arrest a poacher. It may be that Chaplin had done more than threaten because Harris's face had been marked, as one of his children noticed. Perhaps this was the reason that Harris was found guilty of manslaughter rather than murder and sentenced to seven years penal servitude.[78]

'The History of Poaching in Worfield', would be a pretty large tome. Here are some cases from the nineteenth century.

- 1849. Harry Fowler, aged 19, was convicted of stealing a carpet bag at Worfield which was the property of C. H. Molineux. He was also tried for stealing rabbit traps. Having already been in jail for poaching, Fowler was sentenced as follows: three months for stealing the carpet bag, six months for stealing the rabbit traps, and twice to be privately whipped.[79]
- 1863 Four poachers at High Rock Coppice: Isaac Rogers, William Low, George Littleford & Robert Furnell were charged with trespass at Worfield on 13 September last on Sunday morning in search of conies, the occupation belonging to Thomas Smith. Furnell didn't appear. James Barker, rabbit catcher, said that he was on watch at High Rock coppice when he saw the defendants in Penzer's field, stooping down at a rabbit hole. When he was coming up to them they ran off saying, "that is that d....d Jemmy Barker coming, bury the line and bolt". Barker went up to the hole and pulled the ferret out. Police gave evidence of repeated convictions by Low and Rogers and no defence was offered. Fine 40s each. Littleford and Furnell were fined 10s each.[80]
- 1867 Thomas Smith, toll collector, was charged with taking one rabbit in a poaching engine. Mr Gatacre allowed a nominal fine of 6d.[81]

---

[76] *Birmingham Daily Gazette*, 27 February 1945 p. 4

[77] *Hartlepool Northern Daily Mail*, February 1945 p. 8

[78] *Birmingham Mail*, 26 February 1945 p. 4

[79] *Shrewsbury Chronicle*, March 3 1849 p. 3

[80] *Shrewsbury Chronicle*, 16 October 1863 p. 7

[81] *Bridgnorth Journal*, 23 November 1867, p. 5

- 1868 Two men went fishing with Apley's gamekeeper at Rindleford Mill. Bob Ridley the miller (aka Sweet William or Billy Bouquet because his waistcoat smelled of aniseed) kindly stopped the mill wheel. Eventually the men had a good catch of trout but the author writes, "If you want to be a poacher you would be well-advised to try the sluice and backwater at Rowley's Mill." (*Poaching*, Sporting Times 25 January 1868, pp 6,7)

- 1879 George Millard of Hilton was charged with having one rabbit and 2 snares. Fine 10s and 8s 6d costs.[82]

- 1890 John Firmstone of Albrighton was one of a gang of poachers at Worfield found in possession of game [83]

- 1890 John Lamb, William York, John Shinton, Edward Watkiss & James Hill, all of Ironbridge, were charged with poaching at Hallonsford near Worfield and having game. It was the 4th September and PC Briggs was on duty at 4.30am when he saw the men with heavy bags on their backs. He blew his whistle to alert another police were nearby. The men ran a few yards and then threw stones. The policeman tried to search one of the bags but was dragged through the hedge into a field where the gang attacked him with sticks and stones and set a dog on him. His shoulder was injured and his head cut. When the other policeman arrived on the scene the men fled. Each had a £5 fine and Watkiss, Hill and Lamb had six months hard labour in addition for the assault.[84]

- 1895 30 or 40 youths from Bridgnorth were unlawfully beating High Rock and killed pheasants with catapults. Arthur Hall, Percy Tuckley & William Bowen were summoned for assaulting and beating the under-keeper, Sidney Gasper, on 2nd December. Fine 2s 6d each.[85]

- 1895 William and Richard Shakespeare were found guilty of poaching on land off Burcote Lane. The two pleaded their innocence and were outraged at the suggestion that they might be guilty but they had twenty-four previous convictions. Fined 40s each. [86]

- 1898 Harry Lowe and Charles Matthews, labourers, were accused of being in possession of a catapult and stones to kill pheasants. The offence took place at High Rock at 9.30pm and the offenders were caught by Sidney Gasper, Apley's gamekeeper. A scuffle took place. Gasper tried to search one of the offenders and said if he would not allow him to do that he would hit him on the head with a stick whereupon the offender said if he did he would punch him on the nose. Fined 10s each. [87]

---

[82]*Eddowes Journal*, 7 May 1879, p. 9

[83] *Wellington Journal*, 11 October 1890, p.6

[84] *Birmingham Daily Post*, 22 September 1890, p. 7

[85] *Bridgnorth Journal*, 12 January 1895, p.5

[86] *Bridgnorth Journal*, 12 January 1895, p. 4

[87] *Bridgnorth Journal*, 29 October 1898, p. 6

FISHING

It is hard to overestimate the importance of the River Worfe to the Parish of Worfield. Economically it was even more important in the past than it is now, providing a variety of benefits including power to drive mills, water for livestock, nutrients for meadows and food to eat. Until we polluted rivers so badly in the twentieth century ,they teemed with fish and eels. We have squandered what our ancestors looked after with such great care which prompts the question as to how the streams of Worfield were managed in medieval times.

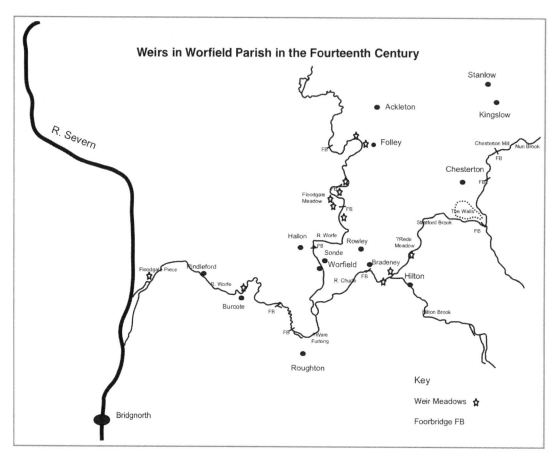

Preservation of the environment was the responsibility of all the tenants of the manor. It was they who had to scour ditches and keep streams in their rightful courses, free from obstructions and pollution. Any man-made structures or changes to the course of a river had to be permitted by the Lord of the Manor.

The fish stocks of all the rivers and streams in the parish were carefully protected. A licence from the lord was required in order to fish and only fish of a certain size could be taken. Fish were caught with flies, rods, nets, and fish traps. Thomas Barker in 1464, contravened two of the local regulations when he put three stakings in streams without a licence from the lord and fished with nets and flies destroying all the young fish in the Worfe and the Churle.[88]

Stones in the Worfe north of Worfield may be indications of a weir

Stakings, or fish weirs, were woven withies driven into the river bed and across the stream in a V-shape or series of V-shapes. The fish would thus be funnelled into nets which hung from the point of the V and a bridge was built over the stakings so that the nets could be hauled out. Fish weirs were dotted all along the streams but at measured intervals so there would be no overfishing. In 1360, John of Eudenas was given permission to build a weir at Eudenas Meadow in Ewke, which was perhaps the same weir which changed hands in 1463.[89] [90]Large sandstone blocks present in the Worfe today may indicate the location of weirs as in the picture

[88] *Shropshire Archives,* P314/W/1/1/325

[89] *Shropshire Archives,* P314/W/1/1/48

[90] *Shropshire Archives,* P314/W/1/1/324

on the previous page which shows such stones at Hallonsford. Even more delicate structures, traces of stakes and wattle have survived in Alveley and Arley.

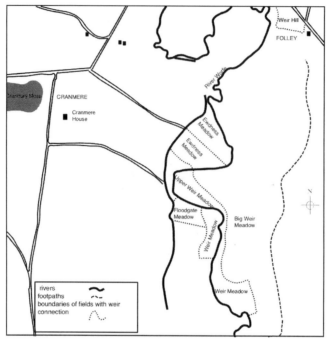

Weir Meadows north of Worfield

There are no weirs shown on the 1839 map but evidence of their former presence is indicated by field names such as Weir Meadow but other records can fill in some gaps. From the Manor Court Rolls we know that a weir place in Chesterton next to the Weir Parrock of John Bradeney, and part of Hilton Walls, was leased in 1456 on condition that no fishing nets were put between Hogemans Meadow and the weir.[91] Other weir references are as follows:

- 1340 A weir in the Churle is claimed by Adam of Beckbury which should belong to the lord (*Shropshire Archives*, P314/W/1/1/20-23)
- 1365 William of Asterhull is given the right to rebuild the fulling mill at Churleford in Wyken which belongs to the Chantry Chapel "and valuing the ancient and customary weir". (*Shropshire Archives*, P314/W/1/1/61)
- 1433 A weir called Watstakyngs and fishery adjoining and a new weir between Redemedowe and Crowmere Heath (*Shropshire Archives*, 5586/1/284)
- 1437 A new weir at Hanging Rock which by 1440 is a weir and a house (*Shropshire Archives*, 5586/1/288)
- 1439 An unlawful weir on the Churle (*Shropshire Archives*, 5586/1/291)

---

[91] *Shropshire Archives*, P314/W/1/1/311

- 1446 Thompkys weir called Snakenale (*Shropshire Archives*, 5586/1/297)
- 1447 Pasteford Weir (*Shropshire Archives*, 5586/1/299)

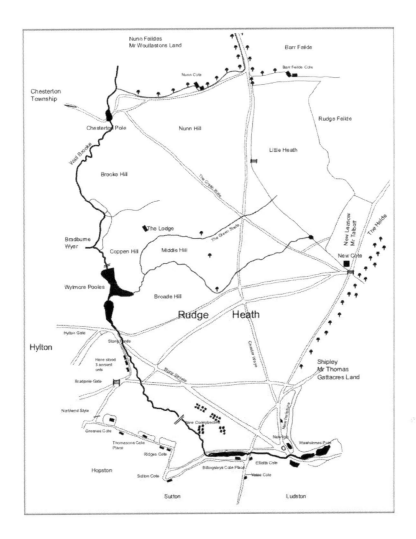

Pre 1635 map of Rudge Heath showing Wylmore Pools (*Shropshire Archives*, 5586/13/14)

- 1447 Weir at Wycheford (*Shropshire Archives*, 5586/1/298)
- 1453 Snell's Weir in Chesterton (*Shropshire Archives*, P314/W/1/1/308)
- 1473 A weir at the end of the Lord's Meadow (*Shropshire Archives*, P314/W/1/1/353)
- 1496 Weir under Wolmore Hill (*Shropshire Archives*, 5586/1/224)

- 1575 Weir between Stapleford and Ackleton & one in Bromley (*Shropshire Archives,* 5586/1/232)

- 1578 Redrock Weir with a fishery up to Bache Brook (*Shropshire Archives,* 5586/1/236)

Weirs had a dual purpose, of managing fishing and controlling the flooding of adjacent meadows. Flooding improved the fertility of waterside meadows thereby increasing yields and offering early grazing. When the floodgates were opened, the water must spread evenly across the surface leaving no stagnant pools which would harm the grass. It was said that the water should flow, "on at a trot and off at a gallop".

Natural and man-made pools provided more fish stocks, again at the discretion of the Lord of the Manor. Some of these pools still exist, such as Hoccum and Barnsley Pools, others such as the Batch, Chesterton and Wylmore Pools have disappeared. Even in my lifetime ponds were so common we took them for granted. Then there was a time, probably in the sixties, when many were filled in because they were a nuisance and no longer needed and others have dried up naturally as the water table has gone down. Even the pool at Cranmere, which was used to drain Cranmere Common when it was enclosed, is now much reduced.

In 1744, Samuel Fletcher and John Eykyn leased the three Barnsley Pools, Hoccom Pool, two at the Batch and all other pools on Morfe Common for twenty-one years. The landlord was Thomas Whitmore and the rent was £5 per year. At the end of the lease the pools had to be left in good order and for each acre of pool (pro rata for larger or smaller pools) no less than twenty brace of store carp six inches or more in length had to remain.[5]

The map on the previous page dates from before 1635 when it was endorsed by John Denham. Although it is of the eastern side of the parish it shows pools which no longer exist. Chesterton Pool is now simply a boggy area around the stream now known as Nun Brook but in 1600 it was known as Wall Brook. Even though Wylemore Pools, on the boundary between Rudge and Worfield parishes, were quite large, they have also disappeared. The Wylmore Pools were created by Edmund Waryng of Leacross in Staffordshire in 1614-1615 when the Lord of the Manor gave Waryng permission to create fishing pools in Hilton at Waryng's own expense. He was given a lease to use the same for twelve years. The pools were to be situated on the waste near to the fields of Hilton adjoining the Lordship of Rudge, and Waryng was allowed to dig turves in Hilton to create dams. The Lord of the Manor would take a proportion of the catch from these pools. In the case of Wylmore Pools, Lord Bergavenny could choose between fish or a monetary equivalent as payment. He reserved the right "at each drawing or fishing of the pond or ponds to one good and convenient dish of all sorts of such fish and there housed stored or kept or the sum of 10s".[92]

Pollution of ponds and streams was a constant concern and in Henry VIII's reign became a problem which he partly created. So great was the demand for hemp, particularly from the Royal Navy, that in 1533, Henry ordered that for every sixty acres of land owned, a quarter of an acre of hemp had to be sown. In 1563, Queen Elizabeth increased the required acreage to an acre of flax per sixty acres. The problem was that the flax fibres had to be broken down and that was done by soaking them in water. Dew on a meadow would do the job but soaking in a stream or pond was quicker although with an unfortunate by-product of pollution. Retting in

---

[92] *Shropshire Archives,* 5586/2/258

streams and ponds was therefore forbidden and the court rolls of Worfield abound with fines for "putting hemp in the common waters".

In the nineteenth century, land at Stableford was flooded due to the invasion of "the American weed." I am afraid I have no idea what the American weed was, but flooding certainly devalued the agricultural value of Stableford land resulting in a bitter court case with the Badger Estate thought to be responsible.[93] The issue wasn't just that the land was affected; fishing was damaged as well, with fish getting caught in the weeds. By this time, the Worfe had gained a considerable reputation for its trout (and eels), providing a good income for landowners. Poaching was a constant issue, with the locals knowing exactly where the trout could be found. William Brown, George Rowley and Daniel Wootton were found guilty of taking three trout out of the stream at Chesterton. One trout each doesn't seem a big crime but the Petty Sessions in Bridgnorth thought otherwise and fined the boys for their misdemeanour.[94]

An outrageous poaching incident was committed by poisoning the Stratford Brook with lime.[95] The poachers on this occasion were a group of men and women who came from Wolverhampton. At 6.30am on the 14 April 1896, Henry Harley of Hilton saw three men taking fish out of the stream. Two of the men were standing in the water either side of the Stratford Brook, across which a net was hung, and another was standing farther up stream floating fish to the side of the brook. Although they were disturbed they were in no hurry to leave and were still there at 10am when a police constable arrived. He recognised one of the men, Hodgkiss, as a travelling salesmen selling salt and besoms. The defendants were found guilty and each served two months of hard labour.

A bill has survived from 1480 which lists various types of fish bought probably for a festival such as Good Friday:

Bread - 3s 9d, ale - 3s 11d, white herring - 11d, red herring - 6d, salt - 16d, saltfish - 22d halfpenny, stuckfish - 10d halfpenny, oil - 4d halfpenny,… 5d, wine and vinegar - 9d, fresh fish - 13d, mustard - halfpenny, reward to the wife - 12d, oats - 2d, for bearing ale from Bruggenorth - 6d.[96] One assumes the fresh fish would have been caught locally and the preserved fish brought by boat in barrels up the Severn to Bridgnorth. Stuckfish were air-dried, red herrings were smoked and salted, white herrings might have been fresh or pickled, and saltfish, as the name suggests, preserved in salt.

In the past, fishing was a much more significant part of people's lives and the pools and rivers of the parish yielded a valuable crop some of which would have been eaten locally and some may well have been sold. Now, of course, the same waters are used for sport and the Worfe still retains a reputation for its trout which our ancestors also enjoyed.

[93] *Eddowes Journal,* 2 August 1871, p. 6 & 7

[94] *Eddowes Journal,* 8 July 1874, p. 8

[95] *Bridgnorth Journal,* May 30 1896, p. 7

[96] *Shropshire Archives,* P314/W/1/1/417

THE NINETEENTH CENTURY

ANTIQUARIANS

Local and family history became fashionable in the nineteenth century and the term antiquarian was coined for these historians. There were many of them and their contribution to our understanding of the past is immense. Three antiquarians deserve special mention in relation to Worfield; the Revd. R. W. Eyton, John Randall, and William Hardwicke.

William Hardwicke

Eyton (1815-1881) was the Rector of Ryton Church and researched the early history of Shropshire which he published in twelve volumes, entitled, "Antiquities of Shropshire".[97] Worfield's history is in Volume 3. Eyton was particularly interested in the period from Domesday to the thirteenth century and examined documents which most of us would find incomprehensible and some of which may no longer exist. It is Eyton's explanation of this early

---

[97] R. W. Eyton, *Shropshire Antiquities*, (J. R. Smith 1860)

history which makes him so useful, for example, enlightening us that because Worfield Manor was once held by the King, this gave it the right to trade without tolls and to manage the manor as a self-governing body operating according to local custom. The manor courts held to carry out this governance are an important source of historical information and fortunately Worfield has a good run of them covering five hundred years. The absence of court rolls and private deeds before 1327 creates a watershed. There is wonderful detail after that date and a very patchy picture before it. Eyton's work became source material for Randall and for Robert Evans in his "History of the Rectors and Vicars of Worfield Salop 1205-1972." One of Eyton's weaknesses is his use of a limited number of sources and failure to give clear references. For examples, the conclusion that Roughton and Chesterton Chapels were both subsidiaries of St. Peter's Church and that Roughton Chapel stood on the Green at Roughton, presumably came from the Surveys of Chantries, Collegiate Churches and Free Chapels in England and Wales 1546-1548, although Eyton doesn't say that. This should not however detract from the value of Eyton's research. If you want to know the early history of any Shropshire parish, Eyton is a good starting point.

John Randall (1810-1910), born in Broseley, was a pottery painter by trade, only retiring at the age of seventy-one when his eyesight began to fail. He then opened a post office in Madeley, sold books and stationery and ran a printing works. No-one could say that Randall was work-shy! Randall was also a keen geologist and a Fellow of the Royal Geological Society. He was offered a post with the British Museum but preferred to stay in Shropshire and his home county was certainly the beneficiary of his talents. Randall's books included a geological study of the Severn Valley, histories of Broseley, Madeley & Shifnal, studies of the local clay and iron industries and, of course, a history of Worfield, entitled, "Worfield and its Townships, being a history of the parish from Saxon and Norman times and including notices of old families and documents contained in the parish chest".[98] Randall is particularly good at painting a picture of what life was like as he wandered around the parish. Perhaps it is the artist's eye for detail which brings Worfield's landscape and its people to life so that the book is still talked about today. A conversation about the history of Worfield with any of its residents of a certain age is soon bound to include the question, "Have you read 'Worfield and its Townships'"?

William Hardwicke (1772-1842) had a particular interest in genealogy. Based on the Herald's Visitation to the County in 1623, Hardwicke drew up about 1500 pedigrees of the gentry and higher status families which he published in three volumes entitled, "Shropshire Pedigrees".[99] Hardwicke is a good place to start for the early history of families, for example his pedigree of the Bradneys of Bradney and Hilton, dates from 1349.[100]

Hardwicke was born in Allscott and later lived at Diamond Hall, although he retained a house in Rindleford for many years, perhaps as his country retreat. He worked as a solicitor in Bridgnorth with the firm of Devey and Hardwicke. This gave him an understanding of legal

---

[98] John Randall, *Worfield & its Townships*, (Madeley, 1887)

[99] Shropshire Archives, *Pedigrees of the Heralds Visitation of Shropshire (3 volumes)*, 6001

[100] Shropshire Archives hold many of Hardwicke's pedigrees, indexed alphabetically

and Latin documents, and access to much local history. Unlike Randall and Eyton, most of Hardwicke's observations on the history of Worfield were not published. Hardwicke writes in a privately published book entitled "Hardwicke of the County of Stafford," as follows: "In Saxon times it appears that the present manor of Worfield was in two distinct manors, and continued as such until after the death of Hugh de Montgomery. One half was as we have noted before, Gurveld or Worveld and the other is noted as Wolferesford from its nearness to the castle which Wulfric Spot had erected to cover the crossing at Hallon Ford."[101] Wolferesford was what is now known as Wyken but where Hardwicke got his information from he doesn't reveal.

It was in Hardwicke's unpublished notes, now held in Stafford Record Office, that I first read about the castle at Hallon on the site later occupied by the pound, and now by Pound House.[102] Hardwicke believed that Queen Aethelflaed, who died in 918, stayed at the castle while her castle on Panpudding Hill was being built. At first I dismissed the idea as fanciful but then evidence for the castle appeared in the manor court rolls , for example:

• 1328 Matilda of the castle brewed.[103]
• 1334 Robert Nelde unjustly threw up a ditch at the castle.[104]

Unfortunately we have no documentary evidence about Aethelflaed or Wulfric Spot being in Hallon so one can only assume the stories were handed down locally through the generations. It would be easy to dismiss Hardwicke's theories out of hand but both Aethelflaed, in Bridgnorth, and Wulfric Spot, a son of Lady Wulfrun of Wolverhampton, were geographically close enough to make a connection with Hallon Castle plausible. There is one other possible link with Wulfric Spot. In his will he endowed Burton Abbey with land in various locations, including Halen.[105] Hardwicke believed this was Halen in Worfield, although experts today think Halen refers to Halesowen.

In 1809, Hardwicke's brother, John Bell Hardwicke, lived in Burcote and while doing some work to remove soil which had accumulated at the base of a rocky outcrop, a cave was revealed in which there were the bones of several people and animals. The cave faced east and was quite large, 30 feet long by 12 feet deep. Hardwicke recorded the event in an article published in the Gentleman's Magazine of January 1810 and dated the collapse to before the reign of Queen Elizabeth, "as several circumstances which took place here in her reign have been handed down in the Saddler family which lived here from 1592 to lately." Unfortunately we are left wondering what those circumstances were.

Hardwicke offers a different perspective on local history from Eyton and Randall because these were families he knew personally and had lived amongst. Sometimes his imagination got the better of him, for example he suggested that the Burcote cave was deliberately filled in by

---

[101] William Hardwicke, *Hardwicke of the County of Stafford,* (privately published, undated)

[102] Stafford Record Office, *Collections for Notes on Worfield,* 350/1-5/40

[103] Shropshire Archives, *Worfield Manor Court Roll,* P314/W/1/1/6

[104] Shropshire Archives, *Worfield Manor Court Roll,* P314/W/1/1/18

[105] P. H. Sawyer ed., *Charters of Burton Abbey,* (OUP 1979)

Christian people who wanted to prevent the bones being used for Druidical worship. The latest effort to locate the cave was in 1960 and to date it has not been found.

One can forgive an over-active imagination when one reads Hardwicke's portrayal of some members of the Barney family. For example: "Francis Barney born October 1698 had no issue. He was very careful with money but could be generous. Once he said to a neighbour 'Are you going to the fair tomorrow?' The man replied, 'No, I haven't the money.' Barney said, 'How much would it take for you to go?' £4 said the man and Barney lent it. The man went to the fair and repaid the money to Francis Barney the following week. Francis Barney left £3,000.

Timothy Barney was a blacksmith at Hallon and died in 1788 at the age of 73 years and he also had a careful streak. His dress to visit an attorney in Bridgnorth would be an old flannel waistcoat with sleeves. This garment saved the expense of a coat. A wallet over his shoulder, a short old leather apron and a torn hat patched with linsey. Timothy Barney was a ringer at the church for fifty years and continued so till his death, even though in his latter years he was too ill to ring. He then subcontracted the bell ringing to an able-bodied man at a lesser wage."

One cannot help but be captivated by Hardwicke's descriptions and by his mentioning facts which would otherwise go unnoticed. Here are a few examples:

- "In 1621, the 19th year of King James's reign, the Manor was most seriously and injudiciously mangled and amputated about due to greed which in the course of a few years led to the almost complete obliteration of oak.

- Rindleford Mill at about 1720 was converted into an oil mill but lately disused, being now altogether used for grinding corn, a large portion of this structure being purchased from the lord of the manor in 18.... Worfield Mill has been lately rebuilt and continuing as the property of the lord of the manor.

- In 1789 there was a survey done of the parish and the acres of enclosed land amount to more than 7015 acres. The survey was done by Messrs Vickers father and son and assessed by John Bishton of Kelsall Salop and Daniel Banton of Shipley in the parish of Claverley.

- On the North side of the Rectory [Lower Hall] is a brick and timber structure, the dwelling of the 6 former vicars since the reformation. On the same point are several miserable dwellings which had been given at times to form a revenue for the priests of chantry who officiated at St Mary's altar. In the first year of King Edward VI' reign [1547/8], the chantry priests were dispossessed and in James 1's reign the churchwardens bought the houses for the poor of the parish. At the North end of these houses is a small meadow.

- Men sat apart from women in the church till 15 May 1796

- On August 13 1796 a plain bob was rung by six Pattingham lads Thomas Shelley, George Shelley and James Shelley, John Salter, William Law and John Law

- The old vestry stood at the North Western extremity, a large square room from whence is the approach into the organ gallery, and in which the Jury of the Lord of the Manor Court of ancient demesne upon all trials respecting land in this manor were impanelled and there sat to hear evidence adduced before the High Steward and assessor and afterwards deliver a verdict upon the case. It was upon one of those important but disagreeable occasions that ...Hoccom of Hoccom was seized with death and expired before he and his companions could deliver their verdict. The partition was taken down, the space filled with pews and then a new vestry built at the east of the St Mary's Chapel.

- A great part of the plot [churchyard] was fenced with pales in James 1 reign but in 1664 was secured by a proper stone wall built by Jonas Groom. George Runnowles was paid for the mortar. 62 wain loads of stone were brought in. Francis Payne was paid for fencing the church.
- The shaft of the medieval cross has long gone, perhaps it went at the time of the Reformation.
- The Grammar School [the building at the end of the church path] was where the half yearly courts of the lord of the manor were held.
- On the North side of the churchyard there aren't many remains. It was generally used for felons and malefactors but almost certainly contains the bodies of the plague victims of 1349 in pits of 12 to 20. The area is called the pest ground.
- Cranmere has lately been drained and nearly made dry.
- Eventually the Cattstreys died out in Worfield in the male line and the property went to the Cox family. The ancient family residence of the Cattstrees is now much improved with considerable additions to the house and modern outbuildings recently erected being now occupied by Samuel Nicholls and the estate has been much increased from the inclosure of the 2 commons."

Hardwicke also recorded some of the tombstones in the Church and Churchyard which have now disappeared.

"The Bell Family
Near this place lie the remains of John Bell late of Roughton who died June 28th 1740 aged 73 years . Jane M. Bell died Dec 20th 1752 aged 51 years, William Bell son of Thomas and Jane died July 9th 1753 aged 16 years, Thomas Bell died April 11th 1754 aged 57 years, William Bell brother to Thomas Bell died 1754 Nov 22 aged 53 years. Thomas Bell son of Thomas and Jane Bell died March 1st. 1770 aged 40 years likewise John Bell his brother died March 27th 1799 aged 74 years

Devey
Near to the principal or south entrance are several Devey tombs but the footsteps of the youths of the school of this parish have obliterated the whole of the inscriptions.

Billingsley
Near to the above in memory of Charlotte Billingsley who died July 16th 1793 also Richard Billingsley gent who died March 9th 1804 aged 64 'A loving husband and wife most dear this tender couple lie sleeping here'.

John Bradney
On the East side of the principal avenue near to the South entrance. Here lyeth interred the body of John Bradney who departed this life in the 80th year of his age AD 1696. Here also lyeth the body of Jane the wife of the said John Bradney who departed this life Dec 12 1712 and in memory of John Bradney of Hilton who departed this life the 28th day of November 1750 aged 55 years also Elizabeth the wife of Joseph Bradney departed this life 9th Dec. 1766

aged 52 years. Life how short, eternity how long. Good God on what a slender thread hang everlasting things.

Thomas Worrall

On a headstone near to the east end of the chancel. In memory of Thomas Worrall late of Oldington departed this life January 31st AD 1753 aged 35

Eykyn

Upon a headstone near to that above.

James Eykyn gent died October 16th 1783 aged 46 Close to the above. Near to this place are deposited the remains of many ancestors of the Eykyn family of Ackleton in this parish particularly of James Eykyn gent and Catherine his wife with several of their children also 3 of their grandchildren James, Elizabeth and Ann who died in their infancy son and daughters of Roger and Elizabeth Eykyn of W'ton Co. Stafford and also of Elizabeth their mother, daughter of Gregory Hickman of Stourbridge in the Co. of Worcs. gent after a long and painful illness which she supported with piety, great patience and resignation died on the 16th Aug 1767 in the 35th year of her age. She was not only amiable in her person, but a most affectionate wife and tender mother, a benevolent Christian and sincere friend"

William Hardwicke retired to Wales and died in 1842 and was buried in Llanaber churchyard, Barmouth.[106] After his death, his widow sold Diamond Hall and the property at Rindleford, the latter being bought by Thomas Charlton Whitmore of Apley.

Eyton, Randall and Hardwicke are just three of the early historians of Worfield who each covered a different aspect of the history of the parish giving us a good starting point for further exploration.

---

[106] Hubert Smith, *A Short Memoir of the Late Eminent Shropshire Genealogist and Antiquary William Hardwicke*, (J. Randall 1879

WORFIELD IN THE 1870s-1890s

Mr Nicholas was the Vicar of Worfield from 1872 to 1898 when he moved to Wombourne parish. The cousin of Edmund Henry Davenport, Mr Nicholas's father, George Nicholas, had married Elizabeth, the third daughter of Edmund Sharington Davenport. Edmund Parry Nicholas, their son, was probably therefore assured of the living of Worfield.

In the 1891 census, Edmund and Marion Nicholas were living at the vicarage with their children, Basil, Ethel, Cecily and Evelyn and three servants. Basil later became a clergyman and there was another child, Stephen, who went into the Indian army. Mr Nicholas wrote as follows in the Parish Magazine.

"So many kind enquiries are often made for 'Master Stephen', that he is not likely to drop out of remembrance in the Parish of which he is so fond...He is happy in his profession ...He likes the Force he is in ('The Hyderabad Contingent') very much indeed."

Robert Evans summed up Mr Nicholas's contribution to the Parish as follows:

The Good:
- Started the Parish magazine 1873
- Hot air heating of the Church 1873
- Night Schools for teaching reading, writing and arithmetic
- Parish Lending Library, located in the school, started 1874
- Sheep excluded from the Churchyard 1875
- Installation of the organ 1876
- Worfield choir boys formed a cricket club and were allowed to use part of Davenport Park by E. H. Davenport in 1876
- Repaired the Churchyard Cross in memory of his father 1877
- The Old Grammar School which had recently been bought by E. H. Davenport was allowed for use by the Church as a reading room and the library relocated from the school. The playground was added to the churchyard in 1880

The Bad:
- Moved the Bromley tombs to the back of the Church where they languished for a very long time and removed the screen around them. "The screen was then cut up by Isaac Tarrant, the carpenter of Hallon. One part was fitted into the chancel arch and the other placed in front of the space under the tower to form a vestry." 1876
- Demolished the stocks which were on a small grass plot outside the North-West gate of the churchyard. Robert Evans writes: "What business it was of his to perpetrate this entirely gratuitous and dreadful piece of vandalism goodness only knows."[107]

Change didn't seem easily accepted by Mr Nicholas. What might seem to us trivial seemed to him of enormous importance, for instance,"Friends have told us that caps and bonnets are

---

[107] Robert M.H. Evans, *A History of the Rectors and Vicars of Worfield 1205-1972*

not to be hung within the Schoolrooms in future and that suitable cloakrooms are to be provided! We shall hope for the best."[108]

Vocational training flourished in the 1890s with cookery, joinery, agricultural and nursing classes all well attended.

Of the nursing training Mr Nicholas wrote in the 1893 Parish Magazine:
"What a source of happiness to those who are seeking happiness and are not quite sure if they are on the right track. Why should not quite a sufficient number of skilled, gentle nurses be found in the homes, scattered about every parish. Kind women who would give up an hour or two daily to go out amongst the sick in their village or near neighbourhood 'to make them comfortable' for the day and to cheer them with true words of sympathy, and to leave with them the glow of their own earnest faith ..."

Sickness was prevalent; and terrifying one can imagine. In 1891 there was an outbreak of scarletina which fortunately was mild and did not spread. Nonetheless, the schools were fumigated and the walls whitewashed. An epidemic of measles in 1892 was very severe, however, and attendance at the Infants School fell from 80 to 40 in two days. Even royalty was not immune from illness and in 1891 the Prince of Wales died from influenza.

In June 1891 in Worfield there were three burials in the Sneyd family of Kingslow; William Sneyd aged 48, Emma Sneyd aged 46 and William Sneyd aged 19. Whether this was part of the influenza epidemic or not, I don't know. Mr Nicholas noted that, "The influenza has made itself felt in our Parish. It soon reduces the most stalwart frame to powerlessness ..."

One has only to read the ages of those who died to see how fragile life was at this time.

- 1890 Charles Gwilliam (the Limbutts) aged 6 months, Richard Everall Pugh (Stableford) aged 2, George Harry Morriss (The Wheel) aged 12 months, George Pinches (the Limbuts) aged 7 months, Edmund John Evans (Swancote) aged 13 days, Edward Timmins (Rindleford) aged 22, Louisa Hinckley (Bromley) aged 24, Thomas Parton (Newton) aged 39, James Sneyd (Ackleton) infant, James Albert Elcock (Ackleton) aged a few days
- 1891 Max Levett (Davenport) aged 3 months. (No other ages are given for those who died)
- 1892 Charlotte Jones (Hilton) aged 29, Mary Martin (The Mere Pool) aged 21, Edwin Pursehouse (Hallon) aged 2, Isaac Maddocks (Chesterton) aged 28, Millicent Snead (The Hopes) aged 3 months, Martha Helena Pugh (Stableford) aged 35
- 1893 Harriet Hannah Price aged 8, Agnes Annie Gertrude Harpur (Ewdness) aged 4 months, Henry Charles Link (Bentley) aged 2 months, William Preece (Chesterton) aged 22, Walter Whitehead Pratt (Stretton) 44, Samuel Thomas (Chesterton) aged 46, Joseph Welsbrey (Cranmere) aged 33, William Richard George Mansell (Newton) aged 1 year, Blanche Gratiana Davenport (London) aged 17, Sarah Evans and Fanny Evans (Stableford), Annie Macefield (Hallonsford) aged 40

---

[108] *Worfield Parish Magazine* (Author has copies)

Injuries and deaths due to accidents were also common. Many were drowned in the Worfe as was Thomas Rogers who was trying to retrieve his hat and Alfred Ridley of Rindleford who fell into the mill race there.[109] Manual labour was brutally hard and who could blame those waggoners who 'rode the shafts,' rather than walk alongside their horses or those who had one tipple too many after a good day at Bridgnorth market?

Accidents could cause life-changing injuries as William Instone knew only too well. Born in Wolverhampton, William was aged fourteen in 1861and an apprentice blacksmith in Rindleford. John Wellings was the blacksmith, Daniel Mobley was a journeyman blacksmith and William Instone the apprentice. The 1871 census records William Instone living with his aunt and uncle, William and Ann Blunt at The Lowe. He is described as formerly a blacksmith and "blinded by hot iron". In the 1881 census he was still living at The Lowe but his occupation was a basket maker. By 1891 he was living with William Fryer, his wife and family at Hillside, Worfield. William Fryer was a shepherd. Poor Mr Instone seemed to have a constant struggle to get enough sales for his baskets, mats and wicker chairs. The vicar made this cryptic comment in the parish magazine: "William Instone's health is improving, he hopes his trade might do the same".

The Vicar advertised other local businesses. In 1883 James Lloyd, the cobbler of Wyken was given publicity. In 1891 it was William Penny's net making business at Rindleford, where he has "two or three strong tennis nets," and in 1895, Annie Lloyd, who had taken in needlework, was looking for more work. "She has also opened a grocer's shop at the back of her mother's house. It would help Annie much if some of her friends would remember this."

The weather in the 1890s was challenging for farmers. Four years in succession there were dry summers. The summer of 1895 was the driest since 1868, "When some of us can remember the weary months of heat and dryness, the constant expectation of rain, the constant disappointment." And then it did rain, a glorious thunderstorm, as Mr Nicholas recalls. But the following year, in 1896, the summer was dry once again.

So that is a taste of life in Worfield in the late nineteenth century, when boys left school as soon as they could to go to work, when, in 1889, a Vicar could take three months off work because of his wife's fragile health, a time when we start to pick up the names of children who will later appear on the War Memorial as casualties of the First World War and a time when the last Squire Davenport, Edmund Henry Davenport, died.

[109] Alfred, the only son of Edward Ridley, was killed when he fell into the mill race in 1861. He was standing watching the mill wheel turn, and there was the possibility that he had gone dizzy or simply lost his footing on the stone he was standing on. The wheel was stopped but it was too late to save the boy. (*Wellington Journal*, Saturday 15 June 1861, p.3)

THE TWENTIETH CENTURY

LOUIS WELLESLEY WESLEY

Louis Wellesley Wesley

Mr Nicholas's successor as the Vicar of Worfield was the Revd. Louis H. Wellesley Wesley who was inducted on 6th August 1898. Robert Evans described Mr Wellesley Wesley thus: "Mr Wesley, a good and sincere man, was handicapped by being a very sensitive person. In a rural parish unfortunate lapses are bound from time to time to happen. Mr Wesley was constitutionally quite unable to encounter these disasters with anything like equanimity of mind. His utter horror and detestation of the sin led him sometimes to treat the sinner with undue severity, for instance when some unfortunate girl got into trouble, charity and understanding would have been a much more efficacious manner of dealing with the problem than mere rigid severity. Mr Wesley was never really able to get on terms with, let alone understand, his more rumbustious parishioners."[110]

---

[110] Robert M.H. Evans, *A History of the Rectors and Vicars of Worfield 1205-1972*

THE TWENTIETH CENTURY Louis Wellesley Wesley

Worfield certainly challenged its new vicar. "A priest's life, even at Worfield, is by no means a bed of roses without thorns," he wrote. Getting parishioners to come to church was not easy. Wellesley Wesley tried starting the evening service at 7pm so that people could come after work, dressed in their working clothes but this had a poor response. There was, however, as the vicar noted in January 1902, one service which the parishioners had no difficulty finding the time or the inclination to attend; Dole Sunday. Even bitterly cold or wet weather could not keep them away. The abuse of a system providing alcohol for the sick and needy, further rocked the vicar's trust in human nature. In January 1900, he wrote as follows in the Parish Magazine. "I gladly provide wine, whiskey, brandy etc. for sick and needy people, but in future I can only give it by the Doctor's order. People must ask the Doctor for a note, specifying exactly what wine is needed, how much is to be given, and for how long."

The highlight of 1900 was the visit of the Future King George V and Queen Mary to Wolverhampton. Sidney Wilson adapted six wagons to provide seating for one hundred and fifty-seven Worfield children. The carts left Ackleton at 7.45am and took them through Pattingham with a twenty minute stop for exercise and refreshment (a glass of milk and a scone) at the Mermaid. "On to Wolverhampton, where the party stopped at the top of the Compton Road and met Mr and Miss Wilson, and then to their vantage point at Chapel Ash where some very thirsty children took advantage of water supplied by a water-cart. At 12.50pm, the procession passed by, to everyone's great excitement.

At 1pm the whole party was provided with refreshment: sandwiches, cake and lemonade which was amply appreciated, and at 1.45pm a start was made, amidst much cheering for Mr Sidney and Miss Wilson, to drive through the principal streets, seeing the decorations en route. Wightwick was again reached at 3.15 and tea was provided at 4 o'clock, teachers and friends rendering invaluable assistance. While at Wightwick the Royal Party drove by, and were again welcomed by loud and hearty cheering. At 5.20 the children left, returning through Pattingham to Patshull Pool, after each one had been presented with a book in memory of the event, the gift of Mr Wilson.

On the return journey the Royal Party passed the children, who cheered them loudly, but even more loudly as Lord Dartmouth passed by. He waved his hand to them until he passed out of sight." All arrived at Patshull Pool at 7.30 and thence went by various routes to their respective homes; some waggons going to Chesterton, Hilton and Worfield, others to the Ackleton District." (Worfield Parish Magazine.)

Louis Wellesley Wesley while he was at Worfield suffered from much ill-health. He resigned as vicar in 1902 and was appointed to a suburban parish in Nottingham. Robert Evans obviously felt this suited him much better than a rural parish such as Worfield. Yet Wellesley Wesley, as the Parish Magazine of 1900 records, did much to improve the appearance of the churchyard by replacing the wooden gates and planting the line of yew trees as well as a number of shrubs and snowdrops. How much he achieved in enhancing the spiritual life of his parishioners is not recorded, but he appears to be an intense young man trying to do his best and one can ask no more.

THE EARLY YEARS

Boy Scouts in Worfield. the date on the back is 1908-1910. Photograph courtesy of Dr. John Turnock

The Bridgnorth Journal was as fascinating in its description of the transgressions and mishaps of people as it is today. The paper was then more of a regional than a local paper with local people only featuring insofar as they broke the law, had an accident, went to war or in the case of the wealthy, had children, married or died. Looking at the Journal in 1900 these are a few of the Worfield incidents which are mentioned. The headings are mine and not those of the journalist.

DISGRACEFUL CONDUCT.

Richard Blakewell, a shepherd from Roughton was summoned for being drunk and disorderly in the parish of Oldbury. The defendant did not appear but sent his little girl. Sergeant Morris said that he saw the defendant at 4 o'clock in the afternoon when he was drunk and his conduct was disgraceful. There were females about. He also cursed and swore at a sheep dog he had with him. The defendant was a shepherd in the employ of Mr Jones of Roughton. He was fined 5 shillings with 5 shillings costs.[111]

COMMOTION AT WYKEN.

In May there was a barn fire at Warren Farm, Rudge, the home of Mr and Mrs Beddoes. On Wednesday afternoon at 5.30 a telegram was received at the Bridgnorth Fire Station requesting attendance at Rudge Warren Farm where a range of buildings was ablaze. The Dartmouth Steam Fire engine went out from Patshull, the manual one from Claverley and a waggonette

---

[111] *Bridgnorth Journal & South Shropshire Advertiser,* 3 Feb 1900, p. 5

carrying the hose and men went from Bridgnorth. Going through Wyken the waggonette collided with the mail cart overturning the latter and throwing its driver into the hedge. The horse bolted, taking the cart at full speed towards Roughton where it was stopped.[112]

CRUELTY TO A CHILD.

Rosamond Payne, a married woman living at Worfield was summoned for cruelty to her child.[113]

SALE OF SHROPSHIRE SHEEP.

On July 28 at Catstree the Catstree flock of Shropshire was sold. Mr J. S. Harding sold his entire lot of shearling Shropshire rams to Mr Robert Miller, Ontario, Canada.

CRANMERE ACCIDENT.

Joseph Sankey, a carter for Mr Ridley of Cranmere fell from his cart and died as a result of his injuries.[114]

The Parish Magazine provided a different perspective from the Bridgnorth Journal. The year started, as the Vicar wrote, " With wars and rumours of wars." Prayers were offered for those fighting in the Boer Wars, namely: William Jones, Corporal Lloyd, William Thatcher, Harry Weaver, Walter Bishop, Corporal Dawes, Milton Talbot, Sergeant Rowley, Verner Grove Horton and George Doran. Henry Mapp and Fred Hallam also enlisted. There was a fire at Hoccum and Mr & Mrs Wainwright suffered loss but it could have been much worse had the wind been in a different direction. Mrs Wainwright's personal bravery was to be commended. James Syner of Apley Terrace who lived in a cave at Apley, died. "The cave he had lived in was a picture of domestic bliss and many of the visitors from Bridgnorth and around ended an afternoon with a picnic on the grass at "Syner's Cottage" In February new churchyard gates were erected, paid for by an anonymous donor, much planting was done in the churchyard. By April the list of those prayed for at war had grown. In May, Sir Francis Marindin of Chesterton died. In June the Relief of Mafeking was celebrated with bunting in Main Street and ringing of the church bells. In August there was the royal visit to Wolverhampton. In September, "those who knew and loved dear, bright, sunshiny, "Little Jim," Jones of Swancote will be saddened to learn that he has died." In October there was a girls versus boys school cricket match and in December, on the coming of age of Hilda Marguerite Davenport, the parishioners gave a diamond tiara, the tenant farmers a diamond pendant, and the cottage tenants a silver inkstand.[115]

---

[112] *Wellington Journal,* 2 June 1900, p. 11

[113] *Bridgnorth Journal & South Shropshire Advertiser,* 7 July 1900, p. 5

[114] *Bridgnorth Journal & South Shropshire Advertiser,* 8 Sept. 1900, p. 5

[115] *Wellington Journal,* 10 Nov. 1900, p. 12

1914-1918

During both World Wars the Recreation Room was used as a convalescent home for servicemen recovering from their injuries. In the First World War the Voluntary Aided Detachment, as it was known, was run by the Red Cross. Dr L'Oste Brown of Shifnal and Dr Hewitt Claverley were the Honorary Surgeons, Mrs Eykyn of Ackleton was the matron, Helen Corbett of Chesterton was the commandant, Mrs W. O. Wilson of Norton the quartermaster.[116] The following are photographs from the First World War a number of which are in Shropshire Archives. None have been found for the Second World War.

Sister Oulton, patients, and unknown others. Photograph courtesy of John Chester

---

[116] Jane Smith, *Worfield. The History of a Shropshire Parish from Earliest Times,* Share our Past Ltd, 2017, p. 147ff.

Catherine Rochelle is the nurse on the right. Photograph courtesy of Mr. Cornes

Sister Oulton seated in the middle I believe. Photograph courtesy of Mr. Cornes

Above: Helen Corbett in the centre. Below: Sister Oulton and patients. Photographs courtesy of John Chester

Interior of the Recreation Room (now the village Hall)

The Vicar, Robert Evans, on the front row and Dr Hewitt wearing an apron

BETWEEN THE WARS

It is 1919 and the servicemen who had fought in the war have returned home. But the joy of returning is tinged with bitterness with the realisation of what they have lost and the swift disillusionment that life would be no different from how it was before the war. There was also tension between those who stayed at home and those who went to fight, highlighted in this poem by Guy Kindersley OBE.

A POEM TO PROFITEERS
"The Shepherds Feed Themselves and Feed Not My Flock."

We died in our millions to serve it, the cause that you told us was ours;
We stood waist-deep in the trenches, we battled with hell and its powers.
Broken and shattered and helpless, we rotted by land and by sea.
For the dream you held before us, the dream of a Freedom to be.

And you? You have gathered your millions; you have lined your pockets with pelf;
You have talked of the Rights of Nations, While you worshipped the rights of self.
Your lands are dunged with our life-blood, Your houses are built with our bones;
Your temples (and would you could hear them) are filled with our children's moans.

Do you think we shall rise and smite you? Fear not! You shall garner your gain.
And we? Will you give us our freedom, just those who have not been slain?
No, the tale is the same as ever, and the world will go as before:
Our sons will be fooled and blinded, as our fathers were of yore.

Fooled tho' we've been by your hirelings - you know that we fought for a lie -
We've fathomed a truth you see not, but one you must learn when you die.
That silver and gold and raiment are things of but little worth,
For love is the heir of the ages and the meek shall inherit the earth.

It was however a time for everyone to pick up the pieces of normal life and in March 1919 the whole village celebrated the wedding of Seaman William Botley to Nellie Turner at St Peter's Church. Main Street was decorated with flags and a banner saying, "Long Life and Happiness to the Fair Bride and Bridegroom." The schoolchildren lined the churchyard walk and strewed flowers in the path as the happy couple left the Church.

St Peter's Church was an important part of parishioners' lives even though it was such a long way for many people to go on a Sunday. Imagine the servants and poorer families walking from Kingslow, Oldington, Ewdness or Stanmore in their Sunday best. I would like to bet that all they thought about in the service was how much their feet ached. Ackleton people were lucky because they had a bus laid on so no excuses there, then.

Sibill Corbett at Stableford. Image courtesy of Sue Riches

In 1919 Sibell Corbett had a farm sale as she was giving up farming the Home farm, Stableford.[117] These were hard times for farmers but the sale at Stableford didn't mark the end of Sibell's farming career. She moved with her sister to Somerset and farmed for the rest of her life. The stock which was being sold was as follows:

7 Waggon horses and colts,75 head of Shorthorn, Jersey and Polled Angus cattle, 34 Kerry and Cross bred in lamb ewes, 1 Oxford Ram, 100 Pure Bred Berkshire and Large Black pigs

One of the delights of the Bridgnorth Journal is that nothing much changes so when I found a court hearing about the stealing of a bike I thought that this could have been in the Journal last week. Small crimes were major events in those days. On the other hand dying as a result of having a knife stuck in your back, as did poor Annie Fellows of Bilston only caused a "mild sensation" in the town. But in the Worfield case, Sidney Wood from The Pleck, Walsall stole a bike worth £4, the property of John Edwin Theodore, of No. 11, Worfield at 12.30pm on 30th June 1925. Theodore was happily mending the road between the Hermitage and Swancote and had left his bike at the roadside. At lunchtime he returned to the bike and found it had gone. The police must have been rather speedier in those days than they are now and the cyclist was stopped as he was going into Wolverhampton. Wood was asked if he had taken the

---

[117] *Wolverhampton City Archives*, D-NAJ/C/1/CO4

bike and he replied "Yes I took it, I wanted to get to Walsall." Bridgnorth to Walsall is some walk, no wonder the bike was so tempting.

In August 1919, Mr F. Capel Cure gave a lecture in the Recreation Room entitled "the Peace Treaty with Germany." A hot evening after a hard day on the farm, hmm. I hope, for the audience's sake, that Mr Capel Cure was a good speaker.

The Claverley Gymkhana sounded a lot more fun with classes for "horse leaping." There was also a two mile pony race in which "there was quite a thrill ...when the lady rider of Gold Dust failed to negotiate the second bend and both horse and rider went through the hedge on to the adjoining road."

Life between the Wars was marked by a strong code of people helping each other. The British Legion gave support to ex servicemen, Friendly Societies supported the poor and needy in the Parish and they and the Church provided the moral code by which parishioners lived their lives. Politically women were active with the Women's Unionist and Conservative Association. Several of the wealthier families such as the Evans family from Wyken and the Corbetts from Stableford, stand out as benefactors and all in all Worfield seems a good place to live.

So many men were killed in the First World War that many women never married. One of those who did was Catherine Rochelle of Bromley who met William Cornes of Alveley, Royal Horse Artillery, while he was convalescing at Worfield VAD hospital where she was a nurse. They married in 1919. Photographs courtesy of Mr. Cornes

THE 1920s

The Wedding of Edna Leighton and Sidney Courtney Cook 1921.
Image courtesy of Wendy & Paul Rylance

Worfield must be unusual in having such a long run of parish magazines. There are several people to thank for this. Firstly, Miss Eykyn, who, in 1923, donated copies of the magazine from 1872 onwards. The intention was that the magazines would then be kept in the vicarage but at some point it looked as though they were going to be put out with the rubbish so Joe Harper took care of them. Joe then ensured the safe keeping of the magazines by handing them over to John Turnock who deserves special thanks for allowing me to photograph them all. Hopefully at some point they will be placed in Shrewsbury Archives.

In 1921, the Reverend Arthur Barrow became Vicar and, as with his predecessors, he seemed to have a constant struggle to get people to come to church. Yes, they would happily attend a tea party but Church services were a different matter. Robert Evans in his book 'A History of the Rectors and Vicars of Worfield Parish 1205-1972 described the Vicar as "a good man and also a cricketeer". He resigned in 1932.

The Revd. Arthur Barrow

What more could a Parish want of a Vicar than that, a good man and a cricketer? Yet it seems rather sad that Robert Evans was not able to say any more about the man himself. The Revd. Barrow's parishioners were always being chided for not coming up to scratch in a Christian sense. Choir boys did not attend regularly and were warned that only those doing so would be eligible for the choir outing. But the Vicar himself did seem to be popular. He held a tea party at the Recreation Room in 1922 when 450 people came, similarly in 1925 which 350 attended but he could only manage to get 250 people to take communion at Christmas. The Vicar couldn't help but point out that he would have preferred more members at communion than at a tea party. This excerpt is in a similar vein. "I wonder if I could manage to get more of the congregation to join in the singing than we do at present, especially in the morning. I am afraid that if the choir were silent there would be hardly anyone making a sound sometimes! ...Will those who sing already continue to do so, and those who do not begin, to lift up their voice? And will everybody please say, "Amen," at the end of every prayer."

After the sadness of the First World War and the economic decline which followed it, Worfield by the twenties was beginning to enjoy itself again. In 1921 the Worfield Flower Show had its best year since the War and the Worfield Brass Band started up again as did the scouts and guides. There were many groups which the parishioners could join, such as, the Working Men's Club, the Guild of the Holy Child, the Mother's Circle, and the Women's Institute which had seventy members at its AGM in February 1923. There was a football club and a cricket club and regular fundraising was done by a sports committee. However, these were not easy times, as the need for a Boot Club, Clothing Club, and soup kitchen indicated. Thank goodness Mrs Morrison bought Nurse Kirby a bicycle in 1924 (for £5 it is noted) or she could never have done all her visits. Friendly societies were popular, too, and in 1923 there was a parade by the

Oddfellows and the Foresters headed by the Bridgnorth Brass Band. The Parade gathered at the Recreation Room and marched through the village. It must have been quite a sight. Normality was returning.

But it was a sour note that was struck in 1923 when the Vicar writes about a case of cruelty to animals.

"There seems to be a strain of the savage in some of the Worfield lads which leads them to show cruelty to animals. One would not expect it from the decent fellows most of them are in other ways. There are few things more blackguardly than the ill-treatment of dumb beasts and it is to be hoped that a recent prosecution may help to put a stop to anything of the kind. I do think that a birching should be served out to any boy or man who wantonly makes any animal suffer."

Lady Hulton from Chesterton who had worked hard at the VAD hospital died in 1923 as did Mrs Booth who had been a staunch supporter of St Peter's. (It was Mrs Booth who embroidered the altar cloths in St. Mary's Chapel.) In July 1924 Stanley Botley was "taken from the family in peculiarly pathetic circumstances". Whether this was illness or accident is not recorded. In the same year, a key figure in the parish, William Henry Foster, also died, a man, according to the vicar, who recognised the responsibilities as well as the rights of ownership.

Reference: Worfield Parish Magazines

Frank Turner, headmaster of Worfield School 1905-1927, and his wife, Rebecca who had been head of the junior school at Worfield. Image courtesy of Joe Turner

WORFIELD IN THE 1930s

The Revd. Barrow was succeeded by Theodore Lunt and shortly after he became Vicar in 1931 he was joined by Cyril Marsden Lee in 1932 as curate and, when the Revd. Lunt resigned in 1934, Cyril Lee became vicar and stayed until 1938.

In 1931 an excerpt from Milton's Comus was performed at Chyknell Hall. Left to Right: Mrs Cotterell, G. Oliver, Miss Wilson, W. Head, Mr Guy. Image courtesy of John Chester

What a glorious time this was for Worfield's Parish Magazine as the vicars reflect on current events and allow their parishioners to speak. It is wonderful to hear people tell their own stories rather than have them told by a third party, ie the vicar. A Choir Boys' Outing was described by Edward Driver, aged 11.

"On the morning of the fifteenth of July I awoke at five o'clock. I did not have much sleep on the night of the fourteenth but lay awake thinking of the trip. I was a bit disheartened at first because it was raining but it soon gave over. At exactly twenty minutes to seven I started out from home to the cross-roads where I was to be picked up. After I waited for about ten minutes the char-a-banc came and I got in. All went well for quite a long time and then we came to a drove of cows and Tom Welsby got out and drove them up a side turning. We stayed in Llangollen for twenty minutes and while some of them went and had a cup of tea I went to the fruiterers and bought some cherries...At about twelve o'clock we arrived at Llandudno and met Mr Lunt outside the Red Garage. We stopped at the fruit shop and Mr Lunt bought a basket of strawberries which we ate on the beach. After we had eaten all the strawberries we bathed and Mr Lunt paddled. When we had finished bathing we went half way up the Great Orme for lunch in a tram. While we were having lunch the sea gulls came and Wilfred Elcock took a snap of them. For the whole of the afternoon we could do what we liked, so I went round the town and into Woolworths. At half past three we bathed again and till five o'clock I sat on the shore. At five o'clock we went and had tea at Summers and had salad and trifle. When we had finished tea we went to the char-a-banc and two boys got lost. We went to look for them and they came back at twenty past six. We had several breakdowns on the way back, the first was on Madley Hill. The petrol would not reach the engine. I arrived back at quarter to one, very sorry it was all over."

The tennis club season started on the 28th April in 1932. The courts were to be opened at 6pm and a dance would follow at 8.30pm. "Subscriptions to the club have been fixed at 5/- and members' guests may use the courts on payment of 6d for a ticket from the Worfruna Garage". It sounds as though the club might have been struggling because A.A.M. writes, "It is hoped to arrange as many matches and tournaments as possible but these, in fact the existence of the club, depends on the amount of support received from playing members."

In 1933 the wedding of the decade as far as Worfield was concerned, took place, but sadly it was not at Worfield. Margaret Leicester-Warren married Major Oliver Leese at Tabley in Cheshire. It was also the year in which Wyken, in particular, and Worfield in general, mourned the loss of Kate Morrison (1848-1933) who had given so much to the parish. The last of the Eykyn line, Peggy Hodge Eykyn, of The Laurels, Ackleton, also died, and the vicar gave a short history of the family who, it would seem, were granted their lands in the reign of Henry 1.

The Cricket Club was having a bad time in 1933 with lack of interest and support. Many of the players "are only fitfully at work and can scarcely afford to bear the whole cost of travelling to away matches or entertaining visiting teams to tea". By 1935, although they weren't winning a lot of matches, the players were having a lot of fun. There were over twenty players to choose from and the problem now was how to give them all a game. "The only danger is that we are certainly not going to get conceited by the large gates which we attract at our home matches. The parish certainly leaves its cricket team severely alone." By 1937 the Cricket Club had a new pavilion and was playing under the captaincy of the vicar.

The choirboys' outing to Blackpool in 1935 was described by Henry Seedhouse, later the village blacksmith. A visit to a zoo was included in the trip and a tigress was everyone's favourite animal. Henry wrote: "She was lovely and clean and in perfect condition. When we got to Blackpool the weather was none-too-good. The sea was rough making it impossible to bathe. Tea was had at Booth's restaurant - ham, tongue and salad followed by trifle." Jean Turner described the Brownies outing to Rhyl and Margaret Botley wrote about other trips.

The Young Peoples' Fellowship had a trip to Dudmaston in 1934 where the young people enjoyed punting on the lake and swimming. "The walking party will start at 2.15 from the War Shrine and go by Hoccum and Bentley (distance about 5 miles), the cycling party at 3 and go by Barnsley Lane (distance about 6 and a half miles). A few who cannot cycle or walk can be accommodated in cars."

The school ran clubs to teach the children the practicalities of looking after livestock. In 1932 the Calf Club began, followed a year later by the Lamb Club. This was Tom Welsby's account entitled "How I Took Care of My Lamb." Tom was 13 at the time and won first prize in the competition.

"When I first had my lamb I got leave from the vicar to keep it in the cemetery. I had to think out a name for him and in the end I called him Bill. I gave him a pound of corn a day which I bought from school. I collected some swedes for the winter and the bad weather. I kept him in Mr Monk's loose box in the bad snow time. I had a hard time in cleaning the shed and putting straw for him to lie on. We got on very well together and he soon was very tame and would follow me about. I used to take him down by the Blacksmith's Shop to graze and Mrs Seedhouse gave him some bread. When the time came to lose him I took him down to school. Although I took first prize it meant I should not see him again. Mr Foster said he was an outstanding lamb as well as fat and clean."

Worfield School Calf Club. Image courtesy of Sheila Fellows

The Revd. Lunt had chosen Mr. Lee as his curate, and a good choice he was; a country man with a zest for life, people and farming. One might have thought he would have been an academic with no practical skills but in fact he was a good horseman and a welcome pair of hands at harvest-time. It is a shame that his stay in Worfield was so short. He followed Mr Lunt as vicar but was in the parish for just six years. Tragically he was killed in a hunting accident not long after he left Worfield. Like many vicars before him Cyril Lee had difficulty getting men to come to church and it was partly for this reason, and because he couldn't find a replacement vicar while he was away that he chose to spend his holidays at home helping farmers with the harvest. "It seems to me," he wrote, " that there is no better way of getting to know a man than by working with him in the harvest field".

Weather was of constant concern in this farming parish and Cyril Lee was a great recorder of the seasons. Here are a few of his entries beginning in 1935 when he became vicar.

1935

May Cold Frosts

June. A story of "three hot days and a thunderstorm."

July. "It has been wonderful weather for getting the hay in and all the hay is in. I saw the first field of oats cut on the 21st July in Ackleton,..I only hope that the hot sun over the past two weeks has dried and not burnt the grain. It is sad to see the Mere Pool quite dried up and hundreds of eels lying dead, some as thick as your wrist." Ewdness Pool was still full but Barnsley & Hoccom pools were very low.

December. "It has been an exceptionally mild and wet December. Not a frost worth the name all winter. So mild that I saw partridges chasing one another in the week before Christmas and some snowdrops already in bloom. So wet, that the Worfe and Severn are once more flowing along bank high and water is standing in the furrows, and the Wheatland side of the river rides very deep and Wenlock and I come back from hunting well bespattered with clay." [The hunter, Wenlock, was loaned from the Fosters of Newton.]

1936

Easter was colder than Christmas. Snow on Good Friday and a sharp frost Easter Day.

June 26 "there was a tornado at Bobbington and Seisdon and hailstones as big as thrushes' eggs cut and battered down all crops."

July. The Lowe and "Chemsull" meadows were flooded. "Brook Lane from Roughton to Hoccom has once again been a river with sand more than a foot deep carried down the road and cars had to be pulled out by horses."

Of the summer as a whole, the vicar notes: "For the record 1936 was a truly wretched summer, the worst since 1912 with rain nearly every day".

1937

"The weather seems so uncertain I have given up the idea of an open-air service for holiday makers on Sunday week. In all probability the weather will be perfect and if so won't you take a walk to church?"

Harvest. "I have had a very pleasant hay harvest on nine different farms & would like to make a score before corn harvest is all home".

October. "Lovely weather for potato and root harvest."

December. Mild & sunny. "Christmas Day was mild and sunny, all the better for the absence of snow and bad weather from the church point of view."

1938 "Will go down in history as having witnessed the warmest first quarter within the memory of anyone now living."

On October 28th 1935, the Vicar wrote: "Easily the most exciting event recently was the fire which gutted the old part of Ackleton malthouses on Saturday evening October 12th. It started before 5pm and was not really subdued until 11pm. At one time it seemed that nothing short of a miracle could save the row of cottages down the road or the two above. The difficulty was to get any water. The Bridgnorth engine got bogged down in the fields near Broadbridge, but Shifnal, after trying to get to Badger Dingle, were successful in pumping water from the Royal Pool through 1200 yards of hosepipe to the malt house. Meanwhile, all the furniture had been got out of the cottages and carried to Mrs Wainwright's yard. Hundreds of sightseers in rows of cars had come from all over the countryside as the blaze was visible from Wolverhampton in the east and from all the high ground in the Wheatland country between here and the Clee Hills. It was a weekend which will not soon be forgotten in Ackleton.

Of an entirely different nature but hardly less memorable to me, was the party given to all the able bodied inmates of the workhouse in the Recreation Room by the generosity of two members of the parish. Foxalls brought them out in two char-a-bancs and after tea the Women's Institute performed an amusing play. Then some of the old men, a little wheezy perhaps and more than a little nervous, sang us songs of fifty years ago - The Farmer's Boy and The Old Arm Chair." [Note: I assume the men were from Bridgnorth Workhouse]

Cyril Lee was an enthusiastic supporter of many of the parish groups and celebrations. There were two national celebrations; the first for the Silver Jubilee of King George V in 1935, and two years later for the Coronation of King George VI. The Mens' Club was struggling to keep its numbers up in spite of sports facilities at the Recreation Room such as billiards, badminton and table tennis. Thomas Turner was doing his best to keep things going but with little help. The WI in contrast was flourishing and Mrs. Cunliffe's President's Day at Bradeney attracted over 100 people. The young people had their own entertainment; Brownies and Guides for the girls, and for older children a new youth group was started by the vicar. A mixed choir and band was begun in Ackleton and there was Worfield choir for the boys.

Events in the Ackleton room were better supported than those at the Recreation Room and one Boxing Day dance at Ackleton attracted 140 people. Not much room for dancing I would think. There were some odd entertainments. In 1934, at the Recreation Room, the Misty Crystals entertained at a choir concert by blowing up a motor car on the stage.

No-one could have worked harder for the parish than the Revd. Lee. Apart from helping with the harvest, he ran services in the remote villages, and he took God's word to the holidaymakers at Rindleford. Yet in spite of his best efforts he was often met with indifference and sometimes with scorn. One collecting box for the church was returned full of cigarette papers. The choir failed to attract new recruits and church numbers went up and down like a yo-yo. That new-fangled invention, the wireless, was luring the congregation to listen to God's word at home so that at one time the vicar was encouraged by the parish's response to his teaching and the next he was despondent.

The parish library was given a boost by a grant of £7 from the Rebecca Hussey Trust towards the purchase of religious and practical books. The library was to be housed in the Old Club room and Geoffrey Cook was to be the Chief Librarian. Later the library moved out of the village to a purpose-built shed at the Recreation Room and was finally closed in the 1990s.

Mains electricity came to Worfield village in the 1930s and was installed in the church and vicarage. Wolverhampton had sunk bore holes for water at Rindleford and had plans to do the same at Hilton. The Revd. Lee feared that this might be accompanied by jerry building . Until mains water was installed, water was delivered by rams and wells. The water at the vicarage was supplied by a ram from Lower Hall but originally by a well some 96ft deep.

Roads were also being improved. "Hilton has at last had its road widened. It has made a better road but taken away some of the picturesqueness of the village. The Lowe Bridge is still with us and so are the potholes down to Rindleford". [Note: Probably the same potholes I encountered when going down to Rindleford in September 2020!]

From the point of view of the history of the parish we owe Cyril Lee a debt of gratitude because he deposited all the old documents which had been in two chests in the church in the Public Record Office. The Revd. Nicholas who had found the documents had never got round to cataloguing them nor to depositing them as he had intended. Cyril Lee wrote:"For I don't know how many years, certainly over a hundred, there have lain in an untidy heap in the old coffer in Worfield Church, a miscellaneous collection of old parchment rolls and smaller parchment scraps. No-one seems to know how they got there nor where they came from. About two years ago Mrs. Cunliffe obtained the services of Miss Auden, who is an expert in such matters, to go through this collection and try to put them in some order … On December 15 & 16 last, with the consent of the Church Council, I packed all these rolls and papers into 3 boxes and took them up to the Public Record Office in London…We have dated and tied into bundles and temporarily labelled the great bulk of them. They form a very interesting collection going back, almost consecutively, to Richard II in 1370…It is my earnest hope in 1937 to seriously undertake this work of translation."

By 1938 Cyril Lee had read through the Churchwarden's Accounts from 1590-1610 and published some of the entries in the Parish Magazine. The items included payments to various workman, "Mr. Compton for a sermon 2/-, Hugh Yate 'for stopping ye pigeons out of ye church 6d,' 'to Mr Oldriche his man for a foxe head.' The Constables' Accounts are no less interesting as these examples from 1614-1615 show.

- For one hue and cry that came from Wheaton Aston after an yoke of oxen that were stollen 2d
- Bestowed upon a poor man that had losses upon the sea and conveying him out of the parish 6d
- Bestowed upon the conductor that had the government upon a company that came in the name of Egiptians according to his passe 2/-.
-

Reference
Worfield Parish Magazines

STANLEY MOORE

Stanley Moore was brought up in Cannock and Rugeley where his father had a general stores. At the age of sixteen he left school and went to work in the shop and when he was eighteen he decided to be ordained. As with Cyril Lee, he went to Cambridge. On the 2nd December 1938, aged only twenty-eight, the Reverend Stanley Moore was instituted as the Vicar of Worfield. It was very likely, therefore, that Mrs. Moore would have been the youngest vicar's wife in the Diocese, if not in England. This part of the story is told by Stanley Moore himself, in an autobiography written for his grandchildren. What follows is the section which relates to his time in Worfield.

"The service of institution was uninspiring, taking place in a cold church on a cold Friday afternoon in December, and the tea party afterwards was frigid. The local gentry only were invited and they were all very old. I wondered what my wife was thinking, but I knew that I had a rose about to burst into full bloom, in a room full of elders who had lost their sheen.

1939 - War

And now an event which cast its shadow before it and which I have never forgotten.[118]

On Good Friday, 1939, I preached in Worfield Church the Three Hours Devotion 12-3; we went back to the Vicarage for our first meal of the day, which was always fish pie. While waiting I switched on the radio and the news came through that Mussolini had invaded Albania. I felt as if I had been struck - the ruler of a Roman Catholic country had defied world opinion, and had chosen Good Friday to attack a small neighbouring State without a formal declaration of war. I feared for the future. I am sure that this event influenced me greatly in offering my services as an army chaplain.

The first Diocesan Conference that I ever attended took place at Ludlow and the Bishop of Hereford in his address, asked that young clergy should offer themselves as chaplains for the duration of the war if it came. We talked it over during a picnic lunch in the Castle grounds. When I got home I wrote to the War Office and was soon commissioned as R.A.R.O. - Regular Army Reserve of Officers. I did not have any doubts that war would come, which it did on 3rd September.

The last week of August, before war was declared, is just a jumble of memories; crisis followed crisis; children were being evacuated from the big cities into the country away from

---

[118] Stanley Moore commented on the build-up to war in the Parish Magazine of April 1939. "As I write, the German troops are in Prague, and Czecho Slavakia has ceased to exist. Such high-handed piracy is a product of our own times, and while many will say that this is a true commentary on the Munich Settlement, it is well to remember that it is always easy to be wise after the event. The true statesman must deal with the situation as he finds it, and this is, of course, what our Prime Minister did at Munich. In the sphere of international relations it is necessary, as in ordinary intercourse, to believe the word of another great country. The fact that our armaments are piling up shows at any rate that our Prime Minister, while willing to believe another great country's representative, meant to leave nothing to chance."

the threat of heavy bombing, and the whole business hung on whether Germany would invade Poland or not. She did, and once again Great Britain was at war with Germany.

On Friday 1st September, in Worfield village itself, our excellent village school master, Mr. S. J. D. Knowles, who with his 'sensible' wife Doris, became our very good friends, was busy planning the arrival of the evacuees, as they quickly became known. I was at the vicarage, among other things listening to various government broadcasts. Eventually it came. My class was called to the colours, and to report forthwith. I already had my orders and knew I had to report to Aldershot.

Next morning Mr. Knowles took us to the station at Wolverhampton and took my wife back to Worfield. I still remember that I put a good suit on - I was still in civilian clothes, to go to war in. After a short period at Crookham the unit had the call to serve overseas but before going overseas I made a quick visit to Worfield, and what I saw made my heart bleed for my poor wife. The Bishop had sent a young priest of 25 years old, to act as locum in my place. He brought with him his young bride, for this was their honeymoon. This could not be helped, but it was hardly the treatment my wife needed after seeing her own husband off to the war. There were five evacuees in the house, four were children and one adult. One of the children was in a wheelchair and my wife had to push him up the steep hill from the village to the house; the

Stanley Moore preparing communion on the bonnet of an army Jeep

woman evacuee simply wanted to sit at her bedroom window all day smoking. My wife had to cook for them all and to crown it all, the children were all bed wetters.

THE TWENTIETH CENTURY   Stanley Moore
Worfield 1938-1953

We landed in France on 26th September but this was the Phoney War and with no casualties, no work for a C.C.S. to do. I visited regiments all over the front and took services on Sundays, sometimes not finishing until 8 o'clock at night. I also played a lot of soccer at regimental level; such prowess as I had, helped my ministry a great deal.

When the British army was evacuated from France in 1940, I came off from Boulogne on a British destroyer, having first seen on board 12 stretcher cases from where I know not. We had been told to leave, and destroy everything behind us. On my last leave I had bought a super 'British Warm' and meant to get it home; I must have looked very odd wearing a superb winter coat on the hottest of June days.

On the voyage back to Dover, I wondered how to let my wife know that I was safe without the sight of a telegraph boy giving her an awful shock. I solved the problem by sending a Greetings Telegram, hoping that she would see the golden envelope before the shock. It worked.

England was now alone and the army had to be reformed and re-equipped; there was nothing for me to do so my wife and I spent six glorious weeks walking the moors on the Devon/Cornish borders in the most wonderful weather

I was demobilised in October 1945, and after a short holiday at Weston went back to Worfield. The Leeses gave us a terrific home party at the Lower Hall to which it seemed all the

Stanley Moore introduced nativity plays as part of Worfield's Christmas celebrations

parish was invited; the doors had even been taken off their hinges to get people in. I found an entirely different Worfield; I had left a down-at-heel farming parish; I came back to a prosperous farming community with contented people for my ministry."

The following information is from the Parish Magazines and recollections of the Moore children, Stephen and Angela.

In July 1952 the belfry was given a spring clean and seventeen handbells were found, most in a poor state of repair. Mr. Fea paid to give them a new lease of life and off they were sent to Taylors of Loughborough.

Mains water came to Worfield in 1951 but in August 1953 there was a less welcome arrival as the Revd. Moore described.

"The Pillar Box is Fat and Red. It wears a Tammy on its Head. At least it isn't a pillar box, but a telephone box which this article is about. Visitors to Worfield will have seen a scarlet red kiosk standing under and clashing with the lovely green of trees and hedges just below the turning from the village towards the Worfe Bridge. That it must be red and standing as an alien amidst the verdant countryside is obviously dictated by someone who sits in an office in Whitehall, thinks only of busy streets with painted crossings, a vivid red against splashing buses, and has never seen the morning mist dispersing in the sunshine and revealing the wonder of tall trees and hedgerows bedecked with flowers, and dewy pearls glistening on each blade of grass. If he had he wouldn't have dared put vivid red in the countryside.

But nemesis struck in the shape of a passing lorry and our telephone kiosk stood humbled and in ruins. The optimists hoped that it would not be resurrected there to stand defiant and ugly, but be moved to a safer and less obtrusive spot. The safety of the occasional telephoner also crossed one's mind, for no-one can mutter sweet nothings or order a load of coal into a mouthpiece of plastic if, at any moment one's life may be cut off in its prime. At least a telephone conversation should be a peaceful occupation, not one which embraces all the hazards of total war.

But we were wrong; officialdom was soon on the move and a 'replacement from stores' stands where its predecessor stood before, not quite so gaunt and ugly, for it is yet an orange which blends, and the man with the official paint pot hasn't come. But we really should feel safer with it somewhere else, where possibly it may be slightly hidden and we can conduct our own personal business in modest privacy."

The highlight of 1953 was, of course, the Coronation and it was right that it should be suitably celebrated. As the Chairman of the Committee, Mr Knowles, put it: "It is fitting that we should actively rejoice and that our children should remember the commencement of the reign of our young Queen, for it is they who, with God's blessing, will march forward through the century with her. It is therefore mainly of the children that we have been thinking in marking this important day and it is hoped that it will prove to be something they will never forget."

The day started with Holy Communion at 8.30am in order to prepare the parishioners for the Coronation itself which they would listen to on the radio or watch on television. Buses collected people for the carnival and sports and returned them home afterwards and a mock trial was held in the Recreation Room in the evening. [See Appendix]

THE TWENTIETH CENTURY
Stanley Moore
Worfield 1938-1953

Mabel and Ernest White helped maintain the large vicarage and its garden; Mabel working inside the house and Ernest in the garden. Ernest and his son Stanley ran a market garden at The Folley, Henry Bath's home, and supplied the Moore family with vegetables. Stephen recalled the visits he made with his father to select the week's vegetables. The vicar might offer a comment on a cabbage which would suit by saying something like, 'that's a nice cabbage Stanley,' to which Stanley would reply, 'don't give it a name sir, don't give it a name.' I assume the explanation comes from not naming livestock destined for slaughter. To put cabbages in the same category seems rather delightful.

Sir Oliver and Lady Leese were great friends of the Moores and on one occasion the vicar received a phone call which went something like this. "Moore, we're going to the desert in the morning for a couple of weeks. Can I leave the mushrooms with you?" No, was not an option but knowing nothing about mushroom growing, the vicar was very concerned. One can imagine his relief to find that, on visiting the mushroom farm the next day, the staff had everything under control and his was just an administrative role.

What children remember is always interesting. Angela was older than Stephen and recalls the unique status a vicar and his family have in a parish. In Worfield, one of the downsides of this exalted status was that Angela had to go to the parties of wealthy children, all of whom had nannies. At tea-time, the nanny would stand behind their charge's chair but in Angela's case it was her mother who stood behind her chair; galling to both mother and child one would imagine.

Etiquette required that due deference was shown to one's superiors. It was perfectly acceptable for Sir Oliver Leese to address the vicar as Stanley but the vicar and his family would always address the Leeses as Sir Oliver and Lady Leese. To his staff Sir Oliver was known as, 'The General,' and Lady Leese was always addressed by Mabel White as m'lady. What five year old Stephen couldn't understand was why Mabel called his sister, 'Miss Angela,' while he was simply, 'Stephen'. Mabel's explanation was simple: "When you go away to school, then you will be called Master Stephen." Times have changed.

Stephen spent the first few weeks of his life being looked after by Mrs Bayliss as Angela and her mother had measles. Reflecting on his childhood in Worfield, Stephen concluded that they were probably the happiest days of his life.

Lower Hall was where the vicar and his family spent their last night in Worfield and Stephen has good reason to remember that night. Having been put to bed, he couldn't get to sleep because Mabel White, kept putting her head round the door to see if he was all right. Eventually Lady Leese said, 'Mabel, leave that child alone,' to which Mabel replied, 'I wish you hadn't put him in that haunted room m'lady.' Sleep must have been very difficult after hearing that!

Acknowledgments
Without the information provided by Angela and Stephen Moore, this article could not have been written. They kindly shared stories about their father and permitted the reproduction of their father's autobiography as it related to Worfield.

THE TWENTIETH CENTURY

Appendix: Worfield Coronation Programme Courtesy of Val Edwards

::¤::¤::¤::¤::¤::¤::¤::¤::¤::¤::¤::¤::¤::¤::¤::¤::¤::

TUESDAY, 2nd JUNE, 1953

Coronation Dance

Recreation Room, Worfield

MODERN and OLD-TIME DANCING from 8 p.m. till 1 a.m.

THE HORLENS TRIO

M.C.: G. MOWBRAY   —   REFRESHMENTS

WEDNESDAY, 3rd JUNE

Carnival

The Carnival will assemble on the Cricket Field at 2 p.m.
There are Four Classes, all for Children
1 — Historical Costume
2 — Mounted Costume
3 — Any Costume other than the above (Boys)
4 —   Ditto   Ditto   (Girls)
There will be First, Second and Third Prizes in each class.

Sports

Commence at 3 p.m.   Open to all Worfield Schoolchildren.
Class 1 — Children aged 5—7 years.
„ 2 —   ditto   8—11 years.
„ 3 —   ditto   12—15 years.

Each class will compete in three events:
(a) A Sprint Race.
(b) A Sack Race.
(c) An Obstacle Race.

Prizes (Cups, Medals, etc.) will be awarded to the First, Second
and Third in each event.

Maypole Dancing

By Children of Worfield School, under the direction of
Miss S. M. Thomas

::¤::¤::¤::¤::¤::¤::¤::¤::¤::¤::¤::¤::¤::¤::¤::¤::¤::

4

::¤::¤::¤::¤::¤::¤::¤::¤::¤::¤::¤::¤::¤::¤::¤::¤::¤::

4 p.m.

Physical Training Display

by R.A.F. Bridgnorth.

The Display will consist of approximately 20 minutes Mat Work,
Box Work, Agility and Chair Exercises. The party in charge of Warrant
Officer C. Brown and Sergeant C. Evans will be : Corporals Parminter,
Roche, Brooks, Stanley, Duncan, Armstrong, Ball, Greaves, Warren,
Baker, Bennett, Sudron, Pitts, Griffin, Hunt and Williams.

4.20 p.m.

Model Aircraft Display

CORPORAL FOWLER

(1) TIPSY JUNIOR — Scale acrobatic control line (70 m.p.h.)
(2) PACER — Class "A" Team race (70 m.p.h.)
(3) MERCURY MONITOR — Semi-scale acrobatic control line
(50-60 m.p.h.)
(4) JUNKERS 87a — Full scale control line (60 m.p.h.)

A/C. MEAGER

(5) SKELTON RACER — Control line acrobatics (65 m.p.h.)
(6) GLO-DEVIL — Control line speed model (100 m.p.h.)
(7) RED STAR — Control line acrobatics. Built from own design
(speed unknown)

Acrobatics include :—Loops, Figure Eights, Flying upside down, and
general capability of pilot.

4.30 p.m.

Horse Riding and Jumping

By R.A.F. Bridgnorth, School of Equitation.

The show will consist of 10 minutes General Riding, and 10 minutes
"B" and "C" Class Jumping.

Team comprises : Flt. Lt. Mayoux, Flg. Off. Rolston, Sgt. Doyle,
and Cpl. Proctor

5 p.m.

Children's Tea at Worfield School

PRESENTATION

All Children of the Parish will be presented with the following to
Commemorate the Coronation of Her Most Gracious Majesty
Queen Elizabeth II. on the 2nd June, 1953:

(a) A Copy of the New Testament of our Lord and Saviour
Jesus Christ:

(b) A Coronation Mug.

::¤::¤::¤::¤::¤::¤::¤::¤::¤::¤::¤::¤::¤::¤::¤::¤::¤::

5

PREB. TOM

On the right is Preb. Tom with members of Worfield Church

Preb. Tom was a larger-than-life character who so many people speak of as the perfect Worfield Vicar, yet surprisingly I had very little material to work with until John Turnock lent me several tapes which he thought I might find useful. This was an understatement; they were exactly what I needed. It's not easy doing oral history. I find that I just let people talk and when the interview is finished I come out wishing I had asked more questions. So I was very impressed with John's work; the way he set out the purpose of the interview and the nudges he gave, very gently, to keep the interviewee on track. The purpose of the interviews was to look at education in Worfield as part of research towards John's Ph.D. This interview with Preb. Tom was recorded in 1992.

Preb. Tom succeeded Stanley Moore as Vicar of Worfield in 1956. Tom says that Sir Oliver Leese encouraged Stanley Moore to move on by saying that if he stayed in Worfield any longer he would be there for life. That is not quite how it happened. Stanley Moore may well have asked Oliver Leese for his advice but he had quite unexpectedly been offered the Rectorship of

Cheadle Hulme in Staffordshire. Although he was happy in Worfield, the stipend was very small for a man with a family. Moore decided that he must leave and hoped that the next vicar would prove "to be a worthier parish priest for you than I have ever been".[119]

Preb. Tom, or Sidney Seward Chartres Thomson to give him his full name, was an unlikely candidate for the Worfield post as he was only in his second year as a curate. On paper therefore, he did not have the experience for the job. Lady Leese was the Patron of the living and whereas today the Patron might rubber-stamp a recommended candidate, in those days the Patron had a more active role. Margaret Leese spoke to her husband and asked how they were to go about finding a candidate and Sir Oliver said, "You need to speak to Harry," and of course, Harry knew someone and the result was that Preb. Tom was shortlisted and essentially lined up for the post.

The Bishop of Hereford was unimpressed with Tom's inclusion on the shortlist and thought he should withdraw his name.Indeed, Tom himself was embarrassed about being put forward for the post but when the Bishop suggested he might not be up to the job he was determined not to withdraw his application. Reluctantly the Bishop allowed the appointment to take place although he refused to induct the new vicar.

S. S. C. Thomson's approach to religion was shaped by the man who trained him, Dr. Alec Vidler, a noted theologian and Dean of Windsor. Their bond remained strong with Dr. Vidler visiting Worfield and delivering a sermon on at least one occasion.

Prior to training for the ministry, Preb. Tom had been in the merchant navy, only retraining for the church in middle age.Unlike the Revd. Moore, who struggled to keep his family on a paltry stipend, Preb. Tom had his naval pension of £1400 to augment the stipend of £750 and so could live quite comfortably. Worfield was to be Preb. Tom's only parish.

Stanley Moore 'eased' Tom into the parish and gave his successor one piece of advice which was invaluable. "Never do anything unless Sidney Knowles approves".

Sidney Knowles was then the headmaster of Worfield School, and was, as Preb. Tom put it, "One hell of a man. Not only was he an outstanding schoolmaster, he was the head of the Rural District Council and a member of Rotary and several other groups. It was Stanley Knowles who taught me how to chair a meeting. Too many chairmen at the end of a discussion say, 'is there anything else?' Knowles' approach was to say, 'well I think we have spent enough time discussing that so let's move on'."

In 1992, Preb. Tom looked back on how the parish had changed. When he came to Worfield in the late fifties, "The parish had at least six people of some consequence who were churchgoers, and that helped me. The school managers included Norman Forbes from Hilton, Sir Edward Foster from Newton, George Ridley, Miss Cunliffe from Bradeney and Lt. Colonel Perkins, who lived at The Batch. The latter was a mild-mannered man who had a DSO and MC. There was also, of course, Sir Oliver and Lady Leese who were a great support to the parish.

On one occasion we needed some money. The General [Oliver Leese] had a cactus farm known as Worfield Gardens, and he would regularly get a thousand people there. Sir Oliver

---

[119] Worfield Parish Magazine December 1955

offered the loan of the Gardens so that we could raise the money we needed. We could have the Gardens on the Saturday and Sunday if, by 10 o'clock on Monday morning, there was no sign that we had been there. He advised that we should insure against bad weather because the weather was unsettled. I wouldn't have bothered but it would have been discourteous not to follow this advice. On the day, it rained a little in the morning and a rain gauge was there to measure how much rain we had. The weather brightened up and I thought no more about the insurance until I received a cheque in the post for the amount we had insured for. It turned out that two of the schoolchildren had topped the rain gauge up! I was in a moral dilemma but decided that least said soonest mended was the best approach.

Apart from its annual Open Day, Worfield Gardens showed at Chelsea and other Flower Shows in the late 1950s and 1960s

When I went to Worfield, the school was effectively a secondary modern. It was in 1963 that it became a primary school when the secondary modern was built in Bridgnorth. Sidney Knowles applied for the headship but he was too old to get it and remained at Worfield. As headmaster of a secondary school, Knowles had been an administrator, and now he had to go back to teaching. He was affected very badly by what he must have seen as a demotion. I went

THE TWENTIETH CENTURY

Preb. Tom Thomson
The 1950s & 1960s

Preb. Tom remembered at St. Peter's

to Shrewsbury Education Department and told them that they had knocked Sidney Knowles' world from under him and they hadn't even had the courtesy to thank him for what he had done. They put that right and Sidney continued at the school until he retired.

The organist when I went to Worfield was Harry Bayliss. He owned a chain of cinemas in Wales with restaurants attached at a time when they made money. He also arranged choir outings to various places in Wales. Harry Bayliss wanted an exclusively boys choir but there were only eight or ten choristers and it wasn't enough. Two or three men also sang, even though Bayliss discouraged it. Bob Adams was one. When Harry Bayliss was away, Michael Lloyd played the organ but Bayliss said it was an outrage because his fingers were too big to play a single note.

When Harry Bayliss died, Michael Lloyd took over as organist. He was unwilling at first because he was playing at Pattingham Church and was not attached there. He liked the arrangement of not being attached but agreed to play the organ at Worfield for a trial period. One thing he did insist on was a four part choir. Lloyd created an excellent choir by all accounts and on one occasion they went to sing at Hereford Cathedral."

Lest the extracts I have chosen make him sound rather meek and mild, his personal opinions were sometimes very definite. He tells a story of going into school to speak to Sidney Knowles and finding him alone in a room drawing a picture on the blackboard. "Well, Sidney, I said, this is completely out of character. I thought all artists were nitwits".

Paul Holt added to Preb Tom's story as follows:

Prebendary S.S.C. Thomson was a driving force behind the planning of a new school building which was completed in 1963. A very capable administrator, he had enjoyed a stellar

103

career in the Merchant Navy before being ordained in middle age. This was a contrast to his predecessors in Worfield who had typically had a conventional Cambridge or Oxford University education. He remained in the parish after his retirement, moving a short distance from the vicarage to Hartlebury.

Here's a fun fact: at the height of the swinging sixties, the Vicar of Worfield owned a Mini Cooper. This startling choice, considering his age and station in life, plus his frequent use of a motorcycle during his early years in Worfield, point to an interest in machinery that he probably retained from his naval days. He had risen to the position of Marine Superintendent, making him more of an engineer than a navigator. He was awarded an OBE in 1944 for his outstanding service, some of it spent in the Far East. It seems likely that Ceylon and Burma were particularly significant places since his first wife, Mrs Doris Thomson, reported spending time there both before and after her marriage. It was in Rangoon that they were married in 1929.

Mrs Doris Thomson very ably filled the role of vicar's wife. In addition to her leadership of various church fellowship groups, it is tempting to wonder if her contribution to the parish magazine extended beyond simply reporting on those activities and included other sections ostensibly written by her husband. It would certainly have been a great loss to him and the whole village when she died in early 1970. Ever practical, the good vicar was nevertheless once again a married man before the year was out. There was nothing unseemly about this however, as the second Mrs Thomson was the sister of the first and was herself recently widowed. He also outlived Mrs Ida Thomson after more than 20 years together.

Preb. S. S. C. Thomson died locally in 1998, aged 96.

Prior to the opening of the Secondary Modern schools in Bridgnorth in the late 1950s, Worfield had educated most pupils until they completed all their schooling at the age of 14. After Mr. Knowles retired he was replaced by Mr. John Sherman who shared the teaching of the senior class with his wife. A feature of Worfield School in the 1960s was the presence of the children of RAF families, making up more than ten percent of enrolment. The RAF base at Stanmore, near Bridgnorth, had closed in 1963 but the married quarters housing remained in use by members serving at RAF Cosford. Many of the children had experienced overseas postings, typically in Aden or Singapore. Mr. Sherman broke with convention by not living in the schoolhouse, choosing to commute from Bridgnorth. Senior pupils were required to record and report daily temperature and rainfall statistics, an imaginative introduction to gathering and presenting scientific data. Mr Sherman might also be remembered for the Turkish-style fez that he kept. He wore it to great comic effect on occasion to entertain the school in the pantomime tradition.

Acknowledgments
Thanks are due to Dr. John Turnock for the loan of the recording made by Preb. Tom and to Paul Holt for his article about Preb. Tom and Stanley Knowles.

LIFE IN THE SIXTIES; A PERSONAL VIEW
by Jane Smith

"If you can remember the Sixties you weren't there," didn't sum up the decade as far as I was concerned. Even though the early years of the Sixties felt like a carry-over from the 1950s and the later years morphed into the excesses of the 1970s, the whole decade was different from that which went before and that which followed, bringing about huge cultural changes in society.

The Telstars, a group from the Cannock area, performed at the Milano's Kabin Klub, Wolverhampton, in 1965.
Photograph courtesy of Mike Shield

The Beatles personified the Sixties; four young men from Liverpool, who could have been the lads next door, created music which inspired a generation and challenged the status quo. A nationwide hysteria was whipped up by the media and love was in the air; the girls were in love with the Beatles and the boys with the music. It was fun and exciting to us, and sometimes challenging to older generations who couldn't understand what all the fuss was about. It's always good to have reflections from someone at the time. My grandfather wrote in 1963:

"Girls in their thousands have gathered hysterically to wait for the 'Beatles' shows. I think their performance on TV to be 'far below proof,' as liquors are graded. I think it was an insult to common intelligence, let be culture. It shows up the mind of the young mass; and the move of sex. For young men are not in the scramble for the performance." It was clear that the touch paper of something had been lit in many young people although I would disagree with my grandfather that this was simply sexual.

The generation of which I was a part was brought together by this new wave of music and in Wolverhampton we met in a tiny coffee shop called the Milano. We drank frothy coffee out of glass cups which had a tendency to burn your mouth, but no-one cared. Upstairs we talked, and downstairs it was all about music. In the daytime, we listened to the latest music on the juke box but in the evening the basement became a night club, the Kabin Klub, where bands such as the Telstars, entertained. It was exciting to be a teenager, perhaps it always is, at least since the days when children had to work twelve hours a day, but it didn't prevent some parents seeing the Milano as a den of iniquity.

The cloud in our otherwise blue sky was the Cold War and in 1962 matters came to a head with the Cuban Missile Crisis. We doubted that anyone could survive such an incident but the British government tried to give us all hope that survival was possible. Someone came to talk to us at school about the preparations we should make. As soon as the two-minute warning was given we were to go to a designated room in our house which would be our bunker, and remain there until the all-clear was sounded. Details were rather vague on how long this period of incarceration would need to last. The bunker would have essential provisions, food obviously, and also a bucket in which we were supposed to do everything. We laughed heartily at the bucket but actually we were terrified.

On the other hand, the assassination of President Kennedy in 1963 had no impact on me at all. Another cliche often bandied about is that everyone remembers what they were doing when J. F. K. was shot. I have no idea what I was doing, nor do I have any memory of discussing the shooting with friends. Our conversations would have consisted of the mundane details of everyday life; we lived in a small world.

In 1964, I left Wolverhampton to study geography at the University of Wales in Aberystwyth, which, I think it would be fair to say, was not at this time in the vanguard of cultural change. It was an uncomfortable time to be a student from England at a Welsh University when the depth of anti-English feeling was great. No matter what terrible things one nation had done to another I didn't see how I was personally responsible but there were times when I certain felt as though I was. This was also the time of Women's Lib, (the Women's Liberation Movement) which promoted equal rights for women. I remember standing on a very crowded bus when a fellow male student, seated, turned to me and said, "You fought for equality and you got it, so now you can stand." Again, personally I had never been an advocate of the feminist cause but caught the backlash nonetheless.

In 1968, I went to Bradford University to study Marketing; a subject for which I had no vocation whatsoever but which sounded fun and fashionable. In reality it was both, as different from Aberystwyth as it was possible to be. Lectures were delivered from notes as current as though they had just been written which they may well have been. Lecturers wore gowns at

Aberystwyth but here the style of dress was much more casual and students and lecturers were on Christian names terms.

While education had begun to respond to changes in society, many institutions were still in a Dickensian world hampered by being bureaucratic and top-heavy. Women's place in industry was generally acknowledged to be inferior to that of men therefore they were paid less and had fewer opportunities for promotion. The good thing was that there were jobs. You could leave a job one week and have another one by the following week.

It was a time of rich cultural expression in films, for example, with the first Ian Fleming film being released in 1962. We also read anything we could get our hands on. The censor finally relinquished his grip on 'Lady Chatterley's Lover,' permitting publication in 1960, followed shortly afterwards by the 'Tropic of Cancer'. When we had had enough titillation we soaked up classics such as 'To Kill a Mockingbird,' and 'Catch 22,' and when we needed some personal therapy we turned to R. D. Laing. We talked endlessly about politics. It was cool to be left wing and to be from the working classes. I was neither so most of these conversations passed me by.

When the Sixties was good it was vibrant and exciting. You could feel that the country had emerged from the dark days of the post-war era into a brighter world. It was a time of empowerment of the individual and frustration that old traditions meant that one's talents couldn't be fully used. It was a time before money became society's God and a time when a sense of community was still recognisable; just.

THE WORFIELD PASSION PLAY

It was in 1973 that Worfield's first Passion Play was performed. One might have expected that the Vicar of Worfield would have been its instigator, but in fact the idea for such a play came from the director of the Worfield Theatre group, Robert Davies.

I have very fond memories of Bobby Davies from the late 1950s to early 1960s. I was in my early teens and crazy about horses as were my sister and brother. In the winter, whenever we

The Worfield Theatre Group flourished from the 1950s until the 1970s. Photo courtesy of Eileen Tracey

could we went hunting with the Albrighton Hunt. We would hack to the meet, our horses in their shaggy winter coats, no overnight stabling or clipping for them. By comparison Mrs. Collis from Stableford was the epitome of elegance, the only woman still riding sidesaddle, beautifully turned out on a bay thoroughbred. Also unmissable was the dashing Mr. Davies dressed in hunting pink and spreading bonhomie amongst the assembled gathering at the meet. A solicitor by trade, I don't know how it was that Bobby Davies from Pattingham came to be running the amateur dramatics group in Worfield, nor why it was that after eight years of directing, he suddenly had a penchant to stage a play within St. Peter's Church.[120] As he was sharing his desire to put on a church play he remarked, "I suppose I will have to chat up the vicar." Michael Lloyd, the organist and choirmaster fortunately overheard the conversation and replied, "Oh, no you won't," he said, "you'll have to chat me up. We'll do a Passion Play at Easter. I'll write it and you produce it".

Michael Lloyd driving "Hilton Queen" on a busy Sunday afternoon

And so it was that over the winter of 1971/72, Michael Lloyd wrote the first Worfield Passion Play. Before training as an engineer at Birmingham University, Michael Lloyd had been at Charterhouse, and drew on his classical studies to include anecdotal extracts to make the

---

[120] Exactly when the Worfield Theatre Group started I don't know, but in the late 1950s and the 1960s the producer was Miss Waite, who had come to Worfield from London. Eileen Tracey, who took the starring role in 'Sailor Beware,' said that Miss Waite trained the Worfield actors to near-professional standards but without losing any sense of the fun of it all. The earliest reference to the Theatre Group I have found in the Worfield Parish Magazine is from January 1959 when the Revd. 'Tom' Thomson wrote of the group: "The members are now relaxed, and the parish in general thanks them for all the work which went into their recent successful production."

play more entertaining. Many people make plans which then get forgotten in the hurly-burly of everyday life. Not so in this case, for a few days after the conversation, Bobby Davies received three pages of typescript, and within six weeks the complete script. Even so, the director thought it would take a year to produce the work. Tragically, Mr. Lloyd died in a hotel fire in Bournemouth in January 1973 and never saw his work produced. The Passion Play was produced six weeks after Mr. Lloyd's death and was a fitting tribute to a man who made an enormous contribution to the Parish of Worfield. Surely, you may say, he made a great contribution to Worfield Church as organist and choirmaster, rather than the Parish as a whole? No, Michael Lloyd's influence was more extensive than this as he was the inspiration behind the Hilton Valley Railway which gave pleasure to a huge number of people. How he found time to work is a mystery.

1974 Passion Play. The money changers in the temple

The play was performed the following year in 1974 but the work involved was of such an order that it was decided to stage it every five years in the Oberammergau style. A stage was built in the Church, lighting installed and about eighty actors recruited from the local area. The construction of the stage nearly gave the vicar, Stephen Thomas, a heart attack. Dan Lloyd (Michael's son) was stage manager for the first two plays and designed the stage. Unfortunately

The 1984 Passion Play

Dan had made an error in his measurements meaning that the front pews and the pulpit had to be removed to accommodate the stage!

Nearly all the costumes were made by Mary Roberts who was a perfectionist. Rather unwisely, when my children were at Worfield School, I offered to help with the costumes for a nativity play. Sewing sessions were held at School for the willing volunteers. I walked into a room where there was a small army of women making costumes which wouldn't have disgraced the Royal Shakespeare Theatre. A hard taskmaster was Mary Roberts but the results were superb.

The 1979 version was again produced by Bobby Davies and new music was commissioned and composed by James Wood whose family lived on the Apley Estate (James's father and the Goulborn brothers who owned Apley were first cousins). Michael Lloyd had taken a great interest in James Wood's career and had hoped that he might follow him at Worfield as organist and choirmaster. In fact Mr. Wood was destined for greater things. After studying at Cambridge and the Royal Academy of Music, he went on to have an illustrious international career. Wood's music for the Worfield Passion Play was controversial in more ways than one. Designed to reflect the play's everyday language, the music was based almost entirely on African-American spirituals and plainsong. Scored for female singers with an instrumental group of flute, clarinet, saxophone, piano, double bass and percussion, the music was pre-recorded by Mr. Wood's London choir, much to the disappointment of the Worfield singers. Some very bizarre sound effects were however produced live. The idea of an angel coming to earth was captured by James Wood enthusiastically lowering a large gong into a baby bath full of water. It would be lovely to know what the audience thought of that!

Some of the actors were members of the Worfield Theatre Group but other actors came from neighbouring parishes such as Claverley, Alveley and Bridgnorth and even farther afield. Some, like John Hollis, a member of the Worfield Theatre Club, were reluctant recruits. Mr. Hollis played Christ in the 1979 version and doubted whether he could do the script justice.

The 1979 play was followed by one in 1984, directed by Scott Whitehead and one in 1989 directed by Rosalind Rawnsley. It was early in 1988 that work began on the 1989 Passion Play and it was felt that the time had come to rewrite the script. The job of rewriting fell to John Buck, an experienced amateur playwright, who was the brother-in-law of John Sharplin who played Jesus Christ in this production. The brief for the rewrite was to emphasise the relevance of the Passion Play to current times and to all people, whatever their age. John Turnock, who was then Headmaster of Worfield School and Director of Music at St. Peter's Church, Worfield was to compose the music and in the main it was to be performed by those from the Worfield community. The Right Reverend Ian Griggs, Bishop of Ludlow, was the Patron.

John Buck wrote the following author's notes in the 1989 Programme. "Those who believe in Jesus of Nazareth as a figure of historical fact have done no more than accept the evidence of historical records …. But the 'Figure of History' engages a far more important and significant role in the whole passion of the world's history than merely an 'Honourable Notable,' from a past age. The spirit, teachings and saving grace of Jesus of Nazareth have lived on throughout the ages and are present, still, in today's world." John Buck sought to present the audience with a play which was neither easy nor comfortable, but one which would challenge each of those involved.

Rosalind Rawnsley, the Director, wrote as follows. "We the players, and you the audience are together reliving the events of Holy Week, and to that extent this is not a play, but a re-enactment of Christ's last journey. Like the original characters in the drama, we try, mock and crucify Christ in our everyday lives, and like them, we do not see the tragic irony, for as Dorothy Sayers put it, 'we the audience are now the actors, and we do not know the end of the play'."

The composer, John Turnock could have used music which already existed but felt that the music should be written as an integral part of the new production. As he wrote in the 1989 programme, "The music should help to reinforce the impact of the triumphal entry of Jesus into Jerusalem, the agony of Good Friday, the stress and soul-searching of the Disciples, and the anguish of Mary, the mother of Jesus."

1989 was the last time the Worfield Passion Play was performed. Time moves on, the world becomes ever more secular and people today perhaps do not have the same interest in community projects such as this. It certainly must have been a huge effort to perform but as someone whose involvement was as part of the audience I can only say that the effort was appreciated.

The cast for the 1989 production was as follows: Paul Beard, Elizabeth Bullas, Jonathan Chuter, Laurence Chuter, Patrick Chuter, Roland Chuter, Ronny Jane Chuter, Nicky Elliott,

The 1989 production left to right: Dr. Patrick Chuter, Emma Handley, Dennis Fincher, Christine Fincher, Kay Lipscombe, Catherine Turnock, Bill Hiscocks, Gill Turnock. Front: Peter Madeley, Sylvia Stoker

Christine Fincher, Dennis Fincher, Betty Fulwell, Norah Glass, Marion Gordon, John Hammersley, Emma Handley, Bill Hiscocks, Caroline Howard, Nowell Howard, Sarah Howard, Jeff Hughes, Peter Madeley, Simon Mondon, Kay Lipscombe, Terry Lipscombe, Andrew Lund, Duncan Peagam, Felicity Peagam, Colin Perks, Philip Perks, Rosalind Rawnsley, Len Robinson, Olive Robinson, Adam Sedgwick, Mike Seedhouse, John Sharplin, Brian Smith, Caroline Smith, Dee Smith, John Stoker, Sylvia Stoker, Ray Thornett, Catherine Turnock, Eleanor Turnock, Gill Turnock, Gwen Warwick, Peter Warwick, Eileen Whitehead, Scott Whitehead and the Pupils of Worfield School

The Production Team was as follows. Director: Rosalind Rawnsley, Musical Director: John Turnock, Producer: Eric Peagam, Assistant Producer: John Hammersley, Choreography: Norah Glass, Stage Manager: Alan Glass, Assistant: Pauline Atkinson, Lighting: Dave Kirkham, Sound Equipment: Chris Bowden, Sound Engineer: Graham Bailey, Costumes: Mary Roberts, Make-up: Sally Handley & Dee Smith, Props: Peggy Fincher, House Manager: Margaret Ball, Front of House: Bridget Hill, Hazel Marston, John Turner, Mary Turner, Geoff Wooldridge,

THE TWENTIETH CENTURY Worfield's Passion Play

Stage construction advice: Dan Lloyd, Musicians: Glyn Davies, Sarah Graham, Sarah Howard, Eric Peagam, Caroline Pritchard, Claire Seedhouse

Eric Peagam, John Turnock and Rosalind Rawnsley working on the 1989 production of the Passion Play

Acknowledgments

Thanks are due to the following.:

John Turnock for sharing advertising material, photographs and the programme for the 1989 play, Dan Lloyd for his input on the early productions, Rosalind Rawnsley for correcting errors and adding detail and Caroline Howard for her memories.

AROUND THE PARISH

ACKLETON HALL

Generally speaking my computer and I get on famously. Every morning my first job is to translate the Worfield Manor Court Rolls for about an hour and a half and normally it's a joy, but not today. I was looking forward to finishing a particularly difficult court roll from 1477 when I found that two days' work had been lost. The positive way of looking at my loss is that it teaches me patience, for now I have to do the work all over again, but not today. For my sanity's sake I need to do something different and I decide to visit Wolverhampton Archives to look at the sales details of the Ackleton Hall Estate.[121] My purpose is to write an article for the Parish Magazine about William Piper who bought the Estate in the late nineteenth century. Thank goodness for the Parish Magazine because no sooner had I written it, and the Parish Magazine been distributed, than I had a phone call from the current owners of Ackleton Hall, Mr. and Mrs. Crawford, inviting me to visit and view some documents which related to the house. To say that I was excited is an understatement. I had no idea where the Hall was in the village and

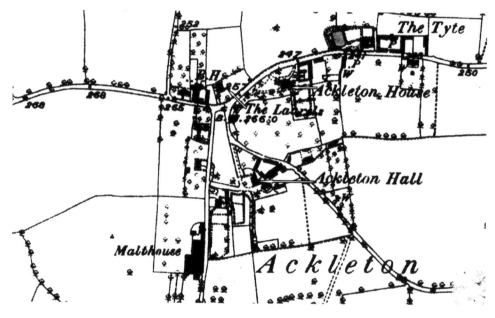

Ackleton in 1883

no preconception of what I would find.

ACKLETON

Ackleton Hall is the oldest surviving house in the village, probably dating from the sixteenth century, thus predating Ackleton Manor, which was built in 1709, and Ackleton House which was built in the late eighteenth century. This is not immediately apparent as the current driveway takes you to what is clearly a Georgian house. In fact this is a replacement of an older part of the house, and there the two halves stand as one; the sixteenth century house and the Georgian.

When Mr. and Mrs. Crawford bought Ackleton Hall in the 1980s, the house was in a poor state of repair but they fell in love with it and have restored it to the beautiful house it is today. The previous owner, Joe Farrier, handed over a pile of deeds and other document relating to the house, and told the purchasers that one of the farm buildings, a long barn, which had already been transformed into a house, was once a malthouse.

The earliest document [see notes at the end of the Chapter] dates from 1760 when Thomas Blakeman surrendered "all that cottage, malthouse, barn, garden, backside and the several lands called Jones's, the Middle of the Field Piece, Somergate Piece and the 3 butts with the appurtenances containing the half of one nook of land in Ackleton aforesaid with the appurtenances" to Eleanor Bradburne.[122] In 1788, after the death of Thomas Blakeman, the above property devolved to Joshua Badger, an innkeeper in Wolverhampton. The admittance of Joshua Badger as tenant took place at the manor court held at the home of John Richards, maltster, whose son was, I believe, responsible for rebuilding part of the house. It is John Richards the son of John Richards who, in 1789, made a surrender in favour of Walter Hollies, a builder. This is a mortgage so one assumes this relates to the new building. The Richards' business seems to be doing very nicely so that when William Richards, maltster, died in 1837, he left his wife Sarah a life interest in several freehold and copyhold messuages (houses with outbuildings & land assigned to their use), dwelling houses, lands, tenements and premises in Ackleton and elsewhere in Shropshire. The instruction was that on Sarah, his wife's, death the property would be sold at auction and the proceeds distributed to the children; Daniel, Jane, John, Sarah, James and Mary Ann. Sarah died in 1847 and it seems that Daniel, being the eldest boy, bought at least three of the properties. In an inventory of the Ackleton Hall Estate following the death of William Piper in 1899, three properties were described as having been bought from Daniel Richards. The first was Clarks Leasowe with two cottages on it. The second was a cottage and land called Goold's land and the third was "a cottage, malthouse, barn, garden and backside, Jones's Piece and the Three Butts. Tenant: James Lowe."

Exactly how or why William Piper came to own Ackleton Hall and its farm, is not clear. William was the son of Moses Piper, an agricultural labourer, and Mary his wife and was born in Wyken. The census enumerator spells it Wicken which may be indicative of how it was pronounced. William went to London and in 1851, aged 26, was a chair maker. By 1861 he was an inn-keeper in Shoreditch and by 1871, a wine merchant in Wanstead. William's elder brother, Moses, was then in Ackleton farming 145 acres. Farming the 150 acres of the Ackleton Hall Estate was Edmund Charles Wadlow and farming 250 acres, probably the Tyte Farm, was

---

[122] Eleanor Bradburn was the daughter of the Revd. Pointon and the wife of John Bradburne. Their last surviving issue was Mrs Mason who died in Shrewsbury in 1871. It was Mrs Mason who left money to Worfield known as Mason's Dole.

ACKLETON

Ackleton Hall

Alan Halby from Shifnal. The Tyte, and over 200 acres of land was owned at this time by the Eykyn family and there was a connection between the Eykyn family and William Piper even before the latter's move to Ackleton . In 1849 William Piper, the chair maker from London, was an executor of James Eykyn's will, along with Marian Eykyn, James Eykyn's wife, and Richard Eykyn his son.[123]

The first map of the estate dates from 1876, when I assume William Piper took over the property from Edmund Charles Wadlow, and it was in his family's hands until it was sold in 1914. The sale in 1914 was prompted by the death of William Piper in 1899, aged 77. The estate at that time consisted of Ackleton Hall & its buildings, with nine cottages and gardens, Ackleton Manor being sold as a separate lot. The sale was overseen by William Piper's widow, Catherine, and the agent was Nock and Joseland. Tom Bowen from Chesterton, acted as the go-between.

The advent of railways and improved roads in the nineteenth century made it much easier to travel around and the Pipers seem to have as strong a family connection with London as with Worfield. Francis Piper, another member of the family, was born in St Marylebone, where his father was a wood cutter. After working with his father he is recorded in the census in Worfield in 1861 working as a wheelwright for his uncle, Thomas. In 1871 he was a wheelwright in Ackleton, at the Folley, and his wife was a beer retailer. It is perhaps not surprising therefore that when Moses Piper left Ackleton he moved to London. In 1881 he was living in West Ham as a retired farmer and on the night of the census, Marian Eykyn was a visitor (born in Whitechapel). Between 1881 and 1891 Moses must have worked as a licensee and in the 1891 census he is described as a retired publican.

The period in which the Ackleton Hall Estate was managed by William Piper, 1876-1899, was one of great difficulty for farmers, particularly those with large estates. From 1853 to 1861, money had been poured into land as the best investment at the time. From 1862 there was stagnation, and after 1874, a period of depression set in which continued throughout the rest of Queen Victoria's reign and beyond. The worst periods were from 1875-1884 and 1891-1899. Between 1871 and 1901, there was so little profit in growing corn, due to foreign imports, that much arable was converted to pasture with no hope of any greater return from livestock. The government, recognising the dire situation, set up a Ministry of Agriculture in 1899 but it was powerless to help. Cheap imported food was not going to go away nor could it be legislated against.

It was against this background that William Piper bucked the trend and built his estate which, in 1881, consisted of 300 acres. He bought land and property from small and large landowners alike and exchanged land to produce a compact whole. The trustees of Lewis and those of Pattrick supplied some land and more was exchanged with the Eykyn family. Other houses and land were bought on Folley Road and Mr. Piper soon had an estate almost equal to that of the Eykyns.

With the downturn in agriculture, Catherine Piper had an estate which in 1899 found no interest amongst buyers and by 1904 it was still unsold. Nock & Joseland, the estate agents, did their best to present an attractive picture to potential buyers, describing the area as follows:

---

[123] The National Archives, *Will of James Eykyn*, 1849 PROB 11/2092/348

"The locality is well known for its game preserves and particularly good for partridge shooting." The estate went to auction in June 1904 but still there was no interest. Poor Mrs Piper must have been at her wits' end. She considered using a London agent but Nock & Joseland warned against this, saying, "There are London agents and London agents. Some are only concerned with the commission and will ruin the property because they are after a quick sale and will do anything to get it. On the other hand a good firm may do good by introducing a bona fide applicant who might assist the chief object, namely that of forcing the hand of the one gentleman who is known to be in the market.

I fancy local folk know the position of that gentleman and that knowledge rather prevents local negotiations and I may tell you that beyond three or four casual enquiries I have not interviewed anyone since the sale who sounds like "business". Please tell Tom that I suggest Major Wilkins being asked to come and look over the estate. I think Tom will appreciate my meaning." I assume Major Wilkins was a stooge to 'encourage' the certain gentleman to get a move on, but I may be wrong.

In 1908 Mr. Beard wrote after viewing the house. "We did not like anything about the place at all. What land we walked was poor, the malt house spoilt the place and the manor is too close and overlooks all the garden and the buildings to the back part of the house are very poor indeed". Another potential buyer didn't mince his words either, saying that there was too much arable, the house was too small, and the price too big.

The Estate went to auction again ten years later on the 17th June 1914 with the sale of Lot 1 to be completed on the 25th March 1915. Mr. Lisle of Star Engineering in Wolverhampton took the Leys at a valuation which Lisle promptly contested in a very protracted wrangle and Mr. Bean of A. Harper Son & Bean bought the Ackleton Hall Estate. Mrs. Piper must have been thoroughly glad to be rid of her burden. She died in 1923 in Abingdon but is buried in Worfield Churchyard. Her son, Thomas Edward, who had farmed at Ackleton, predeceased her in 1920.

We can only speculate on who the gentleman was who is known to be interested in buying the property. Perhaps the estate agent worked too hard in 'encouraging' him to buy, but whichever way one looks at it, at the beginning of the twentieth century the Ackleton Hall Estate was, to use the modern vernacular, a hard sell.

It is unclear when Mr. Bean sold the estate but it was bought by Timothy Owen, a dairyman in Broad Street, Wolverhampton, according to the 1911 census, and sold after his death in 1938 to Mr Iliffe, a Wolverhampton solicitor. The Hall and farm were rented to Joe Farrier who later bought the property and, as we have seen, converted the Hall's farm buildings into dwellings. One of the conditions of the sale of the farm was that a gipsy who lived on the farm should be allowed to stay. "Blue" Locke had worked on the farm and when Joe Farrier grubbed out hedges creating a field of 65 acres, "Blue's Island," as the caravan and its curtilage were known, remained intact.[124]

Sixteen new houses were built in Ackleton, firstly in the1960s, in Rosemount Gardens on the site of Rose Villa and its gardens, and later new houses were built on the site of Wilson's

---

[124] *A Romany's Home is his Island,* Birmingham Daily Post 3 September 1970 p.12

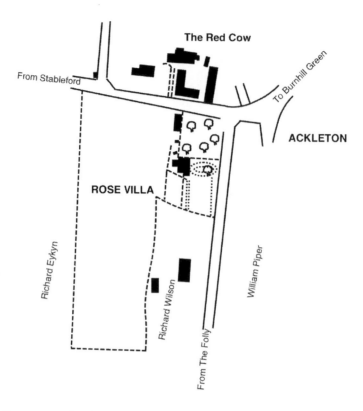

Rosemount Gardens was built on the grounds of Rose Villa

malthouse up to Folley Road.[125] This has made it difficult to imagine what the village was like in the past when Back Lane was an important thoroughfare and Ackleton Hall probably the most prestigious house in the village.

But wasn't Ackleton Manor a contender for the most prestigious house, you may ask? Ackleton never had a manor house as such even though it had an odd status as a separate manor within Worfield as well as being part of Badger Manor. House names are a relatively new invention and at one time may have been called The Mulberries. I may be wrong, but this is my reason for drawing this conclusion. Ackleton Manor was part of William Piper's Ackleton Hall Estate, Lot 2 in the 1904 sale. Extending to just over an acre, the property was let on a repairing lease for fourteen years from 1901. In 1901, Richard Sidney Wilson leased a house called The Mulberries, for the same period. The rent was the same as that of the Manor, £25, the terms the same, and the description; with "stable, coachhouse, cow house, poultry house, greenhouse, out buildings, yard, pleasure & kitchen gardens and tennis lawn adjoining,"

---

[125] *Live the village life*, Sports Argos 22 March 1969 p. 3

remarkably similar to Ackleton Manor. There was also a Wilson family connection. The house had been leased to William Boraston of Wrekin Farm who had married Mary Wilson, R. S. Wilson's aunt, but had been empty for some time.[126] R. Sidney Wilson then sub-let The Mulberries at a "considerably enhanced rental to Henry Valentine Bache De Satgé, Esq.," although in 1902 Mrs de Satgé was looking for staff at The Old House (Hayes Bank), Stableford so perhaps they didn't stay long in Ackleton.[127]

Acknowledgment

Thanks are due to Mr. and Mrs. Crawford for all their help in researching this article & for permitting the inclusion of the following legal documents relating to Ackleton Hall which appear below.

23 December 1760

Thomas Blakeman and wife surrender to Mrs. Bradburne 23 December 1760

Manor of Ackleton. The Court Baron of Clement Kynnersley Esq. Lord of the said Manor held in and for the same on the 23 December 1760 before Walter Stubbs Gentleman, steward there in the presence of John Eykin and John Barney copyholders of the said Manor

To this court comes Thomas Blakeman one of the copyholders of this Manor in his own proper person according to the custom of the said Manor and surrendered into the hands of the Lord of the said Manor by his steward aforesaid by the rod according to the custom thereof All that cottage, malthouse, barn, garden, backside and the several lands called Jones's, the Middle of the Field Piece, Somergate Piece and the 3 butts with the appurtenances containing the half of one nook of land in Ackleton aforesaid with the appurtenances To the use and behoof of … Eleanor Bradburn of Chesterton widow her heirs and assigns for ever Provided always and these presents are upon this condition nevertheless that if the said Thomas Blakeman do and shall well and truly pay or cause to be paid unto the said Eleanor Bradburne her executors, administrators or assigns the full and just sum of one hundred and fifty pounds with interest for the same after the rate of four pounds by the hundred by the year at or upon the 23rd June next ensuing the date hereof then the aforesaid premises be surrendered to Thomas Blakeman his heirs and assigns for ever

And afterwards to this same court comes the said Eleanor Bradburne in her own proper person according to the custom of the said manor and desires to be admitted tenant to the Lord of the said manor to all and singular the premises aforesaid with the appurtenances To whom the Lord of the said manor by his Steward aforesaid by the rod according to the custom of the manor granted the premises aforesaid with the appurtenances and seisin thereof To have and to hold the premises aforesaid with the appurtenances unto the said Eleanor Bradburne her heirs and assigns To the use and behoof of the said Eleanor Bradburne her heirs and assigns for ever subject to the aforesaid condition and at the will of the Lord according to the custom of the manor by the rents, heriots and customary services therefore due and of right

[126] GRO Reference: June Quarter 1852, Bridgnorth, Vol. 6a, p. 1045

[127] *Wellington Journal,* 18 October 1902, p. 4

accustomed and for such estate and ingress the said Eleanor Bradburne doth give 6s 8d to the Lord for a fine and is admitted tenant thereof in form aforesaid ... whereof the steward aforesaid hath hereunto put his hand and seal the day and year above written

Examined by Walter Stubbs Steward

---

16 October 1788

Joshua Badger Admittance

Manor of Ackleton. The Court Baron of Isaac Hawkins Browne Esq. Lord of the said Manor held at the house of John Richards maltster in Ackleton aforesaid 16 October 1788 in the presence of John Richards and Jonah Barney customary tenants of the said Manor

To this court comes Joshua Badger of Wolverhampton in the County of Stafford Innholder grandson and heir at law and also heir in Tail General and Customary Heir of Josiah Blakeman late of Tettenhall in the said County of Stafford Gentleman and Elizabeth his wife both deceased in his own proper person according to the custom of the said Manor And desires to be admitted tenant to the Lord of the said Manor to wit that cottage malthouse barn garden and backside and the several lands called Jones's (part thereof late Eykyns), Somergate Piece and the 3 butts with the appurtenances containing the third part of one nook of land in Ackleton aforesaid with the appurtenances and also all other the copyhold land and premises belonging to the said Josiah Blakeman at the time of his death within the said Manor by his Steward aforesaid by the rod according to the custom thereof hath granted the premises aforesaid to the said Joshua Badger his heirs and assigns To the use and behoof of the said Joshua Badger his heirs and assigns for ever at the will of the Lord according to the custom of the said Manor by the rents, heriots and customary services therefore due and of right accustomed and for such estate and ingress the said Joshua Badger doth give 6s 8d to the Lord for a fine and is admitted tenant thereof in form aforesaid in witness whereof the steward aforesaid hath hereunto put his hand and seal the day and year above written

Examined by Gilbert Brown Steward

Surrender and Admittance

From John Richards the younger to Mr Walter Hollies 4 December 1789

Manor of Ackleton} The Court Baron of Isaac Hawkins Browne Esq. Lord of the said Manor held at the house of John Richards maltster in Ackleton aforesaid 4 December 1789 in the presence of Jonah Barney and Richard Rushton two customary tenants of the said Manor

To this court comes John Richards the younger of Ackleton aforesaid Maltster one of the copyholders or customary tenants of the said Manor and Mary his wife in their own proper persons according to the custom of the manor she the said Mary being first solely and separately examined apart from her said Husband by the Steward aforesaid and freely and voluntarily consented there... and surrender into the hands of the Lord of the said Manor by his Steward aforesaid by the rod according to the custom thereof All that cottage, malthouse, barn, garden and backside and all those lands called Jones's piece (part thereof late Eykyns), Somergate Piece and the 3 butts situate in Ackleton aforesaid with the appurtenances containing the third part of one nook of land (formerly Blakeman's and late Badgers) To the use and behoof of Walter Hollies of Pattingham in the County of Stafford Bricklayer his heirs and assigns for ever at the will of the Lord according to the custom of the said Manor Upon this condition nevertheless that if the said John Richards the younger his heirs executors, administrators or assigns or either of them do and shall well and truly pay or cause to be paid unto the said Walter Hollies his executors administrators or assigns the full and just sum of £250 of good and lawful money of Great Britain Together with interest for the same at the rate of £4 per centum per annum on the 4 June next ensuing the date of this surrender without deduction that then and upon payment thereof the said Walter Hollies his heirs or assigns (at the request, costs and charges of the said John Richards the younger his heirs and assigns according to the custom of the Manor free from all incumbrances to be made or done by the said Walter Hollies his heirs and assigns) shall resurrender all and singular the premises with appurtenances unto John Richards the younger his heirs and assigns according to the custom of the manor free from all incumbrances to be made or done by the said Walter Hollies his heirs or assigns And afterwards to this same Court comes the said Walter Hollies in his own proper person according to the custom of the manor and desires to be admitted tenant to the Lord of the said Manor to all the premises aforesaid with the appurtenances To whom the Lord of the Manor by his Steward aforesaid by the rod according to the custom thereof hath granted the premises aforesaid with the appurtenances and seisin thereof to have and to hold the premises aforesaid with the appurtenances to the said Walter Hollies his heirs and assigns To the use and behoof of the said Walter Hollies his heirs and assigns for ever Subject nonetheless to the aforesaid condition for redemption of the same premises and at the will of the Lord According to the custom of the said Manor by the rents, heriots and customary services therefore due and of right accustomed and for such estate and ingress the said Walter Hollies doth give 4s 5d halfpenny to the Lord for a fine his fealty is respited and he is admitted tenant thereof in form aforesaid In witness whereof the steward aforesaid hath hereunto put his hand and seal this day and year

Examined by Gilbert Brown Steward

Manor of Ackleton George Bennet's Admittance 13 May 1799

Manor of Ackleton} The Court Baron of Isaac Hawkins Browne Esq. Lord of the said Manor held at the house of Thomas Bentley in Ackleton aforesaid 13 May 1799 before Joseph Smith, gentleman, Steward there and in the presence of William Butcher and Jonah Barney two copyholders of the said Manor

To this Court comes George Bennet of Hilton in the parish of Worfield, County of Salop, (shoemaker) oldest son of Thomas Bennett of the parish of Worfield aforesaid, yeoman by Sarah his late wife deceased who was one of the two coheiresses at law of Ambrose Beddart otherwise Bedward otherwise Beddoes heretofore of Ackleton in the parish of Worfield aforesaid yeoman deceased in his own proper person according to the custom of the said Manor and desired to be admitted tenant to all that divided moiety of a copyhold cottage with a new erected tenement and a parcel of land adjoining called the Butt or Yard situate lying and being in Ackleton aforesaid that is to say, the new erected tenement in which Edward Lawrance formerly lived and now in the occupation of James Bently together with that other part of the aforesaid Butt or Yard formerly in the possession of the said Edward Lawrance and now of the said James Bentley. To whom the Lord of the said Manor by his Steward by the Rod according to the Custom thereof hath granted the said divided moiety of the premises aforesaid with the appurtenances and seisin thereof To have and to hold the said divided moiety of the premises aforesaid with the appurtenances unto the said George Bennet his heirs and assigns. To the use and behoof of the said George Bennet his heirs and assigns for ever at the will of the Lord according to the custom of the said Manor by the rents, heriots and customary services therefore due and of right accustomed and for such Estate and Ingress the said George Bennett gives to the Lord for a fine one shilling, swears fealty and is admitted tenant thereof in form aforesaid. In witness whereof the Steward aforesaid hath thereunto set his hand and seal the day and year above written

Examined by me Joseph Smith

1836 Admission. Mary Houlston and Sarah Houlston

Manor of Ackleton} The Court Baron of Elizabeth Browne Widow Lady of the said Manor held at the dwellinghouse of William Richards in Ackleton aforesaid 24 June 1836 before John Jacob Smith, gentleman, Chief Steward there and in the presence of John Richards and John Skett two copyholders of the said Manor

To this Court come Mary Houlston (wife of William Houlston of Wrockwardine in the County of Salop, gardener) and Sarah Houlston (wife of Robert Houlston of Wrockwardine aforesaid, blacksmith), devisees absolutely of the real and personal estate under the last Will and Testament or Testamentary paper of William Whittick bearing date on or about the 7th January 1834 the said Mary Houlston and Sarah Houlston being also the only sisters and coheiresses at law and according to the Custom of this Manor of the said Testator William Whittick late a copyholder of the said Manor deceased (to whom administration with the said Will or Testamentary Paper annexed was on the 20 February 1836 granted by the Prerogative Court of the Archbishop of Canterbury) [come] in their own proper persons and desire to be admitted Tenants to the Lady of the said Manor according to the custom thereof and to all that divided moiety of a copyhold cottage with a new erected tenement and a parcel of land adjoining called the Butt or yard situate, lying and being in Ackleton aforesaid that is to say the new erected tenement in which Edward Lawrence formerly lived and since then in the occupation of James Bentley and now William Ball together with that other part of the aforesaid Butt or Yard situate, lying and being in Ackleton aforesaid formerly in the possession of Edward Lawrence, then of the said James Bentley and now of William Ball together also with all Ways, Waters, Watercourses, Trees, Hedges, Ditches, Fences, Easements, Profits, Privileges, Advantages, Hereditaments and Appurtenances whatsoever to the said Premises belonging or in anywise appertaining or accepted deemed taken or known as part, parcel or member thereof. To whom the Lady of the said Manor by her Steward aforesaid by the Rod according to the Custom thereof hath granted the Premises aforesaid with the appurtenances and seisin thereof to have and to hold the said premises with appurtenances unto the said Mary Houlston and Sarah Houlston their heirs and assigns. To the use and behoof of the said Mary Houlston and Sarah Houlston their respective heirs and assigns for ever as Tenants in Common and not as Joint tenants nevertheless at the will of the Lady according to the custom of the said Manor by the heriots and customary services therefore due and of right accustomed. And for such Estate and Ingress the said Mary Houlston and Sarah Houlston give to the Lady for a fine one shilling, and are admitted tenants thereof in manner aforesaid and their fealty is respited. In witness whereof the Steward aforesaid hath put his hand and seal the day and year above written

John Smith, Steward

1861. Surrender by way of sale of one half of Copyhold Hereditaments in Ackleton
Sarah Houlston, widow, to William Houlston

Manor of Ackleton} Be it remembered that at the office of John Jacob Smith Gentleman in Bridgnorth in the County of Salop on the 6 March 1861 before me John Jacob Smith Steward of Robert Cheney Esquire, Lord of the said Manor appeared Sarah Houlston of Wrockwardine in the County of Salop Widow of Robert Houlston who departed this life on or about the 28th day of April 1859 and was buried at Wrockwardine aforesaid in her own proper person and being seized in fee as tenant in common of one moiety of the hereditaments hereinafter mentioned according to the custom of the said manor and in consideration of the sum of £50 some time since paid to the said Sarah Houlston and her late husband the said Robert Houlston by the said William Houlston as and for the purchase of the fee simple and inheritance of the said one moiety of the hereditaments hereinafter mentioned surrenders into the hands of the Lord of the said Manor by the hands of the Steward aforesaid by the rod according to the custom of the manor one half part of all that divided moiety of a copyhold cottage with a new erected tenement and a parcel of land adjoining called the Butt or Yard in Ackleton that is to say the new erected tenement in which Edward Lawrence formerly lived and since then in the occupation of James Bentley since then of William Ball and now of John Williams together with that other part of the aforesaid Butt or Yard formerly in the possession of Edward Lawrence, then of the said James Bentley then of William Ball and now of John Williams together also with all with all Ways, Waters, Watercourses, Hedges, Ditches, Fences, Easements and Appurtenances whatsoever to the said premises belonging or in anywise appertaining/being the same hereditaments to which the said Sarah Houlston together with her sister Mary Houlston...... 24th June 1836 were admitted as tenants in common in fee according to the custom of the said manor. To the use and behoof of the said William Houlston his heirs and assigns for ever. Nevertheless at the will of the Lord according to the custom of the said Manor. In witness whereof the steward aforesaid hath put his hand and seal the day and year above written

John J. Smith, Steward

1861. Admission of Mr William Houlston to the entirety of certain Copyhold Hereditaments in Ackleton in the surrender of Sarah Houlston and John Houlston, son and heir of Mary Houlston, deceased

Manor of Ackleton} Be it remembered that at the office of John Jacob Smith Gentleman in Bridgnorth in the County of Salop on the 6 March 1861 before me the said John Jacob Smith Steward of Robert Henry Cheney Esquire, Lord of the said Manor appeared William Houlston of the Wrekin Farm in the parish of Wrockwardine in the County of Salop farmer in his own proper person and in pursuance of the surrenders this day severally made for the consideration therein mentioned to his use by Sarah Houlston the widow of Robert Houlston deceased and John Houlston the eldest son and customary heir of Mary Houlston deceased, the late wife of the said William Houlston and desires to be admitted tenant to the Lord of the said Manor according to the custom thereof of and to the entirety of all that divided moiety of a copyhold cottage with a new erected tenement and a parcel of land adjoining called the Butt or yard in Ackleton that is to say the newly erected tenement in which Edward Lawrence formerly lived and since then in the occupation of James Bentley since then of William Ball and now of John Williams Together with that other part of the said Butt or yard formerly in the possession of Edward Lawrence, then of the said James Bentley then of William Ball and now of John Williams together also with all with all Ways, Waters, Watercourses, Hedges, Ditches, Fences, Easements and Appurtenances whatsoever to the said premises belonging or in anywise appertaining (being the same hereditaments to which the said Sarah Houlston together with her sister Mary Houlston were at a court on the 24th June 1836 admitted as tenants in common in fee according to the custom of the said manor). To whom the Lord of the Manor by his steward aforesaid by the rod according to the custom of the said manor hath granted the premises aforesaid with the appurtenances and seisin thereof To have and to hold the said premises with the appurtenances unto the said William Houlston his heirs and assigns. To the use of the said William Houlston his heirs and assigns for ever at the will of the Lord according to the custom of the said Manor by the rents and customary services therefore due and of right accustomed and for such estate and ingress the said William Houlston gives for a fine one shilling, swears fealty and he is admitted tenant in form aforesaid. In witness whereof the steward aforesaid hath put his hand and seal the day and year above written

John J. Smith, Steward

WILL

of William Richards

Will dated 30 March 1838

Testator died

Will proved at Lichfield 26 October 1839

Gordon Nicholls, Bridgnorth

This is the last will and testament of me, William Richards of Ackleton in the County of Salop, farmer. Firstly I desire to be decently buried at the discretion of my executrix and that my just debts, funeral expenses and the charge of proving my will may be paid and discharged as soon as conveniently may be after my decease. I give and devise unto my wife Sarah Richards all and singular my several freehold and copyhold messuages, dwelling houses, lands, tenements and premises with their appurtenances situated and being in the parish of Worfield or elsewhere in the County of Salop to hold to her my said wife for and during the term of her natural life but without power, privilege or authority to mortgage, lease, exchange or encumber any part or parts of the said property and not cut down any timber trees or trees likely to become timber for any purpose whatsoever except or beyond what may be absolutely necessary for keeping in proper repair the buildings and premises before mentioned and intended to be hereby given and devised with the rents and profits thereof to her, my said wife, for the term of her natural life as aforesaid. Also I will and direct that my said wife shall be permitted to have the use of all my household goods and furniture, plate, linen and china for and during the term of her natural life and that an inventory and account should be taken by my executors herein named as soon as conveniently may be after my decease and immediately after the decease of my said wife. My express will is that all my above-mentioned messuages, dwelling houses, lands, tenements and premises with their and every of their appurtenances and also all my household goods, furniture, plate, linen and china and every other matter and thing herein before given, devised or intended so to be devised to my said wife for and during her natural life shall forthwith after the decease of my said wife be sold by public auction and the money or monies to arise from such sale or sales if more than one I hereby will and direct to be equally divided amongst my children, that is to say Daniel, Jane, John, Sarah, James and Mary Ann except only as respects the part or share of the younger daughter Mary Ann which share I hereby expressly charge with the payment of the 2 several sums of money of £50 and £25 and I direct my executors herein after named to deduct the two said sums from and out of her, the said daughter Mary Ann and to pay the said first mentioned sum of £50 so deducted to my daughter Jane Smytheman of Roughton in the said County of Salop and to pay the other sum of £25 to my daughter Sarah or their assigns and which two several sums are to be paid to Jane Smytheman and Sarah Richards in addition to their own proper and respective shares of and in all the before mentioned property herein before directed to be sold and divided as aforesaid. And as to all the rest and residue of my personal estate whatsoever and wheresoever I give and bequeath the same subject to my debts, funeral expenses and testamentary expenses unto my wife Sarah and lastly I hereby nominate and appoint my said Wife executrix and my two sons, Daniel and James executors of this my will and I hereby resolve and revoke and make void any other will or wills by me at any time made and declare this only to be my last. In witness whereof I have set my hand and seal this 30th day of March 1838

Signed by William Richards in the presence of:

E. W. Powell of Worfield and William Trumper of Ackleton

Agreement made on the 8th April 1875 between Edward Cheney of Rudge Hall and Elizabeth Pattrick, widow, of Bridgnorth, of the 2nd part and the Rev. Beaufoy James St. Pattrick of Stockton & the Rev. Reginald St. Pattrick of Sellyndge near Hythe in the county of Kent of the 3rd part

1874 Elizabeth Pattrick had been admitted tenant of one toft and half a yardland & two thirds of a nook in Ackleton being part of one messuage and half a yardland & one toft and half a yardland formerly Browns afterwards Fletchers and lately Daubrie's & also one leasow or flat near Stentwell & one other leasow or flat adjoining Heath Gate formerly the lands of Humphrey Fryer being half a nook of land and to 2 other pieces of land heretofore Toys called Meadowgate Leasow and Somergate Piece formerly in the possession of Thomas Blakeman containing half a nook of land afterwards Fletchers and late Daubries formerly in the several occupations of the representatives of the said Catherine Daubrie, Job Banton & Charles Watkins since then were in the occupation of James Molineux & were then in that of Edmund Charles Wadlow except so much of the premises being the Banks of Badger Dingle as were sold & surrendered to the late Isaac Hawkins Browne then Lord of the Manor by Thomas Backer, John Eykin, Mary Fletcher, Frances Winifred Fletcher & the said Catherine Daubrie at

ACKLETON Ackleton Hall

a court held 3 May 1784 & at that court particularly described. And also to 3 copyhold cottages, tenements, dwelling houses late John Richards the elder & John Richards the younger in Ackleton formerly in the respective occupation of William Beetlestone, William Gallant, William Trumper & the said John Richards the elder since then of William Trumper, William Gallant, Elizabeth Summers & John Walker, afterwards of William Trumper, William Gallant & John Walker and then of the said Edmund Charles Wadlow or his undertenants and also the 2 gardens belonging to the 2 said cottages late in the occupation of the said William Trumper, William Gallant, Elizabeth Summers but not including the garden belonging to the cottage of the said John Walker nor the malthouse erected thereon. And also all that necessary house or privy and the ground whereon the same or privy and so round the same as aforesaid up to the hedge or fence which separates the last mentioned garden from the croft or close of land next thereinafter mentioned And also all that croft or close of land adjoining the before mentioned gardens formerly in the occupation of the said John Richards the elder and John Richards the younger or one of them and since then the representatives of the late Catherine Daubrie and then of the said Edmund Charles Wadlow containing one acre one rood and 24 perches or thereabouts And also the hedge or fence which separates the same from the said gardens all which said premises last described do contain the sixteenth part of a nook of land customary Together with all appurtenances whatsoever belonging to the said premises to hold the same unto the said Elizabeth Pattrick her assigns and assigns for her life at the will of the lord by rent, heriots, customary services and of right accustomed. Edward Cheney is entitled to a chief rent of 16s 4d ... and whereas Edward Cheney has agreed to the sale of the freehold & the surrender of the chief rent for the sum of £80

Whereas) Timothy Owen late of Ackleton Hall died on the 20 March 1938 leaving by his will dated 16 Sept 1934 appointed his wife Agnes Owen sole executrix. Agnes died on 14 April 1938 intestate without having proved the will so letters of administration were granted to the vendors on 5 July 1938. Timothy Owen was at the date of his death seised of the property in fee simple subject to a mortgage. The whole of the property was vested in Dora Josephine Alsop wife of the Rev. Arthur Richard Alsop of Bednal Vicarage, Staffs for a time of 3,000 years.

By a receipt (endowed on the said mortgage) dated 3 Dec 1938 & given by the said Dora Josephine Alsop payment of the principal money and all interest thereon and costs was acknowledge to have been made by the vendors out of moneys applicable to the discharge of the said mortgage.

The vendors have agreed the sale of the property to the purchaser free from any incumbrances but subject as hereinafter mentioned at the price of £6,000. Sale included Ackleton Hall, farm buildings and cottages. Total area of land 195 acres

Conveyance between Zetta Violet Owen, spinster of Ackleton Hall on the 5 Dec 1938 and Gwendoline Kate Jones wife of Oswald Nicholas Jones of 9, Halstead Road in the City of Liverpool, schoolmaster (herein after called the vendors) of the one part and William Marklew Iliff of Oaken Manor, Oaken (herein after called the purchaser)

ACKLETON

Conveyance on the 29 Feb 1956 between William Marklew Iliffe & Joseph Thomas Farrier of Ackleton Hall near W'ton, farmer, the purchaser. Price £10,000 for all that messuage or dwellinghouse known as Ackleton Hall with the farm buildings, 2 cottages, land and premises in Ackleton, in total 194 acres, 11 perches & three quarters of a perch conveyed (with 6 cottages known as Sunnyside, Windynook, 1,2,3 Hall Farm Cottages - OS 111,150 & part 149 sold and conveyed by the vendor)

Further Reference: Shropshire Archives, *Valuation & inventory of implements & furniture the property of John Richards*, 4752/32/70

THE EYKYNS OF ACKLETON

On the 14th May 1921 James Eykyn, aged 71, died at Ackleton House of pneumonia and asthenia. He is described on the death certificate as a landed proprietor. The Eykyns were an old Worfield family and I assume from their name that they came either from Wykyn or Ewyke. The latter was a village which once lay between the Folley and Rowley, west of Rowley Park Farm. The family were in Ackleton from the fourteenth century at least, and in the nineteenth century owned much of the farmland of the village. Today they would be forgotten in Worfield were it not for Ackleton House, the Eykyn vault in Worfield Church, and the following memorials:

- James Eykyn of Ackleton died October 16 1782 aged 47. Martha Eykyn of Ackleton died June 15 1827 aged 85
- Under this stone are the remains of John Eykyn who departed this life in the 71st year of his life on the 22 May 1784. Also of Martha his wife who departed this life on the 18th day of January 1785 in the 74th year of her life
- In loving memory of Richard Eykyn of Ackleton born 1819 died 1902 …Also of Jane Frances born 1816 died 1890

When Peggy Hodge Eykyn, the daughter of Richard Eykyn and sister of James, died in 1933, she left £1,000 to beautify and maintain Worfield church. An altar cross, candlesticks and other items were purchased as a memorial to the family which were always left on the altar table and as I recall were stolen in the 1980s or 1990s.

The earliest reference to the Eykyns is in a charter from King Edward III's reign (1327-1377) which allowed Richard Eykyn to be exempt from jury service as a tenant of lands in Ackleton.[128] We know that the family were still in Ackleton in 1612 when the following payments were made: "Tyror 1s 1d, Eykeyn 1s ½d, Parsons 7d, Bradley 10d ½d, Roger Barnett 7d, Heathill 7½d, Thomas Barrett 11d, in cowshall 6½d, Thomason 7d, Penry/Perry 3d, Brown 7d, Toy 3½d, Blakman and Felton 3½d".[129] By the late nineteenth century Randall notes that the Eykyns have three mansions "pleasingly situated and surrounded by ornamental grounds; two are in the possession of respectable tenants at about a stone's throw of each other but neither seems to present traces of the houses of the ancestors of the family".[130] There is not much more than this in Randall except that, "a regard for the origin, possessions, privileges and home of their ancestors has led the Eykyns to remain and spend their lives at Ackleton." What follows is a little more about the family in the eighteenth century.

There are a number of Eykyn wills of which the earliest I found was that of Ann Eken in 1659. She was a widow and bequeathed to her son Richard one pair of joyned bedsteds now

---

[128]Randall, *Worfield & Its Townships*, p. 45.

[129] Randall, *Ibid*, p. 46

[130] Randall, *Ibid*, p. 47

standing in the chamber over the parlour with one great chest, also two ewes and two lambs and one shilling of money also the rest of her goods - corn, cattell, household stuff, money and debts.[131] Her other sons, Roger and John are minors and in the guardianship of Thomas Bradbourne of Ackleton and John Bassford This sounds as though Ann Eken had one house and some land. Usually with a messuage went half a virgate of land at least - 30 acres.

John Eykyn, a blacksmith, in his will of 1717, gave to his wife Jane Rowley his mare, and to John Dalloway, weaver, of Ackleton, £10 and all his clothes & 6 ewes.[132] To Elizabeth Blackmore of Ackleton, spinster, all his goods including those in the shop [ie workshop] except his smith tools and wool. She also received his cow. To Mary Dalloway 6 half crowns. James Eykyn, his kinsman is made executor of the will.

By comparison, Thomas Tyrer's will of 1711 has definite property assets of messuages, cottages, tenements and land.[133] Tyrer, a yeoman, leaves a wife but no children. The property goes to two of his nephews; Thomas Tyrer of Oldswinford, clothier, and Thomas Onions of Sheriffhales, locksmith. £380 cash is distributed to relatives, friends and servants.

While Randall is correct in claiming that the family held on to land and property in

Ackleton House circa 1900 built by Roger Eykyn

Ackleton, with some members of the family continuing to live there, others moved away. So it was that in the eighteenth century we find both James and Roger Eykyn living in that fashionable town near to Ackleton, Wolverhampton.

---

[131] The National Archives, *Will of Ann Eken*, PROB/292/234

[132] The National Archives, *Will of John Eykyn*, PROB 11/561/167

[133] The National Archives, *Will of Thomas Tyrer*, PROB 11/524/551

St John's Church, Wolverhampton

James Eykyn opened a shop selling soft furnishings and furniture; everything for elegant living. A cabinet maker and upholsterer by trade, he had a shop, workshop and showroom in the best location in town, High Green, Wolverhampton (now Queen Square). Without doubt this was a smart establishment, and there was much for the customer to choose from. The list of items in stock included dozens of yards of furnishing textiles, laces and fringes, 10,000 tin tacks, 57 Dutch tiles & 159 pieces of wallpaper. In the dining room, there were eight round mahogany pillar tables, several chests of drawers, a large mahogany two-leaf dining table and three breakfast tables, 14 mahogany tea chests, 16 mahogany tea boards, 11 dozen bottle boards and waiter, 40 yards of Manchester stripe, counterpanes, 300 pieces of wallpaper & glass and china ware. The premises included a cabinet workshop, a mat room, a stable, a feather room, a timber yard and an accounting house. One of the bedchambers was used as a silvering room for mirrors, and in the attics were more stocks of textiles and unfinished furniture. Four of the six bedrooms were used to store furniture, particularly chairs waiting to be upholstered. No space was left unused and the showroom and living area merged, creating an emporium of the finest goods for the fashionable and wealthy.[134] The only problem in establishing such a business in Wolverhampton was a lack of sufficiently wealthy inhabitants.

James Eykyn died in 1779 and his wife Janet shortly afterwards in 1780. The four houses in High Green were bequeathed to his brother John who enjoyed them for only a short time before he died in 1783. John split the Wolverhampton property, then occupied by John Brazier, George Wainwright, Bettina Falkner and John Foxall, between his brother Richard Eykyn (later

---

[134] Margaret Ponsonby, *Stories from Home, English Domestic Interiors 1750-1850*, (Routledge 2016) p. 106

132

in the document it is Roger Eykyn which I think is correct) of Wolverhampton and his son-in-law Richard Windle of Beobridge. Windle died before he could inherit.

Roger Eykyn (1724-1795), the son of Roger Eykyn of Wolverhampton, became a successful builder and architect.[135]   Described as a master joiner, nurseryman, surveyor and architect, Roger had, early in life, taken an interest in building and he was commissioned to be the contractor in the building of St John's Church, Wolverhampton. William Baker is thought to have been the architect, but Eykyn's experience in this project led him to design St Paul's Church in Birmingham. The churches are very alike, built in the style of St Martin in the Fields. Roger then designed his own house in Ackleton, now known as Ackleton House, built in 1790, which replaced an Elizabethan house on the site. The source of this information is Colonel Beddows who added that the trees in the garden were very fine particularly a Weeping Lime and a number of Copper Beeches. Roger Eykyn died in Wolverhampton at the age of seventy-one in 1795 and the death notice in the newspaper described him as a "nurseryman and formerly an eminent architect and surveyor".[136] The nursery must have been extensive, perhaps there was more than one, for a newspaper advertisement speaks of, "his nurseries at and near Wolverhampton".[137] Trees and shrubs of all types were for sale; 'forest trees, fruit trees and flowering shrubs". All we know of the location is that the Birmingham Canal passed through the nurseries.

Both the Eykyns who stayed in Ackleton in the eighteenth century and those who moved to Wolverhampton prospered and became well respected members of the Society in which they moved. Roger Eykyn left a legacy of two churches and a very grand house in Ackleton. James was a skilled craftsman and salesman, and many of the fine houses of Wolverhampton would have been graced by his furniture. Meanwhile the Eykyns who remained in Ackleton lived out their lives more quietly out of the public view.[138] The Ackleton House Estate was sold in 1922 by Miss Eykyn to Mr Neale, and Francis John Neale sold it in 1937 to Colonel William Beddows.[139]

---

[135] Wolverhampton Archives, *Notes and Correspondence on Roger Eykyn, architect,* D/JSR/44/52

[136] *Wolverhampton Chronicle,* June 26 1795, p. 3

[137] *Derby Mercury,* 12 February 1779, p. 4

[138]Worfield Parish Magazine in 1934 records that there is an Eykyn pedigree in the Bodleian Library

[139]Wolverhampton Archives, D-NAJ/F/22

RICHARD SIDNEY WILSON

Richard Sidney Wilson is a difficult man to categorise; an entrepreneur, definitely, a social reformer, possibly, and a man whose life was turned upside down by events largely outside his control. He was however his own worst enemy, throwing good money after bad in court cases which had little chance of success. Nonetheless, R. S. Wilson has left an important legacy of improved housing for his workmen, and refurbished houses in Kingslow, Ackleton and Chesterton. Sadly, the large malthouse in Ackleton which generated the wealth of the Wilson business, has been demolished.

R. S. Wilson

It was Derek Rowley who first drew my attention to Richard Sidney Wilson as an important benefactor to the parish who gave money to build what is now called the Old Vicarage. In fact, Wilson gave just £125, and W. H. Foster donated nearly half the cost of the construction; £1,000. In addition, when the Revd. Evans was about to be married, Foster paid for a new stable and coach house.

ACKLETON

Richard Sidney Wilson

Richard Wilson

Alice Sparrow circa 1859

Richard Sidney Wilson was born at Ackleton House in 1867, the only son of Richard Wilson and Alice (nee Sparrow). There was one other child, Florence Annie, born in 1863, who we will meet at the end of this chapter. It was R. S Wilson's great grandfather, Richard, who first came to the area, not to Worfield but to Claverley. In 1800, the elder Richard Wilson, aged about forty-six, came from Chaddesley Corbet and took Aston Hall on a twenty-one year lease. One assumes that his wife, Mary (nee Watkins), and children, John, Richard, Mary and William, came with him. Whatever Richard's hopes were for his new life in Claverley, they were to be dashed because he died just two years later. Mary and the family stayed in Claverley and in 1804 she married John Perry of Aston. Mary's eldest son, John, took over the lease of Aston Hall (it was released in 1817), and Richard went back to Chaddesley Corbett for several years. Richard married Mary Wilkes in 1824 at Chaddesley Corbett and their eldest child was christened there in 1827. The family then moved around a great deal. Richard was christened in 1829 at Feckenham, Edward and Edith in 1832 and 1837 respectively at Kinver and James Wilkes and Fanny in 1841 and 1843 respectively at Worfield/Badger when the family were living at Ackleton.

Exactly when the family settled in Ackleton we don't know but the 1841 census records that Richard was a farmer there. He was described in the same way in the 1851 census, farming 470 acres. They lived first at Tyte Farm and later at Ackleton House, both owned by the Eykyn family. By 1861, Richard had died. and Mary Wilson, Richard's widow, was running a farm of 320 acres and employing 17 men. In 1862, Richard Wilson the younger married Alice Sparrow of Nottingham, and the couple came back to Ackleton to live at Ackleton House.

135

ACKLETON
Richard Sidney Wilson

The Wilson malting business started some time between 1851 and 1861 when Mary and

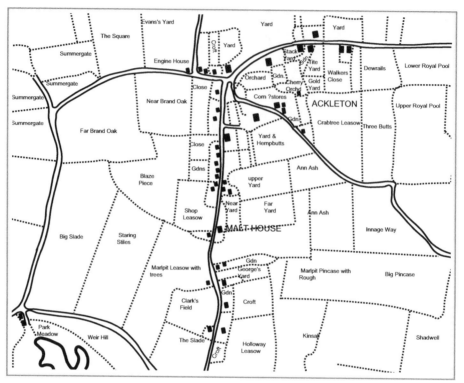

Ackleton Malthouse as shown on Foxall's 1839 Field Names Map

Richard's son Richard, aged 25, is described in the census as a maltster. There were other maltings and maltsters in the village before this date. Brewing occurred in many, perhaps most, households and pubs (the Red Cow included), and along with brewing went malting. In addition there were specialist maltsters. In 1841 John Eykyn was a maltster as was Sarah Richards. By 1851, Sarah had died and John Richards took over the business. It is impossible to know for certain where the malthouses of John Eykyn and Richards were, nor where the Wilson business began. On the tithe map of 1839 just one malthouse is shown, on the right hand side of the road from the Folley into the village. Did this malthouse belong to the Richards family and did Richard Wilson begin malting here before moving across the road to a virgin site giving him enough space to develop the premises? All we can say is that this is possible. The image on page 161 is of the new malthouse but today the only evidence of the location of this once enormous malting business is the road name, 'Maltings Close'.

From, say 1861, and his death in 1901, Richard Wilson built a substantial business in Ackleton which Randall described, in 1887, as follows. "The principal inhabitants in addition to the Eykyns, are Mr R. Wilson, who carries on a large malting business, wetting about 200 sacks a week. Mr Wilson has bored into the red sandstone rock and obtained an excellent supply of good water on the spot and has a large brewery in Bridgnorth where he has formed an artesian well in the rock, the water of which has been tested, and proved to be highly valuable".[140] The brewery in Bridgnorth was the Castle Brewery in Underhill Street.[141] The company also owned eleven inns and beer houses. In 1893, the Castle Brewery was under new management, although Wilson retained ownership[142]

Richard Wilson treated his employees to an annual excursion and in 1900 the trip was to Portsmouth.[143] No expense was spared as this description testifies."The annual trip given by Messrs R. Wilson and Son, maltsters of Ackleton for their employees took place at the end of last week. A special train with saloon attached left Albrighton station on Friday evening to enable the party to join at Wolverhampton the GWR to Portsmouth. On arriving there soon after 6 o'clock, breakfast was the first consideration. The weather was beautifully fine, and by eight o'clock several of the company had been rowed out to Nelson's old flagship, The Victory, each wanting to stand where the famous Admiral fell. Other parties were grouped together, and conducted through the naval ship-building yards where a huge ironclad was shown in course of construction ..., the plate armour being very attractive. Some fortunate ones were taken over the Trafalgar, which was commissioned and under orders to put to sea in a few hours. After dinner different detachments took the steamer over the Solent to explore the Isle of Wight. Driving parties were organised and besides Cowes and Ryde, Shanklin, Sandown & Bonnchurch were visited the return trip being made to the South pier where they listened to the band, while the promenade gave a pleasing glimpse of fashionable life. Various entertainments were afterwards indulged in and great was the merriment when the different parties met, until they finally collected soon after for departure. Albrighton was reached by the return special at 4.30 on Sunday morning. The party were conveyed home in wagons and all were quite ready for the Sunday's rest."

In March 1901, Richard Wilson died, and the business was left in the hands of his son, Richard Sidney Wilson, aged 33. Unmarried, R. S. Wilson continued to live at Ackleton, presumably at Ackleton House, which was his mother's home until her death in 1908.[144] According to his death certificate, James Eykyn died at Ackleton House in 1904, so whether the house was divided I don't know. The 1911 census shows R. S. Wilson still living in Ackleton, aged 43, a maltster, with servants, Sarah Louise Perks, aged 28, Lizzie Gill aged 21 and George Gough, aged 26.

Richard Wilson had not only been a successful maltster, he had also built or improved houses. One cottage in Ackleton bears his initials with the date 1898 (see page 192). Building was a passion his son inherited and which perhaps was his downfall, building up a large portfolio of property without adequate cash to support it. The houses were of good quality and

[140] John Randall, *Worfield and its Townships*, p. 47

[141] *Kidderminster Times and Advertiser for Bewdley & Stourport*, 29 April 1876 p. 4

[142] *Bridgnorth Journal & South Staffordshire Advertiser*, 27 May 1893 p. 1

[143] *Worfield Parish Magazine*, 1900

[144] *Shrewsbury Chronicle*, 1 May 1908, p. 5

ACKLETON   Richard Sidney Wilson

Florence Annie Wilson with her brother Richard Sidney Wilson on the right & their mother and father, Alice & Richard Wilson in the grounds of Ackleton House. I assume the landscaping of the gardens was done 100 years before this picture was taken, & that the trees came from Roger Eykyn's tree nursery.

Richard Sidney Wilson should have been proud of what he had achieved. There was no suggestion that there were any clouds on the horizon except those of an impending war.

In 1914 Wilson was called up to serve with the Yeomanry and in November 1914 went to France where he remained until August 1915. Aged 45 in 1914, Wilson was an older recruit which may warrant some explanation. At the beginning of World War I the country's fighting forces were trained volunteer troops akin to the Territorial Army. Wilson first joined the Royal Garrison Artillery in 1903 where he was Second Lieutenant, and in 1906 transferred to the Warwickshire Imperial Yeomanry at the same rank. As a volunteer Wilson was therefore called to serve in time of war. The trauma of Wilson's army service was quickly compounded with financial problems affecting his business back home. While he was in France he had left his businesses in the hands of bankers, and when the businesses floundered, creditors sued him. Wilson gave his sister power of attorney, authorising her to sign a deed of assignment under which the brewing business was sold on 2 June 1915. This consisted of:

- The Prince of Wales Inn, Walsall Road (between Darlaston & Wednesbury)

138

- The Miners Arms Inn, Ruiton Street, Lower Gornal & two cottages adjoining
- The Swan Inn, Darkouse Lane, Deepfields, Coseley, and two houses attached
- The Barley Mow Inn, Oxford Street, Bilston
- The Rolling Mill Inn, Millfield Rd, Bilston and five dwelling houses
- The California Inn, Hatton Street, Bradley, near Bilston and five dwelling houses
- The Boat Inn, Boat Row, off Park Lane West, Tipton
- The Red Lion Inn, Castle Street, Coseley
- The Summer House Inn, School Street, Roseville, Coseley
- The Cabin Inn, Kent Street, Upper Gornal
- The Folly [later written Folley] Inn, Ackleton
- Cottage residence adjoining the above let to Mr Davies
- The Castle Brewery, Bridgnorth, together with the fixed plant

The money from the sale of these assets was enough to meet the demands of the creditors but perhaps it irreparably damaged the malting business and given different circumstances other arrangements may have been made. When Wilson first heard that creditors were demanding payment he was in France and said that he did not realise the severity of the situation, his own survival being his chief concern.

A reporter describes Wilson's examination at Shrewsbury Bankruptcy Court in May 1916."At that time, he said, he did not see himself as being insolvent. Moreover when he received the communication insisting he give the power of attorney it was the night after the battle of La Chapelle. The whole place was rocking with shells, and one did not take a very long view of life. Therefore it was difficult for a man to concentrate on his financial position. He had no knowledge that his debts had been put down to £10,000-£11,000 and his assets at £13,002. At that time he did not understand the powers that were given by deed of assignment. When he came home from France (in 1915 he returned to England to work in the Army Service Corps) he found that all sorts of extraordinary things had been done to his property - in fact the maximum amount of harm and the minimum amount of good. When he realised his position he applied to the Court to set aside the deed of assignment but his appeal was dismissed and in the meantime a creditor who had got judgment issued a bankruptcy notice. He then appealed to the Divisional Court and the Court of Appeal to have the bankruptcy proceedings annulled, but this was unsuccessful. Replying to his solicitor Major Wilson said that when he left for war he went with the utmost confidence that there would be no financial difficulty".[145]

In 1917 Wilson brought an action against the United Counties Bank claiming that it was their negligence which had caused the bankruptcy and received damages & costs which enabled the payment of his debts. Wilson retired from the army in 1919 on an army disability pension of £4 per week, and in 1923 he recommenced his malting and farming businesses but by 1928 he was again in financial difficulties. These were hard times for any business, but especially for farming, and property in general. Unfortunately virtually all Wilson's assets were in property

---

[145] Bridgnorth Major's Affairs, *Birmingham Daily Post*, 24 May 1916 p. 8

and heavily mortgaged at that. In normal times this might have been fine, but these weren't normal times.

Prior to 1928 R. S. Wilson owned:

A. The Kingslow Estate including Kingslow Hall, a farm, eight cottages and land

B. The Chesterton Estate including a residence and premises, a bailiff's house, a mill, 2 farms known as Bowen's and Marindin and 6 cottages. A & B were subject to mortgages of £22,000

C. A malting house and extensive buildings known as Ackleton Maltings subject to a mortgage of £5,000

D. An inn and premises known as Folly Inn subject to a mortgage of £1,500

E. Certain houses and premises in Wolverhampton known as Halletts Row subject to a mortgage of £500

With creditors pressing, Wilson was advised by his solicitor, Herbert Taylor, to sell the Maltings by public auction so that the creditors could be paid. Taylor recognised that a contingency needed to be put in place if the Maltings didn't sell and it was this: if the Ackleton Maltings weren't sold at auction or within seven days at a price which would enable the creditors to be paid, a deed of assignment of all Wilson's assets would be executed for the benefit of his creditors. Edward Campbell would be the trustee and Taylor's company would act as solicitors in this arrangement. The Maltings failed to find a buyer, and as a result Wilson was forced to sell the whole estate when it was proving hard to sell any property, let alone achieve a reasonable price. Wilson said that his understanding of the situation was that, in the event of the Maltings not being sold, Taylor would make an arrangement with the creditors so that the deed of assignment would not have to be applied. Wilson's only recourse now was to go to the law again. In June 1928, he asked for this deed of assignment to be set aside and claimed damages for negligence from Taylor. On the 16 April 1929 Wilson set down a motion in Chancery to stay the sale of household furniture & farming stock, but this was dismissed with costs. More court applications were similarly dismissed with costs and on the 17 Dec 1930, in the case of Wilson versus Taylor at the Court of Chancery, the Judge made these comments in support of Wilson's counsel:

"He has certainly said everything that could be said in support of the various allegations which the plaintiff has made but when all is said and done neither he nor I nor anybody can make bricks satisfactorily without straw. I think the true solution of this case is there is no straw with which to make the bricks.

The plaintiff with whom one cannot help feeling the sympathy which naturally extends to anybody when he is in a tight corner was undoubtedly in a very embarrassed condition in the early part of 1928. I quite understand what his view was and is. It was this. I have substantial assets and although it is true that I owe £3,000 or £4,000 to public bodies who are not likely to shew me much mercy, it is a cruel thing that my assets, not liquid but represented by landed property, should be sacrificed because of this more or less insignificant demand for ready money.

In sum, he tried to do what anyone would do, namely to make an arrangement with his creditors, but he overvalued his non-liquid assets and although he had friends, some of whom like Mr Taylor …offered to guarantee a debt …, a time came when his friends could do no more and it was time to send out an SOS to his creditors saying 'give him time and he will realise the value of the Maltings'. Unfortunately this was not to be but Mr Taylor has proved a very good friend to the plaintiff in taking over the mortgages of some of the properties."[146]

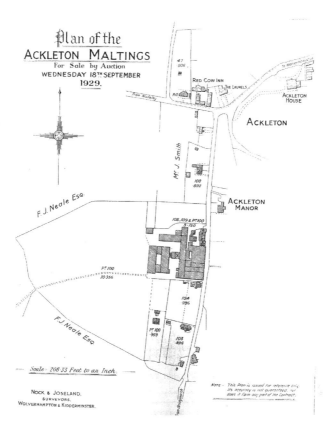

All that is left of the Maltings today is a wall alongside the footpath shown on the plan. See also pages 144 & 162

Wilson's litigious nature was one of the causes of his downfall and is seen in this case at Bridgnorth Petty Sessions in 1903. He was fined £3 for not making weekly returns to the Excise (he had only made two returns since 1892). Wilson had bought 700 sacks of corn from Mr. Instone of Aston at Bridgnorth & his defence was that only a sample was shown to him in Bridgnorth with the contract being sealed in Ackleton. It seems a weak defence in a case which was indefensible yet Wilson's immediate response was, 'when can I appeal.'[147]

[146] *Birmingham Daily Gazette,* 17 December 1930 p. 5

[147] *Shrewsbury Chronicle,* 8 May 1903 p. 8

ACKLETON   Richard Sidney Wilson

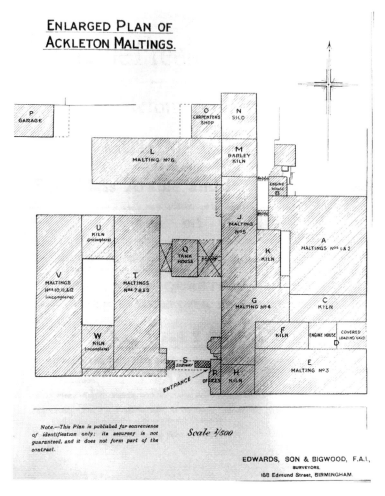

Plan of Ackleton Maltings prepared for the sale in 1928

From June 1928 Wilson was without a job and dependant on his pension and gifts from family and friends. He was declared bankrupt for the second time in August 1931 and in January 1932, the Official Receiver attributed Wilson's position (debts of £8,404 and assets nil) to heavy law costs in unsuccessful actions. R. S. Wilson was then living in Hornchurch in a house called 'Kingslow'. In 1938 he tried to bring another case but the Judge stopped it and described Wilson as a man with a passion for litigation. By then he was living at Ardleigh Green Road, Hornchurch, but at some point Wilson returned to the Midlands and lived at the Elms in Pattingham looked after by his faithful servant, Miss Perks. Even in 1944 he was still claiming an interest in the Ackleton Maltings bringing an action against Harry Nock of Brierley Hill for alleged breach of contract. It was a crazy case to bring and needless to say Nock said Wilson had no rights in the property after it was sold at auction. Richard Sidney Wilson died in 1955 and is buried in Worfield Churchyard.

The demise of Wilson's fortunes in 1928 prompted the sale of the Kingslow and Chesterton Estate of 900 acres. We think today of the Apley and Davenport Estates as being the major estates in the parish but the Kingslow Estate was very impressive.

The estate was parcelled up into the following lots:

1. Kingslow Hall 16.851 acres
2. Home Farm, Kingslow 149.639 acres
3. Small Holding, 37 and 38, Stanlow 21.733 acres
4. Two cottages and gardens 35 and 36, Kingslow 3.818 acres
5. Piece of arable land 18.199 acres
6. Eleven enclosures of pasture and arable 44.507 acres
7. Chesterton Mill Farm 67.512 acres
8. Chesterton Mill Cottages smallholding 7.790 acres
9. Chesterton Bowen's Farm 197.889 acres
10. Chesterton Holding 79.721 acres
11. No 25 Chesterton Cottage .225 acres
12. Chesterton House Farm 105.755 acres
13. Useful Grain Farm 165.498 acres
14. Chesterton House 6.279 acres
15. Cottage & Garden & Blacksmith's shop .278 acres
16. Old Chapel Cottages (2) .439 acres
17. The old House, Chesterton 2.330 acres
18. Growing timber (Phillips Wood) 8.023 acres
19. Growing timber (Deepdale Coppice) 9.407 acres

The intention was to sell the Kingslow and Chesterton Estates as one lot, which was probably wishful thinking. All over the country big estates were being sold and their break-up enabled many people to buy their first homes and farmers to buy the farms which they had tenanted for years. Not everyone saw the change as a good thing, Rolf Gardiner being one of them.[148]

So what happened at the Kingslow & Chesterton auction? Lot 1, Kingslow Hall, failed to sell at auction but a man called Sydney Guy was interested in buying it. It was a meeting of ascendant fortune in the case of Sydney Guy and descendant fortune in the case of R. S. Wilson. Sydney Guy was born in King's Heath, Birmingham in 1885, started work in Birmingham as an apprentice at an engineering company, then worked at Humber in Coventry before joining the Sunbeam car company in Wolverhampton in 1909 as works manager. Production increased dramatically and by 1913 Guy felt that he had earned a pay rise. This was refused so he started his own company manufacturing lorries. The First World War

---

[148] Gardiner, Rolf, *England Herself,* (Faber & Faber) 1943

increased demand for vehicles and engines and Guy Motors prospered. After the war life was much more of a struggle with a surplus of lorries for sale at very low prices. In spite of the terrible economic situation which prevailed across the country, Guy Motors survived, making charabancs and buses as well as lorries.

An aerial view of Ackleton Maltings estimated to be from the 1960s, courtesy of Mr & Mrs James.

Guy's agent visited the Hall in July 1929 and gave his assessment of the property.[149]

"To make the necessary alterations and improvements to suit your requirements a very considerable expenditure would be required and when these had been effected you would not then have a desirable or saleable residence... In my judgment the present buildings comprising Kingslow Hall are valueless."

The agent put a price of £1,500 on the Hall purely because of the site and advised Guy that if he did decide to buy the Hall he should also consider buying Lots 2,3,4, and probably 5 in addition. In the event Guy offered £2,000 but added a clause that:"Neither Major Wilson, Miss Perks, nor any relation of theirs should be allowed to occupy the Bailiff's house." Guy made it clear that this was his final offer and it was not accepted. [Note: the Bailiff's House is shown on p. 192.]

---

[149] Correspondence in private hands. Included by kind permission of Sheila Carver

ACKLETON   Richard Sidney Wilson

While Sidney Guy didn't buy Kingslow, as the shrewd businessman he was, he did buy Chesterton Mill Cottages and some land (Lot 6) . Having ascertained that he could evict a 'service tenant,' he then sold them to William Perry of King's Heath, Birmingham.

Kingslow was sold to Norman Tailby who is reputed to have had a party for three days to celebrate his purchase. The next buyer was Reginald Tildesley who died locally in a tragic car accident in 1953. Kingslow was then bought by George Davies and his wife who later sold Kingslow Hall to Roy and Sheila Carver.

Notes on Chesterton Mill

Chesterton Mill became a paper mill some time in the early eighteenth century. There is the baptism of a son of Richard Adams, of Chesterton, paper-maker and Elizabeth, on March 9th 1728/9. Eight further references to Richard Adams appear up to 1753, and in all but one he is recorded as a paper-maker. His place of residence is recorded as Chesterton (four times), Kingslow (twice) and Worfield (twice). Another paper maker appears in the parish registers in 1747 when Richard Cowell and Hester Millingchamp were married. They were 'both living at ye paper-mill at Chesterton.' On 24 January 1753 the burial is recorded of Thomas Phillips 'apprentice to Richard Cowel of Chesterton, paper-maker'. After that there are no further references to the paper mill or to paper makers, suggesting that the paper mill may have closed down around 1750 and become a corn mill and the paper makers moved elsewhere to work.

In 1937 Mr T. F. J. Parton was the tenant of Mill Farm. He had been at the farm for fourteen years and when he came to the farm the disused machinery of the corn-mill was still in position suggesting that it was still in use not long before 1923. H. Cook, a bricklayer's labourer in Bridgnorth in 1937 said that he remembered the mill grinding corn when he was a lad about fifty years before. The following is a description of Chesterton Mill as it was in 1937, written by Dr W. Watkins-Pitchford in an article in the Transactions of the Shropshire Archaeological Society Vol XL1X entitled 'Paper Making in Shropshire, 1656-1912.

'The ruined buildings of the mill stand some way below the present farm-house, athwart the Nun Brook; this comes down from the Great Pool of Patshull, and joins the Worfe between Hilton and Worfield. The buildings are small and almost entirely of brick. The bricks do not seem very old. The overshot wheel is of iron, small in diameter but elongated into a cylinder. There is a plentiful and constant supply of water. The machinery formerly turned by the wheel has been removed, but parts of it - including large iron cogged wheels and a massive wooden spindle - are lying among the nearby weeds and bushes. The appearances suggest that the mill was rebuilt some hundred years ago - perhaps when it was converted into a corn-mill. Just east of the mill, on the North side of the brook, are one or more old cave-dwellings excavated into a low sandstone cliff. The face of the adjacent cliff to the East is cut vertically and shows signs of having formed the back wall of some sheds.'

Acknowledgments

My thanks are due to James Hewitt for supplying much of the material for this article, to Sue Burns and Derek Moorhouse for their extensive research, to Sheila Carver for additional material and to Mr and Mrs James for the only known images of Ackleton Maltings.

FLORENCE ANNIE WILSON

Florence Annie Wilson

Out of the blue an old acquaintance, James Hewitt rang one day and asked if he might have a copy of the first Worfield book. I knew that James's mother had lived for a while at Stableford Hall but knew of no other connection with Worfield, so I was rather surprised by the request. I should, however, have made the connection from James's surname, for Dr. Hewitt was a doctor in Claverley for many years. During the First World War, when the Worfield Recreation Room (Village Hall) was used as a hospital for injured soldiers, Dr. Hewitt was one of the doctors who cared for the patients. His practice served Worfield in addition to Claverley, and it was, so family history tells, while walking through the fields at Ackleton that he met and fell in love with a charming young lady, Florence Wilson.

Florence was born in 1863 so was four years older than her only brother, Richard Sidney Wilson. She must have had something of a charmed upbringing at Ackleton House, enjoying as she did, country life. Both Dr. Hewitt and his bride-to-be were very popular and judging from

146

his performance at a Claverley concert in 1898 Dr. Hewitt had quite a sense of humour. 'Razors in the Air,' was one of the songs he sang; with a bone accompaniment, of course.[150] But although Worfield Church would have been full had the wedding been held there, the couple wanted a quiet wedding and their choice was a London church. They were married on the 28th January 1904 at St George's, Hanover Square. The Vicar of Worfield wrote in the Parish Magazine that,"the weather was dull, but the wedding party was independent of it, they had their own sunshine."

Thomas Henry La Nauze Hewitt was born in Ireland in 1865, the second son of Thomas Pierrepoint and Elizabeth Hewitt, and did his medical training in Dublin, qualifying in 1895. Around 1898 Dr Hewitt came to Claverley to work with James Torrens whom he had met when he was at Dublin. Dr Torrens was living at the Lodge in Claverley High Street and initially Thomas Hewitt lived at Sunnyside, Claverley, with his widowed mother and his Aunt Sophia.

Dr. Hewitt and Florence Wilson

In addition to the duties of looking after the infirm of Claverley and Worfield, Dr Torrens was appointed Medical Officer to the Quatt District, and Medical Officer and Public vaccinator for the Bridgnorth Union in 1897, replacing T. W. Haslehurst who had resigned. Dr.

---

[150] *Bridgnorth Journal*, 23 April 1898 p. 5

ACKLETON   Florence Annie Wilson

Hewitt was also Medical Officer of the Trysull Workhouse and No 2. District Seisdon Union, Medical Officer No 5 District, Bridgnorth Union and the Medical Officer of South Shropshire Schools and finally the vaccination officer for the Bridgnorth and Seisdon Unions.

The partnership of Torrens and Hewitt was dissolved in 1903 with "all the debts to be received and paid by T. H. La Nauze Hewitt by whom this said practice will in future be carried on".[151] At that time, presumably, Dr. Hewitt moved into the Lodge, and his mother and aunt continued living at Sunnyside. There were two children from the marriage; Mark Wilson born in 1904 and Geoffrey La Nauze Pierrepoint born in 1907

The Lodge , Claverley

Dr. Hewitt died in 1925 and was buried in Claverley Churchyard but his memory lives on, and my personal connection with James leads me to imagine that at least some of the latter's gentleness and sparkly humour came from his grandparents. The Wilson malting and brewing tradition was carried on by Thomas and Florence's son, Geoffrey and their grandson James, both of whom were brewers at Mitchells and Butlers.

Acknowledgments

My thanks are due to James Hewitt for sharing his family history and to Sue Burns and Derek Moorhouse for their research.

---

[151] *London Daily Standard,* 5 August 1903 p. 8

HENRY BATH

I hope that by the time you read this article (February 2020) the floods will have subsided. In a farming area like Worfield, it's not just people & their homes who are affected. I feel sorry for the livestock and the farmers doing their best to keep them fit and well in these abnormal weather conditions. The damage to the growing crops is yet another worry.

It was quite a shock to hear that Worfield Car Sales and Servicing has closed. Apparently Dave Jones had worked there for almost forty years and perhaps he could be persuaded to write a history of Worfield Garage. That would certainly be worth reading.

Cars are the theme for this article, the story of one family associated with the motor car trade who made their home in Worfield. I am indebted once again to Paul Holt for writing on this subject and have slightly rejigged his article to fit this format.

One can imagine Henry Bath off to work in a car of this style

In the early days of the twentieth century, new residents moved to live in Worfield, enabled by the fact that they could drive to work. Before the car, everyone lived within walking or driving (pony and trap) distance of their work. The car made it possible to live farther away and commute to work. Railways had, to a certain extent, opened up this opportunity, but it was the motor car that offered the flexibility we take for granted today.

These were exciting times for the internal combustion engine and it is fitting therefore that one of those who would settle in Worfield in the early years of the twentieth century, was Captain Bath and his family. Henry James Bath was a Director of Sunbeam Motors in Wolverhampton, and had the new house built at Folley, Ackleton, in 1911 or 1912. A couple of points may need to be clarified. Firstly, the Folley was originally part of Stableford and not Ackleton, and secondly it was the hamlet which was called Folley/Folly, and not the pub, which in 1911 was called The Spring Gardens. Prior to the new house being built by Henry Bath, the only house opposite the pub was the farmhouse to Folley Farm the occupant of which, in 1882, was E. Ridley,

Henry Bath was born in Swansea and was part of the family's copper smelting business there before moving to Wolverhampton as Consulting Engineer and Director of Sunbeam Motors. It is not hard to imagine the excitement created by this new-fangled mode of transport but these early cars were by no means easy to drive. The Evans's 1912 Sunbeam, for instance, only had brakes on the front wheels. To make matters even more dangerous, anyone could drive without training since it was not until 1935 that driving tests were introduced.

Bath was one of the early adopters of a commuting lifestyle and soon the family were playing a part in the local life of Worfield, with Henry acting as an accountant for the Worfield Nursing Association (1925). There was a family interest in medicine as Mrs Bath was the daughter of Dr. T. D. Griffiths, an eminent Swansea surgeon and President of the BMA in 1903. The Bath family attended St Peter's Church and Mrs Bath served on the Parochial Church Council. Mr Bath also generously supported School initiatives in the 1930s led by the innovative headmaster, Mr A. A. Matthews. Beyond this I can find very little out about Captain Bath.

We do know a little more about Henry's daughter, Olive, who in 1909, aged just seventeen, married another engineer and director of Sunbeam Motors, Louis Coatalen, aged thirty-one. This must have been something of a whirlwind romance because the exceptionally talented Mr Coatalen only joined Sunbeam in 1909 having moved from Coventry.

The marriage took place at the Birmingham Registry Office in September 1909 as Louis Coatalen has been married before. The new Mr and Mrs Coatalen lived at 39, Finchfield Road Wolverhampton in 1911 but it was to Worfield Church that the children were brought for their churching in 1913 and 1916. The two boys were christened Hervé Louis and Jean Louis. The marriage didn't last. Louis Coatalen separated from Olive in 1918 and went to live with the wife of a friend. At this time the Coatalens had a house in France and one in London, and it was from there, in 1919, that Olive wrote a heart-rending letter to her husband, beseeching him to return, saying how lonely she was and how she was sure they could be happy together once again. Louis replied that he thought they couldn't be happy together and Olive then filed for divorce which was granted in May 1921.

Coatalen was a design engineer of the highest order and in 1914 he became joint managing director of Sunbeam with William Iliffe. Coatalen's work on the development of the internal combustion engine was so significant that one cannot understand why he is not better known today. The First World War gave a great boost to the Sunbeam business as Coatalen designed aero engines for the war effort. The opportunity the war created must have been a design engineer's dream and Coatalen did not let the opportunity pass him by. After the war, the aero engines were used in Sunbeam cars.

Louis Coatalen behind the wheel of the Sunbeam Nautilus in 1910

Coatalen loved racing cars and in 1912 Sunbeam cars were successful but by the following year it was Peugeot who dominated the sport. Visiting Wolverhampton in his Peugeot, the racing car driver Dario Resta was unwise enough to park the car near to Coatalen's house. Overnight it was stripped, and by morning put back together, each part having been measured and sketched. In 1914, Sunbeam were champions of the racing circuit once again.

Coatalen must have been good company. W. O. Bentley described him as "not only a first class businessman who made (and lost) a great deal of money in his active life with Sunbeams; he had other qualities which I liked even better; he was highly educated and amusing and a tremendous raconteur, and he was dedicated to motor racing." Sadly, there is no record of the impression the dashing Mr Coatalen made in Worfield. Arriving at Church in the latest Sunbeam would alone have been enough to turn heads.

Mr & Mrs Bath's son, also called Henry James Bath, was born with a paralysed right arm and although he was described on his army record as a farm student, his employability must have been limited. Henry Bath remained at the Folley after his parents' deaths in the 1940s and he too was involved with Worfield Church, helping to maintain the churchyard, and acting as a sidesman. He died in 1964.

151

The Evans Sunbeam taking patients from the VAD Hospital out for a ride

Mary Foster nee Bradburn remembered the Coatalens when they lived on the Finchfield Road and it was not a flattering memory. "My mother's family had a farm in Finchfield and delivered milk to the Coatalens and I remember mother saying that they wouldn't pay their milk bill. My childhood memory of the Baths was that we sat behind them in church and later, when I married Mark Foster, my husband used to fish a stretch of the Worfe which Henry Bath owned. Unsurprisingly it was known as the 'Bath Water'."

Mary's other memory was about the Sunbeam car owned by the Evans family and shown above. The car was built in 1912 and was bought by Mark Foster from Mrs Evans in the 1950s. In spite of a number of offers, Mrs Evans had refused to sell the car. Mary's husband, Mark was one of those who wanted to buy, and spoke to the Vicar, Preb. Tom, about how he might persuade Mrs Evans to sell. Preb. Tom's answer was that he thought Mrs Evans would sell if Mark agreed to give the purchase price to the church. "But how much should I offer?" said Mark. "£25 should do it," said Preb Tom. And so it was that the Evans' Sunbeam changed hands for a very modest price

MEMORIES OF WORFIELD
By
Ted Walker

I am known as Ted Walker to Ackletonians and as Eddie Walker by the rest of the world. I am an only child and I was born in June 1936. My paternal grandfather came from Cleobury Mortimer.

My earliest memories go back to when I was two and my earliest memory of No. 26 Winchester Road,Wolverhampton was me climbing these enormous uncarpeted stairs and saying at every step "this is a nice house this is"....So this would have been 1939 I think. I remember being very worried about the news of impending war which I listened to with my parents each day. Then War was declared but despite hearing several sirens nothing much happened. My father dug a hole in the back lawn for an Anderson shelter but it immediately filled with water.

I think it must have been in 1940 that Spitfires used to startle me as they took off from Perton Aerodrome almost taking the tiles off our roof. Then German bombers started coming up the nearby canal reflected in the moonlight to bomb Boulton and Paul's Aircraft factory nearby but they didn't hit it once during the whole war. They did however scare me and my terrified mother to death as they were fitted with sirens to frighten the populace. My mom used to take me in her arms and hug me in the cupboard under the stairs as the staircase was often the only part of a house which remained standing after an attack. My mother was a genius at making money although she only went to school till the age of 8 but she always kept it quiet and lived a humble quiet life. She decided she had to get away from the town and we walked along the Bridgnorth Road looking for somewhere to live. We found nothing till we got to Worfield where we went to the church. There the Vicar persuaded one of his Choristers, Ernest White, to take us in as winter was coming on. So we lodged with him, Mrs White and their son Stanley (who later became organist at Badger church).

If we start at the Folley Inn. Directly opposite lived Mr Rowley who later delivered our milk when we lived in our own cottage half way up the Room Bank in Ackleton. Moving towards Wellington the next house was that of the Whites situated at the foot of Mr Bath's drive. Mr White worked for Mr Bath who lived in The Folly [ie the big house on the hill opposite what used to be the Folley pub].I still have prizes of books given to me by Mr Bath for attendance at Sunday school.One was a book on birds, another was called 'Moving Things for Lively Youngsters.' By Spring my mother wanted her own home and my father found one for us at the Limbutts cottage. The Limbutts was situated six fields from the road at Cranmere Bank opposite Charlie Wainwright's. It was on the edge of Newton Common, just inside a wood, with pools of crystal clear water and little streams running down to the brook. Mr Chaplin was the gamekeeper here and was murdered shortly after we left. The cottage belonged at the time to Mr Ward at Crowgreaves Farm and was tied. My father could drive so he became a tractor driver at the farm. Mom also worked on the farm and absolutely loved it! I went with her and

ACKLETON

Ted Walker

rode enormous cart horses and generally had a lovely time. I can still smell the potatoes and feel the sandy soil in which they thrived. Dad started a big vegetable garden having helped his Aunt Nelly on her smallholding on the Titterstone Clee each year as a boy. In the towns there was rationing but we wanted for nothing. We kept ducks as there was an adjacent brook which entered the Worfe a little way down stream. Dad grew fruit and vegetables (he loved gardening all his life). We caught a feral cat and re-domesticated it, kept two pigs (Jacky and Jimmy) and the wood in which we lived was full of game. Life was truly idyllic.

The Limbutts cottage had a scullery with cobbled floor, a sitting room, dining room, and two bedrooms. Oddly the cottage had church windows ie an arch over each window. It was soundly built and in good repair and there was a tap in the scullery. The toilet was outside and was simply a seat over a cesspit. My Dad read me a book called "Stepping Stones to Literature" and just by his reading it to me and pretending to get it wrong in places he taught me to read though I have absolutely no recollection of how this miracle happened.

After about two years, in 1943, a cottage became available in Ackleton and we rented it. The rent was tiny, 1/6d a month I think, but I could be mistaken. The landlord, Mr Iliffe, happened to be our solicitor from Waterloo Road Wolverhampton and when he put the row of cottages up for auction a few years later, my parents bought our cottage for £200.

To the left of the cottages and adjacent to the road there was a coal house on one side and a brew house on the other. The cottage on the left hand side was occupied by Mom, Dad and me, the previous occupier being Miss Hand who died at the age of 90. According to Mrs Holdsworth, Miss Hand died with the blacking brush in her hand beside the Victorian grate installed into the inglenook fireplace which evidently had been there since the cottage was built (of sandstone). So it was originally one up and one down the fireplace being set in the left wall as one entered facing the road. The cottage was extended in brick at some time and the living space doubled as far as the second drainpipe although Miss Hand had not used this and neither did we until after the war. Immediately to the right on entering the front door was a door which led down to the cellar which I sometimes used as a study. To the left of the cellar door was the door to the extra room. I have no idea when the cottage was first built or when it was extended but I would love to know. When we decided to redecorate, the number and style of many coats of wallpaper were revealed, and we guessed at the dates each one might have been applied. Upstairs my parents occupied the old bedroom and I the new.

The second cottage down was very small, being one up and one down. The lower cottage had two up and two down and was occupied by old Mrs Holdsworth who in her youth had actually lived on Newton Common. Her son lived at the top of Room Bank. She told my mother that, "On the night our young Jim were barn the pot froz on the ob"!

Despite our efforts the pump never worked and as we had no water, electricity or sanitation I was the water carrier and had to go down a path parallel to the road but behind the houses of people living further down the hill towards the Folley Inn for about 200 metres until I reached a board covering a hole into which I hung my bucket to scoop up some water from an underground river. I then climbed back up the hill with my bucket of sandy water and left it to stand for about an hour when the sand settled and the water became crystal clear. It tasted so much better than the water in my taps now! Water for everything but drinking was collected in butts located behind the cottage. Ours was the only cottage to have a back door. Below the

ACKLETON

Ted Walker

cottages and to the rear there were the usual toilet facilities which were emptied into trenches dug in the garden by my father and me every week. Our light was provided by an Aladdin paraffin lamp.

My father (like his father) loved gardening and we never went short of vegetables, fruit or flowers.He would rise each morning at 6.00 am and whistle like a bird before going into the garden. At 8.00am he went to work in Wolverhampton returning at 6.00pm. We also kept chickens, tended by me. No pigs though, as killing Jackie and Jimmy had proved too much for me and my mother to bear!

I started school at the age of seven, attended Worfield School for just over a year, and then attended the preparatory school which was part of Bridgnorth Grammar School. I passed the Eleven Plus at the age of 9 and in consequence was always just under 2 years below the average age of my class.I was also bottom of the class until the O Level Exams loomed large when I was obliged to do some work to avoid being ejected. As I didn't fancy a life on the land I decided to go to University with several of my mates. So I thought I would do the least work possible by passing everything at 50% (the pass mark at that time). So it is that I have nine O levels. When my maths master Mr Swan asked me what subjects I intended to take in the sixth form and I said English, French, and Latin, he replied "Thank God for that" and walked away inwardly rejoicing! My mother had received little schooling being obliged to leave school at the age of eight to act as mother to her younger siblings as her mother kept a shop. She wanted me to "have letters after my name". Her idea was that I would then put a brass plate outside my house saying E W WALKER.BA. or whatever and live happily ever after. I was happy to oblige her and expected to go with my school friends to Birmingham University this being the local University for us at that time. Mr Moore however had suggested that he might be able to get me an introduction into Fitzwilliam College Cambridge to read French and Spanish. In the event I took the easy route and attended Birmingham.

We had a Boys Club at Ackleton in The Room.It had a library and various games including a shooting gallery with an air rifle. Some of the boys used the books for target practice and I felt that this was "not on"! I therefore reported it to Mr Moore and as a result he gave me the library. It was mainly of Victorian authors such as Dickens and Mrs Gaskell. Other organised events which took place were dances and whist drives; pleasurable not just in themselves but for the walk back to our cottage. As mother and I strolled home I marvelled at the incredible number of stars above me; there was no light pollution in the country then. Our local playground was the Malthouse which I remember with deep affection as I played in every room of it as well as walking on the roof. It would not have been such a magnet were it not for the dire warnings of my mother not to enter it and the delicious dangers it represented which rendered it quite irresistible!

I was a choirboy at Worfield from1944 to 1953 and was Harry Bayliss' chief boy soprano soloist until my voice broke. Every Christmas he used to invite me to visit his house in Chesterton to sing for his friends.My mother considered that I had "the voice of an angel" but I suspect she may have been biased! I believe I was a favourite of Mr Bayliss and when he chose to walk back from church I accompanied him while pushing my bike. Goodness knows what we talked about but we talked non stop until we reached the Folley Crossroads where he went straight on and I turned left for home.On reflection we may have talked about music.I had a

ACKLETON

Ted Walker

decidedly catholic taste and he was very keen on Berlioz. Choir sports days were held at Chesterton, choir practice was never on a Sunday and we never got paid!

The only angelic thing about me was my voice and I shudder to think of what a little thug I was! The first thing I hasten to do on seeing childhood acquaintances is apologise (especially to females of the species!)Fortunately a miraculous transformation occurred somewhere in my late teens.Before that, like Satan in Paradise Lost "Evil was my Good."

We were very trusting in those days, not locking doors or bikes. I used to cycle to the Royal Oak at Rudge Heath to catch the bus for Wolverhampton. Returning from Wolverhampton on one occasion my bike was missing and I reported this to the police.They found it in Wellington with a note of apology from the phantom thief thanking me for the loan and explaining that they had been desperate to get home.

A group of angelic choristers on a choir outing. Angela Moore is in the middle of the front row. On the back row from the left is Florence Bayliss, the Revd .Stanley Moore, not known, "Pupson" Jones, the sexton & Harry Bayliss, the choirmaster. On the next row is Mrs Moore

ACKLETON
Ted Walker

During school holidays I worked for Mr Neale, a "Gentleman Farmer," so called because he spoke so far back it was sometimes difficult to understand him. [152] Mr Neale farmed at Tyte Farm; some 400 acres of Ackleton land, growing carrots, potatoes, sugar beet and grain. At first I worked for nothing because I enjoyed it. I helped Eric Plain, one of a large and delightful family who lived in the "Back Lane". Eric drove either Prince or Derby (two gentle giant shire horses) either pulling a cart or harrowing and sometimes I led the horse or rode it back to the stable when work was finished. This trip took place over the headlands of fields and whilst the drive to work in the morning was restrained, that of the evening was undertaken at an alarming speed as the animal anticipated the delights of the nosebag to come! When mounted I hung on for dear life! I also worked with a Mr Bennett who lived next to the Plain family and with Helmut, a German prisoner of war. When harrowing the fields to break up clods of earth we used to take turns in guiding the horse over the fields and dozing in the hedge. I suppose Helmut was not worried about losing his job.

Later Mr Neale decided to pay me the full wage of £5 per week which shows he was a gentleman but I cannot think of any other farmer I have known who would be so generous! I was an enthusiastic worker and used to outwork the other men to such a degree that I was warned by them and had occasionally to curb my enthusiasm! Many of the jobs were backbreaking and boring, such as pulling beet (sugar beet) and potato picking, although the latter was done mostly by women. I remember becoming so rich that I made my parents a loan at an exorbitant rate of interest (which amused and secretly delighted them). My mother did however insist that I buy myself a new suit. Blue was fashionable and my chosen attire was very blue indeed requiring my father to shade his eyes whenever I wore it!

We moved from Ackleton back to Wolverhampton in 1953 but my heart has stayed there ever since.

---

[152] The Neale family farmed in Ackleton from the 1920s to the 1950s. The family had moved from Sussex having bought Ackleton House, the Tyte Farm and a number of cottages alongside Ackleton House, and some cottages down the Back Lane. I assume Mr Neale bought the Ackleton House Estate from Miss Eykyn when it was sold in 1922, James Eykyn having died at Ackleton House aged 71 in May 1921. The farm itself was substantial, amounting to about four hundred acres. The father, Francis John and his wife Rosa, had several children. The three boys went by the distinctive christian names of Francis Seward (born 1895), Gordon Seward (born 1898), and Beresford Seward (born 1904). It was Beresford Seward who took over the running of the farm. Mr Neale (senior) left Ackleton House on October 28 1935.
Michael Roberts, whose father also worked at Tyte Farm, tells of a generous boss whose employees could take home whatever vegetables and milk they needed, and who didn't forget the children of those who worked for him, treating them to a party at Christmas time. Many men, women and children from Ackleton were employed by Mr Neale, enhancing the sense of community in the village. One of Michael's jobs was to clear the brassicas of cabbage white butterflies for which he was paid 6d for 100 butterflies. Mr Neale took the village through the bleak 1920s and 30s and then through the war without any great hardship for the villagers and it is sad to think that such a benefactor is today forgotten. Of course he still had to make money but he sounds about as far from a ruthless businessman as it is possible to be.

ACKLETON

Ted Walker

Ackleton mothers and children on Coronation Day 1953

Chippine Breeze nee Hartley supplied the names of those in the photograph above.
1. Graham Ward, 2. Doreen Plain 3. Des Plain, 4. Alma Hartley, 5. Michael Roberts, 6. ? Roberts, 7. Geoff Clinton, 8. ... Jones, 9. Rosemary Hartley, 10. Bernie Plain, 11. Ivan Reynolds, 12. Clive Bray, 13. Shirley Lett 14. ...Martin, 15. May Plain, 16. Kennie Weaver, 17. Doreen Plain, 18. Ruth Martin, 19. Doris Savigar, 20. Mrs Martin, 21. Mrs Roberts, 22. Mrs Mary Clinton, 23. Ron Plain, 24. John Dovey, 25. Martha Neale, 26. Yvonne Reynolds, 27. Pat Reynolds, 28. Joyce Lett, 29. Mrs Nellie Walker, 30. Mrs Mary Savigar, 31. Susan Brown, 32. Mrs Lilian Briscoe, 33. Celia Jones, 34 Mrs Smith (Mary Holdsworth), 35. Mrs Jane Roberts, 36. Gillian Dovey, 37. Maurice Perrin, 38. Mrs Edith Bray, 39. Chippine Hartley, 40. Edward Walker, 41. Mary Savigar, 42. Dennis Jones, 43. Nancy Dovey, 44. Billy Harper, 45. Stanley White, 46. Mrs Perrin, 47. Molly Brown, 48. Mrs Reynolds, 49. John Carter, 50. Iris Lett, 51. Elizabeth Neale, 52. Harry Savigar, 53. Margaret Dovey, 54. Fred Hartley, 55. June Perrin, 56. Jim Holdsworth, 57. Marion Brown, 58. Mrs Brown

ACKLETON IN THE SECOND WORLD WAR
By
Chippine Breeze née Hartley

The Hartley family moved to Ackleton in 1939 from a house in Cosford with a large garden to one of the six houses in a row facing the main street. The Ackleton house was a shock to say the least. We moved in November and I remember my mother's words when she went into the dark little cottage. She looked out at the back to a view of the pig sty and the ruin of the malthouse [burned down in 1935] and said, 'Harry, Harry, what have you brought me to.' Whatever my father had told mother about the cottage clearly hadn't prepared her for this. Mother came from a good family, her father was a farmer and she had been educated at a convent in Ireland and then trained as a nurse. Father's words were reassuring. 'Don't worry, Dot, this is only temporary, we will soon be moving to somewhere much nicer.' The cottage was to remain my parents' home for the rest of their lives.

Our only modern convenience was a sink in the kitchen but there was no running water. The cottages were known as 'Tub Row' to the other villagers, because in each of the back yards was a water butt to catch the rainwater. This was used to do the washing but first had to be sieved through muslin to catch insects and debris. When the tubs were empty water had to be fetched for washing which was done in a copper boiler built into a corner of the kitchen. There was only one water pump for the six houses and when that ran dry, the pump had to be primed. This was quite a job. A bucket of water was poured down the well and people took turns to pump the water up. If their efforts failed, it was a case of carrying water from the road, about 150 yards away and down the "shut," an alleyway between two houses and the fire-damaged malthouse. Your feet can get very wet playing that game.

There were electric lights in the cottage but a hurricane lamp was needed to visit the lavatory which was in a brick shed in the back yard. No flushing toilet here, just a bucket which had to be emptied regularly and the toilet paper was newspaper squares.

Clothes were ironed with a flat iron heated over the fire and then the base covered with a tin shield. Oh, the joy of dropping soot on a newly pressed shirt. Baths were taken in a galvanised bath or in the enamelled hip bath. The water had to be heated on the fire and scooped out of the bath afterwards.

The good thing was that we were never short of food. Behind the malthouse there was a large allotment which was invaluable in the war. Father was a good gardener and supplied enough vegetables for all the family. We had our own chickens at the allotment and even today, egg and chips are always a meal for when you are hard up. There were rabbits aplenty, unaffected in those days by disease and a roast rabbit was a meal to remember. The pig kept in the sty was another source of good food. The pig and the hens were fed on tiny potatoes and vegetable peelings which were cooked in the wash-boiler. Harry Bray, our roadman friend, butchered the pigs. The meat was shared with other villagers and when their pig was killed you got a piece in return. The pigs were very large and yielded a lot of lard - real pork scratchings in those days. Hams and bacon were cured with saltpetre for several weeks on the large settles in the pantry and then hung, covered in butter muslin, from great hooks in the kitchen wall. Only my father was allowed to cut the ham from the bone.

Cooking was done on a range in the kitchen and what a terrible smell there was if a pan boiled over. The soot had to be cleaned from the pans each time they were used but the oven was excellent for baking and the fire was perfect for toasting bread. The Sunday evening supper of toast with dripping from the Sunday roast was an absolute delight. It never tasted so good when we had an electric cooker.

We were not allowed to do any work on Sundays but after breakfast we children dressed in our best clothes and went for a walk on the roads whilst mother prepared dinner. This was Sunday dinner with no pretension about lunch.

Our new life in Ackleton had begun and I was to move schools from Donnington a mile down the road from our home in Cosford, to my new school in Worfield. The journey to school couldn't have been more different from what I had been used to. In the mornings it was dark, and in the war, with Double Summer Time, it was even worse. The first morning my brother Fred and I were going to school, mother said to Fred, 'hold hands and be good' and off we went with the other Ackleton children, down Room Bank, along the unmetalled road from the bottom of the hill to the Dudley Road, through Rowley's Farm and then over the fields. Mr Rowley disliked the children going through the farm and put cattle in the field as a deterrent. 'Be careful of those cattle,' he would shout. In winter we were soaked by rain and in summer by the dew from the crops as we walked along the narrow pathway. The crops, taller in those days, were sown across the footpath and the only track was the one which our little feet made.

I remember one morning my brother was taken by some dewdrops sparkling in the sun on quaking grass. He picked a bunch for one of the teachers but was very disappointed when he got to school with just a bunch of rather dull grass! Another morning the Acklonites, as some of the teachers called us, were tempted by the beautiful weather with the idea of taking our sandwiches down to the stream. In the end, we couldn't bring ourselves to do it and hearing the church clock chime we realised we would be late for school. My brother held my hand and we ran together until I could keep up no longer. At this point Fred left me and ran on with some of the others to make sure he would be on time, which he was. The boys who were late had to line up for the cane. 'You, too, Fred Hartley,' said Mr Knowles, the headmaster. 'But I wasn't late,' said Fred.' The reply was, 'You aren't getting the cane because you were late but because you didn't wait for your sister!'

Walking home after school we were tired and the older children would look after the little ones and sometimes give them a piggy back. When it rained hard the Worfe would flood and one day after school we reached the bridge and could see that the ground beyond it was flooded. We all held hands as we walked through the water which was lucky because suddenly there was no ground beneath my feet, only water. Had someone not been holding on to me I would have drowned. When we got home mother said, 'I suppose you came round by the road.' She was horrified when we said that we had taken our normal route. It is amazing to think that the teachers, knowing that there were floods, hadn't offered us any advice at least.

Sydney Knowles, the headmaster, taught all the children to write properly. There were no biros then but nib pens and inkwells. I used to get ink all up my right forefinger. There were six classes at Worfield School. Miss Thomas taught the youngest, the five- year olds, and in her classroom was a big doll's house. We knitted rugs and bedcovers and learned other basic skills.

Ackleton Maltings. Image courtesy of Mr and Mrs James

In the next class Mrs Brudenell taught us to embroider. A group of girls embroidered a tablecloth for a local lady. When Mrs Brudenell went to tea at the house she mentioned that the cloth was upside down. The reply was what every embroiderer wants to hear, 'I can't tell which side is which.' I remember the cloth so well because I worked on it and when it was finished the lady brought a bag of carefully saved sweets for the girls who had done the embroidery. Unfortunately I was away from school on the day the sweets were handed out and none of the others saved me any. We also collected sheep wool and made it into a rug on a loom.

Big girls were taught to cook and to clean a house properly and the boys did woodwork and gardening. In the summer we had some lessons outside. We would sit in a big circle on our chairs in the playground and take turns to read. We had nature walks and outdoor painting lessons. When I first went to Worfield, the school leaving age was fourteen and then it went up to fifteen. There were scholarships to Bridgnorth Grammar School. We scholarship people

The row of cottages known as Tub Row

were very looked down upon in the early years but when it was necessary for everyone to pass an examination to attend, the snobbery ceased.

One day someone came to school to warn us of the dangers of incendiary bombs. The reason for the visit was that they had been dropped in the Rowley Woods area. We were told to be careful and not touch any if we saw them. Inevitably, after this we went round looking for bombs but never found any. Ackleton in the war was much smaller than it is now. There were, and still are, several big houses in Ackleton. In 1939, Miss Mabel Wainwright had left Tyte Farm following the death of her mother and was living at The Laurels and Mr. Neale had bought the farm. At Ackleton House were the Beddows family. Colonel Beddows was a Wolverhampton timber merchant. At the end of World War II, his son Ian was the youngest colonel in the British army. The Hickmans lived at The Manor and Major Hickman was also a timber merchant. The Harpers lived at Rosemount where there is now a housing development of that name. Mr. Harper's land was used as a market garden although by trade he was a bookie based in Wolverhampton. Mr. Harper owned a horse called Grock and a large, ill-tempered billy goat who chased me and who had a taste for my mother's washing when it was on the line. Miss 'Gertie' Matthews ran the Red Cow public house. She used to go out in her pony and trap with a big Alsatian dog for company. Mr. Farrier farmed Ackleton Hall Farm and supplied milk twice daily to the big houses close by. Cottages had a morning delivery but more could be collected from the farm in the afternoon. At the other end of the village, considered to be Ackleton but actually Stableford, Mr Henry Bath, a director of Sunbeam lived at The Folley, and rented Folley Farm to Mr Rowley. Mr Bath taught at the Sunday School for several years.

The malthouses and many of the cottages were owned by Mr Nock who lived in the Bilston area. In 1939 there were two malthouses on the hill at Ackleton, an old malthouse which had burnt down in 1935, leaving just a shell, and a new malthouse which was saved from the fire. The latter would be a landmark for miles around for another two decades until it was demolished to make way for a new housing development. The consequence of the fire, started I believe by a cigarette carelessly dropped on some straw, was that Mr. Nock's capital literally went up in smoke and the malthouses remained as they were after the fire. There was no money to clear the ruins of the old malthouse which became a playground where we children would happily play despite threats from anxious parents. The new malthouse, however, was destined to play an important role in the war and one which is now forgotten.

As far as I know there was no warning that the men were coming. They arrived one day, soldiers returning from the Battle of Dunkirk, and many, including one prisoner of war, were billeted in the new malthouse. Others were billeted in houses throughout the village as temporary accommodation. We had eight soldiers in our house. One morning my father arrived home after a night shift with the air ministry police at Cosford, to find a stranger shaving in our kitchen. The stranger said, "Who are you?" Father replied, "more to the point, who the hell are you?" After a while more permanent living quarters were sorted out. [

Nissen huts were erected in the field next to the telegraph exchange and the telephone box and the field became known as Soldiers' Field. How the soldiers arrived in Ackleton I don't know. Perhaps they came by train to Albrighton or Bridgnorth and then walked, or were brought by vehicles. The women of the village ran a canteen for the soldiers in part of the old malthouse which was still standing, an area with a lovely tiled floor. I can only suppose that the army supplied the food, but the women of Ackleton made sandwiches and baked cakes. For us children all this activity was very exciting. The soldiers trained by marching up and down the road and I remember sitting on our doorstep watching them. The fuchsia bush was in bloom and I kept popping the buds until mother caught me and stopped my fun.

I said there was one prisoner of war in Ackleton. Why he was there I don't know. He was housed in a room above a reservoir in the malthouse. One day he walked across the loading bay going towards the main building and fell through a trap door. He fell a great height and broke his ankle. There were German and Italian prisoners of war in Worfield and they came to work on the farms. On Mr. Neale's farm in Ackleton there were three German POWs, Helmut, Billy and Dieter. One was a fisherman by trade, one a farm boy far from home and the third was one of the ruling classes, a fact he liked you to know.

Another group of strangers were the evacuees. A girls' school was evacuated to Worfield and the children went to the village school. I remember a girl called Sadie teaching us to sing 'The White Cliffs of Dover.' At home we also had evacuees for part of the war as did most of the other villagers. I don't know how my mother managed. They, a mother and two sons, used the big front room and the bedroom above. That left one medium and one small bedroom for my parents, brother, small sister and me. (My youngest sister didn't arrive until 1941.) We lived in

163

the kitchen with the range for cooking and boiler for washing. Between washes the boiler was covered with a lid and a cloth and usually a pile of books. If we had an unexpected visitor, mother would shove everything into the copper and put the lid on. Two or three clear surfaces and a room looks tidy. There were always books. Dad's mother said that, 'we were all pen and paper at our house,' covered in ink or with our noses into books. Dad worked shifts and often in the long winter evenings mother would tell us stories and teach us poetry. There was an ongoing tale of Pommy Larndus. We never knew if she invented him. We also made rag rugs, played cards and darts and mother made our clothes. I remember making a fireside rag rug which we raffled to get money to help pay for the party to celebrate the end of the war. It was won by Mrs. Farrier at the farm and I saw it years later still in use in her parlour.

I was the first girl in our village to wear wartime clogs. Shoes were on coupons, clogs were not. Marian and Molly Brown went home laughing their heads off about mine but their mother said, 'I'm glad you find them funny, yours are in the cupboard.' We soon learned to pad the toes and play ballerinas. My baby sister was too young for clogs but she later became a ballerina, married a GI and went to live in America.

There were infrequent church services in the Recreation Room at Ackleton. The building was given by Mrs Morrison as an offering of thanks for the birth of her grand-daughter. In the room was an altar at one end which was screened off during the week. At the opposite end of the room there was a stage and between the two was a dance floor. Whist Drives and dances were held and there was a youth club in the 1940s and '50s with exchange visits with Beckbury Youth Club. The Parish Church was Worfield and after the war there was a coach once a month to take us to Evensong. The coach would be packed with people. Ackleton people have often worshipped at Badger Church which was much nearer home and I recall walking through the Dingle with parents and friends to take my sister to be christened there in 1941. In those days the Rector was the Revd. Archibald Dix and his wife came regularly to visit the people of Ackleton. Mrs Dix had an ear trumpet as she was rather deaf. Her eldest daughter Margaret was in London training to be a medical missionary but after training to be a surgeon was very badly injured in the Blitz. Margaret Dix went on to become world famous for her research into hearing and balance. Her younger sister, Imogen, taught the Sunday School at Ackleton and rewarded regular attendance with chocolate saved from the ration by herself and 'Nanny Harrison.' My mother considered this bribery. Try explaining that to a sweetless youngster.

After the war the Revd. Stanley Moore was Vicar at Worfield. He was very good about house to house visiting and would just arrive. I recall that one day my mother was redecorating a bedroom and when the Revd. Moore arrived I said that mother was upstairs. 'That's all right,' he said, 'I will go up,' and he bounded up the stairs. Mother said afterwards, rather euphemistically, 'that it might not have been convenient.' Fortunately for both of them, on this occasion it was 'convenient'. Years later I heard from another clergyman that Mr. Moore had felt rather a failure at Worfield but he was held in high regard by the parishioners. I remember the time we were talking about Remembrance Day, he said, 'Do not glorify battle; those men did not go willingly to die. They went, often cursing and swearing, to do their duty.' He always had time for the 'little man' and to talk to children.

There were three gypsies living in Ackleton. In the field just above The Folley lived Mr. & Mrs. Lee and on the edge of the village on the Pattingham Road lived Mrs. Lee's brother,

ACKLETON

Chippine Breeze

Bluey Locke. We never knew his true name but his nickname came from his very blue eyes. Mr and Mrs Lee had a horse and cart and would travel around the local area selling pots and pans, bowls, buckets, brushes and so on. Mr and Mrs Lee lived, as did Mr Locke, in a gypsy caravan. Mrs Lee used to give me her radio battery to take to the garage at Worfield to be recharged. It is many years since Mr Bentley's old garage was demolished and no-one has batteries like those now. After they were recharged I would take them back again, riding one handed on my bicycle and holding the battery well away from me by its thin wire handle. The battery was about five inches square. All went well until my mother found out and was cross because I could have been badly burnt by the acid if I had fallen off my cycle.

Before the war my father had worked on various farms, including that of Mr. Austin, which is how we came to be living at Cosford. As an employee father would do anything he was asked to do, providing he was asked politely. If not, he was off to another job. Unfortunately with the job went the house. Our new home belonged to Mr. Nock and was not a tied cottage. When father started his new job as an air ministry policeman at Cosford he worked shifts so he still did some farm work. He was an excellent hedge layer and would hoe and later pull sugar beet and do other jobs as needed. As well as his farming activities he helped Mr. Mason, the coal man who lived below the Room Bank, with his deliveries and of course there was not a weed in his allotment. After the war the air ministry wanted father to go away and train as an inspector. However when he was away training as a a sergeant, mother had a dreadful accident; she slipped on the back yard near the pigsty and ripped the skin off her back. The injuries were so bad that mother's life was feared for and with three young children to look after, father was naturally anxious about going away again. So rather than train for promotion he took redundancy and got a job at the malthouse which was operating as a grain dryer. Father was a good worker and all went well until one day a group of workers were talking about how bad the pay was. The gist of the conversation was that they needed a pay rise or would go on strike. Father said, 'It's all very well your sitting here talking about it but who is going to ask?' 'You're good at putting things, we thought you might go,' they said. Father stated the case to management who heard him out and then the boss said, 'pick up your pay and your cards on the way out.' That was the end of father's job at the malthouse but the incident with management epitomised my father, a man of principle and much-liked by all who knew him. After the malthouse experience he did a variety of jobs until he had a serious motorcycle accident in 1957.

These are some of my memories of Ackleton during and just after the war. By 1946 there was a school bus and I suppose in the end it was the car which changed the village, making it less of a community and more of a group of houses with people living separate lives. The war and pre-war years were hard times but there were simple pleasures which have now gone in the fast pace of life today.

Note: Colonel Beddows added the following information. "After Dunkirk a regiment from Ulster was billeted in the old Malt House for several months. They had very little equipment as it had been lost in the retreat. The regimental HQ was in the stables at Ackleton House and 5 officers including the Commanding Officer were billeted in the house."

WILLIAM HARDWICKE

Allscott is now a tiny hamlet which, according to Hardwicke, shrank in size at the time of the enclosure of the common fields when several houses were demolished. This is his account of the village.

"Alscote used to be called Alvercote. Walter de Alvercote died possessed of a messuage and a half yard land. He died of the exterminating pestilence [the Black Death] which in the 23rd year of the reign of King Edward III went through the country. The Barrets and Bullocks were also in Alscote. The Barret family lived there up to 1723. The Whites from Badger lived here, one of them marrying a Slater. The Alscote enclosure took place in 1703."

The Ancient Mansion of the Ouseleys & birthplace of William Hardwicke 1772 at Allscott - South Front. When this photograph was taken circa 1879 the house had been split into two for the use of farm workers but as the tenant of the farm remarked to the author, H. Smith, "it would have been a lot more convenient and a better residence than the modern farmhouse which now goes with the farm".[10]

ALLSCOTT

William Hardwick

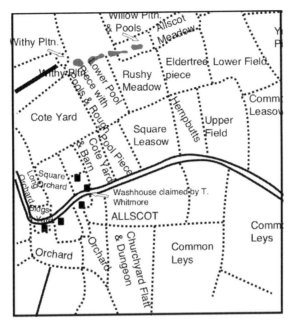

Allscott drawn from the Foxall's 1839 map

"The copyhold proprietors got together, and divided the old open fields. Before this it was open field farming. There is a field called Churchfield not because there was a church here but because the footpath goes towards St Peter's Church. In the village of Alscote there had been several farmhouses which were knocked down, leaving only two main farm houses, the one on the West rebuilt (around 1720) by and belonging to Thomas Slater, and the one on the East where William Hardwicke was born ('the house where I had my being.') The house had been rebuilt by William Beech, Merchant of the Staple of Calais, around 1680. There was a green at Alscote. and a small house there called the Greenhouse which was on the North side and this was lived in by a Rowley.[153] This side of the family was from Newton and they were a younger line than those at Stableford and a scion of the original family from Rowley. Soudley Common was lately a wild heath and thus particularly noticed in the Commonwealth. Between Alscote and Rindleford were several curious earthworks of an early camp and vestiges of ancient warfare. Whitning house was owned by the Townesend family very early on. The James Marshall estate was bought from Allan Pollock of Alscote."

The Greenhouse is mentioned in the court roll of 1477 when Roger Whitbroke and Agnes his wife surrendered into the hands of the lord the cottage in Alvescote called the Greenhouse formerly John Trysell's to the use of William Wever and Agnes his wife, daughter of the said Roger and Agnes.[154] In 1513/1514 John Heuster of London, a mercer, took from the lord a cottage in Allscote called Greenhouse Yard & land.

---

[153] *Shropshire Archives,* 5586/1/225

[154] *Shropshire Archives,* P314/W/1/1/384

A CHAPMAN'S TALE

Contrary to popular belief, even in medieval times people did move around the country. In 1455 when Henry VI was on the throne, Thomas Bullock, formerly of Allscott was convicted of, "diverse felonies and other malefactions at Aylesbury in the County of Buckingham, for which his goods and chattels here were forfeit". Thomas held during his life, a messuage and virgate of land (about 30 acres) now seized by the bailiff for the lord but apart from farming, Thomas Bullock was a chapman, a travelling salesmen. Eventually Thomas's crimes caught up with him but it is extraordinary to think that his work took him so far from home.

Edith and Margaret Stevens of Worfield had carried on a nice little sideline in theft for seven years before they were finally caught, and charged in 1430 with theft. Unlike Thomas, their business was carried out locally. The goods which were seized were as follows:

"One piece of red cloth 18d, 12 flannels price 4d, 1 other flannel price 4d, 1 hand towel price 4d, 4 smocks price 2s, 3 aprons price 8d, 1 other hand towel price 6d, 2 rugs price 16d, 1 foot of linen cloth 2d, 6 hurden rugs price 18d, 1 old towel price 1d, 2 graters 2d, 1 cloak 2s, 1 bed hanging 4d, 1 old coverlet price 4d, 1 other coverlet 8d, 2 old pillows 4d, 1 small chest , 1 piece of felt 4d, one parcel of wool and yarn 8d, 1 old bench cloth price 1d, 1 old small hood 1d, 1 hemp price 10d, 2 brass pots 6d, 1 brass dish price 4s, another brass dish price 12d, 2 brass skillets price 6d, 1 small posnet price 8d, 1 iron drag 1d, 1 brass skimmer price 2d, 2 frying pans price 10d, 1 tripod and 1 hachet price 3d, 1 pair of combs 2d, 1 old pair cards price 1d, 1 bushel measure for grain price 6d, 2 pails 4d, 2 large bowls price 2d, 1 parcel of tallow price 1d, 1 barrel for verjuice [acid brew of crab apples] 1 drinking glass price 4d, 1 jug price 4d, 1 small parcel of flax price 1d, 2 sacks of leather 4d, 1 parcel salt price 1d, 1 chesevat, skabett and strainer price 6d, 1 turner for cloth price 5d, 1 chest 12d and another 8d."

By comparison, Thomas Bullock's goods relate to farming, namely, grain and hay in his barn at Allscott, a cart with wheels bound with iron, a coulter for a plough, a horse, a brass bowl, 2 chains, 1 barrel, 1 scythe, 1 lantern and a protective jacket.

Thomas Bullock's house and land were also seized which Joan Bullock his wife tried to recover in 1464; 1 messuage and 1 virgate of land in Alvescote and 1 toft and half a virgate of land in Wynchecote.[155] This must have been unsuccessful because, in 1473, John Bullok, a son of Thomas Bullok tried to recover one messuage and one and a half virgates of land in Alvescote and Wynnescote[156] and in 1477, Joan Bullock brought a plea of land against William Rowlowe of Newton.[157]

Thomas Bullock was probably hanged in Buckinghamshire but from Hardwicke's recollections it seems that his family stayed in Worfield. With the loss of Thomas Bullock's property, life for the remaining family must have been hard.

---

[155] *Shropshire Archives,* P314/W/1/1/325

[156] *Shropshire Archives,* P314/W/1/1/353

[157] *Shropshire Archives,* P314/W/1/1/384

MABEL & TOM TURNER

Sometimes people are reluctant to share their family history because they didn't come from Worfield, yet I doubt there are many families who can trace their ancestry back to medieval times. In which case we are left with stories of migration from other parts of Shropshire or farther afield. This is the story of how one couple, Thomas and Mabel Turner came to Worfield in the early twentieth century from west Shropshire. Thomas Turner became the village policeman and after his retirement, he and his wife settled in a cottage in Barnsley. The history has been shared by Sue Dewhurst, Tom and Mabel's great granddaughter and Sue's mother Jean has kindly edited the script.

Sue has many family photographs, although most of the older ones are unnamed. Some, such as that below, give a wonderful impression of life in this part of Shropshire at the turn of the twentieth century.

Cardington Harvest Home. Photo Courtesy of Sue Dewhurst

BARNSLEY

Mabel & Tom Turner

Mabel Turner's maiden name was Williams, and her father, Thomas Pardoe Williams, was a farmer in Cardington. Thomas's father was William Turner, also a farmer, in Clee St Margaret. The marriage of Thomas Turner to Mabel Williams took place at St James's Church, Cardington, on the 7th June 1910 at which time Thomas Turner was a policeman at Nesscliffe.

Census Returns can take the family back farther and as Mabel was born in 1884 we would logically look at the census of 1891 to find the family. We find them living at Edgton in the district of Clun. Thomas Williams, the father, is a farmer, born at Hopesay in 1848. The other family members are Fanny, his wife, aged 30, and children, Mabel, aged 6, Amy Elizabeth, aged 5, Richard F. aged 3 and Elsie, aged 1.

The Turner family at Clee St. Margaret. Photo Courtesy of Sue Dewhurst

By 1901, a search for Mabel Williams in Shropshire reveals nothing, nor does a search for her father. In fact, Thomas Pardoe Williams had died in 1896 at the young age of 48, and his wife remarried, becoming Fanny Bethell. William Bethell, had been a farm worker but now took on the role of farmer. Also in the household were Gertrude Williams, 9, Thomas Williams, 7, and Clara Williams, 5, and there is William Bethell, aged 1. Mabel is not living at home; indeed without the internet her whereabouts in 1901 might have remained a mystery. Aged sixteen, Mabel was working as a nanny for John Holland and his wife Katy at West Parade, Huddersfield. John Holland, was a dental surgeon, aged 34, from Huddersfield and his wife,

Kate, née Hayward, aged, 33, was from Oswestry. The children were Kathleen, aged 5, Henry, 3, and John H.

Mabel Turner. Photo Courtesy of Sue Dewhurst

On the death of her father, I assume that Mabel had to find work; perhaps it was always her intention to do so. We know from a collection of postcards, that Mabel worked all over the country as a nurse/nanny. In 1904, Mabel was in Huddersfield, and in 1908, in Devon, Cheshire and Stockport. Even when she had moved on, Mabel's colleagues seem anxious to tell her how her patients were progressing. Mary at Stanton Lacy Vicarage writes, " Just to let you know that Peter is better but Bobbie and Miss Jocelyn are both in bed with chicken pox". There is the usual talk between employees about their employers. Mary (perhaps the same person who wrote the previous card) wrote from Easthope Cottage, Much Wenlock, in 1910 as follows: "I dare say you have heard that I left Stainton and have a new place but I don't care for it much yet. It is too quiet".

On her Marriage Certificate, Mabel's place of residence was given as Waterloo, London, where I presume she was working as a nanny. In 1907 Mabel sent a card to her mother at Hill End Farm, Cardington. "Just a line to say I am having some material for white dresses sent from Manchester as I want FD to make them for me. Shall try and come on Sunday if possible." One wonders if this was this a trial run to see if the dressmaker was capable of making a wedding dress. A newspaper cutting about the wedding reveals that Thomas Pardoe Williams farmed at Wilderley Hall Farm and that 40 guests were at the reception at the bride's home. Whether this was Hill End Farm, Cardington, where Fanny and the family were living in 1911 or Wilderley Hall Farm, it is impossible to know

BARNSLEY

Mabel & Tom Turner

Thomas Turner came from Glebe Farm, Clee St. Margaret. His father was William Turner and his mother Emily. In the 1901 census William Turner, aged 36, was the head of the family, Emily, aged 28, was his wife and the children were, Thomas, 16, Emily, 14, Ernest, 12, William 10, Florence 4, Wilfred J., 2, and Cecily K. 10 months.

Thomas Turner moved away from the family home in 1906 when he was staying on a dairy farm near Shrewsbury. He may have been working on the farm or perhaps these were lodgings as he was training to be a policeman. This postcard sent to Tom from his sister, Emily in 1906, gives us no clue why he was living near Shrewsbury but is interesting in other ways. 'Dear Brother, so glad you have landed safely. Hope you like your new place but I wish you were here. I do so miss you. I had a letter from my little sister this morning. She is very lonely.' At the time of his marriage Tom was a policeman at Nesscliffe and this was the first home for the happy couple. The newspaper cutting reveals the gifts the bride and bridegroom gave to each other. Mabel gives Tom an easy chair and Tom gives Mabel a very practical present, a sewing machine.

After Nesscliffe the couple were posted to Shifnal and Claverley before moving to Worfield where they enjoyed a long and happy life.

Tom & Mabel Turner at Barnsley. Photo Courtesy of Sue Dewhurst

BRADENEY

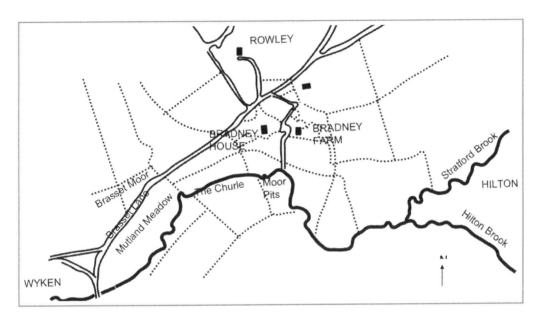

Bradeney taken from the 1839 Field Names Map. Dotted lines are field boundaries

Today, Bradeney House and the new houses associated with it so dominate the tiny hamlet of Bradeney that many think this was the original location of the village but they couldn't be more wrong. Behind Bradeney House, once a family home, and now a care home, is the original hamlet. Bradeney is the older spelling but sometimes, as on the nineteenth century map below, it is Bradney.

Margaret Gelling believed the name Bradeney came from the Anglo Saxon meaning a broad island and it is true that Bradeney is on a rise above the river. In the thirteenth century Bradeney was important for its fisheries, five stakings in the River Churle, that section of the river between the confluence of Stratford Brook and Hilton Brook and the Churle's confluence with the River Worfe at Wyken.[158] The name Churle is also Anglo Saxon, ceorl, meaning a freeman.

---

[158] *The National Archives*, SC 12/14/24

BRADENEY

In 1327, Robert of Bradney held half a messuage and half a virgate of land (about 15 acres), and in 1329 Matilda Colet held a messuage and 3 nooks of land.[159] In 1340, Richard of Wystanesmere and William his son surrendered an enclosed plot of land in Bradeneye so that Thomas his son could build on a plot of land roughly 40 feet square. At this time there seem to have been the following houses or messuages: a pair of semi-detached houses, one detached house, one newly-built, and one called the Moor House. Perhaps the track shown on the map above leading to Moor Pits, once led to or from the Moor House. There may well have been other houses of course but in medieval times the village was probably about the size it was before the building of the bungalows in the early part of the twenty-first century.

In 1349, the Black Death struck in Worfield and Bradeney did not escape. Reginald Collettes, Matilda's son, died, as did Richard Bradney and a man called Galion. It was a long while before the country as a whole recovered, let alone Bradeney. Yet the tiny village did recover and a hundred and forty years after the Black Death a new house of some status was being built; not Bradeney House, but Bradeney Farm. Thanks to dendro-dating, and to the painstaking work of Madge Moran and her team, we know exactly when the original house was built; 1487.[160] Now a four-bay house with a cross-wing and extensions, and a lobby-entry, Bradeney Farm was once a two-bay cruck hall with a louvered opening in the roof to release smoke from a central fire. If, like me you only have the vaguest notion of what cruck construction is, here is Madge Moran's explanation. "Cruck: a pair of inclined timbers, usually wrought from a single tree, forming an arch. The roof is supported on the back of the cruck 'blades' and the walls are independent." A bay is the distance between two pairs of crucks. The oak was felled in 1486, and the timber sawn and erected while it was green, normally within a year of felling, hence the date of building; 1487.

Bradeney House is of more recent origin, probably dating back to the eighteenth century and was built, I believe, by one of the Billingsley family. William Billingsley of Cann Hall, and later of Ludstone, acquired property in Bradeney in 1571/1572 when John Yate surrendered one messuage and a quarter of a nook of land here, and three cottages in Hallon.[161] The Bradeney property then changed hands successively as follows:

- Thomas, William Billingsley's son
- Thomas Billingsley, born 1698
- Margaret Billingsley and thence to William Congreve of Sutton Maddock on her marriage. Margaret died at Bradeney in 1809
- Abigail Congreve, daughter of Margaret and William and thence to Thomas Marshall on her marriage
- John Marshall, son of Abigail and Thomas Marshall
- Abigail Marshall who married Vice Admiral Brazier R.N. & predeceased him. He died in 1866 but his second wife lived at Bradeney until her death in 1877.

---

[159] *Shropshire Archives*, P314/W/1/1

[160] Madge Moran, *Vernacular Buildings of Shropshire.*, Logaston 2003, pp. 56,351 et al

[161] John Randall, *Worfield and its Townships*, Madeley 1997, pp. 63-65

BRADENEY

- Captain Goodwin, through the female Marshall line. He died in 1892
- Captain Alastair Gilroy 1896
- W. G. Leighton lease 1898[162]
- James Arbuthnot lease to 1907
- Lt.Col. John Williams Cunliffe and Florence Evelyn Cunliffe née Adderley. This was the last family to live in Bradeney House before it became a care home.

There are two doles or charities associated with Bradeney. One was set up by Thomas Billingsley and the other by Robin Littleford (1768) to support those who had been servants at Bradeney. Thomas Billingsley, the grandson of Thomas Billingsley described the charity as follows: "My grandfather & father's dole was the interest of 5 houses each which they left for the yearly interest of 10s to be distributed by the head of their family at Bradney to such poor people that had been or might hereafter be servants to their family at Bradney or their heirs on Good Friday for ever & I Thomas Billingsley have hitherto given the same by their direction and have settled the same for ever to be paid out of my freehold estate in Wyken and for the year 1733 gave to the following:

Widow Taylor, Widow Piper, Widow Billingsley, Widow Morrall, Widow Greenhouse, John Billingsley, Thomas Littleford, Humphrey Harris, Thomas Barney, Widow Burrows each 1s".[163]

The Bradeney Dole continued to be paid annually and was administered by Thomas Billingsley's successors until James Brazier decided that it would be much better left in trust to the vicar and churchwardens of St Peter's Worfield. The dole was either to be given to Bradeney servants as before or to nine poor people. The Bradeney Dole was paid from the interest of houses the Billingsleys owned in Wyken but there was no charge on the properties themselves so when the houses were sold by the family I assume the Bradeney Dole ceased. Robin Littleford left £10 in his will the interest of which was to be distributed annually to servants who had lived at Bradeney for over a year. As with the Bradeney Dole this was to be administered by the Billingsley family. At the time of the will this was William and Margaret Congreve.

Note
The Bradney Farm Estate was sold in 1947 (*Wolverhampton Archives*, D-NAJ/F/47)

---

[162] *Bridgnorth Journal & South Shropshire Advertiser,* 5 November 1898

[163] *Shropshire Archives,* M1286/2/1 and P314/Q/7/1

THE CUNLIFFE FAMILY

The Cunliffe family were the last family to live at Bradeney House before it became a care home. In 1908, Lt. Col. John Williams Cunliffe, his wife Evelyn, and their only child, Margaret, moved from London on his retirement. All three had been born in London but Worfield must have suited them well because they stayed in Bradeney for the rest of their lives until the last of the line, Margaret, who never married, died in 1978.

John Williams Cunliffe was born in 1857 and married Evelyn Florence Adderley Harris, born 1875, in 1903. The previous year Evelyn's father had died leaving her £10,000 in trust. A quick Google search tells me that this would be worth one and a quarter million pounds in 2020. There may have been other money which came to Evelyn from her mother's family, the Adderleys who made their fortune in the Bahamas, where Evelyn's mother had been born. A plantation, later known as the Adderley Plantation, was granted to the family in 1790. John Cunliffe, who was born in 1857, had been a Lieutenant Colonel in Lord Cardigan's Militia, and practised as a barrister in London as did his father but the Cunliffe family had its roots in Lancashire and Yorkshire.

Both the Cunliffes and the Adderleys had connections with Worfield which may have influenced the choice of Bradeney as the family's new home. On the Cunliffe side, The Revd. Henry Cunliffe started his career within the church in 1850 as Curate at St Peter's Worfield. So when , as Vicar of Shifnal and Rural Dean The Revd. Cunliffe preached the first sermon after the Restoration of Worfield Church in 1862, he had the benefit of speaking from his experience as a curate.[164] The Adderley connection came twenty years later. Paul Holt takes up the story. "It is possible that Evelyn first visited Worfield from London as a child, two decades before settling at Bradeney. Her uncle was Sir Augustus Adderley and he and his wife lived at Davenport House in the late 1880s.[165] [166]The reredos, the decorative marble sculpture behind the church altar was largely funded by the generosity of Lady Adderley. As contemporaries of Edmund Henry Davenport, the last great Squire Davenport of Worfield, they would have moved in the same circles in London and shared an international outlook."

It would be lovely to have photographs of the family at Bradeney but unfortunately, after Miss Cunliffe died, her papers were consigned to a bonfire. Only a few letters, postcards and one copy of a Chancery case have survived. The Chancery case dates back to 1697 when property was left in the will of Nicholas Cunliffe of Lancashire to John Cunliffe of Wakefield. The latter died when his only child, a daughter, was still a baby and the Chancery case alleges, probably quite rightly, that she was deprived of her legacy. A number of letters have also survived which are interesting because they throw light on the times. This is part of a letter from Robert E. Cunliffe of Manchester in 1861. "I have been much put out since Monday

---

[164] *Wolverhampton Chronicle & Staffordshire Advertiser,* 12 February 1862, p. 7

[165] *Wellington & Shrewsbury News,* 28 May 1887, p. 7

[166] Shropshire Archives, 4752/50/99

when one of the officers of the Salford Union came to inquire of the latest address of Mrs. Dulston to whom it would be necessary to give notice of her removal from the lunatic ward at the union where I was paying for her, and believed her to be comfortable, to the County Lunatic Asylum at Prestwich. Her removal was to take place the next day. It took some reconciling to the move but eventually I feel that she would be in better surroundings than at the Union." R. E. Cunliffe wrote another letter in 1861 about Christmas celebrations which he is worried will be ruined by snow. "I am expecting 24 to my annual oyster supper on Christmas Eve." Apart from that there are postcards from friends and family from all over the world indicative of the Cunliffe's status in society, but tantalisingly little to get one's teeth into.[167]

When the family came to live at Bradeney House they were good supporters of the community; pillars of the Church, members of various committees and, of course, did their bit to promote the Conservative Party. Life must have been very pleasant at Bradeney with a number of servants, some of whom came with the Cunliffes and some of whom were local girls. The 1911 census shows the following servants at Bradeney House: Clara Muggeridge, aged 18, from Sussex, Percival Muggeridge, aged 27, also from Sussex, Ann Leach, aged 38, from London, Edith Hall, aged 19, from Bridgnorth, Ethel Corns, aged 18, from Worfield, Annie Gayton, aged 31, from Trowbridge, and Frederick Viner, aged 30, from London.

Bob Adams remembers how well the gardens were tended by Maurice Reece and Tom Carter from Hilton. There were large kitchen gardens on three sides of the house and to the left of the lane leading to Bradeney Farm, another patch of ground was cultivated. Bob reminded me that the daffodils for Church on Mothering Sunday were always supplied by Bradeney House. The indoor staff in Bob's time were: Annie Leach, the housekeeper (who threatened to resign over mice in the kitchen), Mr Muggeridge (originally the footman), the cook, and at least two girls. Latterly, two ladies came in daily; Mrs Clinton and Mrs Downes, and Mrs Hill worked there towards the end. John Williams Cunliffe died in 1928 and Evelyn Cunliffe in 1956.

Miss Cunliffe's death in 1978 was a sad end for a woman who had helped with the VAD hospital in the War and was a stalwart of both the Church and Worfield WI. She served on the Bridgnorth Rural District Council and was involved with the local Conservative Association. In a different age, Margaret Cunliffe would have had a career and been able to cope with a life without servants. Instead, having always been looked after, and the major decisions of life taken care of by others, it must have been terribly difficult. By the time Miss Cunliffe died, the house was overrun with cats, which she had adored, the fabric of the building was in a very poor state of repair, and the smell of something very undesirable cooking on the stove, still permeated the air.

In contrast to the privileged lifestyle of the Cunliffes, was that of the Herberts who moved into Bradeney Cottages in 1910. Mr Herberts had been a collier but was currently a casual farm worker, and without a regular income the family was starving. They had only been in their new home for six weeks when they had a visit from the local policeman enquiring about the theft of a gate in the area. The farm manager had been carrying out a nightly check and found a gate missing. It was a strange coincidence that in the previous six weeks five oak gates and a

---

[167] A collection of Cunliffe papers in private hands of which the author has copies

number of rails had also been removed. The tell-tale signs of the gate being dragged across the field led to the Herberts' house where some of the missing gate was already fuelling the baking oven. Selina Herberts was found guilty of the theft and fined £1 and if she failed to pay, would have to serve 14 days' hard labour.[168]

Note

The journalist who was present at the Revd. Henry Cunliffe's sermon at the restoration of St Peter's noted the following alterations to the church.

"After extensive restoration the church was opened last Thursday for worship. The Rev. H. Cunliffe, of Shifnal preached an excellent sermon. The collection was just over £65.

Instead of the blank north wall, the small east windows and the corinthian altar pillars, mullionless south window, plastered ceiling and square parlour pews which distinguished the old church, there are now 3 new windows on the north side, four on the south and a beautiful 5 light window at the east, and all fitted with exquisitely painted glass the work of J. Alexander Gibbs of London. The chancel is laid with encaustic tiles the work of Mr Mawe of Broseley, the reredos tiles being from Messrs Minton's. The communion rails are cut out of old oak and most exquisitely carved from a design of the architect, Messrs Francis of London. The whole of the stalls, 14ft long were cut out of one oak, felled on the Long estate."

---

[168] *Bridgnorth Journal & South Shropshire Advertiser* 10 December 1910, p. 5

ERIC ROCHELLE

Eric Rochelle was born in Bromley, Worfield, in 1912 and his story is told in a book called "Over the Farmyard Gate," by G. K. Nelson which paints a wonderfully personal portrayal of what life was like in the 1930s.[169]

Eric's first memory was of the farmhouse in Bromley where he was born. Looking up at the ceiling from his bed there were three staples which he found out later were part of a pulley system rigged up so that a bed-ridden man could lift himself up. The farmhouse was an idyllic place to grow up, and he and his siblings raced up and down the long corridors on their scooters. The first school Eric and his sister Mary attended was run by a Mrs Cunnington at 52, Mill Street, Bridgnorth. It was a three mile walk there and back, a long way for a boy of seven. Bad weather was no excuse for not going to school, just a reason to add more layers; on one winter's morning a coat was made out of an army blanket.

Just down the road from Bromley is Rindleford, and as a child Eric would lie in bed on a summer's night and listen to the rhythmic sound of the blacksmith's hammer hitting the anvil. No less pleasurable was watching the horses being shod. There was the unforgettable smell of burning hoof, and as the blacksmith beat the horseshoe into shape on the anvil, the sparks flew.

Charlie Powell at Rindleford Mill was another craftsman Eric loved to watch as he sharpened the mill stones. There were three sets; two in use and one being sharpened. Charlie always wore glasses to protect his eyes but his hands were unprotected so that fragments of stone embedded themselves into his skin giving the appearance of a rather randomly conceived tattoo. Charlie also had a threshing machine which was so heavy it took six horses to pull it up to Woodside. All the children were excited when the threshing machine arrived and Eric's job was to clean the chaff from under the box; surely the dirtiest job ever. The waggoners were sent to collect coal from Bridgnorth, at £1 a ton. One old wagoner called Pugh always came back from Bridgnorth the worse for drink.

When my father first went to Bromley there were two old people who lived in the big house down The Batch. They told him there was supposed to be a box of gold buried there and repeated a ditty which started promisingly:

"In a valley between two fields
there lies a box of gold concealed."

Unfortunately, apart from, "three fields down from the crossroads on the Wolverhampton Road," Eric could remember no more.

Eric was part of a large family and his mother had difficulty making ends meet. Like so many farmers' wives she had her own flock of hens and she could keep the income they generated. On one occasion she had saved up enough money for a trip to Stourbridge to visit Eric's half-brother Walter. Not having a car of her own, the garage owner in Low Town was the chauffeur. He collected the family in a shiny, open-topped Model T Ford. Off they went at

---

[169] G. K. Nelson, *Over the Farmyard Gate; Country life in the 1930s,* Sutton Publishing, 1995

the breakneck speed of about 25 mph whilst his mother held on to her hat. Even at this speed, the journey seemed endless, and Eric worried they would never find their way home again.

When Eric was eleven he attended the Blue Coat School in High Town to which he travelled on a second-hand Rover cycle his mother had bought for 30s. The headmaster, Mr Blakemore, used the cane liberally which was terrifying. "One day he made two boys bend down in front of the class and thrashed them all round the room with the dust flying off their backs." The crime for which the boys were punished was serious. Milk was sold from a tank and poured into the housewives' own jugs or cans via a tap. The boys had drained the tank by leaving the tap open. Eric himself had the cane one day for not being able to spell. It was probably not surprising that he left school on his fourteenth birthday.

Eric's mother had taught him to save and gave him 1s a week to save in the school savings bank. On leaving school he had the princely sum of £7 with which he very sensibly bought a pig. The sow gave birth to eleven piglets and he sold them to his brother Jack (who was at one time the miller in Worfield) for £22. This money was then invested in a motor bike, much to his parents' concern, as his brother Leslie had been killed on one at the age of twenty-seven.

Eric's first job at Bromley earned him 7s.6d. a week. Since much of his time was spent catching rabbits and moles, his mother arranged for him to go and work for his uncle at Westwood Farm near Much Wenlock. One of his first jobs was swede cutting, a particularly unpleasant job on frosty mornings but he was also introduced to tractors, namely a 1925 Fordson which could pull a two-furrow plough and plough two acres a day.

In 1933 Eric's uncle and his father died (his mother having died in 1930) so it was time to move on from Westwood Farm. His brother-in-law, Reg Rivers, offered hime a job driving a lorry and he went to live at Nordley with his newly-wed sister Mary and her husband Reg. The wages were small but the few pigs he kept got him by.

Times were very hard in the Thirties for farmers and their labourers. The average wage for a farm labourer was 35s. a week and they usually kept a pig and grew their own vegetables to make ends meet. Prices for produce were at rock bottom. Eric sold a ton of potatoes at Wolverhampton Market one day for 30s and these low prices left many farmers heavily in debt and others bankrupt. When Eric's father died he was £750 in debt which Eric's brother, Ernest, inherited when he took over the farm. It was a burden for many years. Housing was also very basic with no sanitation or running water.

Reg and Mary took the tenancy of St James Farm, Bridgnorth which had two hundred acres and with so many people unemployed, Eric jumped at the offer of a job with a wage of £2 per week and a cottage rent-free. Dole queues were often 100 yards long and 6 deep and people were so desperate for work they would queue all night for the chance of a job.

When Eric married in 1938, Reg offered Eric the tenancy of 27 acres of pasture at Danesford. With capital of £200 borrowed from his cousin, Eric bought several old cows and calves and turned them out to single suckle. It was a big mistake. By the autumn, several of the cows were very thin and he lost three by the spring. The £200 investment was now worth £100 so Eric's only choice was to start milking to get some income.

It was then that Eric had a disagreement with Reg who told him to look for another job, and as the house went with the job he would have no home either. Fortunately Ernest had a cottage vacant at Woodside with which Eric and his wife fell in love. Along with the cottage went a

BROMLEY

Eric Rochelle

part-time job at Bromley Farm, driving the tractor for a wage of £1 per week. Six cows still had to be milked by hand at Danesford twice a day so Eric travelled on his old Levis motorbike. This continued for several years until he had gathered a small herd of good cows and store cattle.

There was no electricity in the cottage at Woodside so it was lit by oil lamps and a candle to light them to bed. A well at the bottom of the garden provided water, and the lavatory was "a little wooden affair at the bottom of the garden". Hot water inside the house was provided by a boiler alongside the grate which heated two gallons of water with a twenty gallon boiler outside in the washhouse. The fuel was mainly wood. The couple's first daughter was born about a year after they moved to Woodside on a cold January night with deep snow and a hard frost. With no car to take his wife to Bridgnorth Hospital, there was only one solution; to walk to Bromley (with a hot water bottle under his coat), put the water in Ernest's old Austin car, drive to Woodside, collect his wife, and then on to Bridgnorth hospital. The trip was made without incident. His wife was safely delivered of a daughter later that night and the car was safely returned to Bromley without anyone being any the wiser about the trip it had made. Two years later a second Rochelle daughter was born; very sensibly in July

By this time, milking had become tedious so Eric decided to try growing peas. Ambitiously, he planted six and a half acres but it was a gamble that paid off as he made a profit of £500. Eric was now farming sixty-two acres at Danesford and dealing in cattle. A group of thirty made another £500 which enabled him to finish milking and concentrate on pigs and cattle dealing. The farm prospered so that Eric was able to build a bungalow at Danesford. Having spent his life living in and around Bromley, Eric met a number of characters.

Bob Bodger lived in a thatched cottage in Bromley with his sons, Alf and Bob. He was a mole-catcher and made pegs for the housewives in the village. His two sons worked on the farm until Alf had a breakdown and was taken away in a 'Black Maria'. Eric was then aged about eight. Eric's father was friendly with Bob the son, visiting his house every evening at 10 o'clock. One day Eric peeped in through the window to see the two men sitting either side of the fire drinking. The room had a flag floor and was sparsely furnished with a table and a few chairs. On the table was some bread and cheese and crockery which looked as though it had never been washed. The room was lit by an oil lamp and there were mole skins nailed to boards around the room. Bob himself was very dirty and unkempt and in consequence stunk to high heaven but he lived to a ripe old age.

Mr and Mrs Meyrick lived in a cottage at the High Rock coppice. Mrs. Meyrick was the local midwife and very fat. When she was called to a case her clients knew they had to get plenty of stout in because she wouldn't go up the stairs until she had had a pint. She would sit and drink it very slowly in spite of cries for help from her patient saying, "All in good time my dear, all in good time". Her husband, William, worked part-time at Bromley Farm and was a particularly good hedge layer, a fact which Sam Jones, who lived in a cottage in Bromley, would dispute. Sam thought he was much better at the job and would criticise Will''s work saying,"Youne killed that bloody hedge Will." Will's appearance was distinctive as he had snow-white side whiskers. Sam's distinction was in his height; he was well over six foot, and his skin was brown and wrinkled. One summer's day in the Second World War they were making hay when there were planes flying overhead. Sam looked up and said "we um bound to have some rain before long with all them old airyplanes a buzzing about".

There were also two Davies brothers known as the Jacky brothers. They were what we would call, 'of no fixed abode,' and lived in farm buildings. They did very little work except to collect old rags and sell them in Bridgnorth and survived by scrounging food. At one time they had a donkey and cart to collect the rags but when the donkey died Fred pulled the cart. He was giving Jack a ride along Underhill Street one day when he had had enough and threw the shafts up in the air thus depositing Jack in the middle of the road. They would wear any decent coat they were given, one on top of another, each tied up with binder twine. Jack was once summoned to Bridgnorth for trying to obtain money under false pretences and when he arrived he was wearing four coats and two pairs of trousers. When he left the court the police were seen spraying the area with disinfectant! At Christmas, Jack would sing carols while Freddie played the mouth organ. Jack was once heard to say, "I've got five hundred acres of carol singing to do this year". They stayed in the building at Woodside all one winter during the war with the cattle keeping them warm, until Eric was fed up with them and decided to move them on by mentioning that the Home Guard wanted to recruit them. That did the trick, they were gone for 6 months across the river.

Old Jim Cuerton first came to Danesford in October 1940. Eric set him to pull five acres of sugar beet and he settled himself in one of the sheds with an old stove and plenty of straw for his bed. All went well until he received his first wage packet. Off he went into Bridgnorth and came back as drunk as a lord & very objectionable. His route to the pub along Riverside puzzled Eric so he asked why he took that route. He said it was because that way he came to the grocer's shop before the pub otherwise all the money would be spent on beer. When he was sober Jim was a gentleman, and he came back for fourteen years to pull beet. The final year he came a month late and the job had been given to someone else. Eric gave him £1 and the last he heard of Jim he was blind drunk under a hedge in Oldbury.

Note: In October 1932 there was a big fire at Bromley Farm which destroyed a six-bay Dutch barn containing the produce of eighty acres. Lichfield Mercury 7 October 1932, p. 2

DOUGLAS HAWTHORNE

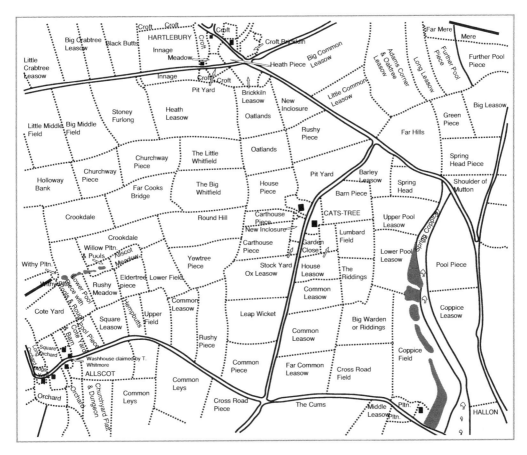

Catstree drawn from the 1839 Field Names Map. The hamlet at this time consisted of two farms, one of cruck construction and the other more recent, perhaps eighteenth century. Such a tiny settlement seems rather unimportant today but the tree ending may denote that it was an administrative meeting place in Anglo Saxon times.

Just after Christmas I had a telephone call from one of the churchwardens who passed on an enquiry about Douglas Noel Hawthorne who had lived at Worfield some time in the early twentieth century. My heart sinks at the thought of searching for information in the twentieth century. We are very fortunate in having the Parish Magazine archive but the magazines have not (as far as I know) survived for the period I was looking at and unless I could find someone who remembered the family, I was frankly not optimistic that this was going to lead anywhere. The enquirer told me that Douglas Noel Hawthorne had lived at Catstree Farm and that he had been married to Eleanor Langley. There were two children of the marriage , both born in Worfield; William Douglas Hawthorne, born 1920, and Eleanor Joan, born 1918.

CATSTREE
Douglas Hawthorne

Douglas Hawthorne I found on the internet when he was on a committee to decide the nature of a memorial to those killed in World War 1. It was an invaluable piece in the jigsaw as you will see. A parish meeting was called to discuss the matter of the World War I memorial and it was 'fairly well attended'. I was someone taken aback by the apparent lack of enthusiasm. Perhaps people were fed up with war, but Douglas Noel Hawthorne fortunately did attend the meeting and when a small committee was formed to further the memorial idea, he was the farmers' representative, along with Evan Ridley. Mr Hawthorne's contribution to the discussion related to the siting of the memorial. The suggestion was that the memorial should be on the terrace in the churchyard and that the large chestnut trees should be removed. Everyone on the committee agreed except Douglas Hawthorne who said that the wishes of the people of the parish were that the memorial should be near the gate at the entrance to the Churchyard and facing the street. I warm to the man from that statement alone; a man of principle methinks who was prepared to speak out for the people of Worfield and to go against the prevailing opinion. It was agreed that both sites would be considered, not that they were ever going to be; such is the nature of committees.

The next reference to Douglas Hawthorne was in the Parish Magazine of 1921 when he was a sidesman at St. Peter's. (There is a gap in the archive from 1915 to 1921 so there may have been earlier references.) In January 1923 he became the Lay Representative at the Ruridecanal Conference. The Vicar of Worfield wrote, "We are sure to find Mr. Hawthorne worthy of the office." It is mystery therefore that by May 1923 he had been replaced in this role and no longer featured in the Parish Magazine.

In the 1911 census, Douglas Noel Hawthorne was 20 years old and a farm pupil. He had evidently decided not to follow his father, William Henry Hawthorne, into the family business, Cannon Iron Foundries, of which William was co-owner. Douglas's mother, Ada Florence Hawthorne née Millward also belonged to a family of industrialists who owned an iron foundry in Newcastle -Under-Lyme. More locally, the Millwards owned a malthouse in Station Road, Albrighton (the building still stands at the time of writing), another in Wednesbury, and sixty pubs and off-licences. It must have come as quite a surprise to the family when Douglas, educated at Wolverhampton Grammar School and Wrekin College, decided to become a farmer.

In 1917, Douglas married Eleanor Langley, the daughter of William Langley, a farmer, and Charlotte Langley his wife, of Shipley in Claverley parish. There were just the two children, already mentioned, from the marriage. In Douglas's obituary he is described as having been a farmer at Catstree over a long period and for the twenty-five years prior to his death had been employed by the Birmingham Siphon Company. That would put the date when he left Catstree as 1930.[170] At the time of his death in 1955, Douglas Hawthorne was living in Albert Road, Wolverhampton.

Douglas & Eleanor's son, William Douglas Hawthorne, became an estate agent by day and a band leader by night. He lived at Wightwick but retained a strong attachment to the area and was a member of Claverley Church.

---

[170] *Birmingham Post*, 15 January 1955 p.17,

CHESTERTON CHAPEL

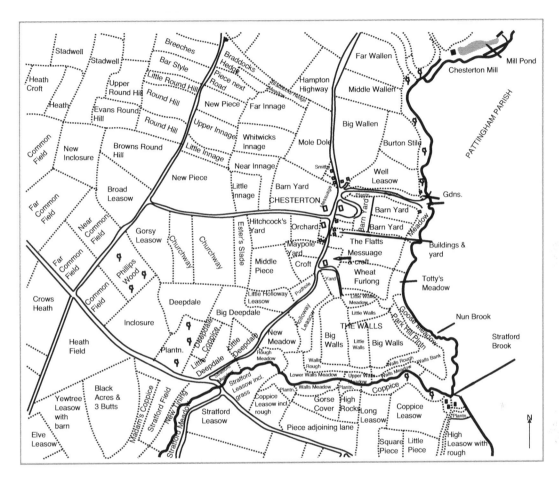

Chesterton from the 1839 Field Names Map

The former Chesterton Chapel is now Chapel Cottage and incorporates several features of the old building, notably the stone-arched doorway on the South side, and the remains of old windows on the South and West. Historic England dates the building to the fifteenth century but a chapel was well-established when, in 1394, the Bishop of Lichfield and Coventry included the oblations of Chesterton Chapel and the corn tithes of Chesterton as part of the endowment of the Vicar of Worfield.[171] Before this date, Chesterton Chapel and its incumbent were maintained by the chapel's gifts and all the township's tithes. One might imagine that after this date the funds of the chaplain were seriously depleted but if there was a new chapel or the

---

[171] Randall, John, *Worfield and its Townships* pp. 26-27

rebuilding of an older one in the 1400s this perhaps suggests otherwise. The following affray at the Festival of St. John the Baptist would further indicate a thriving religious community and a chapel with influence beyond Worfield Parish.

"Chesterton presents that several strangers came here on the Feast of the Beheading of John the Baptist [29 August 1446]. Richard Togge of Areley in the County of Stafford Thomas Togge of Areley of the same county and William Togge of Glazeley in the County of Shropshire all yeomen Richard Wade of Midleton in the County of Shropshire yeoman Thomas Heye of Bridgnorth shoemaker John Carbonell of Upton in the County of Salop yeoman with many others unknown were hostilely armed with daggers, spears, arquebuses, arrows, poleaxes, bill-hooks and long bows and other arms in the manner of an insurrection in the 25th year of the reign of King Henry VI against the peace of the Lord King and then and there assaulted and wounded Thomas Mylles Rector of Cleobury and evilly carried him off so that his life was despaired of and other outrages inflicted to the grave danger of Thomas Myles and in great disturbance to all the Christian people who came here to honour and praise God and St. John the Baptist at the time of the said Feast."[172]

Poor old Chesterton suffered another violent incursion two years later when "William Weston and Peter Weston of Lychfield in the County of Stafford, yeomen, came on the 12th day of March in the 27th year of the reign of Henry VI at the township of Chesterton aforesaid and here by might and arms namely gleyves, swords, crossbows and arrows took 15 hurdles price 40d against the peace of the lord King of the goods and chattels of Simon Hichecokes and further it is said that he is plundered and has damages to the value of 40s etc."[173]

Chesterton Chapel had its own cemetery as we can see from the Manor Court Roll of 1453-1454. John Snell came to the court and "took from the lord the whole of the waste land lying by the cemetery of the Chapel of St. John of Chesterton extending up to the gate of Thomas Gerbot here with one parcel of land called Bele Yard".[174] Does that imply there was also a separate bell tower, I wonder?

The origins of Chesterton Chapel are lost in the mists of time and most of the documentation relating to it was probably destroyed at the time of the Reformation. We cannot know for certain whether or not Chesterton was built as an outlying chapel of the Parish church of Worfield or whether it was linked to Rudge where there was an outlier chapel to Pattingham.

The track from Chesterton to Rudge is well-used, even today, and we accept that it crosses the Nun Brook and goes past Nunfield, without thinking of the significance of these names. Eyton gives us the explanation. "White Ladies Priory must have acquired a small estate at Rudge... some time before 1292 as in that year Prioress Sarra (Sarah) sued William of Rugg, the lord of the manor for denying her use of common pasture. ...The jury found that William had contravened his tenants' historic rights and deprived them of pasture they required for

---

[172] *Shropshire Archives,* P314/W/1/1/298

[173] *Shropshire Archives,* P314/W/1/1/313

[174] *Shropshire Archives,* P314/W/1/1/308

their animals through enclosures designed to improve his estate. He counter-sued the prioress and others for breaking down his fence but Sarah and the other tenants won their cases".[175]

We can be certain that by 1646 when John Bradburne surrendered a cottage called Chesterton Chapel, there was no place of worship in Chesterton but whether it was the Reformation or the Civil War which brought about the Chapel's demise, we cannot say. [176]

Note: The Manor Court Roll of 1374 (P314/W/1/1/94) held in Shropshire Archives records a surrender of half a nook (about seven acres) of land by Henry Newe in Chesterton, of Bishop's land.

[175] R. W. Eyton, *Shropshire & its Antiquities Vol. 3*, Shropshire 1856, *pp 208-209*

[176] *Shropshire Archives*, P314/W/1/1/304

BUILDING IN THE TUDOR STYLE

The drive to Long Knowle, Chesterton

There are many house names around the Parish which throw up interesting lines of history. Some refer to previous owners or occupiers, such as Baker's cottage in Bromley and Marindin House in Chesterton. Others point to an occupational use, such as the Malt House or Mill Cottage, whilst Old Forest Lodge in Barnsley Lane is a remnant of the Forest of Morfe, which once covered half the parish. Other names, one imagines, have been chosen simply because they are pretty. One such I always thought, was Long Knowle in Chesterton. I might, had I stopped to think, wondered why this name was chosen when the house didn't appear to sit on a long hill, but I never really gave it a thought. In fact, without someone telling me the derivation it would have been nigh on impossible to work out.

Long Knowle sits just behind Chesterton Farm and was built by George Bradburn. It was named after the Bradburn's farm in Wednesfield I was reliably informed by Mary Foster née Bradburn. Mary told me of another house with the same name in Wightwick, which many of you, I am sure, will have gone past and thought, 'what a beautiful house,' but nothing more. I had never realised that this house was also called Long Knowle but the name is clearly there, set into the stone wall.

Long Knowle, Wightwick, named after long Knowle Farm, Wednesfield

As I write this piece in 2018, the Wightwick house is up for sale, which makes it easily spotted and, of course, easy to see the interior of the house online. This Long Knowle was built by a local architect, J. R. Wooddisse, for his own personal use, from material reclaimed from demolished properties. The house is full of features we would recognise as Tudor in origin, mullioned windows, oak panelling and flooring, and a magnificent staircase. Most of these timber features came from Long Knowle Farm in Wednesfield which was dismantled in the 1930s. Other material was of later origin, such as the wainscoting at the top of these stairs, rescued from the Brick Kiln Methodist Church on the corner of Lord Street, Wolverhampton, when it was demolished.

Many old properties were demolished in the early part of the twentieth century, providing a ready supply of building material. The Cole family in Bilston extended their demolition business into a reclamation yard selling building materials and effects. I remember my mother picking me up from school one day and whisking me off for an impromptu visit to see this bizarre builder's yard. Mother was laughing and saying that I wouldn't believe what I was about to see. I begged to know more but apart from the fact that there were some animals in cages I was kept in suspense. Mother was right, this was the most crazy builders' yard I had ever seen with chaotic piles of demolition detritus surrounded by cages containing a variety of animals. Towering over them all was a huge cage containing a tiger who paced up and down wondering how he had come to be in this hellish jungle.

Kenneth Hutchinson Smith architecture in Castlecroft Gardens, Wolverhampton

In Wolverhampton at this time, Major Kenneth Hutchinson Smith was viewing this disappearing heritage with an architect's eye, and would leave a very different legacy from that of the Cole family.[1] Major Smith came to England from Canada with the Canadian Cavalry in 1915, married, and settled in England after the First World War. To earn a living he decided to design and build houses. These were to be no ordinary houses but individually designed and built by craftsmen using the best reclaimed material which could be found. The result was a house which looked as though it had been there for centuries but finding the craftsmen who were able to work in the manner required was no easy task. For example, not all bricklayers could lay small uneven medieval bricks with lime mortar, often with stone worked into them.

Smith's carpenters, too, had to be rather special, for he would not allow the use of modern tools or any method of mass production.'[177]

Material came from near and far. Tong Castle provided much of it and Montgomery Castle was the source of some of the material used in building the 'Tudor' house at the bottom of Histons Hill in Codsall. The Butter Market in Shifnal was moved lock, stock and barrel to Castlecroft Gardens, and The New Ship Inn in Shrewsbury was reincarnated in the Ridgeway, Springhill, Wolverhampton. Pattingham Hall was restored and extended in 1938. Sadly the house was demolished and the only legacy is in the name of a road - 'Hall End Lane.'

There is no doubting the beauty of Major Smith's houses in Finchfield Gardens, Springhill Lane and Castlecroft Gardens. 'The Ridgeway' in Springhill Lane is a spectacular example of Smith's work. Not all the houses were built in a half-timbered style, those with a more contemporary look were just as stylish. If you ever have a moment to spare it really is worth searching these houses out for they are exquisite and so typically English.

In 1929, Mr Brockbank, the manager of the Wolverhampton Steam Laundry, and his wife, were travelling from Bridgnorth to view Hilton House with the intention of purchasing. The house did not suit, and as they were travelling back towards Wolverhampton, they stopped at the brow of the hill in Hilton, and looked over towards the Titterstone Clee. The view clinched it. Mrs Brockbank fell in love with the spot and determined to have a house built here. One day, as stone was being quarried from the garden to build a wall, Mrs Brockbank heard a lark singing and suddenly the house had a name; Larkstone. And who should they have to design this new house, you might ask. Only the best would do and that, of course, was Major Kenneth Hutchinson Smith.

Richard Wilson's initials on a cottage next to the Malthouse site in Ackleton dated 1898

Richard Sidney Wilson's initials on an extension to Chesterton House

[177]Ron Davies, *One Man's Dream. The Architectural Art of Major Kenneth Hutchinson Smith*

CHESTERTON Building in the Tudor Style

In Worfield, the Tudor style of building was endorsed by R. S. Wilson at the start of the twentieth century although in this case it was the mock Tudor style with which we are so familiar today. Kingslow village seems to be the embodiment of Wilson's dream; a village which includes a distinctive mansion, renovated, of course, and houses built in the mock Tudor style.

The family interest in architecture began with R. S. Wilson's father, Richard Wilson who built a cottage in Ackleton in 1898, helpfully dating and inscribing it with his initials, and continued with the building or improvement of the Tub Row houses in the village (see page 165). Richard Wilson's interest in housing seems to have been to provide his employees at the Ackleton Malthouse with quality houses and his son, R. S. Wilson, continued in the same manner, improving and building houses across his Kingslow and Chesterton Estates. Today we can follow R. S. Wilson's work as each house he worked on was dated and marked with his initials.

The Bailiff's House, Kingslow

Kenneth Hutchinson Smith never made a fortune from his chosen career, and R. S. Wilson's financial fortunes have already been discussed but this should not overshadow the legacy of either men. Hutchinson Smith built a number of beautiful houses in Wolverhampton and the surrounding area, and Wilson created a portfolio of properties in the parish which are still sought after today.

GERTRUDE JEKYLL IN CHESTERTON AND THE WEATHER IN 2017

If people are not talking about football at the moment, then it's the weather which is most likely to be the topic of conversation. For sun lovers it is heaven, for farmers, gardeners and the water companies who supply water, it is a terrible worry. The comparison in conversation is always with 1976, and the question is whether this is going to be a repeat of the drought conditions of that year, with hosepipe bans and washing-up and bath water being used to water gardens.

R.S. Wilson Cottages at Stanlowe 1928 (Sales Catalogue 1928)

Like many of you, I remember 1976 well. To be honest, I remember it very selectively, as it affected me. I do remember the glorious sunshine so welcome at first. It meant that jobs such as haymaking and shearing could be done without the usual stopping and starting caused by rain. Geoff Parton remembers haymaking at Chesterton; cutting a field in the morning and baling it at 4pm the same afternoon. Sometimes the quality was impaired by the heat as the hay burned rather than dried. The early enthusiasm for the fine weather soon turned to dismay as the rains

CHESTERTON   Gertrude Jekyll

failed to materialise and pastures dried up in the searing heat. There would be no second crop of hay and grazing was non-existent.

By the 5th July it was clear that the country was facing the worst drought in 250 years. Other droughts had occurred in the twentieth century, notably in 1911 and 1921, but none on the scale of 1976. What made that year particularly bad was that it had hardly rained since January, so rivers and reservoirs were already short of water before the summer even started. By August, England's green and pleasant land had turned into a landscape of various shades of brown. Autumn sown cereals fared much better than those sown in the spring and many of the potato crops were ruined. Some livestock farmers were feeding hay to their stock in August and wondering how they were going to survive the winter. Soft fruit farmers who had looked at potentially good crops in early summer saw the fruit literally cooked by the intense heat.

Working in the heat was a nightmare. Some companies changed their working hours to a more continental system, starting earlier in the morning, but farm workers often had no choice but to work in the heat of the day. Mary Taylor was overcome by the heat after a day pulling Lambs' Quarter or Fat Hen out of a field of sugar beet off Shepherd's Lane, Rudge. 'I struggled to walk through the weeds and as I pulled them the leaves stuck to me. I was so hot, and I hadn't taken any water with me. By the end of the day I thought I would never get home.' How Geoff Stephens fared that year with his shearing I can't imagine, but I have always been amazed at how he copes with heat normally. I have never heard him complain, as though to do so would simply be a waste of precious energy needed for the job in hand.

Inevitably in 1976 there would be shortages of some food items. There was talk of a bread shortage and there was certainly a potato shortage. Imports would be required to fill the gap and I am sure it will be the same this year. My small garden is usually a jungle of vegetables with peas reaching four foot and more. This year they have struggled to reach two foot and with nothing like the normal crop. Spring onions are literally burning at the tips and root crops are particularly badly affected with no carrots or beetroot. It remains to be seen whether I have any parsnips at all.

The good news in 1976 was that, contrary to predictions, the drought did not last until December but broke in September. The rains came, the land cooled and the pastures greened. And then, in one corner of Worfield, at Littlegain, a miracle appeared to have happened. One morning the fields were white. Snow seemed to have fallen on seventy acres. Of course, it wasn't snow, but mushrooms. They covered every field and we set up a stall at the end of our drive to sell them. I remember the price; 30p per lb. As fast as we cut them they grew again and that year we made £30 from this God-given crop.

A couple of weeks ago I was visiting my daughter in Great Warley, Essex. Opposite her house is the garden which was created by a famous gardener, Miss Willmott, who died penniless, having spent her entire fortune on her thirty acre garden. I found my mind straying back to a story I had heard, that Gertrude Jekyll, the famous garden designer, had designed a garden in Chesterton. It was always uncertain which garden she had created, whether it was that of Chesterton Farm (now Hall) or Marindin House. The client, apparently, was a Mrs. Thompson of Chesterton, and the date was 1919. Many of the gardens commissioned by Miss Jekyll's clients at this time were in remembrance of those who died in World War 1 but whether this was the case in Chesterton I don't know. Which begs several questions; who was Mrs

CHESTERTON
Gertrude Jekyll

Chesterton Hall

Thompson, whose stay in the parish seems to have been short, which garden did Miss Jekyll design, and was the garden ever created?

Although both Chesterton Farm and Marindin House were possible contenders, a member of the Rowley family confirmed that Hilda Rowley had worked for Mr and Mrs James Thompson who rented the house. Miss Jekyll's notes for the design of the Chesterton garden are for :a) a border facing north by the side of the tennis court, b) a border facing west, c) a north garden: long border by building, d) & e) north garden already planted, f-m) north garden.[178] Whether all were planted is another question.

Miss Jekyll collaborated with Sir Edwin Lutyens and, as Paul Stamper writes, "while there is no evidence of his involvement at Chesterton, there remains a possibility that, through Miss Jekyll, gates of a Lutyenesque character were made for estate buildings in the hamlet."[179]

[178] *Godalming Museum*, Gertrude Jekyll notebook 25

[179] Paul Stamper, *Historic Parks. Gardens of Shropshire* (Shropshire Books 1996)

HARRY SCOTT BAYLISS

Harry Bayliss lived in Chesterton from 1940 to the time of his death in 1960 and it was from here, as managing director, that he ran Paramount Picture Theatres, a cinema chain which stretched across the Midlands and Wales. It is odd that he located himself in Worfield but it was the parish's gain as he became the organist and choirmaster at St Peter's.

A choir outing from the 1960s. In the centre is Harry Bayliss and to the right of him is his wife, Florence, a German visitor and Mr Jones, the sexton. To the left of Harry Bayliss are Mrs Doris Thomson & the Revd. Thomson. Photograph courtesy of Ron Cornes

Harry Scott Bayliss, to give him his full title, came from Wolverhampton. In 1911 the Bayliss family were living at 277, Dunstall Road, the end house in a row of terraced houses, modest in the extreme. The family consisted of Harry's father, also called Harry, an electrical engineer, Alice his mother, Harry Scott, aged 21, a solicitor's clerk, Percy, a manufacturer's clerk, Annie, aged 19, a draper's assistant, Gertie, aged 18, a clerk, and Edna, aged 6. In 1915 Harry Bayliss married Norah Bradshaw who died just four years later, and he then married Florence Martin in 1920. Florence and Harry met at a church in Chapel Ash, Wolverhampton, perhaps at St Marks, where he played the organ and Florence sang in the choir.

How Harry Scott Bayliss rose from the role of solicitor's clerk to run a chain of cinemas is a mystery. Mary Foster (née Bradburn) who lived opposite Marindin House, thought that he had a brother-in-law who ran a large cinema in Birmingham. Wolverhampton Archives has a picture of the staff of Dunstall Road Picture House, taken in the 1940s,. The cinema had opened in 1934 and was very close to the Bayliss's home.[180] Imagine my surprise when I saw that the chief projectionist was Harry Bayliss. All too soon I realised that this man was too young to be Harry Scott Bayliss but could this have been a relation?

Harry Scott Bayliss died in 1960 and in his obituary we learn that he "was the founder and MD of the Paramount Picture Theatre Circuit which operated cinemas in many Midland towns including Cannock, Bilston, Worcester, Gloucester, Rugby, and Leamington Spa. He then turned his attention to Wales which he felt was badly served for entertainment, apart from the larger towns, and opened 20 cinemas there."[181] It was an extraordinary achievement.

The Majestic Cinema, Caernarfon

In 1930 Harry Bayliss bought Morville Hall where he lived until 1936. That is some meteoric rise from a house in Whitmore Reans. During the six years he was at Morville, Harry Bayliss made a number of alterations to the house, which makes it rather surprising that he moved to the much more modest and run-down house in Chesterton.[182] Work was carried out on Marindin House prior to the Bayliss's moving in, but just as the work was finished in 1940, a fire caused significant damage. Until Marindin House was made habitable, Harry and his wife lived at 24, Chesterton, next to Mr. and Mrs. Harris. Several people have noted the sumptuous

---

[180] *Wolverhampton Archives*, P/7944

[181] *North Wales Weekly News*, 25 February 1960, p. 15.

[182] *Morville Hall*, The National Trust information leaflet

CHESTERTON   Harry Bayliss

decor of Marindin House during the Bayliss's time there which all attributed to Harry Bayliss. He may have come from humble beginnings but the man had excellent taste.

For the next eight years, Paramount Picture Theatres was run from Chesterton but in 1948, with fifteen cinemas in Wales alone, the headquarters were moved to Welshpool. Harry Bayliss stayed in Chesterton and put Guy Baker in charge of the North Wales circuit. Jeff Hughes, who appropriately lived at Marindin Cottage, Hallon, joined the company in 1943 as an administrative assistant after leaving school and stayed until he went into the forces in 1945. Jeff rejoined the company after the war, working in Chesterton and Welshpool, and eventually became the Circuit Relief Manager.

Harry didn't drive but had a chauffeur/gardener, Bill Grocutt. Florence most certainly did drive, and while Harry Bayliss walked at some speed to church every Sunday, Florence always drove. One of Florence's passengers from Chesterton was Derek Rowley, a choirboy, who recalled that she would knock the car out of gear at the top of Bradeney Bank and freewheel down the hill; sensible woman, with petrol in short supply.

The organist and choirmaster held choir practice every Wednesday and Friday between four o'clock and five and on Sunday after the morning service. High expectations from the choir boys (as they all were) were on one side of the equation but the choirmaster was generous in his rewards. Marindin House was the scene of the choir's annual Sports Day and there was also an annual trip paid for by the choirmaster. Without this help most of the choirboys simply wouldn't have been able to afford to go. Derek Rowley remembers going to the Isle of Man, Whipsnade Zoo, Snowdon and Caernarfon and there were regular theatre trips to the Grand and the Hippodrome theatres in Wolverhampton. Jeff Hughes organised the trips from Paramount Picture Theatre's point of view and recalled the following. "There was an annual outing for the whole choir, usually to North Wales, with a meal at the Majestic Cinema in Caernarfon and a boat trip on the Menai Straits."

The cinema and theatre scene flourished throughout the thirties and continued to do so after the war. However Harry Scott Bayliss had got into the industry he was certainly right in thinking there was money to be made. What an exciting business it must have been, too, with stage appearances of up-and-coming actors such as Richard Attenborough. Harry Scott Bayliss was, by all accounts a gentleman, a man whose humble beginnings never held him back, and someone who never flaunted his position either. After her husband's death, Florence went to live at Wightwick, Wolverhampton.

Acknowledgments
Thanks are due to Cyril Rowley, Derek Rowley, Ron Cornes, Richard Willoughby and the late Jeff Hughes

198

VALENTINE VICKERS

Valentine Vickers the Younger with a pair of oxen of which one was the famous 'Bowman.'

This is the story of a very unusual marriage at the beginning of the nineteenth century. Normally the status of husband and wife were pretty evenly matched but in this case the upper class bridegroom chose a gipsy as his bride. There is no record of the reaction of friends and family but one can imagine that some will have laughed at him and others must have thought he had taken leave of his senses. How could this new wife, of such lowly birth, fit into the business and social world in which Valentine Vickers moved?

Three generations of Vickers had lived at Cranmere. Valentine Vickers the Elder, died in 1821, his son, Valentine Vickers the Younger, died in 1814, and his son, Valentine Vickers junior, who was born in 1786, died in 1846. The family were estate managers of both the Davenport and Apley Estates and also ran a successful surveying business. Valentine Vickers the Elder was, for a time, in partnership with John and George Pritchard of Broseley and Bridgnorth, bankers. Vickers withdrew from the partnership in 1824.[183] In due course

183 *Aris's Birmingham Gazette*, 19 July 1824, p. 4

CRANMERE

Valentine Vickers junior joined the family business as you will see on the promissory note below by which he promises to pay Valentine Vickers senior £5.

Around the end of the eighteenth century, large areas of common land across the country were being enclosed by Acts of Parliament and there was no shortage of work for surveyors. Worfield was no exception and its common land was parcelled up and awarded to those who were entitled. One of Vickers' most prestigious clients was the Marquis of Anglesey but he also worked across large areas of the Midlands and North Wales. The Parliamentary Enclosures made the Vickers family extremely wealthy but there was no suggestion that they acted improperly or took advantage of the situation.

Promissory Note issued at Cranmere 1800/1806

However, while Valentine Vickers was a successful and respected business man, there was one part of his life in which he was unfulfilled; he had failed to find a wife. First he approached a local woman but she rejected him, and then he resorted to a very unorthodox method of acquiring a wife. Riding back home to Cranmere, he saw a child outside a labourer's cottage in the parish of Astley Abbotts. He stopped his horse and made a proposal to the girl's parents that he would educate the girl and then make her his wife. The girl's parents must have been pretty shocked by the offer and could easily have been drawn into accepting. After all, it's not every day that a wealthy young man comes along and offers to take your daughter off your hands. The parents sensibly refused the offer. Young Valentine must have been pretty downcast by yet another refusal. He rode on towards home, across the Severn and then, near the toll gate by the Worfe Bridge, he had a very bad fall from his horse. A young gipsy girl tended to his injuries and on his recovery Valentine Vickers made the same proposal that he had made to the Astley Abbotts' parents, namely that he would educate the girl and make her his wife. This time the gipsy girl's parents had no objection and Valentine Vickers was true to his word. Anne Millar became Mrs. Vickers and the newly-weds settled at Cranmere. Mrs. Vickers' eldest niece, Margaret, who according to Randall was a most beautiful woman with an amiable temperament, also went to live at Cranmere. Both women were excellent horsewomen and were regularly seen on horseback at the Morfe coursing meetings which took place in the area around Stanmore Grove and Mrs. Vickers also went to Bridgnorth Races in her carriage drawn by four dashing ponies.[184]

Anne Millar proved to be a real handful and much as Valentine might have been a dutiful husband, whether his wife was quite the 'true and attached wife … of this romantic marriage,' as Randall's described her, I somehow doubt. Mr. and Mrs. Vickers moved from Cranmere to Ellerton Grange, near Newport and Margaret Millar went with them. The marriage was childless and Anne Vickers died as the result of an accident aged just forty-eight years.

There are two versions of the accident. Randall must have got the picture of the four spirited ponies stuck in his head because he repeats this detail in his version '… [she] met her death near Newport whilst endeavouring to leave her carriage, being unable to control her four spirited ponies, which had run away.' This is definitely incorrect. The details given in the following newspaper report describe what actually happened. The reporter would have attended the Coroner's Inquest and heard the witness statements. On the 18th August Anne Vickers drove from Ellerton Grange to visit friends in Newton and all went well on the way to Worfield, but on the return journey disaster struck. The carriage pulled by a pair of horses was descending a hill at Woodcote near Newport when the reins broke. The coachman leapt off and tried to stop the horses but without success. Without anyone in control, the horses galloped on. Perhaps Mrs. Vickers thought she might be able to grab the reins and stop the horses because she also jumped out but unfortunately she caught her foot as she did so and presumably landed on her head. The horses carried on for another three miles before they or the carriage collided with a lamp post outside the Crown Inn in Newport. A group of helpers, accompanied by the family surgeon, went in search of anyone who might have been injured, and found Mrs. Vickers lying in the middle of the road bleeding profusely from her mouth. She was taken to the Crown Inn, Newport, where she died in the early hours of the next day.[185]

The obituary paints a picture of the bereaved husband, family and friends.

"On the 18th last, at Newport in Shropshire, in consequence of a fall from a carriage, the horses having taken fright, Anne, the faithful and beloved wife of Valentine Vickers, late of Cranmere, now of Ellerton Grange, Staffordshire, deeply regretted by a numerous circle of friends as well as by her relatives, by whom her loss is felt to be irreparable. She will long live in

[184] Randall, *Worfield & its Townships*, p. 68

[185] *Shrewsbury Chronicle*, 21 August 1846, p. 3

the affectionate remembrance of her survivors, who deeply deplore the fatal event by which she has been so suddenly removed from them".[186]

It was two years later, in 1848, that Valentine married Julia Whitby. The couple were married in Meretown, Newport and had three children. Valentine Vickers died on the 13th November 1867. The Death Notice simply said: "At Offley Grove, Staffordshire, aged 80, Valentine Vickers Esq of Offley Grove, Staffordshire and Criggion, Montgomeryshire, and a magistrate for Staffordshire".[187] Julia Vickers died at Meretown House, near Newport, Salop, on the 1st January 1903, aged 88.

[186] *Eddowes Journal* 26 August 1846, p. 2

[187] *Wellington Journal* 23 November 1867, p. 1

THE DAVENPORTS AND LEICESTER-WARRENS

Davenport House in the 1930s from a collection in private hands

As the only child of Edmund Henry Davenport and his wife Margaret, Hilda Marguerite Davenport was the sole heir to the Davenport Estate. Marguerite's father should never, had things gone smoothly, have inherited the Estate, because he was the second son of William Sharrington Davenport and his wife, Catherine Louisa, nee Marindin. There were five children from this marriage:

- William Bromley, born 1836, died 6 November 1865, aged 29
- Louisa Marindin, born 1838, died 1853, aged 14
- Edmund Henry, born 1839, died 1890, aged 51
- William Davenport, born 1848, died 1916
- Charles Talbot Davenport, born 1848, died 1919

DAVENPORT   Davenport & Leicester-Warren

William Sharrington Davenport died on October 1st 1871 predeceased by his eldest son, William Bromley Davenport who had received his army commission in April 1854 as an ensign in the 62nd (Wiltshire) Regiment of Foot. While serving in the Crimean War, William Bromley received horrific injuries to his face during the battle of Sevastopol and as a result of his actions in battle was promoted to the rank of Lieutenant. His next posting was in Canada on garrison duties and in 1864 the regiment returned to England and was posted to Tregantle Fort, Plymouth. William Bromley was now a Captain but his war wounds had taken their toll causing brain damage and severe disfigurement. His already fragile mental health was exacerbated by the death of his mother in June 1865 and in November of that year, after an evening meal with his colleagues, he went to his room and shot himself. He was just twenty-nine years old.[188]

So it was that, on the death of his father, that Edmund Henry Davenport became the new squire of Worfield. Whether the young man wanted this position we will never know, but after staying in England in 1871 and 1872, presumably to sort out affairs of the Davenport Estate, he went to work on cattle and sheep ranches in Australia. This was a time when the likes of Ned Kelly and his gang put the fear of God into law-abiding citizens and when livestock rustling was commonplace. Readers of newspapers would be familiar with notices such as these:[189]

- "I hereby give notice that any person or persons interfering under any pretence whatever, with any of the cattle or horses on or belonging to the Cuerindi or Mundoway Runs will be prosecuted. 1873.

    E. H. Davenport Cuerindi"

- "This is to give notice that no-one has the slightest claim to any such cattle [branded double L at or on Manilla Station], and that the only person authorised to take possession or charge of them is E. H. Davenport, Esq., of CUERINDI. Any person found in unauthorised possession of the above branded cattle will be prosecuted with the utmost rigour of the law." August 1st 1873.

- "Anyone found trespassing (whether in pursuit of stock or not) on either the Cuerindi or Mundoway Runs without a WRITTEN ORDER from myself or GEO. FARQUHARSON Esq., will be prosecuted as the law directs." January 1874

When Worfield's squire left for Australia, Davenport was rented out to a man who had just returned from that continent, Theophilus Joseph Keene. The new tenant of Davenport had been a 'Shepherd King' of such power in Australia that one author referred to him as 'Theophilus the First'.[190] Keene worked as chief executive in partnership with Charles Hotson Ebden, managing 50,000 sheep on a sheep run of half a million acres in Victoria. The Davenport Estate must have seemed like a small garden by comparison. Fortunes were made from sheep and Ebden once said,"I fear I am becoming disgustingly rich". In 1867, Ebden died in Australia. His wife and children had been living in London and remained there, and his

---

[188] *Army & Navy Gazette*, 11 November 1865, pp.2,3.

[189] These newspaper cuttings were obviously kept by E. H. Davenport but there is no record of which newspapers they are from. The cuttings, of which the author has images, are in private hands.

[190] Rolf Boldrewood, *In Bad Company & Other Stories, Reedy Lake Station*, Macmillan 1903)

204

partner, Theophilus Keene returned to England. Ebden's widow fell in love with Keene and there must have been talk of marriage because Antoinette, one of Ebden's daughters begged her mother not to marry Keene until she was twenty-one. On reaching the age of her maturity in 1871, and perhaps inheriting the £20,000 left in her father's will, Antoinette, far from wishing her mother well in her proposed marriage, eloped with Theophilus Keene herself. They were married in Brussels. With a thirty-five year age gap, and the scandal of eloping with a man old enough to be her father, Davenport must have seemed the perfect bolt hole. In 1872, Antoinette Ebden Keene, the couple's first child was born. I assume the family must have remained at Davenport until 1875 when Edmund Henry Davenport returned from Australia. There is only one story which relates to Worfield, handed down through the family. "Having gone to seed after his exertions in Australia, Theophilus had become very fat, and one snowy evening (on occasion of a big party in his house, if I remember), when using the outside lavatory, he had to open the door and step outside to get his trousers back on; whereupon the layer of snow on the sloping roof slid off and deposited itself in his trousers."[191]

At this time, Edmund Davenport was still in Australia where he met his bride-to be, Margaret Ann Smith. They were married at St David's Cathedral, Tasmania in 1875. In the same year, the couple came to England to live at Davenport. The villagers were ecstatic about the return of the Squire and his wife.[192] Bunting and flags flew from every cottage and floral arches spanned the roads. One arch was even lit up at night by Chinese lanterns. As the couple arrived by carriage at Wyken, about half a mile from Davenport House, the old custom of 'drawing in state' was adopted. The horses were taken off the carriage "and about forty pairs of strong and willing arms - chiefly labourers on the estate - took the place of the horses to draw the carriage from that place, round by the old Wheel Gate and over the first entrance to Davenport. Here one minute's breathing time allowed a glimpse of the happy couple who were perfectly surrounded by an eager crowd of welcomers... Another start was made, and the procession, headed by the Bridgnorth Rifle Corps Band ... wended its way round the lovely drive which leads to the dear old home." Life must have been so different in Worfield from Australia and perhaps Edmund was in nostalgic mood when he sent a piece called "Moonlighting Cattle" for inclusion in the Parish Magazine. This appears in full at the end of this section.

On December 9th 1879 Edmund and Margaret Davenport's only child, Hilda Marguerite Davenport, was baptised privately at Davenport House and on the 21st July 1904 she married Cuthbert Leicester-Warren at St Peter's Church, Worfield. The happy couple drove from the Church to Davenport House, a short distance of about a quarter of a mile and the village was very much part of the celebrations. On the Friday after the wedding, Mrs. Davenport entertained 200 children and 50 parents to a party at Davenport. The schoolchildren presented a tortoiseshell and silver letter clip to the happy couple and the Mother's Union gave a Copeland candelabra. The newly-weds left Davenport for their new home in Cheshire and, whilst frequent visitors to Worfield, from now on Davenport would be their second home. Two

---

[191] Henry Sire, a descendant of Theophilus Keene, kindly supplied the details about Keene and the story from Worfield. He added that Theophilus moved to a house in Somerset in 1877.

[192] *Bridgnorth Journal*, 2 October 1875

children of the marriage survived to adulthood, Margaret Alice, born in 1904 who died in 1964, and John Leighton Byrne born in 1907 who died in 1975. The youngest child, Edmund Cuthbert was born in 1915 and died in 1917.

The parishioners of Worfield must have been delighted when Margaret Leicester-Warren, who had been brought up at Tabley, came to live in Worfield. For five years the couple lived at Burton Court, Chelsea and then, in 1938, they were given the tenancy of Lower Hall.

Margaret Leicester-Warren & Cuthbert, her father,
at Tabley, 1944 from a collection in private hands

In 1954 both Cuthbert Leicester-Warren and Hilda Marguerite died. The Reverend Stanley Moore, Vicar of Worfield, wrote in Worfield Parish Magazine:

"Within twelve months of her husband being laid to rest, Mrs. Leicester-Warren has been taken from us, to the great grief of her very large circle of friends and acquaintances. She was the patron of the living, and although she went away to live with her husband in Cheshire, Worfield always had a very secure corner in her heart, and she was so happy to come back for the remaining years of her life. Under her, Davenport became again in these latter years a centre of gracious living and generous hospitality.

With her vivaciousness and energetic manner we were apt to forget that she was an old lady, but I used to wonder sometimes, when she looked far from well, whether she ought really to have been in her place in Church. But she belonged to a generation who were taught to do their duty, cost what it may in personal feelings or human frailty, and she remains to me - as to a great number - a living memory of a gracious lady, a devout Christian and a loyal friend"

John & Margaret Leicester-Warren, Nancy Hatch, Hilda Leicester-Warren

MOONLIGHTING CATTLE
by Edmund Henry Davenport

It was a dry season - word of fear only known in its true meaning to an Australian squatter. The sun had licked up the few remaining spots of muddy water, scorched the grass, and turned everything but the bare earth to a sort of rusty blue. The plains, filled with great cracks and holes, and destitute of a vestige of any green thing, had been scraped and trodden by the starving sheep till they looked like fresh-dug flower beds and the thunderstorms which mocked us on the horizon every night, were only too sure signs that this sort of thing might last for months yet. What with the shepherds giving up their flocks in despair, or worse still, losing them for want of energy to walk round them, I had a hard time of it; night after night out riding one tired and starved horse after another, shifting sheep stations, sinking holes in the river-bed, trying to keep some life in the wretched stock that staggered and tottered along the dusty plains, followed by some cranky, dejected shepherd, whose whole soul was bent on the calculation of how soon his time would be up, and himself at liberty to go and drink his cheque at the public-house in the township two hundred miles off.

The wild cattle, brutes that had already lived long enough to have forgotten the hot iron on their sides, and that laughed to scorn all attempts to head them to the yard, had long been a nuisance on the run. They had by long impunity so increased that the scrubs round Mount Breakneck were full of them, and their numbers were always being recruited by stragglers from the quiet cattle of the place, which, in these dry times, often wandered a dozen miles from their own camps to look for better pasture, or followed the beds of the dried-up creeks, scraping up the sand in the faint hope of coming on water which, even in the worst season, is generally found running below.

It was just Christmas time, and in consequence steaming hot. The thermometer registered over 100 in the verandah of the "Coburn Humpy," or squatter's house, which, built of weather-board and raised from the ground on piles, was, except perhaps the huge wool-shed lower down the creek, the coolest place for many miles. We, that is the cattle overseer and myself, in our little bachelors quarters, had been trying in defiance of flies, mosquitoes, and the tarantula spiders that disported themselves on the rafters, to sleep all day, and to fancy that we were enjoying our Christmas; and, in default of anything else, had been brewing large jorums of lime-juice and water to drink the health of diverse people who were at that moment snoring peacefully beneath the bed-clothes under the influence of Christmas cheer at home, while big coal fires glowed in their bedrooms and the landscape was cold and white under its load of snow. Jack, after moralising on his hard fate, and describing the dances that his people always had on Christmas Eve, was suddenly brought back to a practical sense of the duties of this life, by the black bullock driver putting his head in at the window and saying, "Hi! plenty me been see um cattle! big fellow mob! that been come along o' the water this side little fellow myall scrub. I believe me and you go look out that fellow."

Now the gentleman who condescended to take our fat cattle at £4 per head, and who retailed them to the good people of Sydney at 4d per pound, had been grumbling fearfully about their quality lately, and had even threatened to transfer his custom to our next neighbour, between whom and us there was war and much chaff, so that a chance of getting a really prime lot for Christmas was not to be despised. And if, after we had got to them, they were found to be too wild to drive to market, that was the butcher's look-out - nay, might even put a pound or two into some of the very empty pockets of my mates and myself, for seeing them safe over the range which was the particular bane of all drovers, with its precipitous track, and the prickly scrub which ran right into the road. At least it was something to relieve the eternal monotony of counting two flocks of sheep, morning and evening, and we were equal to the occasion.

Springing off the bed and putting a spur on the right boot, while my mate put the other spur on his left - an ingenious and wholly Australian way of dividing our forces - and rolling up the sleeves of our, to say the truth, not very clean flannel shirts, we dispatched Quondong, our black friend, for the working horses, and making the courtyard re-echo to the sound of our stock whips gave the signal for the stock-men to turn out, put their blankets on their saddles, and with many growls and much lighting of pipes, swagger down to pick up something that had still a little flesh on its bones, to carry them to the camp we proposed making that night at Hungry Jacks' Gully, some eight or ten miles away.

The only water-hole accessible to the wild cattle was separated from the scrub by a mile of level plain, cut and gashed by the sun's heat into a thousand holes and fissures; and the cattle, as soon as darkness concealed their movements, used to steal across this, following stealthily in one another's wake like Indians on the war-path; and having drunk enough to last them till next night, would scamper back again across the plain till they gained the friendly shelter of the scrub; and these sorties into an enemy's country must at least have had the charm of excitement in them, as the least sound, such as the distant gallop of a mob of wild horses or a possum scuttling up a tree, was quite sufficient to entail a headlong *sauve qui peut* of about a mile at racing pace. The only thing to be done with these brutes, whose every faculty was sharpened by thirst and aided by the unnatural stillness of the bush, was to get a lot of, say a hundred, quiet cattle and post them inside the scrub down-wind, and do our best to drive all the wild ones into them, and then trust to luck and good horsemanship to keep them.

And so, in about an hour from the first alarm, we found ourselves well on to the plains driving our wretched "coachers," as they are called, before us by the last rays of a red lurid sun, which threatened to sink suddenly behind Mount Breakneck, and leave us to the mercy of the Southern Cross or any other friendly stars, to show us the way to where our little bushyard of strong saplings lay, far up in a secluded glen, as our base of operations.

Every man mounted on a stout little horse of about fifteen hands, in a big ring snaffle, blanket strapped across the saddle, quart pot and hobbles hanging behind, and short pipe in mouth, we rode along, keeping close to our rather refractory charge.

Crawling through the belt of myall, whose drooping branches fringed the scrub, and carefully threading the tall pines that lay behind - guided always by the black fellow, whose eyes seemed only to begin to be in their element as the darkness drew in, and who was mounted on an old white horse, celebrated in all that countryside for his high qualities in scrub-riding - we at last reached our little sapling yard, and throwing down the rails put our coachers inside; and after watching their attempts to knock it down or jump over till they found it was hopeless, we lit a fire behind, and putting on the quart pots in the ready blaze of small sticks & bark, made our frugal supper of tea, damper, and very salt beef. [Note: damper is an Australian soda bread cooked in the embers of a camp fire]

There were eight of us, all told: my mate Jack B-, the overseer, two stockmen, great authorities on all matters of bush life, three of those nondescript, straight-haired, slab-sided lads who seem to have been born in moleskin breeches and cabbage-tree hats, and who unite the most reckless courage on horseback with a calmness of philosophy, and a grim humour, only to be found in the backwoods of America or the Australian bush; your humble servant, myself, and last, but by no means least, Quondong the black tracker whose whole life was spent seeing things utterly insensible to a white man, the faintest trace of any living beast to him an open book to be read at the gallop. We drew lots with pieces of stick as to who should keep awake, walk round the yard occasionally, and wake the rest of the party when the moon rose. Close at hand two possums kept up a wordy warfare, chattering like two cats; every now and then the faint cry of the "Morepork," the Australian night cuckoo, came softly out of the intensely black scrub behind me; while far away in front, through a gap in the pine trees, I could see the Mulally Plain stretching into the distance.

Having secured and saddled up our bones as quietly as possible, we threw aside the slip-rails of our yard, and let the coachers draw out, led and kept back by Quondong, and went silently down a mile or two to where the myall again began to fringe the edge of the plain. Here we stationed our two boys in as open a place as we could find, behind a thick patch of prickly 'mulga' and leaving the cattle in their charge, followed each other silently along the outer edge of the scrub, the trees still keeping us in the shadow of the moon's slanting rays.

Presently we came to one of the beaten tracks used by the wild cattle on their midnight expeditions to the water; and Quondong, jumping down and carefully examining the recent hoof marks, informed us that a mob had only just gone down, amongst which several large tracks showed the presence of the much desired fat bullocks.

Silence was now the word; our hobble chains were tightly secured (they should have been left in camp) so they should not rattle, and even our pipes were put out so that the cattle, whose noses get as keen as a red deer's, should suspect nothing till we had time to see them first, and form our plans for surrounding them.

Suddenly a halt, and a few hurried words from old Jack, and we found ourselves within a couple of hundred yards of a mob, that had already heard us, and were now altogether in a close ring with their heads up, waiting for the boldest to begin his dash to the scrub.

Now was our time. Sitting close to our saddles and cramming our hats on our heads, we darted at them in single file and, ringing them up as close as we could jam them together, set them galloping in a circle contrary to our own so they didn't know in which direction the scrub lay. Every now and then one would charge headlong out of the dense mass, but by the time he made his mind up which horseman to attack, another would have taken its place, the superior speed of our horses enabling us to keep the pace up in a much larger circle than the cattle could manage; and yet we almost brushed their horn in our mad gallop, and still kept circling on in the half-light, looking neither to the left nor the right but only intent on keeping our circle unbroken.

I know many exciting things in life - the first start from a cover …, with a good fox running straight, and a jealous field all riding for a start - the last few yards of a long and weary stalk to a royal stag, when your hand trembles, and a hot and cold perspiration breaks out all over you alternately - the finish of a well rowed boat race; but I can confidently recommend to anyone who has never tried it, the excitement that springs from a knowledge that the slightest mistake of your horse will bring an infuriated mob of cattle over your devoted head, while you still keep galloping madly after a flying figure whose hat, blown back off his head, flaps and flaps in front of you, with his head down, and himself sticking to the saddle like wax, his little horse scattering the black earth behind him; and by your side a moving panorama of snorting heads and flashing eyes, with a rattle of the long horns that would instantly be down on you, if you allowed them a moment's breathing time.

But this cannot last; the pace is too good, and Jack's wary eye has already shown him that the cattle, for the present at all events, are his own. With a dexterous sweep he puts himself at the head of the mob, and without once stopping to form line, we seem to fall by instinct into our places, and by the light of the moon, now rising in all its glory, thunder across the plain towards the coachers looking like an army of phantoms, as no one speaks, and no sound is heard but the steady gallop of our game little horses and the heavy breath of our captives, that find the pace a little too hot for them. But they have not time to stop. Before we can realise it we are upon the tame cattle, which have silently brought as near to us as possible the boys in charge, and, shifting round the other side, we await the charge of the newcomers, that often try to force their way straight through the little herd, and break away on the other side; but here the coachers themselves come to our assistance. Uneasy at being off their own camp, and thoroughly out of temper with the whole thing, they meet the charge of the strangers gallantly, and with hoarse grumblings, close round them till, what with the confusion of their ideas, and their curiosity as to what has brought all these other beasts on to their domain, they give it up as a bad job, and in half an hour's time are a mile or two from their own haunts, and ready to act as coachers for fresh victims.

And now, having recovered our equanimity, we scrutinise our captives, and find ten fat bullocks among them - old rascals that have lived with impunity through a life longer than is appointed to bullocks, and whose hides bear a big "A.T." the brand of a previous owner.

I think I need not describe all the expeditions we made that night - how "Scrub Bill" and his mate Tommy both got falls in the treacherous melon-holes and how, my girth breaking suddenly, I found myself sitting disconsolately on the plain, with a good pigskin saddle between my legs, and the tail of old "Schemer" that had carried me so well, vanishing in the dark, to the sound of many trampling hoofs. Every raid we made into the enemy's country was successful, and we found ourselves masters of some seventy or eighty beasts, which we now had to steer to the station. Cattle driving has a peculiar charm. The old moss-troopers, who used to scour the border country for cattle, as they pricked along with their spears a good fat lot, belonging to some Northumbrian farmer, must have felt much the same as we did, warily watching our hard-won charge; although we indeed had stock whips instead of spears, a decided advantage for cattle driving, for it would take a good long spear to get within reach of an Australian scrubber.

All round us were troops of wild mares and foals, in much the same state as the cattle, in companies of twenty or thirty together, each constituting the harem of some old horse, that would allow them to approach within two hundred yards of us, and then dashing in between, with his long main and tail flying in the wind, would round them up and drive them before him like a flock of sheep, stopping every now and then to trot a little nearer to us, and snort, and strike the ground in defiance of our steeds.

And now away in the distance we see the dim shadowy line of the head-station creek-trees, raised by the mirage above the line of the true horizon, and looking like a faint cloud hanging in mid air. Lower and lower it drops as we approach, till it joins the earth, and the huge zinc roof of the woolshed begins to glitter in the rays of the sun.

In another half-hour the massive rails of the stock yard, closing behind our charge, give us good security for their safe keep; and breakfast, with its hot tea and fried steaks makes up for our frugal supper of the night before. There! it looks simple on paper, but let me tell you if you have a tolerable seat on a horse, have as many spare necks as other people, and want to combine amusement with profit, there are worse ways of spending a night than "moonlighting cattle."[193]

E. H. Davenport

---

[193] The original, which I have photographed, is in private hands

THE BISHOP FAMILY
By
Geoff Tomlinson

Anne & John Bishop

Henry Tomlinson, Harry to his friends, was born on September 25th 1908 at Davenport, Worfield, where his maternal grandfather, John Bishop, was the Head Gardener. His grandmother, Ann, assisted the cook, Mrs Rogers, in Davenport House's kitchen. Harry's grandfather, John Bishop was born in Shifnal in 1840. In 1862, in Stockton church, he married Ann Thomas from Wren's Nest, Linley, in the parish of Astley Abbotts. Ann's father, William Thomas, was a stone mason. Sadly, while restoring the steeple at a church in Old Swinford in 1836, he fell and was killed; he was just forty-five years old. Ann's mother was in service for George Whitmore, presumably at Apley Park. John and Ann set up home in Stockton, where John was gardener to the local vicar. Over the next fourteen years they produced nine children, after which they moved to Davenport. The Head Gardener's cottage at Davenport was situated close to Davenport House and adjacent to the wonderfully productive walled garden, where peaches and apricots covered the south-facing wall. It was John Bishop's task to supervise his substantial team of gardeners to ensure a continuous supply of fresh fruit and vegetables for the tenants of Davenport House: Mr. & Mrs. H. Reginald Cooke and their son Vincent.

John and Anne Bishop's eldest son, Thomas, became a marine engineer; he was apprenticed in Liverpool in the mercantile marine, later moving to Cowes on the Isle of Wight, to serve on Lord Ashburton's yacht White Ladye. After service as Chief Engineer on other yachts belonging on Lord Ashburton, he eventually became the Chief Officer on Sir Thomas Lipton's 1,240 ton yacht Erin, a position he held for eighteen years. In this role he travelled the world

212

until, in 1915, when the Erin was commandeered by the British government, heavily armed and renamed as the Aegusa. After dangerous trips to Archangel, the ship was moved to the Mediterranean where, while hunting for submarines in 1916 it was torpedoed and sunk. Six crewmen were drowned but Thomas survived, only to die as a result of the trauma a year later in June 1917.

Eng. Lt. Tom Bishop 1863-1917

Thomas left a widow, the daughter of Captain Tom Lashmar RNR, and seven children; one, Basil, only a few months old. Thomas was buried in Cowes, where the funeral was attended not only by friends and relatives but representatives of the Osborne Lodge of Freemasons, Cowes Conservative Club, senior naval officers and members of Cowes yachting fraternity.

The second son, Edward (1864-1956) emigrated to South Africa in 1902 and eventually settled in Port Elizabeth. There were three daughters: Anne, Marion and Sarah-Louisa. Marion and Sarah-Louisa married and moved away from Worfield. Two boys died while still babies. John & Ann Bishop's youngest son, Walter, was killed while fighting in the Boer War.

Walter was baptised on 16th September 1877 at Stockton, Salop. In 1891 he was the only child still living at home and, at the age of 13, was working as a gardener's assistant, presumably with his father at Davenport House. In the Boer War he served as a Private with the 10th Hussars, probably arriving in South Africa in December 1899. In this letter to his parents reassuring them that he is well one can't help feeling that they would have feared for their son's safety.

3959 B Squadron, 10th Hussars,
S. African F Force Kimberley
Monday Feb 21st 1900
My Dear Father & Mother,

You will be pleased to hear I am safe & sound at Kimberley. In my last I told you we were making a quick move somewhere. Well we started due south from Modder, did about 25 miles & halted at a farm for the night, next day we marched about 15 miles - these two days we were rather badly off for water, but as the Doctor pronounced the pool water alright we were only too glad to drink with our horses. I cannot tell you the particulars, so well as the papers will, for I almost lost count of the days.

We had a sharp skirmish with the Boers at Modder River but when they saw our number they made off like the wind leaving several loaded wagons behind. We stayed here for rest - 24 hours & as each man carried his own rations we were glad to look around for something to eat, they had left some flour behind so we got a sack of that in the lines & each tried his hand at making cakes. I had a tin of Treacle in my wallet so made a dumpling in my mess tin with that. It didn't rise much but was a change from biscuit, being thirsty the biscuits wouldn't go down at all, one would last me all day. By this time we were within a days march of Kimberley, expecting a big fight, and we were not mistaken, for soon 6 Boer guns were banging into our Artillery, ours soon began to slacken their fire & now came the move that astonished the Boers. The dash had to be done & Gen. French meant to do it.

The two Cavalry Brigades moved forward & made across the open country between the Boer positions. We had to gallop over four miles most of the way under rifle fire & didn't the bullets whizz about, we (the 10th) were in the centre - its wonderful that none of us were hit but several horses were hit including mine. I heard the bullet hit, but thought it was in my saddle pack. She carried me well out of danger & then I found it had gone clean through her one thigh. We halted for the night just outside Kimberley. Then the two brigades moved off after the Boers up the Free State. I had to stay here, as it was not safe to take the horse, though it is quite healed up again & she is not lame. I was lucky wasn't I ? Those whose horses fell had to run leaving everything. I haven't heard the casualties, but don't think they were heavy. I believe the Kimberley people could not believe their own eyes when they saw us coming over the Veldt, there was great rejoicing when it became known who we were.

They expect the railway will be open today so hope to post this. They couldn't have held out much longer. It's a sight to see the blacks come round the camps for dead horses, they had one of ours this morning that died in the night & they carried it all off like beef, one said he didn't mind it, for it was just like beef. Yesterday we had a heavy thunderstorm & having no tents everything was soon wet through, that made it rather a miserable night for us.

The town sent out a wagon laden with tanks of soup for us, goodness knows what it was made of but we had our fill of it, for it tasted very nice. It is a hard matter to say when we shall see our regiment again, for they must be some way up the States by this *(sic)*. I shall not be able to stamp this letter for those you sent me are in my kit bag at Modder River, the bit of paper I've carried in my haversack about 100 miles. I am very glad I brought it. Please let Brothers and Sisters know I am well. I hope yourselves keep quite well.

Walter Bishop was wounded at the battle of Diamond Hill on 11th June 1900 and died on 19th June at Pretoria, South Africa, aged 22. He is commemorated on the Boer War memorial in Worfield church.

He was awarded the following: Queens SA Medal and Clasps. Johannesburg (31 May 1900), Diamond Hill (11-12 Jun 1900), Relief of Kimberley (15 Feb 1900), Orange Free State (28 Feb-31 May 1900), Natal (11 Oct 1899-17 May 1900).

Walter George Bishop

Anne was the fifth of the nine Bishop children. She left Davenport aged twenty-one and moved to Nuneaton to help her brother Edward's wife look after the children. After a few years she moved to Aston to help her sister, Sarah-Louisa, take care of her offspring. During this period she met John Richard Tomlinson with whom she quickly produced four children. Early in 1908, aged thirty-eight and pregnant, she was suddenly widowed. In dire financial straits she returned to her parents' home at Davenport where Harry was born. Initially, he was a sickly child, however it is reported that a diet of sherry and raw eggs soon helped him regain his health. Harry started at Worfield School in 1914, when Mr. F. Turner was the Headmaster. Mr. Turner was also the choir-master at the church, so all the good singers were recruited into the choir - or else! The first hour of each school day was spent on prayers, hymns and scripture. "Sums" followed until the break, after which it was Composition time. At midday Harry would collect a loaf from the village shop and then run up through the Park where his mother would have his lunch waiting. Many afternoons were spent marching, drilling and learning how to salute; the Great War dominated everyone's minds. Learning by rote was also a vital part of one's education and even in his nineties Harry could still entertain by quoting great chunks of Shakespeare. Digging the Headmaster's garden and keeping it tidy was also considered a necessary part of a country schoolboy's training. Conveniently, the Headmaster's house was immediately adjacent to the school. Holidays and weekends were spent roaming around the Park, looking for birds' nests and collecting firewood. Harry's Grandfather didn't encourage him to do any gardening, though he did cultivate a patch where he grew lettuce to feed his pet rabbits. Harry would chat with Mr Rogers from Bromley, busy around the estate scratching a living from catching moles. Mr Rogers was also noted as the local pig killer and dresser, for most country folk kept a pig in those days. In the summer tennis courts had to be prepared, with John Bishop supervising the proceedings. A pony would be fitted with leather shoes before towing a mowing machine, carefully guided by one of the gardeners, walking between the shafts. The court would be marked out and then the young gentry would descend. The butler kept everyone supplied with soft drinks while Harry was kept busy retrieving tennis balls. At the other end of the social spectrum, also during the summer months, gangs of people would descend on the stream at the foot of the Park, where the watercress grew. They would load up their sacks before struggling back to the Wheel for the return bus journey to Wolverhampton, no doubt supplementing a meagre income by supplying the market.

Four of the five Tomlinsons: Annie, Norah, Claude &
front right, Harry

DAVENPORT The Bishop Family

Harry's older sister, Annie, eventually left home and went into local Gentleman's Service. In 1921 she married Stanley Botley and had a daughter René. In 1925 Stanley was working on the railway line when he was hit by a train and killed. Annie married Worfield resident, Harold (Tan) Onions in 1929 and had two sons, Douglas and Derek. Derek and his wife Jean were well-known Bridgnorth florists. Harry's sister Nellie moved to the Wirral and Norah, after training at Radbrook College, to Cross Houses near Shrewsbury.

Annie's wedding to Tan Onions in 1929 – Harry, the Best-Man at the groom's side. There are many well-known local residents including: Jack & Nellie Wilcox; Charles Onions; Charles Morrel; Doug Clarke: Jack Williamson; Crick Onions; Kate Onions (Minshull)

Harry's brother Claude remained in the area all his life, when he left school he went to work at Enville Hall, then owned by Lady Grey. Later he moved to Rowley Farm and then the Sonde, from where he was married. Mabel, his bride, was born in Bishops Castle, they had three daughters: Joan, Margaret and Rosemary. Later Claude and Mabel moved into the old Rectory, from where they served cream teas for several years to the many tourists who flocked to see the wonderful church of Saint Peter. Claude was a bit of a dare-devil in his youth and once, when the church spire was being repaired and the workmen had gone home, he clambered to the very top, where he clung waving to his pals far below! Towards the end of his working life Claude helped Robin Evans at Yonder Wyken, while living in a cottage at

DAVENPORT The Bishop Family

Roughton. In their eighties both he and his wife, Mabel, moved to West Wales, next door to one of their daughters and it was here, after a long life, they both died.

Each year Mrs Cooke would hold, at Davenport, a Christmas party for the school children, until the family eventually moved to Dallicote Hall, taking over from Major Gilroy. There would also be an annual outing to the seaside. On one trip to Rhyl the children were seated on benches on the back of one of Gatt's lorries, a tarpaulin fastened over the top, in case it rained. Gatt's was a firm in Hilton dealing with poultry and eggs, there were two sons Sydney and Charlie. The lorry-load of excited children was accompanied by the Headmaster on his motorbike, his wife ensconced in the sidecar. Every twenty miles or so the driver of the lorry would stop and beg a bowl of water from a nearby cottager, to throw over the wheels to cool the brakes! No Health & Safety laws to be troubled with in those times.

Harry was present when the Great War memorial was opened at the edge of the village, opposite the Davenport Hall entrance. He was a member of the choir that sang as a part of the ceremony. The list included his uncle, Tom Bishop - and by coincidence the uncle of his wife to be - one Harry Price. Poor Harry, trained as a sniper was killed by one in 1916, aged twenty-three, on a desolate Belgian field.

In July 1922, aged fourteen, Harry left school and was sent to work on Mr Chester's farm at Rowley. He walked the two miles from Davenport to Rowley each day, arriving in time for the 06.30am start. He carried a shoulder bag, known as a Frail, containing a sandwich and a bottle of tea, wrapped in a sock. He was put in charge of an elderly heavy carthorse called Topper. The huge collar was almost more than Harry could lift but a relationship developed and the old stallion would lower his head to make it easier! The old horse quickly got short of breath when harrowing or haymaking, so Harry would let him stop and recover and the relationship grew deeper. The long working day continued until five o'clock and on a Saturday until noon. At the end of work on Saturday the men would gather at the farmhouse door until Mrs Chester would appear in her white apron. Her gathered-up apron contained the pay-packets. The Waggoner was paid first, then the Cowman, the Stockman and finally Harry; this was 1923 - eleven shillings for a fifty-eight hour week!

Harry had only been working at Rowley for three months when Mrs. Chester told him, as she gave him his pay, one Saturday lunchtime, that he would not return on Monday, as Mr. Clarke wanted him to work in the village shop! Neither he nor his mother was consulted, indicating that in 1923 feudalism was alive and well in Worfield! Harry had very mixed feelings at the thought of longer hours for the same pay, the only upside was the carrot of being able to drive a model T van Mr. Clarke was buying. The village shop was also a bakery and so a great deal of heavy lifting was involved, especially when collecting sacks of sugar, tea and flour from Bridgnorth railway station. When he was seventeen Harry was let loose on the van - no lessons, no test. Soon he was a familiar sight, as he made deliveries all around the area.

Harry's grandmother died at Davenport in 1914 and was buried in Worfield churchyard. John Bishop continued to live at Davenport until his death in 1924 aged eighty-four, he had been a resident at Davenport for thirty-five years.

DAVENPORT The Bishop Family

In 1929 Mr. Clarke died leaving his widow and two sisters to run the business. About that time Harry met two directors of Boswell Builders who used to come to Davenport to shoot pheasants and to fish. From them Harry learned of a huge building project in North Wales and that they were short of drivers. So Harry talked himself into a job and left the shop. He collected a brand new lorry from Guys in Wolverhampton and set out for Penmaenmawr. Harry worked on the project for six months before returning to Worfield where he did odd jobs: painting, beating for the pheasant shooters and digging graves. One day while filling in a grave, one of the relatives of the deceased said that the Pearl Assurance needed an agent in the area. Next day Harry went to Bridgnorth and talked himself into a new part-time job. This needed transport, so Harry purchased a motorcycle and toured the area collecting premiums. This soon developed into a full-time job and he married the young lady whom he had met dancing at the Recreation Room and moved to Much Wenlock. In 1935 their first son was born and in 1939 the family moved to a brand new house in Victoria Road, Bridgnorth, where Harry remained for the next sixty- five years.

Harry's wife Ivy Price was the third child of Charles and Mary Price's nine children. Charles was born at Tettenhall Wood in 1880 but later the family moved to Hallon, where they lived close to the blacksmith's forge. Charles was always keen on horses and later became groom to Lord Berwick. Later he moved to Bickford, near Wheaton Aston and it was here that Ivy was born. When he was drafted into the army, Charles moved his family to Penkridge. He saw service in France and Belgium but thankfully returned home unscathed in 1918.

By this time Ivy had been sent to Bridgnorth to be brought up by Charles' sister Fanny and her husband Wilf Overton. They had no children of their own. Ivy attended St. Leonard's School, where she was a top student and desperately wanted to be a teacher. The Overtons would not or could not find the money for the Grammar School and so at fourteen Ivy was sent to Waterloo House to train as a tailor. She remained at Waterloo House until it was eventually sold. During the war, like so many Bridgnorth housewives, she worked at the RGD. [Note: Radio Gramophone Development.] Later in life she taught dressmaking and tailoring at the Bridgnorth College. Ivy was an enthusiastic member of Oldbury Women's Institute for many years, up until her death in 1998, aged 89 years. Charles Price's sisters remained in the area, one of them, Annie, married Joseph Plant and lived at Davenport. After their demise, their son, Eric Plant, continued to live at Davenport.

In 1939, as the war began in earnest, Harry was drafted into the Police Reserve and he worked out of the Bridgnorth police-station in Whitburn Street until 1946. He returned to the Pearl Assurance after the war but later transferred to the Prudential, with whom he remained until his retirement in 1969. Harry and Ivy had a second son, John, born in 1949.

During his retirement Harry was a keen member of the Bridgnorth Bowling Club and served as President. Harry died in 2004, five months before his 96th birthday. His ashes are buried in Worfield churchyard, a stone's-throw away from the house where he lived as a teenager - almost full circle.

219

CAMP DAVENPORT
By
Mick Powis

About the Author

After being educated at Coleg Harlech, Aberystwyth University and Warwick University, Mick Powis's career encompassed a variety of roles as engineer, trade union official, social worker and part-time Open University Lecturer. He has written many magazine and newspaper articles on a range of historical subjects including two books on military history, "Zeppelins over the Midlands," (Pen and Sword 2016) and "Defeat of the Zeppelins," (Pen and Sword 2018) as well as a chapter on the Zeppelin Raids, in "Wolverhampton's Great War 1914-1921," edited by Quintin Watt (Wolverhampton Society 2019).

Camp Davenport in Worfield Shropshire was one of dozens of tented camps used in 1944 as transit camps for troops waiting to join the Allied Armies in Normandy. Generally troops taking part in the invasion on D-Day were based on the south coast near the embarkation ports around Southampton. Troops due to land later were housed further north. Most men of the US Third Army, which was not due to land until July or August 1944 after the capture of Normandy, tended to be based in the English Midlands or Wales, housed in temporary summer camps, though others were billeted, with civilians in towns. Like the Roman Army, the US Army built its camps to a standard pattern. There were streets of six-man tents; with more permanent building generally Nissan huts for the administrative block, guardhouse, mess halls, latrines, showers, and cookhouses. Most camps were erected in the grounds of stately homes or large country houses.

There were 21,600 American troops in Shropshire in May 1944, mostly in camps such as the one at Davenport. There were camps at Stanley Hall, near Bridgnorth, Chyknell House, Coton Hall, and Kinlet Hall, near Cleobury Mortimer. There is a full list in the book, *The U.S. Army in South East Shropshire 1944*, by Adrian and Neil Turley. They also have produced a similar work, *The U.S Army at Camp Bewdley and locations in the Wyre Forest Area. 1943-1945*.

A standard camp had a capacity of about 1,250 men; an infantry regiment or artillery battalion. Davenport was a double camp taking about 2,500 men. As access was fairly good, and the ground firm, Davenport tended to be used by artillery battalions which had tanks and guns, and heavier vehicles.

I went around the site in 2004 with Clyde Kennedy, from Granada, Colorado, who I have known for over 20 years. He married a Wolverhampton woman, and they used to spend four to six weeks every two years with relatives in Wolverhampton. As he is now about 95 I'm not sure if they will come again, but he was able to remember much of the layout of Camp Davenport. As you go up the drive to Davenport House, you will see a downward sloping dip on the hillside making what appears to be a natural amphitheatre. This is where the troops of the 90th infantry

Division were addressed by Generals Patton and Bradley. If you go to the Cricket Club you will see a grass mound, that looks like a castle motte. It was, in fact, a bullet stop used for rifle practice. According to Clyde, a lot of material was buried there when the 90th Division left, so it may be an archaeological treasure trove. It you walk towards Davenport House from there, you can still see the remains of some of the concrete bases of the Nissen huts. The soldiers lived in tents to the side of the buildings whilst the area from the cricket ground to Davenport House was used to park the tanks, guns, and vehicles. The entrance gate was where the present-day entrance to the farmyard now is. Most of the camps were built by general service troops from December 1943 to March 1944, and from April 1944 troops destined for the Normandy landings were moved in. Camp Davenport housed the artillery battalions of the 90th Infantry Division, the 343rd, 344th, 345th and 915th Field Artillery Battalions. It was some time in April 1944 when the soldiers of Camp Davenport were joined by those in local camps, to hear an address by Generals Bradley and Patton. The inmates of Camp Davenport moved out in early May 1944 to camps in South Wales, near to their embarkation point.

Camp Davenport was then used to house troops of the 135th Combat Engineer Battalion, the 274th Armoured Field Artillery Battalion and the 741st Field Artillery Battalion between early July and mid August 1944. They were taken by truck to Southampton and Weymouth and shipped across to Normandy, to chase the retreating German Army to the German border.

Jim Duffy at the Eagles Nest

A FRIENDLY TIGER
by
Mick Powis

On the 14 July 1944 three 19 year old American G.I's got out of a truck in Queen Square, in the centre of Wolverhampton. They had arrived the day before at their transit base, Camp Davenport in Worfield, Shropshire. Hundreds of American troops were transported every evening to the centre of Wolverhampton, the nearest large town, for a night out. The journey of the three friends from Cincinnati, Ohio, Jim Duffy, Joe Corry and Dick Barth had started over a year before when they were drafted into the 274th Armoured Field Artillery Battalion, part of General Patton's Third Army. They were part of Operation Bolero, the invasion of Europe after D-Day. The West Midlands were a huge transit area for hundreds of thousands of Allied troops. As the Normandy Beachhead expanded they were to be shipped to France.

As young men do, Joe, Jim and Dick decided their first priority was to find a pub. They followed a crowd of other soldiers down Worcester Street, but found all the pubs in the town centre, like the Gifford Arms, were full of G.I's. They walked right out of town until they found a quiet pub. It was the Tiger Inn, in Church St, near St Johns Church. For the rest of his life Jim Duffy remembered it as if it were yesterday. He said: "We weren't there very long, but it was long enough to really get to know some of the folks. At times we could hardly understand the Black Country accents of the older men, but could easily talk with the women". They felt so much at home that they returned almost every night during the next month. Jim said: "We would sit around a long table in the tap room with everyone else. We met a lot of friendly people, but I guess some didn't like our habit of drinking too fast. The pub was rationed on liquor and I think they only got their spirit allowance every two weeks". The three G.I's made friends with a number of people and visited their homes in the Great Brickkiln Street area. Looking back it is easy to see what happened, the Tiger Inn became a home from home for them. Many , like Jim, Joe and Dick were homesick teenage boys, but in that summer of 1944 they grew into men as they were trained to do what soldiers do, to kill and be killed.

Late at night on 16th August, the 274th Armoured Field Artillery left for Southampton, to be shipped to Utah Beach two days later. The job of the 274th was to provide artillery support for the thrusting tank columns of Patton's Army. Jim, Joe and Dick, the temporary regulars at the Tiger Inn, never returned to Wolverhampton. A month after leaving the pub, Dick Barth was killed in action. On the 24th September 1944 he went out on a patrol to repair the telephone wire to an artillery observation position forward of the front line near Metz. The patrol was hit by mortar fire. Dick was killed and many soldiers seriously wounded. When the patrol returned it didn't diminish Dick's heroism or the grief his friends felt for him to know the whole thing was an example of what the G.I's called SNAFU:- situation normal all fouled up. The observation post had been pinpointed by the Germans, making it defunct and dangerous for anyone approaching it. It had been abandoned and its telephone removed. That message never got to the officer who sent the patrol out. Richard Barth is buried in the American Military Cemetery at St Avold, France.

Jim and Joe remained friends in Ohio for the rest of their lives and they often talked about the good times in the Tiger Inn. Joe Corry died peacefully in 2003. Jim Duffy died a few years ago aged 86. For most of his life he was a stalwart of the 274th Veterans Association. He spent a lot of time each day on the internet, facilitating communication between members of the Battalion and people interested in its history. I got to know him in 2002 and we corresponded several times a week. I was lucky enough to visit him a few years before he died. He said that, "Everyone from the 274th who spent time in Wolverhampton remembered it with affection". His memory was that Wolverhampton was warm and almost idyllic. He read the local news paper, the Express and Star, most days on the internet. For him the month he spent in Wolverhampton, was perhaps the end of his youth, he went from home from home to the horrors of war.

Today there can be very few people in England who remember Jim, Joe and Dick. It is a sad fact that while the presence of American troops is part of the history of most British towns, few people, know much about them. To some there were only three things wrong with them, they "were overpaid, over-sexed, and over here. To others they were kind, interesting and exciting. For the most part they enjoyed the temporary pleasures of the pub, the dance hall and snatched romance.To most they were a large anonymous group, known to the locals as the 'Yanks', waiting to go over, never to return. After they left people knew little of their battles, little of their history. For some they left a more personal impression. Some married local girls, some left illegitimate children. Some older people remember the large numbers around in 1944, along with Dutch, Polish and Empire troops. The Yanks were by then the largest group, they were for most people a ubiquitous group. People may have known individuals; they knew nothing about the units they served in, of what happened when they 'went over' to France. Many people have seen films like 'the Longest Day' or 'Patton' or 'Saving Private Ryan'. Yanks based in or near many English towns took part in some of the actions depicted; hardly anyone knows which.

Finding the whereabouts of US troops in Britain is not easy as there are few records. During 1944 there were over a million men stationed all over the U.K. Many were stationed in temporary camps, or billeted in private homes. Camp Davenport a tented camp in the grounds of a stately home is perhaps typical of the thousands of temporary camps. Because of wartime secrecy, units were rarely identified in the local press. There is no central record of the location of units. The Imperial War Museum which has masses of wartime records has very little on the location of individual US units.

The small mobile artillery unit based at Camp Davenport, the 274th Armoured Field Artillery Battalion was an altogether unremarkable unit, its wartime role was to provide artillery support for other units.For this reason it took part in many of the most notable and savage battles fought by the US Army in the European Theatre of Operations. It was very difficult to find out about this small non-divisional unit. The unit appears quite literally in the footnotes of other works. The unit history proved to be invaluable in my research. Entitled: "Longneck. A History of the 274th Armoured Field Artillery Battalion 15 April 1943 to 2 September 1945," it was produced by a Battalion history committee, edited by Captain Jack K Morrison and privately published in Chicago in 1946. It is very well written, full of pathos and humour, as well as descriptions of war. It helped me understand the human element in what until then had been the plain facts of military history. There were hundreds of unit histories privately published just after the War. Soldiers awaiting demobilisation, probably with journalistic ambitions, were given the task of preparing unit histories. These were mainly intended for circulation to troops who had served in the unit. Very few are widely available. They are, however, invaluable for an understanding of the G.I.'s War. While they lack much detail about the wider tactical role of their units, they offer an insight into the personalities and feelings of the ordinary G.I., experiencing the mixture of horror and comradeship that was war.

M7 grenade launcher of the 274th Armoured Field Artillery Battalion 1945

The 274th Armoured Field Artillery Battalion was part of Patton's Third Army. It took part in the pursuit of the Germans from Normandy, the Lorraine Campaign, the relief of Bastogne and the crossing of the Rhine. It finished the war in May 1945, in Bavaria, just across the River Inn from Hitler's birthplace, Braunau am Inn. Tracing the path of these soldiers from Worfield to Austria helps us appreciate the part the Americans played in the war. Many gave their lives to help deliver the World from the evil of Nazism.

TOUGH OMBRES
by
Mick Powis

The Siegfried Line showing the tank defences known as 'dragons' teeth.'

Worfield Cricket Club in rural Shropshire epitomises Englishness. Although it is only ten miles from Wolverhampton and the Black Country, it is as pastoral as you can get. White-clad players gently compete in the grounds of Davenport House, a mansion built in the early years of the eighteenth century. On the other side of the trees you can see the spire of St Peter's, the parish church. The Union Flag blowing lazily from the flag pole adds to the feeling of timelessness.

In 1944 before D-Day, things were very different. The grounds of Davenport House were covered with Nissan huts and tents. Camp Davenport as it was known was home to over a thousand G.I's, along with their tanks, guns and trucks. The Stars and Stripes flew from the flagpole which was brought over in 1944 by the US 90th Infantry Division. That flagpole is now at Worfield Cricket Club, a link with the wartime past.

Camp Davenport was home for its three artillery battalions. The 90th Infantry was made up of troops drafted mainly from Texas and Oklahoma whose insignia was made up of the letters T and O, giving them the nickname, 'Tough Ombres'. The Division was in Worfield from March to May 1944 when, as part of Operation Bolero, the troops were moved to the South coast to embark for Normandy and the invasion of Europe.

In the main the soldiers time at Camp Davenport was the quiet time of their war. Most G.I's spent their evenings in Wolverhampton, taken there by convoys of trucks. The Express and Star has published the story of Clyde Kennedy, a Sergeant in the 90th and Marie Arrowsmith who met at a Civic Hall dance, married in Wolverhampton after the war, and moved to Clyde's home town in Colorado. They have now been married 70 years.

Clyde remembers one day at Camp Davenport very well. During the spring they had a visit from the top brass, General Omar Bradley, and the man none of them would ever forget, General George S Patton Junior. Patton was often called, though never to his face, 'Old Blood and Guts,' and his visit told them one thing; they would soon go to war.

General Patton

DAVENPORT

About 15,000 men assembled for Patton's speech . The staff officers from their base at King Edward's School in Birmingham, the 357th Regiment from Kinlet, the 358th Regiment from around Bewdley, and the 359th Regiment from around Leominster.

General Bradley spoke briefly and modestly but the star of the show was Patton. His speech was seemingly off the cuff, but actually was well rehearsed. Clyde Kennedy remembers it very well, "Not like anything we expected from a General, full of profanities, more like a football coach doing a team talk.

His last words were carefully calculated to make his audience appreciate their place in history. "You men can be grateful for one thing, in 30 years time when you have your grandson on your knee and he asks 'granddaddy what did you do in the great World War Two?' you won't have to cough, turn away and say,
'I shovelled shit in Louisiana'."

Lt. Bob Wittstruck with his Piper Cub, 'Cup Cake II

In the next year that may have seemed a very appealing option for many of the infantry men of the T O. The 90th Infantry was one of the few Divisions continuously in action from D-Day to VE-Day. Out of a paper complement of 14,000 men, it lost 21,371 killed wounded or missing in action. Clearly many of these were replacements sent to replace men already killed or wounded.

The Tough Ombres landed on Utah Beach, and fought through the Bocage of Normandy. They spent the autumn besieging and capturing the fortress city of Metz and helped defeat the Germans in the snow of the Battle of the Bulge. They broke through the Siegfried Line in the spring, and finally drove across Germany, liberating the concentration camp at Flossenburg on the way.

The 90th Division finished the war in Czechoslovakia near the city of Pilsen. There they met the Red Army. Clyde Kennedy remembers the Russians very clearly. He said "we shook hands, they hugged us, and we slapped them on the back. We gave them cigarettes, they gave us vodka. We didn't speak each other's language but we got on well, like real comrades. It's funny the way history has worked out".

But history never guarantees happy endings. The late Alan Garner, a Wolverhampton councillor for many years, often told a story about his friendship with a soldier from the T and O. In 1944 when he was a teenager waiting to join the Army, he got talking to a young G.I called John Snead, perhaps just a year or two older than he was. He was very proud of his unit, saying 'people call us the Tough Ombres' John asked a favour. Before he left home his mother had made him promise to write to tell her where he was but military censorship prevented him from doing this. He asked Alan to write to her, in a town called Alamogordo in New Mexico. He did, and a few weeks later got a letter back thanking him for his kindness.

Alan always remembered John Snead and he in his turn remembered Alamogordo because it sounded strange and exotic. A year or so later the world knew about Alamogordo because it was the nearest town to the site of the first Atom bomb test.

Some 50 years later while doing research which led to this article, Alan and I decided to try to find out what happened to John Snead. Using modern technology it only took a few days to find out that on 20th March 1945, PFC Snead of the 358th Regiment of the 90th Infantry Division was killed near Mainz in Germany. He was one of the last of the 3,871 members of the T and O killed in action. He was wounded in combat, but killed when the ambulance jeep taking him to hospital was fired on by a German patrol, even though the war was clearly lost. Probably the Germans were teenage boys too.

2004

DAVENPORT PRISONER OF WAR CAMP

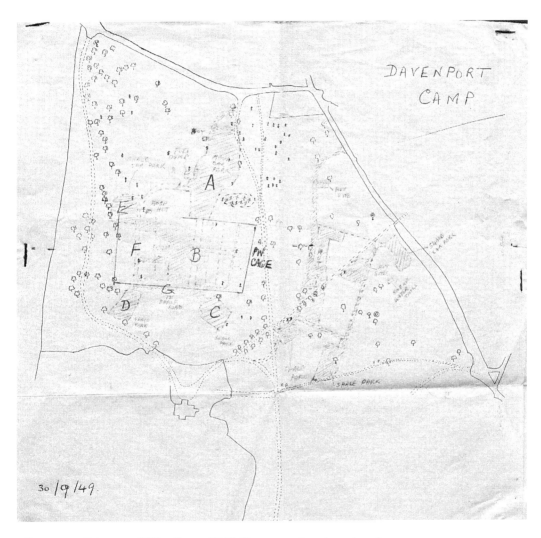

Davenport Prisoner of War Camp 1949. Document in private hands.

THE WORFIELD I KNEW from 1943 to 1966
By
Eileen Tracey

Sonde Farm

I am proud to say that I am an old Worfrunian. I lived at Sonde Farm until my parents retired to live in the village of Quatford although their hearts were always in Worfield. They are buried in Worfield Cemetery, but that's another story.

I remember before I started school, going with my father on his milk round. The villagers left out their milk jugs; with weighted muslin netting over them. There was no such thing as Pasteurised Milk. I grew up on untreated cow's milk. One of Father's calls was to the POW

Camp at Hallon. I don't think the POW's were locked up as I remember them coming to the farm for binder twine which they dyed different colours and made it into slippers.

Lt. Gen. Sir Oliver Leese was my nearest neighbour. At about the age of four I helped him paint some of the Bailey bridge over the Worfe. I remember him sending me home to get an apron which my mother made out of an animal feed bag, BOCM's best - nothing wasted. I remember the paint was dark green, army colour. Before Sir Oliver had the Bailey bridge built, there was only one way a vehicle could get to Sonde Farm; over the cricket field. This was a very useful alternative road when the River Worfe was in flood. The footbridge was a rickety old wooden one. Many a time on my way to school I had the privilege of seeing Kingfishers fly under that bridge.

Sir Oliver and Lady Leese used to give local children Christmas Parties. Every child was given a gift. The Revd. Stanley Moore would hide in the fireplace dressed as Father Christmas to hand out presents. One Christmas we had a coach trip to a pantomime in Wolverhampton. When I caught Measles and was off school, Sir Oliver came to see me bearing gifts. He was such a kind man. Sir Oliver and Lady Leese travelled widely. How I wish I had taken more care of the postcards they sent me.

Worfield School and the Church were part of my life. The vicar, the Revd. 'Tom' Thompson was the first to admit girls into the choir, of which I was one. In summertime we went to either Hereford or Worcester Cathedral to take part in Evensong. Those were great days. The choirmaster Michael Lloyd always had individual packets of sandwiches and drinks for us. There was great excitement in Worfield village when the BBC recorded Evensong in 1969. I still have this recording on an LP.

I married John Tracey from Exeter. I wanted nothing more than to be married in Worfield Church, even though I no longer lived in the Parish. I left for the church from Crow Cottage. My dad had been Bell Captain for many years, and my brothers, sister-in-laws and nieces were involved with the church in one way or another. The choir and the bells were a wedding gift. John and I walked down the village street to our reception at the Dog, and villagers were standing on their doorsteps to wish us well. I have often wondered if any other bride and groom have walked down the street the way we did on that April afternoon.

Moving on to the twenty-first century. My husband was the first to suggest that I collect post cards of Worfield as a hobby. To date I have sixty-three postcards of the village and surrounding areas. These include the China Bridge, Chestnut Drive, the School with the Mill in the background, The Wheel Inn and Old Toll House, Lower Hall, and different ones of Worfield Main Street. I have one of Davenport House, which was posted in Canada. The sender tells the story of being in Worfield at the time of a big wedding with many bridesmaids. Could that have been Sir Oliver and Lady Leeses' wedding?

During the Second World War, as I have mentioned, Camp Davenport was used to house prisoners of war and one of the most exciting finds so far is a letter written on a pre-printed POW form. Found by an internet search, the letter had been sent by a Werner Schrimpt HA 112 119 from Satellite Camp, Worfield, Near Bridgnorth, Shropshire, England. Werner was writing to his Grandma and Mum and Dad. I had it translated, which was difficult as it was written in Old German. The letter is as follows:

"Today is the fourth Advent. I will now start this letter. Thank you very much for the last three letters. I had the letter from Belgium. Thank you very much. Letters dated 22, 23, 24. I received as well as Birthday letter. Number 1 Number 2. I have received. 3, 4 and 5 which you sent to Belgium, I also received a letter from Aunty Freda received on the 15/11. Also 2 post cards from Belgium. (I was told that Werner could have been interned in Belgium before coming to Worfield). He writes. I hope you will be ok. Elfreda it is clear to me she lives from money from us. Her letters were not clear, but I have written to her and I am waiting for an answer. That is all for today. She has written to him but it did not make sense to him. Unfortunately, this is not the last letter. Please write again."

This may have meant he was not yet free to go home in 1947. The date of the letter looks like this: am 14/1/47 The address on the letter was to Frau Klara Christiani, Erfurt, Thuringen, Thomasstrasse 4, Germany, Russian – Zone. I have looked up Erfurt on the internet. Before the war it was part of Germany, after the war it was behind the 'Iron Curtain'. I have wondered ever since what Werner Schrimpt found when he returned home after the war was over. The letter was translated by Ingrid whom I met at my local U3A. She said it was written in Old German which she was not familiar with even though she was in her seventies. I

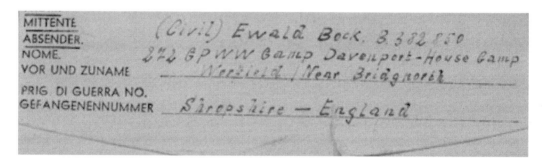

Envelope of a letter sent by a Prisoner of War from Worfield

asked her about her life in Germany during the war. She said she lived in the Hanover area, which was given to Poland. She and her family were told to take only what they could carry, which was difficult as her mother had three children. She said they walked for a week, and wore down their clogs, sometimes having to remove great piles of snow. Eventually they boarded a train, which did not move for two weeks. People came to bring water and remove the dead. She had to collect the bread rolls – there was little food. Once she bit into her bread roll and lost her two front teeth; there was a piece of brick in the middle. She said it was rubble due to the bombings. Overall she was out of education for four years. Sadly Ingrid passed away earlier this year. What she told me of the hardships she had suffered brought tears to my eyes.

I have done many things since I left Worfield. The most important was raising our two sons. In 1997 I became a volunteer for the Witness Service at my local Magistrates Court and I also worked on a successful Lottery bid of just over £200,00 to purchase Victim Support their own property in Dudley. In 2007 I was invited to Buckingham Palace, to celebrate Victim Support and Witness Service volunteers, and presented with a pin by Princess Anne who is Patron of the Victim Support Charity.

I will keep looking for more postcards of Worfield Village as I am certain there must be many more waiting for me to collect; they are an important part of the social history of Worfield.

2014

EWDNESS

Ewdness drawn by Jeff Flanc from a drawing by Stanley Leighton in 1899 when the house was owned by W. O. Foster

Ewdness was given special status in the thirteenth century when a man could live rent free there if they accompanied the sheriff of Shropshire when he took the ferm (rents) of the county to London. In 1443-1450 there was a chancery case between Roger Clerk, plaintiff, and John Hilton the younger, defendant, great-grandsons of John Ewdenas relating to Ewdenas and Asterhill which their great grandfather had held.[194] In 1553-1555 Ewdness was the subject of another Chancery case between William Felton and his brother, Richard, concerning the detention of their father's (Richard Felton's) title deeds for Ewdness.[195] William Felton's widow, Jane, married William Berkeley of Cressage and during the Civil War Thomas Berkeley had a troop of horse at Ewdness and the £90 to maintain it was paid to William Felton of The Lowe, Wem. The house now at Ewdness was built in the sixteenth century by Mr Fletcher whose daughter, Jane, married a Berkeley. Sir John Astley sold the Ewdness estate in 1764 to Apley consisting of: 3 cottages, 6 gardens, 4 orchards, 150 acres of land, 40a. meadow, 80a. pasture, 14a. wood, 60a. heath, in Ewdnes, Oldington, Hartlebury and Worfield.[196]

---

[194] *The National Archives,* C/1/15/45

[195] *The National Archives,* C/1/1350/5

[196] *Shropshire Archives,* 4387/3-4

NEW LODGE FARM

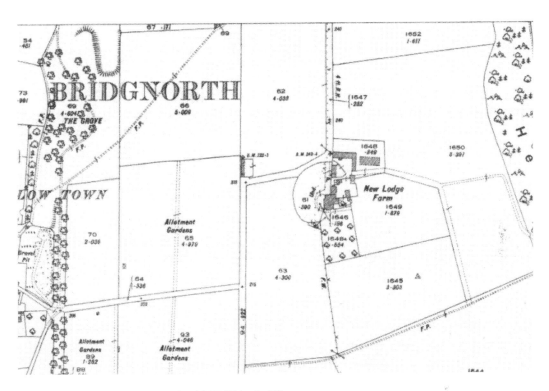

New Lodge Farm shown on the 1927 25 inch OS map

Half way up the Hermitage, just off the A454 from Bridgnorth to Wolverhampton, is Lodge Farm, an estate of houses dating back to the late 1960s or 1970s. I don't like to think how many times I have driven past, or visited the place, without giving a moment's thought to where the name, Lodge Farm, came from. I would have remained in this state of blissful ignorance had Rosemary Maiklem not got in touch and given me the answer.

In the 1920s, the Maiklem family came to Worfield from Scotland. Rosemary Maiklem's great aunt had married David Gray of Swancote, so this may have been the reason for the relocation. Rosemary lived at New Lodge Farm until it was demolished in 1966, by which time the fabric of the house had deteriorated so much that, as she lay in bed, Rosemary could hear the sand trickling down inside the rendering which covered the outside of the building. The Lodge Farm estate was then built on the New Lodge farmland and is now part of Bridgnorth, although it was formerly in Worfield Parish. There were two lodges in Worfield Parish; the Old

Lodge was on the border of Claverley and Worfield parishes near the junction of the Bridgnorth to Stourbridge Road and the road to Barnsley and Roughton, and the New Lodge at the Hermitage. Both lodges are shown on the 1613 Forest of Morfe map. [197] In the more recent past the term lodge was often given to the gate-house of a mansion but in medieval times a lodge was where the warrener lived who looked after the rabbits. The Old Lodge was also where the Forest of Morfe courts were held.[198]

New Lodge Farm looking towards Bridgnorth

To any farmer and gardener today, rabbits are a scourge. They have a voracious appetite for almost anything that is sown and seem happy to live on the ground or burrow below it. If they still had a value as a cash crop we might think more kindly of them, but as they don't, the humble rabbit has few friends. This wasn't always the case. Rabbit meat has been valued for centuries and until recent times the skins were used as well. In hard times, such as just after the First World War, many a farm rent was paid for in rabbits. The irony of this, of course, is that the rabbits on tenanted farms were the property of the farmer. In medieval times, rabbits were highly prized and bred in artificially created warrens managed by the warrener. Rosemary recalls that there was a mound at New Lodge Farm which would probably have been a pillow mound, part of a second wave of warren building dating from the late medieval period.[199]

It was thought until quite recently, that rabbits were introduced into this country by the Normans. In fact, it was the Romans who brought them here although it was perhaps the Normans who managed the animal for its meat and pelt. It is hard to imagine that rabbits at first found the English climate so inhospitable they didn't thrive and required careful management to get them to survive and breed, hence the need for purpose-built warrens within

---

[197] *Shropshire Archives,* 4296

[198] *The National Archives,* DL39/1/26, 1377-1509

[199] *Royal Commission on Ancient and Historical Monuments in Wales,* HMSO Cardiff 1982, p.321

which they could live. It would be a long time before rabbits wandered from these havens. Warrens were often replaced because they became physically unsustainable, being a honeycomb of tunnels, or because the rabbits succumbed to disease but we don't actually know why there was a need for a new warren at the New Lodge or indeed for the New Lodge itself. In the late fifteenth century it would appear that there was a population of rabbits living outside the confines of a warren, since two men were fined for hunting them with dogs and ferrets.[200]

New Lodge Farm in the early 1960s

The sandy soil of Worfield suited rabbits well but even so the warrener who looked after them needed much skill to keep them alive and healthy. Culling would generally have been done with ferrets at which time the warrener might have needed extra help. The main period of culling would have been when the rabbit fur was thickest. In the winter, gorse was a cheap source of extra food, and it was sometimes planted specially for them. As the rabbits began to acclimatise they fed off nearby crops. Perhaps this was a reason for the late enclosure of the Hermitage/Stanmore areas; people had just given up the battle against the rabbits and left the land as waste. The job was also dangerous, with poachers being a constant threat. Living on site was essential, hence the need for the lodge. When the Forest was under royal ownership the warrener received a wage but once it was in private hands, the lodge and its warren were leased out for profit. In 1658 Sir William Whitmore leased to Thomas George a parcel of waste

---

ground in the Forest of Morfe where "conies were lately planted," adjoining the old warren.[201]
The term was for the remainder of a term granted to John Bromley.

In 1761 the lord of the manor leased the warren and lodge to William Bates of Bridgnorth
for twenty-one years at an annual rent of £41 6s. The following is a summary of the terms of
the agreement.

William Bates agrees to rent "all that dwelling house or lodge on the Forest of Morfe and in
the Parish of Worfield in the Co. of Salop with the garden buildings and appurtenances thereto
and that warren of coneys or parcel of the said forest or waste used for a warren extending and
lying in length between a certain rock or mountain called Pendlestones Rock near the town of
Bridgnorth on the north part the highway leading from Bridgnorth through a late hospital of St
James's near the said town of Bridgnorth on the south part and in breadth from a late
hermitage there and the top of a mountain above the said hermitage called Broaditch on the
east part and to the town of Bridgnorth on the west together with all rights ... and
appurtenances whatsoever to the said warren and ...other premises belonging or appertaining
to and also on that warren or parcel of coneys or parcel of wast ground being part of the Wast
of the Forest of Morfe lying adjacent to the Old Warren extending itself to Gattacre Highway
on the north to a place called Round Hill and Yew Tree Hill on the south to a footway leading
from the said town of Bridgnorth to the town of Quatford on the west part ...together with the
use of all such trenches and coney burrows as are made therein with free liberty to plant, breed
and preserve coneys in the said ground and all the coneys in and upon the same and the
increase gain profit and advantage yearly arising coming, growing and renewing by reason
thereof and all other privileges and libertys belonging to the warren of coneys all with the said
dwelling house or lodge, warrens and premises were heretofore in the occupation of James
Currier and Elizabeth Currier, widow and John Andrews afterwards of Thomas George and
Walter Kidson and late in the tenure or holding of John Smith or John Bourne ...and now in
the possession of the said William Bates his assign or assigns undertenant or undertenants
accepting and always reserving out of this demise unto Sir Thomas Whitmore his heirs and
assigns and his and other agents and followers free liberty of ingress, egress and regress for him
and them to enter into and upon the said demised premises ...with dogs and guns and the game
of coneys there to course kill and carry away without any protestation or contradiction (and
pay to William Bates) for every couple of coneys that he or his agents or followers shall kill and
carry away the sum of eight pence of lawful money also accepting and always reserving of this
present demise unto the said Sir Thomas Whitmore his heirs and assigns all quarries of stone
mines and minerals ...opened or unopened now or at any time ....with free liberty for him and
them and his servants, agents and workmen with horses and carriages and other materials at all
times to enter into and upon the demised premises ...to dig, delve, handaise carry away and
enjoy sell or dispose of to his or their own proper use without any law suit or hindrance of or
by the said William Bates his executors, administrators etc."[202]

---

[201] *Shropshire Archives,* 5586/2/1/367

[202] *Shropshire Archives,* 5586/2/1/493

After William Bates, The Lodge was leased to Joseph Corbett, a Bridgnorth grocer, on similar terms. There were 400 pairs of rabbits in the warren. The probability is that this is the number of pairs put into the new warren.[203] However, by 1799 the Lodge and warrens of the Forest of Morfe, having been let to William Hallen by Thomas Whitmore, were in a "disused and uncultivated state." Poor Mr Hallen was bankrupt and there was little chance of recovering the arrears of rent so he had to forfeit his lease.[204]

Farmyard at New Lodge Farm
The Winter of 1963

This was the winter when it started snowing on Boxing Day and the snow lay until March

Acknowledgment
Thanks are due to Rosemary Maiklem without whose help we would know so much less about New Lodge Farm.

Further References
Mark Bailey, *The Rabbit and the Medieval East Anglian Economy*, (The Agricultural History Review Vol.36:1, 1988).
T. W. Turner, '*Memoirs of a Gamekeeper*,' (Geoffrey Bles, London 1954).

[203] *Shropshire Archives*, 5586/2/1/496

[204] *Shropshire Archives*, 5586/2/1/512

LITTLEGAIN

Millfield Cottages, Ackleton, later called Millfield Farm, a typical pair of nineteenth century farm workers' cottages photographed in 2013

Nock and Joseland, a Wolverhampton firm of auctioneers and estate agents, deposited a bundle of letters in Wolverhampton Archives relating to Littlegain. The letters date from 1894-1896 which was a time of extreme poverty for many people. Long spells of bad weather; cold summers in 1891-1892, a drought in 1893, and a dreadfully cold winter in 1894-1895, during which the River Thames froze over, exacerbated peoples' misery, and farmers were further hit by low prices for their produce.[205] The nearby town of Wolverhampton was in no better state economically than its rural neighbours with the decline of old industries such as mining and the iron trades on which Wolverhampton had depended.[206] Some of those who couldn't afford lodgings nor find a place in the workhouse turned to vagrancy and in January

---

[205] R. E. Prothero, *English Farming Past and Present* , Longmans & Co 1912, p. 382

[206] Jane Smith, *Accidents. Nineteenth Century Accidents in Wolverhampton*, Share our Past 2015, pp. 6, 7

1914 the death of a vagrant at Littlegain was a reminder of the plight of many at times of economic recession .[207]

The Nock and Joseland letters relate to the letting of property owned by Captain Smythe and his sister, who had lived at Hilton House but were at this time living at the Manor House, Trysull.[208] Will Bowen from Chesterton was acting as rent collector for his uncle & aunt, the Smythes, a thankless job at the best of times but even worse when the tenants were impoverished and the housing substandard.

By 1870, Public Health had become a national issue and the poor state of the country's housing, was one of the contributory factors. Bridgnorth's Rural Sanitary Authority, later Bridgnorth District Council's Sanitary & Nuisance Department, waged war on houses unfit for human habitation, inadequate drains, pigsties next to living accommodation, privies with inside cesspits, uncovered cesspits and uncovered wells.

The nineteenth century saw extra powers being granted to local authorities to ensure that homes had clean drinking water and a safe system of disposing of sewage and refuse. Local authorities were also obligated to inspect for nuisances and order action to remedy them. Bridgnorth District Council's Sanitary & Nuisance Department's comments shed more light on how people lived.

Littlegain cottages dated from the nineteenth century and were tiny, ramshackle, brick-built dwellings some of which were built into the sandstone rock. They were encroachments into the Lord of the Manor's land, essentially squatters' houses. [209] Apart from Littlegain Cottage and a cottage opposite, the remainder were down an unmade lane leading to Stratford Brook.

An inventory taken at Littlegain Cottage gives some indication of how the tenants lived.

• "Front kitchen

> 1 good deal table about 4ft by 3ft (7/-), 1 verey good round oak table (about 28 in diameter), 1 good corner cupboard, 4 shelves, 3 kitchen chairs, 1 old oak sideboard, 3 drawers (poor condition), 1 good large tray, one breadboard, 4 plates, 3 small basins, one glass sugar basin, one small pewter tea pot, 5 odd tea cups without handles, 3 tea saucers, 2 small salt cellars, one small looking glass - oval, 14 small photographs

• Back kitchen

> 3 mole traps, 2 wooden benches, one kitchen sofa with back (only wooden frame), 2 old brooms and scrubbing brush, one good bucket (6/-), one small fire shoval, one small fring pan 2 tin candelsticks, one brass candelstick, one tin bowl, one wooden harvest bottle, about 4 odd bottles and jars

• Bedroom

> One good large iron frame bedstead (one castor broken), one broken looking glass, one broken box."

---

[207] *Bridgnorth Journal,* 3 January 1914

[208] *Wolverhampton Archives,* D-NAJ/C/1/SM6

[209] Littlegain Cottage may have been an exception; a toll house, perhaps. Jane Smith, *Worfield, The History of a Shropshire Parish from Earliest Times,* JS Books 2017, p. 114)

The Smythes' tenants at Littlegain included Hannah Richards, and Messrs. Calder, Corbishley, Richards and Simmons. For various reasons, the Littlegain tenants seem to have fallen on hard times. J. J. Corbishley had lived and farmed at Warren Farm so he had definitely come down in the world, Mrs. Richards had been ill for some time and unable to work, and Mr. Calder had so little regular work that his rent arrears to Lady Day 1895 were £30. The landlord must have suspected that this wasn't quite the whole story as regards Mr. Calder and had him followed to see where he spent his weekends. Perhaps Calder was 'encouraged' to leave Littlegain Cottage because by November 1896 Elizabeth and John Richards were the new tenants. In September 1896, the rents due at Littlegain were as follows: Richards H. £6. 5. 0, Richards E. £8. 5. 0, Calder J. £9. 5. 0 and Corbishley J. J. £5. 10. 0. The following correspondence was received by the agents[210]

From H. Richards (Littlegain) to Nock & Chase

Thursday 6 October 1894

"Mrs. Richards has received word from Captain Smythe that the one quarter that was due before the half year belonged to him and if she had paid it to you he should make her repay it to him. Hannah Richards knows there were three quarters rent due up to 29th of last month but Captain Smythe claims the one quarter, but if you can't stand the racket with Captain Smythe I will pay it to you but I cannot afford to pay the two. Richards wants the repairing done very bad but if you are coming down this way I wish you would call."

From Will Bowen, Chesterton to his Uncle, Captain Smythe

6 April 1895.

"Dear Uncle,

I have just been to Littlegain, I found them all in but have only got Edward Richards' rent and they grumbled a lot about paying it, he said he expected 10/- taken off the rent, a new gate and the poplars at the bottom of the garden felled and a shed for coal or straw put up, or else they wouldn't stay. Calder said that he had so little regular work that he had not been able to get the money and Mrs Richards had been seriously ill for some time and had only just got to work again but would soon be able to pay one quarter's rent, she is now living altogether in Miss Smythe's house now."

From Bridgnorth District Council's Sanitary and Nuisance Inspector re: H. Richards' house

November 1895

"Please look at the state of wash house floor and yard surface and down spout and gutters."

From Bridgnorth District Council's Sanitary and Nuisance Inspector

28 January 1896

"I was here again [H. Richards' House] investigating into a case of scarlet fever but found nothing done to improve washhouse floor and yard surface leading thereto. The yard drain outlet ought to have been made to empty to a properly built and covered cesspool and not as it does now to an open hole in garden and there causing a most offensive nuisance."

From Jas. O. Davies to Nock and Chase.

7 September 1896

---

[210] *Wolverhampton Archives,* D-NAJ/C/1/SM6

Sir,

"I have made enquiries respecting J. Caulder has you spoke to me about on Saturday and find that he comes into Bridgnorth on Saturday night and stayes at George Corfield, 7, River Side and leaves on Monday morning again for the week."

And there the story ends, for there is no more correspondence about Littlegain. A light is shone, all too briefly, on the less than idyllic lifestyle of many at the end of the nineteenth century.

Note

Joseph Corbishley of Grindle occupied 3 farms of which one was Warren Farm, a short walk across Rudge Heath from Littlegain. In the 1880s, there were two incidents which Mr Corbishley brought before the court. The first was in 1883 when James Hartel, a higgler & fruiterer from Gornall Wood, was held on charges of obtaining a ton of potatoes from Warren Farm. Corbishley was then living at Hatton near Shifnal and it was the farm bailiff, Charles Rawlins, who dealt with Hartel. He told Rawlins that he had come to collect a load of potatoes for Mr Jones of Bilston. The story was plausible because Jones had a contract with Corbishley for a large quantity of potatoes, some of which were bagged ready for collection. Hartel left with a ton of potatoes and paid £2 for them, convincing Rawlins that this was the price Jones had agreed, whereas in fact it was £2.15d. The second case, in which Corbishley claimed a breach of contract, came before the Shropshire Spring Assizes in 1888. He sought damages from William Morgan, a potato merchant from Whitchurch. The previous April, Corbishley had a large quantity of potatoes to dispose of and in May a price was agreed with Morgan of 36/-. Of this there was no argument, but was this for the entire lot, as Corbishley claimed, or just for 20 tons as Morgan later claimed? The potatoes were to be delivered to a local railway station in Morgan's sacks, and Morgan's agent, Graham, was to work with Corbishley at Warren Farm to ensure smooth delivery. Graham was then to make arrangements for onward transport of potatoes to other areas of the country. On the 14th May Corbishley received a letter from Morgan as follows: 'I have received the 20 tons of potatoes I have bought from you. Enclosed please find cheque for the same. Trade is over for the season and I will buy no more. They cook very black and I cannot sell them.' His Lordship found for the defendant which left Corbishley with 70 tons of potatoes to dispose of at the wrong end of the season. The potatoes (Magnum Bonums) were stored in clamps at Warren Farm and sold by Nock and Chase on the 3rd July 1888 at the Fox Inn, Shipley. It was a struggle to find buyers, even at the low prices achieved; between 11/- and 13/- per ton, and 10 tons were left unsold. The Corbishleys weathered these storms and J. Corbishley was still at Grindle in 1893 with Joshua Corbishley in residence at Warren Farm. £2.15.[211]

---

[211] *Bridgnorth Journal* 29 July 1893, *Wellington Journal* 10 Nov 1883

THE HILTON VALLEY RAILWAY

From the left, Gary (surname unknown) is driving Lorna Doone, Michael Lloyd,
standing, Bren (surname unknown) is driving Hilton Queen, and "Pop," standing

In 1954, the Lloyd family lived at Hilton House, and in that year, Michael Lloyd began a
$7^{1/4}$ inch miniature steam railway which for the next twenty-five years, gave pleasure to a large
number of children and their parents. 25,000 people visited annually and it is hard to believe
now that the cars queued up Hilton Bank to visit this attraction. Dan Lloyd, Michael's son,
explained how innovative the railway idea was. "At that time there were only a few
miniature railways operating. But the miniature railway passion was being born. In later years
miniature railways were being operated all over the country."

The engines which hauled the carriages were steam driven. In one advertisement in 1969 it
was called the "Stronghold of Steam, the only railway in the Midlands operating steam-hauled
passenger trains."[212] Fortunately there was no shortage of volunteers to help out. There was
much work to be done to create the Hilton Valley Railway as a professional operation. Track

---

[212] *Walsall Observer and South Staffordshire Chronicle*, 29 August 1969, p. 11

had to be laid and an electrical signalling system installed. Volunteers maintained and drove the engines. "Pop," the father of Rita Hartley who with her husband, Peter, were licensees of the Black Lion, ran the shop, another volunteer was needed to take the entrance money, and Michael Lloyd, of course, oversaw the whole operation. Visitors parked at Hilton Station, and for a standard fare of 1/- in pre-decimal money and 5p in decimal, passengers were conveyed for nearly a mile across the meadows alongside the Stratford Brook. The journey took about twelve minutes.

Two volunteers, Bren and John who gave up their weekends to help at Hilton

Lorna Doone was the first engine that Michael Lloyd bought, a Pacific LNER style locomotive built by Louis Shaw in 1925. "The engine ran at Mablethorpe before the war and after a period of neglect she came to Hilton and became the foundation stone on which the whole railway has been built." (Guide Book) She was restored at Hilton and ran reliably for many years, being once again restored in 1969 by A. J. Glaze.

Other engines followed, for example:

• Locomotive Number 2, Hilton Queen, was bought in 1964. It had been built by J. N. Liversedge of Herne Bay in 1950, and ran on the Herne Bay Pier for a season.

• Locomotive Number 3 was begun by Trevor Guest to a Greenly drawing of a Canadian prototype and built in the training school at F. H. Lloyd in 1959 under J. T. F. Naylor. Named after the founder of the firm, the locomotive was rebuilt by A. J. Glaze.

• Locomotive Number 7 was inspired by Great Western and built by A. J. Glaze. The Guide Book says the locomotive "is testimony to Mr Glaze's unrivalled skill and experience as a steam locomotive engineer."

The 1972 season had been a successful one for the railway but in January 1973, Michael Lloyd tragically died in a hotel fire in Exmouth. He was just 63. An article in the Birmingham Post recorded that he had only been Chairman of F. H. Lloyd for three years but in this short time had reorganised the thirty loosely connected companies which comprised it, into a coherent group.[213] He had also made the Hilton Valley Railway one of the top tourist attractions in the area. After his father's death, Dan Lloyd continued to run the railway for another six years until he moved it to Weston Park.

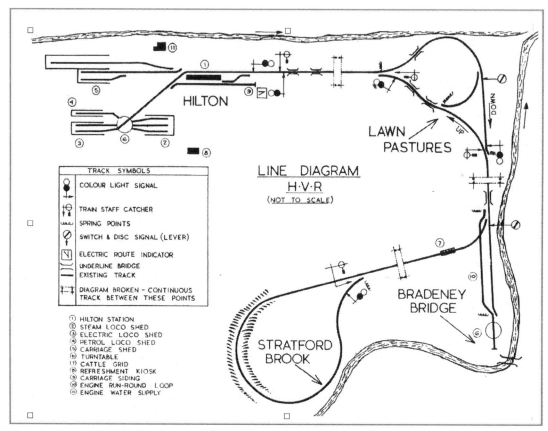

Route of the Hilton Valley Railway taken from the Guide Book

Acknowledgments

Thanks are due to Dan Lloyd and Nigel Gandy for the images used in this article and for the information they kindly provided

---

[213] *The Birmingham Post*, 22 January 1973, p. 3

ISABEL BASELEY

Isabel Baseley

Isabel Baseley, junior, was four when she came to Woundale near Claverley. The family relocated from Deptford when Isabel's father, James, took a job as butler for Colonel Legh at Chyknell. Isabel's mother (also called Isabel) didn't want to leave London, and cried all the way to Claverley. A butler warranted a better house than most, but there was nothing to endear the tiny, remote hamlet of Woundale to Isabel senior, when all she wanted were the bright lights of London. To make matters worse, none of their neighbours would speak to them because they were outsiders. Mrs Baseley didn't help matters by refusing to show the same deference to her master and mistress as the other servants did. The protocol was that if a servant was carrying a bucket of water when the master or mistress passed by, the bucket would be put down, and the servant curtsied. Mrs Baseley simply refused to do that. Before she had married, Isabel senior had worked as a cook in Kensington where there was no expectation to curtsey and if it wasn't the custom in London she certainly wasn't going to start it in Chyknell.

HILTON
Isabel Baseley

In 1910, James Baseley took a new job at Hensol Castle in South Wales and the family moved to 2, Hilton, on the A454. There were so few cars that it was safe for children to play in the road with hoops and marbles but there were plenty of horses and carts passing through Hilton so there was not the same sense of isolation there had been at Woundale. The road surface was very rough and not macadamised and at intervals along the road there were piles of large stones which a man had to break up to fill in the holes. The house at Hilton was lit by candles and oil lamps, drinking water came from a well, and rainwater was collected for washing clothes. The children walked to school, of course, past the Wheel Pub run by the Bithells who had two boys who went to Worfield School. Bentley's garage hadn't been built and there was no toll house at Wyken which must have been demolished by 1910. The children often had wet feet when they arrived at school and there was a supply of slippers they could wear while their wet shoes were dried around a coke stove. Worfield was the children's whole world, and they knew little of what was happening elsewhere. One day during the First World War, the headmaster said to the schoolchildren, 'I wonder how many of you know that there is a war on?' No-one knew. Isabel would have known soon enough that there was something different as the walk to and from school went past the Recreation Room transformed into a VAD hospital for injured soldiers in 1915. The children's contribution to the war effort at school was to wind skeins of khaki wool and knit socks..

Marriage of James Baseley to Hilda Price in 1939. Isabel Baseley,the bridegroom's mother, is on his right. Image courtesy of Graham Gatt

When she was fifteen, Isabel junior went to work for the Cartland family at the Priory, in King's Heath, Birmingham. She didn't like it but, "there was nothing for country girls in Worfield. The boys went to work on farms, the girls went into service. I started as an under-

248

housemaid at 3/6d and moved up to housemaid." One of the visitors to the house was Barbara Cartland who was a great niece of the owners of the house. Miss Cartland was then aged about 19.

In 1932, Isabel Baseley junior married John Richard Smout of Chesterton. They were living in Oldington in 1949 when John Smout died aged forty-six. Isabel remarried in 1955, her second husband being Thomas Weston of Rindleford, and they moved to Shrewsbury.

Isabel senior never went back to London. Her husband, James, died in 1935 and is buried in the Upper Churchyard in Worfield, and Isabel senior stayed at Hilton and became the postmistress there, delivering post to the villages well into old age. She died in 1961 and is buried near her husband in the Upper Churchyard.

Opposite Number 2, Hilton was the Hilton Post Office. At the time of the 1911 census four sisters lived at the Post Office. Three were widows: Mary Hodgkiss, Hannah Jenkins and Eliza Selleck. Ann Ebrey, a spinster, ran the post office. There was just one large room downstairs and a screen provided the only privacy. When this photograph was taken in the 1930s, Sarah Bull was running the Post Office.
Image courtesy of Graham Gatt

Acknowledgments
Thanks are due to Graham and Sheila Gatt and to Tony and Jane Mills.

THE BROWNS OF DEEPDALE

Jane Brown, William's wife

The Brown family have lived and worked on the Apley Estate for at least four generations. Ralph's great great grandfather was an agricultural labourer and woodman from 1827, his great grandfather was a general labourer and blacksmith and lived at Apley Forge, and his grandfather, William Joseph Brown was a blacksmith at The Batch. Ben Brown and his wife started the farm at Deepdale and had two children, Ralph and Audrey. Ralph Brown had lived all his life at Deepdale on the B4176 until a few years ago when the owners decided to sell the land. Farming is a way of life which can generate an income but not necessarily enough capital to buy a farm. There was no way that a small farmer could compete on the open market, especially with the easing of planning restrictions which allowed for a change in use, so Deepdale Farm became Chesterton Valley Golf Course. This has given pleasure to many but took away the Brown's livelihood.

Until recent times, Deepdale was scrub and not farmed at all. It was War Ag which cleared the Deepdale land and gave the Browns the opportunity to have their own farm and it was here that Ralph Brown and his sister grew up. Worfield School which they attended sounds idyllic. There were withy beds where the bungalows are now and the children were sent out to gather the withies and make baskets. The Worfe wended its way through the Sonde and in times of heavy rain came right up to the school wall. Mrs Brudenell knitted socks for the war effort while she was teaching. Ralph said,"You could watch the sock grow, she went like the clappers." It was probably much more interesting to watch the knitting than to pay attention to the lesson. Another diversion from school work was when there was a delivery of coke for heating Oliver Leese's mushroom sheds. The coke was tipped in the middle of the road alongside the school and volunteers were sought from the schoolchildren to shovel it into wheelbarrows and put in a shed.

Another enjoyable wartime job was taking the bread from Clarke's bakery to Davenport House. The demand for bread had increased considerably with the arrival of John Groome's Orphanage. The loaves were double the normal size, square in shape for ease of cutting and the reward for delivery was the choice of a cob or a currant bun. Mr James was the baker and

William Joseph Brown outside his home at The Batch.

by the way everyone talks about how delicious the bread was, he must have been very good at his job.

Church took up most of each Sunday, with two services a day and Sunday School in the afternoon. Sunday School was either at Mrs Bradburn's house in Chesterton or at Hilton Manor, the home of Mrs Banister.[214] Sometimes Ralph and his sister Audrey would attend the Mission Hall in Ackleton and if they were really lucky the young curate would give the children a lift home on his bike. Audrey would sit in the basket and Ralph on the crossbar and they would go at breakneck speed down the hill from Ackleton towards the Folley. As the road whizzed by the terrified children prayed they didn't come off or they would surely die. Speed wasn't the only terror of the ride, the wrath of the children's step-mother if she saw the children on the bike was best avoided, so the last part of the journey was done much more sedately on foot.

The Brown's house at The Batch which was derelict in 2018

---

[214] Mrs Banister moved to Scotland in 1951 to live near her son and was sadly killed in a car accident not long afterwards. We are indebted to her for preserving the picture doors and the benefaction tables which now hang in the Vestry.

HILTON

The Browns of Deepdale

There were strangers in Worfield in wartime. Walking to and from Worfield village past the Recreation Room, the patients in the VAD hospital were often out and about wearing their bright blue uniforms. Evacuees lived in the parish and they often found it hard to connect with what the local children did. Many of the children had no idea where their food came from, never having been outside a city. One child even thought that eggs grew on trees.

But what a good job the evacuees came because Thelma was an evacuee and she and Ralph became a strong partnership. After they had married, they had an idea of emigrating to Australia but felt obligated to stay and help Ben, Ralph's father, on the farm. Thelma loved the farm horses but sadly they were sold two weeks before she moved in. Tractors had taken over the work done by the horses and one couldn't afford to keep both. The dairy cows were Dairy Shorthorns and were excellent until TB forced the sale of them all. Their replacements were a much poorer group, "absolute rubbish," as Ralph described them. In farming, the consequences of decisions have very long lasting effects but the business survived and Ralph and Thelma raised their six children at Deepdale. It can't have been easy, yet in spite of the hardships, the answer to the question, "Do you still miss the farm," was an unhesitating, "Oh yes."

The Ford at Deepdale where the Stratford Brook once crossed the B4176.

Acknowledgment

Thanks are due to Thelma and Ralph Brown for the information which they provided for this article in 2011

THE HILTON ESTATE

Hilton House, now Hilton Manor

On the 20th June 1917, the Hilton Estate came under the hammer.[215] This was another large estate broken up in the early twentieth century which changed the landscape of Worfield. Sold by Fowler, Langley and Wright, the auctioneer was Thomas Barnett of Wolverhampton, and the agent was E. O. P. Copley of Brewood. The estate was described as: "a commodious country residence, 2 excellent mixed farms, and 16 cottages". There were 549 acres in total, bringing in a rental of £812.9s.0d. Seven cottages with large gardens at Hilton and Littlegain were being sold separately by auction. Most of the property was copyhold of the Manor of Worfield and the rest was freehold. Copyhold property was held at the will of the Lord of the Manor and in 1926 all such property became freehold. The sales particulars emphasise that, "The estate generally has been considered one of the best partridge and pheasant shoots in the district. It is within easy reach of 3 packs of hounds and excellent trout fishing". Some of the sales lots were as follows:

- "Lot 1 Hilton House. Mr Knox is the occupier of the house and the cottage/bungalow is occupied by Mrs Weaver. Charming gardens, stabling, motor house and a one storey cottage or bungalow. The outbuildings are a small greenhouse, 2 stables with 6 stalls and lofts over, harness room, coach house, fowl house and 2 dog kennels. On the opposite side of the road is a 2 storey brick building comprising a motor house and cart shed with granary over.

  There is an extensive kitchen garden which is well-stocked with fruit trees, a greenhouse, brick built frame, a walled garden and an old stone-built cottage used as a store.

---

[215] *Shropshire Archives*, 1485

Hilton Farmhouse

- Lot 2 Hilton and Littlegain Farm. Adjoining Hilton Farm is a 4 stall stable and loose box with a loft over, a barn with 2 bays, 2 cowhouses, calf and turnip houses. New Barn Building has a 3 stall cart house, stable and loose box with loft. Cow houses to tie 27, barn with 2 bays, turnip and chopping houses, cart shed with granary over, large open feeding shed with an iron roof and a wooden foal house. Littlegain has a barn with 2 bays, a 3 stall stable and loft and large feeding shed.
- Lot 3 Hilton Grange. 155 acres, farm buildings include a 3 stall Hackney stable, 4 stall cart horse stable and a motor or trap house.
- Lot 5 Two Cottages. 2 enfranchised copyhold 2 storey brick built cottages adjoining the Black Lion. One house has 2 sitting rooms, 3 bedrooms and a cellar, the other has a kitchen, pantry, 2 bedrooms and a cellar. Also included are coal places and privies, 3 pigsties, brick built motor house, store room with iron roof and lean-to open shed."

The sale was prompted by the death of Georgiana Smythe, nee Allardyce, who died in March 1917, aged eighty-eight years. She was the widow of Captain George Smythe R.N. who had died in 1894 aged eighty-four. Georgiana was from Cheltenham where her father James Allardyce was a physician, but the Smythe family had been in Worfield for generations. Randall refers to the fact that they can be traced in the manor court rolls to 1327, when a William the Smith had land at Bromley.[216] [217]In 1587, Thomas Smyth appears in the Regarders Accounts holding land in the Forest of Morfe in Hilton.[218] When the Hearth Tax was assessed in 1672,

[216] John Randall, *Worfield and Its Townships*, p. 93

[217]*Shropshire Archives*, P314/W/1/1/2

[218] *The National Archives*, E32/149

HILTON The Hilton Estate

Hilton eleven households were liable to pay the tax. John Smyth and eight other households had one hearth, John Lilie, five hearths, and Widow Norton and William Beech each had two hearths..[219]

By the nineteenth century the Smythe family were the main landowners in the village and there are a number of memorials to them in Worfield Church. The font and tiles around it were given in memory of Lieutenant Thomas Smythe who died at Trysull in 1879 aged seventy, and also of Mary his wife who died at Hilton in 1862, aged 35. There is also a plaque to John Groome Smythe, father and son, which reads:

"This tablet is erected to the memory of John Groome Smythe Esq of Hilton in this parish, a Deputy Lieutenant for the County of Salop who died on the 4th December 1835 aged 64 years. Also of Anne his wife daughter of Thomas Park Esquire of Highfield near Liverpool. She died at Stretton Hall in the County of Stafford on the 14th November 1852 aged 82 years. She was interred in General Monckton's vault in Stretton Churchyard. Also of John Groome Smythe second son of the above, a Lieutenant in the H.E.I.C.[The Honourable East India Company] 27th Regiment of Native Infantry on Madras Establishment who died at Ellore in the East Indies on the 25th July 1839 aged 30 years and was interred in the churchyard attached to the station."

In 1851, according to the census, Anne Smythe was living at Stretton Hall and Henry Monckton was the head of the household. Anne Smythe was Henry Monckton's mother-in-law, and with an age gap of twenty-five years between Henry Monckton and his wife, (in 1851 he was 70 and she was 45) Henry was nearer his mother-in-law's age. There were five children, including sons, of Henry's marriage so the Monckton succession was assured. Also at Stretton Hall was George Smythe, Henry Monckton's brother-in-law, and the butler, who went by the unforgettable name of Oliver Cromwell.

In the 1881 census, George Smythe was retired and he and Georgiana were living in Marine Terrace, Aberystwyth. Perhaps this was their permanent home enabling Hilton House to be let to Arthur Monckton, the second son of Henry and Anne, and his family in 1901, and to Mr Knox and his family at the time of the sale in 1917.[220]

[219] W. Watkins-Pitchford, *The Shropshire Hearth-Tax Roll of 1672: being a list of the householders in the County*, Shropshire Archives, XLS47

[220] 1901 Census

SNIPPETS

An uncivil case

Thomas Wilcox, farmer, Hilton versus Elizabeth Caddick, greengrocer of Pattingham. Plaintiff claimed for 6 bags of potatoes at 6s a bag. Wilcox had dealings with Caddick up to April 1891. She came to the farm and wanted to buy some potatoes. The agreement was that she would pay for the potatoes when she removed them from the farm. The potatoes were removed without payment and Mrs Caddick later offered a reduced price, saying that the price of potatoes had fallen. Mr Wilcox swore at her and said there wasn't an honest person in the parish of Pattingham. She said he hoped he would withdraw those words as there were some big gentlemen in the parish of Pattingham which was 700 or 800 strong. The payment was eventually made at the Darlington Arms. Joseph Charles Vaughan, an ostler, was a witness and when Mrs Caddick gave Wilcox the money he went into a rage and say that it wasn't enough. He threw the money at Mrs Caddick, she didn't pick it up, but others did. Mr Wilcox called her a liar, a thief and a rogue.

The Judge remarked on the folly of leaving debts for four years and found for the defendant.

Bridgnorth Journal & S. Shropshire Advertiser 6 July 1895

At the Bridgnorth Licensing Meeting, R. F. Haslewood appeared on behalf of Thomas Meredith of the Black Lion beerhouse, Hilton, to make an application to renew. The licensee has held the licence for many years. Superintendent Walters was instructed to oppose the application and had issued Mr Meredith with a notice of objection on the grounds that he was not a fit and proper person to hold a licence having been convicted at Bridgnorth Magistrates and fined £1 and costs for allowing drunkenness on licensed premises on Boxing Day.

The Bench renewed the licence.

Wolverhampton Chronicle 14th September 1898

Thomas Perry, Hilton, tailor, bankrupt 1831. Sussex Advertiser, 21 November 1831, p. 1

A TRAGEDY AT HOCCUM

James Meredith was born in 1700 and married Elizabeth Thomas of Claverley. The couple had a son, Thomas Meredith, born in 1728, and three more children, including John who was born in Hilton in 1731, and James born in 1735. Thomas married Sarah Mecham of Wolverhampton in 1756 and had a son James Meredith, who we will call James Meredith (2), in 1759.

James Meredith (2) moved to Wyken where he was, for a while, steward of Wyken Manor. He farmed in Wyken and married Sarah Nicholas, also of Wyken, in 1781. The couple were living in Hilton when their son, John Meredith was born in 1796.

John Meredith was farming in Hoccum in 1836, having married Jane Ebrey, and the couple had eleven children. The 1851 census confirms that Hoccum was a farm of 180 acres with five men and two indoor staff employed. In 1853, John Meredith died, prompting a sale of his property, implements, and livestock, and in 1861 John's son John, aged 36, took over Hoccum farm which was now 250 acres. Another son, James, already a widower at the age of 35, was farming 160 acres at Brook House Roughton. James had been a solicitor's clerk in Wolverhampton and whether the death of his wife was what caused the return to Worfield where he was born, we don't know. As a single parent, with three children to support, unsurprisingly the eldest two being called John and James, life must have been hard.

And then something went spectacularly wrong. The 1871 census reveals that John Meredith of Hoccum was still living at Hoccum but is a "farmer, unemployed," and James Meredith of Brook House, who had moved to Woundale, over the border in Claverley parish, is similarly described. With a new wife, Emma, and two more children, one can only assume that both became casual labourers.

The intriguing question is what happened to bring about their demise. The answer was, I am afraid much worse than I had imagined, and found in a short article which appeared in the Shrewsbury Chronicle, December 29, 1869, concerning an outbreak of Foot & Mouth Disease. Amongst the premises listed as being infected was that of the "Farmyard of Mr John Meredith, Hoccom". There were a number of diseases in livestock which concerned the authorities at this time, such as pleuropneumonia, rinderpest (cattle plague), and foot and mouth. Imported cattle were often the source of infection and in 1864-1865 there had been an outbreak of cattle plague which resulted in the slaughtering of huge numbers of livestock. Foot and mouth disease, up to this point was of the least concern because livestock did recover, albeit not always to full health, but cattle plague had raised the authorities' awareness of the devastating effects of such diseases. The concern of the government was the poor value of the carcasses of infected animals and they recognised the need to prevent the spread of disease. In 1869, farmers were required for the first time to provide a clean bill of health for their livestock. Whether Mr Meredith was unlucky to have foot and mouth in his livestock or whether it was a common disease I don't know but following the sale of livestock and implements at Hoccum life would henceforth be much harder for both John and James Meredith.

Hoccum Farm was mortgaged which we know from the will of John Meredith, the father, and I assume Brook House was the same. It seems likely, therefore, that without any means of maintaining the payments on the mortgages, both properties were repossessed by the mortgagees.[221]

It is twenty years since the last foot and mouth outbreak which affected Worfield and many other areas of the country. The disease strikes fear in farmers as much today as it would have done in 1869 when John Meredith first heard the devastating news that his farm was affected. Without any government support, the Merediths lost everything they had built up.

---

[221] A number of deeds relating to Hoccum came into my hands just after writing this article which will be deposited in Shropshire Archives. An abstract of title concerning William Hoccom confirms that under the terms of John Meredith's will of March 1852, he gave and devised all his copyhold and freehold properties to John Joynson and William Nicholas to be sold.

SARAH JANE SMITHYMAN

Sarah Jane Smithyman and her brother Rowland are buried in the Lower Churchyard at the back of Worfield Church

As I was researching accidents in Wolverhampton in the nineteenth century, I came across a newspaper report about the death of Sarah Jane Smithyman, late of Roughton.[222] This was not an accident but apparently death from natural causes. Miss Smithyman's sister requested an inquest which she was perfectly entitled to do, of course. She was, I suppose, shocked by her sister's relatively short illness, and suspected foul play. She may also have been suffering some guilt, perhaps, that she hadn't seen her sister in three and a half years. Nor, it would seem had the deceased made a return visit to Roughton.

Sarah Jane Smithyman, aged 50, unmarried, now of Shottery Villas, Waterloo Road North, and formerly of Roughton House and Farm, had come to live in Wolverhampton three and a half years before her death. She was living on her own means. The Coroner was notified of the death of the deceased not by the police but by her relatives, who as has been mentioned, had requested an inquest.

The following is a summary of the evidence provided by witnesses at the inquest.

Mrs. Mary Addison, widow, of 10, Drummond Street, New Hampton Road, aunt of the deceased, said that the deceased had lived at Roughton House from birth until three and a half years before. After the death of her brother some years previously, the deceased farmed the land at Roughton on her own account. Her household at Wolverhampton consisted of a servant girl and Mr. Richard Batho formerly farm bailiff at Roughton. Mr. Batho lived with Miss Smithyman until her death.

Mrs. Addison had not seen the deceased for nearly twelve months when Sarah Jane Smitheman sent for her. Mr. Batho came for Mrs Addison to stay with the deceased while he

---

went to fetch Mr. Scott, a surgeon. Mrs. Addison went in the evening and her niece was in bed, conscious, but in great pain in her back and the lower part of her body. The aunt stayed for several hours and returned the next day at the request of the deceased. She stayed with her a short while and Mr. Batho was present. She visited again on the Sunday, Monday and Tuesday, and on the latter day, Mrs. Woolrich of Roughton, sister of the deceased, came after hearing from Mrs. Addison about her sister's illness. Mrs. Addison went again on the Wednesday and on Friday evening and learnt that Miss Smithyman had died the previous night. During Mrs. Addison's visits, Mr. Batho gave the deceased her food and medicine. Until she came to Wolverhampton, the deceased had enjoyed very good health having been a strong, robust woman.

Mrs. Mary Ann Wolrich, wife of Henry Wolrich, of Roughton House, said that she had not seen her sister to speak to since she came to Wolverhampton on Tuesday last. She came after being told what a dangerous state her sister was in. She found her sister dying, and the inquest was held at her request as she did not know the cause of death.

Mr. J. W. Scott, surgeon, was questioned. The deceased had been a patient of his since February. When he first saw her he found her suffering from general illness and a chronic abscess in the chest and also suffering from congestion of the liver and stomach. He called in Dr. Totherick on the first of the month. Miss Smithyman died on Thursday last and he certified the cause of death as primarily due to an abscess of the liver and secondly to blood poisoning deriving from it.

Mrs. Sarah Moore, wife of Thomas Moore, a carpenter, was engaged to nurse the deceased from the 3rd September. Mr. Batho hired her. She stayed with the deceased a great deal during which time Miss Smithyman complained of internal pain and a vomiting disposition. While Mrs Moore was there, the deceased took no food but only milk and brandy and soda water. She only had medicine three times while she was there.

Mary Botwood of Tettenhall was Miss Smithyman's servant and said that three weeks before her death her mistress was able to get about. She had very little to eat, her chief diet being brandy and milk but who mixed it she did not know. The witness never saw her eat any solid food. She was never the worse for drink. The deceased was taken ill a week after Mary Botwood was employed.

The inquest was adjourned for two weeks.

After a post mortem it was found that the Miss Smithyman's right kidney was diseased. The liver and left kidney were healthy. There was no evidence that the deceased had died from the effects of poison and the jury were clear that death was from natural causes. The initial diagnosis of Mr. Scott was therefore incorrect although a death certificate had already been issued by him.

THE STOKES FAMILY

As you are driving from Wolverhampton to Bridgnorth on the A454, having travelled through Wyken, your eye will probably have been taken by the beautiful house on the left hand side of the road which stands on a hill in Roughton. Roughton House, as it is called, was built by the Stokes family and occupied by them from the late eighteenth century until the last of the Roughton line, Louisa Stokes, died in 1914, aged eighty-four.

The Stokes' connection with Roughton began in the eighteenth century when William Stokes of Tettenhall married Anna Bell, the daughter and heiress of William Bell of Roughton in 1742 at Codsall Church.[223] With the marriage came his wife's estates in Roughton. Anna died in 1757, and on the death of her husband the estate passed to William Stokes their son.

William Stokes' marriage to Nancy Freeman of Kingswinford in 1781, brought property further afield, in Alveley and Worcester, and a "messuage, barns, stable, orchard etc in the parish of Totnell co. Staffs at a place called the Dippens with … approximately 145 acres.[224] " Sadly, William Stokes died in 1784, just three years after his marriage and the estate then devolved to Stokes's five sisters who passed it on to their cousin, William Smith Stokes of Oldswinford, who became the second husband of William Stokes' widow.

William Smith Stokes and his wife Nancy had three sons who lived to adulthood and three daughters. Two of the sons died young. The eldest son, Lieutenant James Marshall Smith Stokes, died in the Peninsular War in 1812, the year in which William Smith Stokes also died. Another son, Lieutenant William Smith Stokes RN, who had been at the Battle of Trafalgar, died in 1826. Since neither of the elder brothers had married, the estate fell equally to the youngest son, Michael Smith Stokes and his three sisters; Jane Eleanor, Louisa, and Mary Ann. When William Smith Stokes made his will in August 1811, he and Nancy were living apart, William in Beckbury, and Nancy at Roughton House. The relationship was acrimonious. Nancy wanted to bequeath the estate to certain of the children while William was adamant that it should be equally shared. There was a lot of property but much of it was copyhold, and there was a hefty mortgage of £2,000 to be paid off. The Stokes' property portfolio included some inherited from Francis Stokes, of Red Hill, Oldswinford, and some via the maternal line from Francis Smith the architect. 'Smith of Warwick' as he was known, specialised in the design of elegant country houses such as Davenport House, Patshull Hall, Dudmaston Hall, Gifford House in Wolverhampton and Chillington Hall.

Perhaps it was the Smith connection which inspired William Smith Stokes to build Roughton House on its elevated site facing towards Davenport Park. We may never know whether this was a new house on a virgin site, as Randall believed, or a house which Smith Stokes extended, but a roof tile dated 1798 confirms that building work was being done at this time. When William Smith Stokes made his will in 1811, Nancy was living in Roughton House

---

[223] *Gentleman's Magazine*, Mrs Stokes, Vol. 163 1838 p. 435

[224] *Shropshire Archives*, 1067/7

and had a life interest in the Stokes' property and to make sure the household goods of Roughton House remained in situ, an inventory was taken[225]William Smith Stokes was buried at Tettenhall.[226] Nancy Stokes died in 1838, aged 86.

The Smith Stokes property in Roughton grew and shrunk over the years. Before Roughton House was built, William and Nancy lived in a house with thirty acres, formerly William Brookes's which may have been Willowbrook.[227] At this time they also owned a toft and buildings with about 120 acres of land called Brookes's Farm; Brook House, perhaps, or Roughton Farm.[228] Both the barn and lower part of Roughton Farm appear to date from the late eighteenth century and was built using local, handmade bricks. The upper storey seems to be of a later date, perhaps early nineteenth century. Both the farmhouse and its associated farm buildings reflect a profitable period in farming which certainly wasn't the case when the family tried to sell the property in 1893.[229]

The Stokes family benefitted from the permitted enclosure of the Forest of Morfe and acquired The Old Lodge, and Old Lodge Farm from the Earl of Shrewsbury.[230] Thanks to Randall's work that we have a description of what the Old Lodge, sometimes called the Old Forest Lodge, looked like. When he visited Miss Stokes, she showed him what remained of the Old Lodge. By this time, in the 1890s, not much remained of the building except for stout strong walls and cellaring. Miss Stokes said that it had had large, cheerless rooms and a fireplace big enough to roast an ox on. The tenants asked for the Lodge to be turned into cottages so the old fireplace was bricked up and some of the building demolished.[231]

The Stokes family at one time held much property in and around Roughton but in 1911, when the Census was taken, Louisa Stokes recorded that she was 'living on scant means,' a sad end to a family which had once had so much standing in the community.

---

[225] *Shropshire Archives,* 1067/18

[226] *The National Archives,* PROB-11-1536-164

[227] *Shropshire Archives,* 1190/3/173 [undated] Admittance to 1 mess. and 1/2 yard land formerly William Brookes's where William Smith Stokes & Nancy dwelt plus the Upper Garden, The Brooke Meadow, Hoccom Meadow, Hayes Meadow; plus 1 mess., 1 toft, 2 yard lands called Brookes's Farm & Hell Dole (comprising Breeches Meadow, Oak Meadow, Alder Moor, Nettle Barrow, Barn Field, Middle Field, Crow Field, Brook Field, Birch Furlong, Alveley Hill); all in Roughton & Hoccom. [For the William Brookes house see the Forest of Morfe Map 1613, SA 4296/1]

[228] *Shropshire Archives,* 679/30

[229] The valuer wrote: "I think if Pritchard's trustees don't buy it will probably remain unsold for some time as owing to the depression agricultural land is not selling so well as it has done and at present there is no sign of recovery."

[230] John Randall, *Old Sports and Sportsmen,*Madeley, 1873, p. 30

[231] Worse was to befall the Old Lodge. The house was rebuilt in the 1940s and in 1979 only a small patch of painted stonework remained of this important building. (Shropshire County Council HER Number (PRN): 03592)

A 1918 WEDDING

Sheila Fellows née Myatt saw a photograph in one of the Worfield Parish Magazines of The Lodge to Roughton House and rang me up to say that this was where her father had lived. Mrs Fellows wondered if I would like to see a family christening glass engraved with her father's name; Bernard Myatt Roughton 1890. This was an interesting item and it was good to learn more of the Myatt family in Worfield, particularly of a wedding which took place in 1918.

The Miners Arms in Madeley. William & Harriet Myatt & from
the left: Bernard, Frank & Martha. Date estd. 1902

Bernard Myatt was born at Roughton and his parents were William and Harriet. In the 1891 Census William (aged 27) was a coachman/domestic servant to the Stokes family. In 1901, the Myatt family were living at 39, Penn Road, Wolverhampton, where William was a gardener. By this time there were two more children, Martha Florence, aged 8, and Frank, aged 6. William seemed destined to be a servant for the rest of his life but then he took a sharp change of direction and became licensee of the Miner's Arms, Madeley. Harriet's family, the Wakelams

264

were licensees of the Royal Oak at Rudge Heath which may have been the reason for William's career change.[232]

William's son, Frank, became a miner but what Bernard did for a living is not exactly known. He worked in a steelworks as a grinder and at one time worked in Sheffield. In the diary account which follows, Frank Myatt speaks of going to 'The Works.' Lizzie Dovey, the woman whom Bernard was to marry, lived at Rudge Heath, and worked at Ludstone Hall where she was ladies maid to Mrs Gratrix and also her kennel maid. This might seem an odd combination of jobs but Mrs Gratrix used to show Cavalier King Charles Spaniels and Pekingese dogs. Lizzie went to the Shows and on holiday with the family.

Lizzie Dovey

One might have expected that Bernard and Lizzie would have got married at Worfield or Claverley Church but in fact they were married at Ixworth in Suffolk. The Gratrix family, in addition to owning Ludstone Hall, also owned Ixworth Abbey in Suffolk. Lizzie went to work at Ixworth for a time which explains why the marriage was there rather than in Shropshire.

---

[232] There was a brewery in Wolverhampton started by John Francis Myatt in 1900 which at its peak served 100 pubs. It was taken over by the Holt Brewery in 1926. Whether the two Myatts were related I don't know

ROUGHTON

In 1918 Bernard and Lizzie were married, and Frank Myatt travelled, I assume, from the Madeley area to Ixworth to give Lizzie away. Frank kept a diary of this very special week and not only is it a delight to read, it is also important historically as we get a glimpse of London in the First World War. Aerial attack on civilian targets is not something we associate with the First World War but London was badly affected causing nearly 5,000 casualties. Nonetheless, theatres stayed open and Frank went to see the highly acclaimed 'Zig-Zag' at the London Hippodrome and the less highly acclaimed, 'Damaged Goods'. The latter was a propaganda film made by the War Office about venereal disease. This was costing the British Army a lot of money since the sufferers then had to be discharged from the army. I notice Frank makes no comment about the film. The wedding ceremony itself wasn't without incident, with a plane going overhead just as the parson was about to put the ring on the bride's finger. Even worse, the vicar nearly married Lizzie to the best man, Frank, rather than the bridegroom. I can't explain why Frank's return journey took him to Cardiff Street, Pennfields but that would explain why he walked down Lichfield Street to the Station. What is also charming about the diary is the obvious affection Frank has for his brother and new sister-in-law.

Frank Myatt's Diary

"Monday Jan 28th 1918

5.30am left home for the mine. 12.30pm finished. Took train at 2.58 ex Shifnal for Wolverhampton. Left Wolverhampton 4.15pm arrived Euston 7.30. Caught the Highgate tube landed at No. 26 Archway Road at 7.45. Maroons [Air Raid warning signals] sounded 8.5pm took cover at No. 23 Whitehall Mansions until 10.50pm. I wrote a letter home whilst raid was in progress, went back, called again at 11.20pm until 1.00am. Went back again. All clear given. Shrapnel fell heavily round us.

Tuesday Jan 29th 1918

Rose at 8.15. Had breakfast. Went to Elthorne Rd. Caught train at Liverpool Street at 12.00pm. Changed at Cambridge arriving 3.30pm. A most long[?ed] for ride. Met by the Bride to be, went by car to High Street Ixworth to Digs and had tea. Went to the Abbey. Introduced to the Girls. Acted as Cook General in the kitchen. Explored the abbey, Went up High Street with Devy. Had supper at the Abbey retired 9.20. Wrote to Mother and others.

Wednesday (the Eventful) Jan 30th 1918

Rose at 8.30 had breakfast. Went to Abbey. Back and changed, back to Abbey. Introduced to Mrs Laidon. Took Bride to Church 11am. Parson Canon Warren. Aeroplane passed over the Church just as parson was putting the ring on finger also liked to have married the wrong man. Came out Walked round the grounds had Breakfast (Swank) Speech by Lt Col Chadwick, youth and Beauty etc. Left at 3.20 en route for London, a most memorable journey with a new and Dear Sister landing at Archway Road at 10.00pm thus ending the beginning of a new era of a happy couple.

Lizzie pinched sugar on Cambridge Station [Note: sugar would have been scarce]

Moving staircase poor sister [Note: Apparently Lizzie was always terrified of escalators]

Nearly missed tube owing to luggage

Thursday Jan 31 1918

Went shopping with Lizzie had dinner went to Works and to City at Night.

Went to ZigZag. Simply great. Jack Edge, Daphne Pollard. Splendid

Friday Feb 1st 1918

Rose, had breakfast, went out on lonesome, came back and went with Mr Crump to see Leicester Square, Piccadilly Circus, Oxford Street, Trafalgar Square, the Strand, St Paul's, John Bulls Wreck, Covent Garden Floral to see wreck and other notable places in West End. Went to see Damaged Goods at the Marlborough. Home, had supper and to bed.

Frank & Bernard Myatt and Lizzie Myatt nee Dovey. Photograph taken in 1918, I assume

Saturday Feb 2nd 1918

Went to Works, came back and dined off Pheasant. Changed and went to Westminster. Saw Houses of Parliament, Westminster Abbey, Thames Embankment, notable buildings. Had tea in the Strand. War Rations. Visited Madame Tussauds, Baker St. Station, home by Bus and had from 9pm to 2am talking of pleasant reflections, the happiest period with brother and sister, 5 hours of solid talk of ups and downs, pleasant and dark hours of Lizzie and Bernard at home.

Sunday February 3rd 1918

Went after some milk and prepared for home leaving Euston at 12.00pm rather a dull journey landing at Cardiff St [Wolverhampton] at 5.00pm. Saw tart going down Lichfield Street as fast as could walk. Caught 7.45 for Shifnal. Met at Station by Mother with Mrs Harris and Bruce. Quite a joy ride back. One hour on the way. Landed home at 9.40 thus ending a memorable week. Glad to be back in my little grey home in the hills. END"

Acknowledgment:
Thanks are due to Mrs. Sheila Fellows for sharing this charming story

MAUNDY MONEY

1976

An application had been made that Mrs E. L. Shepherd of 1, New Cottages should receive Maundy money at Hereford Cathedral

First Distribution: allowance in lieu of clothing contained in a green purse for women and a white purse for men £3

Second Distribution: allowance in lieu of provisions £1.50 & for the redemption of the Sovereign's gown worn on the day of distribution £1 contained in a red purse

The Queen and Prince Philip were in attendance and a large number of those attached to the Royal Almonry. Mrs Shepherd received the alms money from the Queen[233]

---

[233] The alms money and correspondence are currently in St Peter's Church, Worfield

ROWDALE

Most of the Worfield items in Wolverhampton City Archives are part of the Nock and Joseland collection. Situated in Queen Street, Wolverhampton, Nock and Joseland ran the livestock market there and dealt with property sales and rentals. One of the items in the archive was the rental of a property called Rowdale Cottage.[234]

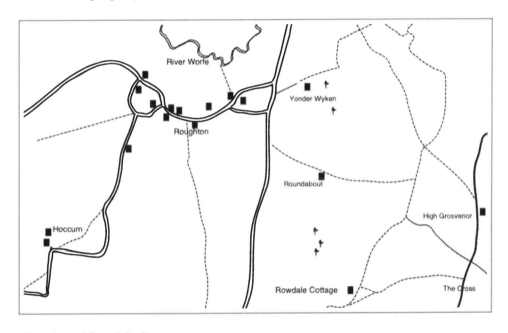

Location of Rowdale Cottage

Rowdale is a house which stands not far from the boundary with Claverley. It was either a late eighteenth century or early nineteenth century cottage built on the Morfe Common and had few amenities as we will see. In 1869, Rowdale was in the possession of Mrs Smithyman and in 1870 Elizabeth Bradley lived there, renting the house from the Stokes family. This was quite a roomy cottage, with 2 sitting rooms and 4 bedrooms and attached to it were a dairy, small stable, cowhouse, pigsty and four acres. The description as, "very healthy and prettily situated for a summer residence but somewhat out of the way in winter," tempted potential tenants until they saw just how isolated a place it was. At that point most of them ran as fast as they could in the opposite direction. Fred Holes and his wife from Wednesbury, who visited the cottage in February 1907, were typical. "I would have taken it, she won't, it's far too lonely," he wrote. It wasn't just the fact that site itself was isolated, there was no easy access as the description in one advertisement pointed out. "The nearest approach is by a cart road over one field and Wyken lane and by a foot road which is a little shorter." There was no easy way to get one's goods to the house.

Letter from Mr and Mrs Roberts. Ironbridge Oct 23 1892 to Nock and Joseland

"Just a note to say that I will meet Mr Bowen without fail in the Wheel of Worfield tomorrow."

Oct 28 1892 from Mr and Mrs Roberts to Nock and Joseland

"Your letter to hand quite safe. I am prepared to take the Rowdale Cottage at once providing you do all repairs and also the pumps which are in a very bad condition. I may mention that you did not mention which was my right road and I am very anxious as to which way I can get my goods there as I have 4 tons of goods to get there and as Mr Bowen will tell you it is an awkward place to get to. I have had a man there and he is at a loss to know how to get the goods there by going across the fields. I am prepared to give you 6 months rent provided you give 3 months notice on each side and I shall want it done as soon as you possibly can. I am very anxious to get there before the bad weather sets in. I am prepared to meet you and would be glad if we can get this sorted at the earliest convenience."

Perhaps Mr and Mrs Roberts didn't move in for the next letter is dated 1894

From: Keary, Wyley and de Wend (land agents and surveyors) 23 April 1894 to N. & J.

Worfield Tithe rent charge

"As recommended in your letter of the 29 Jan we have made application by post (and paid 6d extra for delivery fee) to Mrs Hughes for the tithe due from her to Mrs Davenport but we cannot get any reply so we conclude she does not intend to pay.

We hear that she has had to be summoned for poor rates. We understand you are going to offer her property by auction on the 25th inst. If it is sold we shall be much obliged if you will arrange with the solicitors for the amount due to be paid to us as per statement on the other side also kindly send us the name of the purchaser."

By 1900 the property had been inspected by Bridgnorth Council and various improvements ordered. A new cesspool must be built, properly bricked and covered to prevent water getting in. Inside the house the sink should have a waste outlet, the eaves and gutters should be cleaned, and work done to the back door to prevent damp. The inspector adds, 'I trust a thoroughly good job will be made of the water well. A draw well would be best.' The owner of the property wasn't in a rush to carry out the work and the inspector was angry when, two years later, the work hadn't been carried out. The Inspector writes in December 1903 that, 'the wells haven't been done nor much other work.'

Mrs Davenport puts her point of view in a letter to Mr Nock:

"I think there must have been a misunderstanding as to the well at Rowdale. The well referred to by the inspector must be a hole dug by the tenant at the bottom of the field and not the former source of supply several fields away. Had I better instruct Richards to do the work to this and the other items mentioned in the inspector's letter and shall I write Hughes (the Inspector) asking for more particulars of the covered cesspool he asks for.

The water from the sink falls onto the floor and then goes through a hole in the wall but I had told Richards to put a bit of pipe in. Perhaps the Inspector didn't notice or perhaps Richards forgot.

The cesspool is a big job I am afraid and in my opinion a mistake as the water which went through the cesspool would easily drain into the field.

The hard water well is a hole dug deep through soil and rock. There is no brickwork … It wants stemming for 8 and a half feet. I don't know what he means by a draw well but that is practically what it is at the moment."

Finally the work was done but the inspector was not impressed; he had expected better. As time went on the property deteriorated and the damp caused the wallpaper to peel off the walls. A firm of Bridgnorth surveyors offered to buy the property at the right price but they withdrew their interest believing it to be "a very unletable place because it is so isolated."

"In the early part of 1901 we corresponded about a small house and 4 acres of land called Rowdale occupied by Mr Mansell.

I am afraid it is in a much worse condition now than it was then. Are you disposed to offer it at a very low figure in which case I think I could do business with you?

Signed H. J. Wyley"

The property was not sold and was offered to Major Legh of Chyknell who again hopes to get it for a song.

From Major H. C. Legh of Chyknell to N&J

"Dear sir

"I am in receipt of your letter of the 17th inst. concerning "Rowdale" It is not a valuable property as far as I know but if you would kindly inform me of the price for purchase and the rent for letting I would like to inspect the property. So far as I remember the land if I had it would make a sort of excrescence on the … Morfe property and I would not care to pay a fancy price for it.

However I am obliged to you for giving me the opportunity. Kindly let me know the state of repairs, water supply, amount of tithe and rates etc."

The terms were £250 and Major Legh returned the letter in high dudgeon. 'It is quite useless for me to go into the question of purchase or rent on the basis you mention.'

In 1903 Mr T. Mansell, the tenant, offered to do the painting. He wrote to N&J

"If you have not made arrangements for the painting of Rowdale I will offer to do it as I can do it satisfactory. Has [as]I have been three or 4 years painting. I will do all the outside work with 2 coats with the exception of the stone for £3.5.0"

In July 1903 the water supply needed attention and hinges for the back kitchen window which had been forced by tramps. In January 1904, E. H. Bowen, Nock and Joseland's agent for the property wrote:

"I heard yesterday morning that the wind had blown in a large pane of glass. I haven't been to look but expect to find Mansell waiting for me."

Perhaps this was the last straw for Mansell because Miss Cal, a new tenant, arrived in September 1904. Bowen wrote to N&J that:"several of the rooms are in a bad state with damp coming through the walls. She will take it at £10."

How we take modern comforts for granted!

THE ROWLEYS OF ROWLEY

The township of Rowley is hidden now behind electronic gates and consists of a farmhouse and converted malthouse and barns. Once this was a hive of activity, not just with the regular farm work but with traffic to and from the malthouse in Rowley and also through the farmyard to Rowley Mill on the Worfe.

Rowley's House, Shrewsbury

When John Rowley married Mary Barret of Astley Abbots in the sixteenth century, the Rowleys were already affluent but this marriage brought with it more wealth and property. The couple had two sons, Roger, the elder, who took over Rowley Farm, and John, the younger, who lived at Severn Hall on the western side of the River Severn. Roger married Ann King, the daughter of William King of Birmingham, and the couple had three sons, William, John and Roger. Of these three, William Rowley is the best known, as a maltster, brewer and draper (cloth merchant) in Shrewsbury. He built a huge timber and brick house in the town in 1616-1618, known as Rowley's House, which until recently housed the Shrewsbury museum. John Rowley, the least well known of the three brothers, was a maltster at Ackleton and in 1623, aged forty-seven, he became a merchant in London. Roger Rowley (died 1624) remained at Rowley and, like his brothers, also ran a successful malting business. The businesses of the two (and perhaps three) brothers were linked, with malt being sent up the Severn to Shrewsbury to be used in William's brewing business. William Rowley, a staunch puritan, found himself on the wrong side of the fence in the early stages of the Civil War when Charles I entered Shrewsbury in 1642. This had serious consequences for William's business but the Rowley business at Rowley continued to flourish. It was Roger Rowley's son, Roger, who is thought to have improved Rowley farmhouse, and in 1645 he paid £583 for Sir William Whitmore's Apley estate when it was sequestrated by the parliamentarians in the Civil War.[235] Forrest describes Rowley farmhouse and the malthouse as follows:

"The dwelling house appears to have been largely rebuilt about the time of Charles I or Cromwell, but parts of it, including the kitchen, with its chimney stack, are older, probably Elizabethan. The drawing room is completely panelled, and has an elaborate carved overmantel consisting of two panels each with a large oval boss in the centre, surrounded and crossed by scrolls and other conventional ornaments. The centre bosses are in high relief. ... The panelling etc. was put in during the later Cromwellian period. The kitchen fireplace originally had a very large ingle with an open hearth but this is now filled up and occupied by an open range. The front and back doors of the house are ancient, consisting of oaken planks, vertical on the outer face and horizontal on the inner - nailed together without any framing, and they still retain the old iron latches and strap hinges. Both doors probably belonged to the Elizabethan building. There are some good Dutch tiles in the drawing room grate. The bricks used in the older part of the house for the chimney are of the thin Elizabethan type, whilst modern bricks have been used to replace decayed wattle work etc. So far as can be seen, no part of the existing house is of older date than the latter part of Queen Elizabeth's reign, though, of course, there may have been an earlier house on the same site, since we know that the Rowleys were here as far back as the 13th century.

To turn now to the substantial stone building [in the farmyard] opposite. Up to the early part of the nineteenth century it was used as a malthouse and a careful study of the structure leads us to the conclusion that it was originally designed as a malthouse and not a dwelling house.... The entrance was by a small door on the left close to the front corner, and the opening has a flat Tudor arch. All the details indicate that the building was erected late in the Tudor period, about the year 1600." Shortly after the malthouse was built, the main malthouse was extended on either side by two annexes, and the stonework of the gable end was replaced by brick. On the left hand side, the annexe was brick on the ground floor and wattle and daub above. It created a corridor with steps down to the cellar of the main building and stairs to the upper floors. On the other side was a large brick and stone annexe built with stone taken from the gable end of the main building which was rebuilt in brick."

[235] H. E. Forrest, *Some Old Shropshire Houses and their Owners*, Shrewsbury 1924

AMBROSE AND ALICE BARON

Alice Edwards & Ambrose Baron leaving Rowley Farm for their
wedding at Worfield in 1909. Photo courtesy of Alec Brew

It was in 2008/9 when I was completing a survey of gravestones in the Lower Churchyard
of Worfield, that I was approached by Margaret James who was looking for the grave of her
grandmother, Alice Baron. I was working from a previous survey carried out by the WI but I
just couldn't find the headstone. Margaret had visited the churchyard many years before and
thought she knew exactly where the grave was and her memory served her well. She took me
straight to the grave at the back of the Old Club Room. I had already seen the photograph

above of Alice and Ambrose's wedding, in Alec Brew's collection but this meeting in the churchyard gave me more details of Alice's short and tragic life.

Born Alice Edwards, the Edwards family lived at Rowley Farm, but when Alice was of working age she took a job in service in North Staffordshire, on the Staffordshire/Cheshire border. Here Alice met and fell in love with a miller, Ambrose Baron. Aged only eighteen, Alice's parents felt she was too young to marry but Alice was very headstrong and prepared to live with Ambrose whether or not her parents gave their approval. Reluctantly Alice's parents gave their permission for the marriage and in 1909 the couple were married at Worfield Church. After their marriage, Mr and Mrs Baron returned to North Staffordshire/ Cheshire where Alice gave birth to the couple's only child, a daughter, Edith. Shortly afterwards Alice became ill and came back to Rowley with her daughter. She was suffering from TB. Ambrose came to visit but six months before she died, Alice wouldn't allow him to go into the house for

Edith Baron on the bicycle outside Rowley Farm 1912
Photo courtesy of Alec Brew

fear of infection. He was allowed as far as the garden gate but no nearer. In 1912 Alice died of TB. She was just 21.

Edith was brought up by the Edwards family and whether Ambrose Baron played any further part in Edith's life is not known. The photograph above was taken at Rowley Farm but by 1919 the Edwards family had moved to Westbeech, Pattingham.

FREDERICK HODSON JOYNSON

The painted west window in St Peter's Church is dedicated to Samuel Joynson and his wife, Elizabeth, who lived at Rowley, and in the Lower Churchyard are memorials to other members of the Joynson family, including Frederick Hodson Joynson who died on April 14th 1910, aged 75. The name is an unusual one in these parts but better known in Cheshire, Liverpool and Manchester where some members of the family were involved in the cotton trade. I have been unable to discover what first brought the Joynsons to Rowley where two generations of the family farmed in the nineteenth century. In a sense this is a story about beginnings and endings; the arrival of a family in the parish and the last Joynson to be buried in Worfield over a hundred years later.

I neither know why Samuel Joynson came to Rowley Farm, nor when he did so. Samuel died in 1824, aged 82, and we know from his will that he was then living at Rowley and bequeathed the tenanted farm to his wife, Elizabeth. The couple had a large number of children, one of whom, also called Samuel, was running the farm in 1841, together with Edward Bowen and his wife Catherine. Samuel the younger died in 1849, aged 70.[236] He had married Martha Stokes in 1832 and the couple had no children. The wills of both Samuel and Martha show how intertwined Worfield families at this time. The four executors of Samuel the younger's will were his brother, Peter, his nephew, his brother-in-law William Stokes, and his friend John Meredith of Hoccum. After her husband's death, Martha Joynson continued to live at Rowley until her death in 1855 with her sister Catherine Bowen. Martha Joynson died a wealthy woman owning freehold property at the Sonde, namely, a freehold house and buildings, occupied by Thomas Whiston Powell, which she bequeathed to her sister Catherine Bowen, and a freehold cottage or dwelling house which she left to Ann Perry of Shipley. Two cottages in Heathon, Claverley were left to Mary Ann Perry, and of the household effects, Elizabeth Onions of Bridgnorth, another relative, received a mahogany bookcase and its contents. The will was witnessed by Moses and Thomas Piper of Wyken.

One of Samuel the younger's brothers, John Joynson, took over a 300 acre farm at Chesterton which, again, his widow continued to run after his death.[237] Frederick Hodson Joynson was the eldest son and remained at home helping to run the farm until he was in his late twenties. At some point between the censuses of 1861 and 1871 Frederick gave up farming, and moved to Wallasey, Cheshire, working as a cotton broker.[238]

The cotton connection was strong, as already mentioned. In 1851, Peter Joynson, Frederick's uncle, was living in Salford and working a cotton trader, and in 1861 he was living in a

---

[236] *Wolverhampton Chronicle*, 10 March 1830, p. 1

[237] UK Census 1841, 1851

[238] UK Census 1861, 1871

community of cotton workers in Eccles. In 1861, Ann Holt, Frederick's grandmother was living at Chesterton and described herself as a muslin manufacturer's widow.[239]

Just as we have no idea what prompted Frederick's career change, so we have no idea what brought him back to this area, but in 1881 he was living in Church Street, Bridgnorth, working as a general merchant. By 1891, still in Bridgnorth, Joynson described himself in the census as a retired farmer.[240]

In April 1910, Frederick Joynson, as he frequently did, caught the bus from Bridgnorth to fish in the Worfe.[241] He walked to the Davenport Arms, arriving around noon, had a glass of sherry and some biscuits, and told the licensee, George Eden Reynolds, that he was going to fish under Rowley Wood. His intention was to return to Bridgnorth at 3pm but if he didn't do that he said he would have a cup of tea with George Reynolds before his return.

Arthur Powles, the gamekeeper, was walking alongside the Worfe at 2.15pm and saw a fisherman's basket and a man's overcoat. He did not at that time go nearer but when he saw these items in the same place at 4.30pm, he investigated further and found Mr Joynson face down in the Worfe. Here, there were pools in the Worfe where the water might be six or seven feet deep. The gamekeeper enlisted the help of Harry Fryer, the sexton, who with the help of Mr Price, got the body out of the river.

The verdict of the jury was that Joynson's death was accidental. It was likely that he had just begun to fish for trout when his line caught on a bush and, whilst trying to release it, slipped into the stream. Joynson had been in ill-health for some time but had recently improved somewhat and it was thought that he was not strong enough to save himself.

The inquest was held in the Worfield schoolroom before the coroner, R. F. Haslewood, and the jury: William Bluck (foreman), William George Leighton, John Whitefoot Wilcox, Harry Langford, William Thatcher, John Milner, Thomas White, John Bishop, George Thomas, Harry Tarrant, Isaac Tarrant and Frank Turner.

From medieval times, jurors had always sworn the oath together as one, but a recent Act had been passed requiring each juror to swear the oath separately unless all members of the jury objected when they could swear as one. Haslewood obviously hadn't much time for this change in the law and encouraged the jury to object by saying that most juries objected and if they chose to be sworn one at a time they would have to swear a long oath to be repeated after him which would take twenty minutes to complete. It would have been a brave set of men to have gone against the coroner's direction. The jury, needless to say, objected and were sworn as a whole. Before the evidence from witnesses was heard the jury had to view the body which was lying in the Reading Room.

The Joynson story takes us beyond the confines of the parish to the cotton mills of northern England which it would be fascinating to investigate further. Arthur Oatley Joynson, Frederick's son, who died in 1951 was the last member of the family to be buried at Worfield.

---

[239] UK Census 1861

[240] UK Census 1881, 1891

[241] *Bridgnorth Journal & South Shropshire Advertiser,* 23 April 1910, p. 5

STABLEFORD HALL

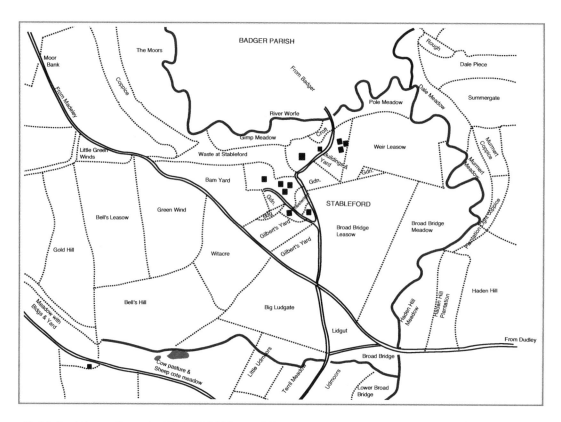

Stableford drawn from the 1839 Field Names Map

Stableford Hall was called Stableford House prior to its name being changed in 1905. John Randall, writing in 1887 refers to the House as follows: "The former residence of the Jasper family which was of red brick, is still part of the present house, Mr Smith having added to it."[242] [243]

---

[242] Shropshire Archives PR/3/503, a watercolour of Stableford House by A. E. Everitt (1824-1882) purchased by Shropshire County Library in 1970

[243] John Randall, *Worfield and its Townships*, Madeley, 1887, p. 113

John Jasper inherited land and property in Stableford through his wife, Sarah, née Foxall.[244] Sarah was the eldest daughter of Hezekiah and Sarah Foxall both of whom died in 1754, There were no sons of the marriage so Sarah inherited the Foxall land in Stableford when she married John Jasper. The Jasper line continued through three generations of John Jasper, until we reach the last John Jasper who married Elizabeth.[245] There were no children of this marriage so when they both died in 1864; John Jasper on the 29 June and Elizabeth on the 20 August, their nephew, Thomas Smith, inherited the Stableford Estate.[246] [247] Thomas Smith was the son of Captain Smith of Tong and was farming with his uncle when the 1841 census was taken.[248]

Shropshire Archaeologists have dated Stableford House/Hall and its associated buildings as a farmstead of early nineteenth century origin.[249] This is at odds with the sales particulars of the Stableford Estate in 1876. Stableford House which was part of the Estate, was then described by the vendor, Thomas Smith, as having been built ten years previously. The Estate at that time consisted of:

"A modern, substantially built mansion, extensive and complete farm homestead, three comfortable villa residences and numerous cottages together with 286 acres. The mansion which was built about ten years ago is approached by a carriage drive through grounds well laid out and adorned with valuable ornamental trees and shrubs. The house has twelve bedrooms and three dressing rooms, bathroom with hot and cold water, two wc's, housemaids closets etc., stabling for seven horses which can be extended, large coach house, panelled harness room etc.

244 *The National Archives*, PROB 11/270/437, Will of Roger Foxall, 1650, "a yeoman, a number of amounts of money to his daughters and son, John, who has already received"

245 *The National Archives*, PROB 11/1663/230, Will of John Jasper 1817 (codicil 1822), gentleman. The copyhold property is put in the trust of John Jasper, his son, John Clare of Bushbury and John Clarke of Ackleton to provide for his three daughters, Elizabeth and Harriet who are unmarried, and his married daughter, Frances Smith. The property is to be mortgaged if necessary to release cash of £1,050 for each of the daughters. His son John Jasper has been provided for elsewhere. The property to be put in trust is: "all that messuage or dwelling house with the gardens and appurtenances belonging in Stableford late in the occupation of Mrs Jane Cox widow but now in the occupation of Mr Valentine Vickers the elder together with liberty for my two daughters Elizabeth and Harriet and their servants to fetch water at all times from the well near the door of the dwelling-house now in the occupation of John Richards and also all that piece of parcel of land adjoining to the said dwelling house and garden called Gilberts Yard now divided into two pieces with the barn thereon together with the garden now in the occupation of the said John Richards and also all that piece or parcel of meadow land lying on the south side of the road near Broadbridge called Little Broadbridge Meadow now in my own occupation all which said premises are in Stableford subject nevertheless to a right of road for my said son John Jasper his heirs and assigns over the said piece called Gilberts Yard to my other lands for all purposes except driving sheep, pigs and loose cattle to hold the said premises subject as aforesaid."

246 *Bridgnorth Journal*, 30 July 1864, p. 3

247 *Bridgnorth Journal*, 10 September, 1864, p. 4

248 *Hereford Times*, 24 December, 1853

249 *Shropshire Archives*, HER No. 26082

The farm buildings are very conveniently arranged, fitted with steam power and …are so situated that they may be occupied with or without the mansion… The villa residences are very conveniently situated…The estate lies in a ring fence in a high state of cultivation having been in the owner's occupation for many years."[250]

The question remains as to when Stableford Hall was built and who built it. Rebecca Madeley, the daughter of a previous owner of the Hall concludes that the house was built as a whole since the cellars cover the whole of the house, with just a new front being added later. Perhaps it was this which Smith added, or did he actually built the house from scratch, having demolished a previous building? The estate and the livestock, 320 Shropshire sheep and fifty Shorthorn cattle, were sold, and Mr Smith left the area to live at Beaumaris.

The new owners of Stableford Hall were Charles Chandos Pole and his wife Anna Constantia. Mr Chandos Pole died in 1881and his wife in 1894 and the Stableford Estate was again sold in spite of Mrs Chandos Pole's brother, the MP, Mr Staveley Hill contesting the will on the grounds that his sister was not of sound mind.[251] The estate was described as follows: "By order of Trustees at a low reserve. A spacious mansion with over 300 acres of farmland, farmhouse and numerous cottages … and two other residences and numerous cottages forming the entire hamlet of Stableford; about 260 acres with the farm villa and homestead are let and the remainder of the land is held with the mansion." Also three miles of trout fishing.[252]

[250] The Field, the Country Gentleman's Newspaper, July 22 1876, p. 9

[251] *Wellington Journal and Shrewsbury News*, 2 November 1895, p. 6

[252] *Wellington Journal and Shrewsbury News*, June 9 1894, p. 1

And there we could leave the story, confident in the fact that the Stableford Estate belonged to the Jasper family except for a rather annoying fly in the ointment. In 1860, Thomas Nock sold the Stableford Estate, "A house called Stableford House, four cottages and over two hundred acres".[253] There are a number of references to the occupants of Stableford House before this. For example, in 1846, Henry Hill of Stableford House married Maria the daughter of Edward West of Worcestershire and in 1845, Robert Taylor son of Robert Taylor died, aged 25, at Stableford House.[254] [255] Mr Nock's Stableford House was described as follows in one newspaper. "There is a comfortable Farm House and suitable buildings, erected on a pleasing and elevated site."[256] If Jasper had bought Nock's Stableford Estate in 1860, this could explain why Thomas Smith built Stableford Hall when he inherited the Estate in 1864.

In 1865 Thomas Smith brought a case against of obstruction of the highway, on a Methodist preacher from Dawley. On the Sunday in question, Mrs Smith and a servant were driving to Worfield Church and the preacher's wagon was parked in the middle of the road at Cranmere surrounded by about fifteen people who were praying and singing psalms. The pony refused to go forward until Mrs Smith's servant led it past. Smith said the congregations were a frequent occurrence and caused great annoyance to residents but denied that he had said he would personally move the congregation on or turn his cattle in amongst them. However, it was true that he had dismissed one of his staff for attending and would do so again. The case was heard in Bridgnorth with a large number of people in court to hear that Smith had lost the case.[257]

Further Reference

There is a box of uncatalogued material in Shropshire Archives called Title Deeds of Worfield which contains some Stableford information. P314/Q/1/2/8 (Box 1) and D3651/B/7/2/37, a schedule of deeds and documents relating to the Stableford Estate situated at Stableford and Ackleton in the parish of Worfield the property of Richard Cecil Corbett also in Shropshire Archives

---

[253] *Eddowes Journal*, 20 June 1860, p.1

[254] *Hereford Times*, 30 May 1846, p 6

[255] *Eddowes Journal*, 24 December 1845 p. 2

[256] *Shrewsbury Chronicle*, 17 August 1860, p. 1

[257] *Bridgnorth Journal*, 10 June 1865. p. 5

GITTON'S FOLLY

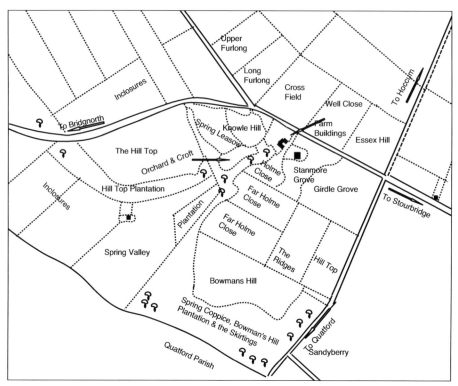

Stanmore drawn from the 1839 Field Names Map

When Stanmore Hall was offered for sale in 2020, it occurred to me that I knew nothing about its history. It is easy to forget that this is part of Worfield Parish because it lies on the Quatford side of the A464 Bridgnorth to Stourbridge Road. As regards its history, even the National Heritage List is vague; "circa late eighteenth century and later," is all they offer.[258]

Estate agents do little better when describing the Hall. The 2020 description says that Stanmore Hall was a "19th-century seat of the powerful Whitmore family of Apley Park, whose wealth derived from a 16th-century ancestor, William Whitmore".[259] The narrative continues with more information about the Whitmore family but few facts about the history of the house. When the Hall was sold in 2008 it was described by the estate agent as, "An

[258] *www.historicengland.org.uk.* Stanmore Hall, listing number 1367568

[259] *Country Life,* October 24, 2020

impressive Georgian country house of great standing".[260] Neither description is entirely accurate as we will see.

Stanmore Hall. Illustration by W. Hallam

Until the beginning of the seventeenth century, Stanmore was part of the Forest of Morfe. The land was of poor quality; a stony moor, dotted with isolated farms, and separated by open common. Morfe Common, as it was then known, was enclosed as part of the Parliamentary Enclosures by an Act of 1806.[261] The fields with straight boundaries shown on the map above, are typical of these late enclosures.

The first mention I have found of Stanmore was an indenture between John Owseley and Sarah Richards, widow, and Thomas Richards, gentleman, in 1691.[262] In 1727, Stanmore came into the hands of Thomas Gitton, a Bridgnorth solicitor who had built up a large property portfolio both in Bridgnorth and the nearby parishes of Highley, Chelmarsh, Chetton and Claverley (Ludstone Hall). Thomas Gitton died in 1766 and most of the property devolved to a

---

[260] *Shropshire Star*, March 27, 2008

[261] *Shropshire Archives*, BB/C/4/2/12

[262] *Shropshire Archives*, 1190/3/350

cousin, Thomas Powis, who was the son of Edward Powis and Mary, his wife. Mary was the daughter of Thomas Gitton's uncle, Henry Gitton.[263] Thomas Powis, under the terms of Thomas Gitton's will, was to change his name to Thomas Gitton and so it was that Thomas [Powis]Gitton, solicitor and banker, came into possession of Stanmore. Thomas [Powis] Gitton married and had a son, rather unhelpfully for us also called Thomas Gitton, who was born in 1774. Thomas [Powis] Gitton died in 1781, and in December 1794, his son inherited Stanmore, a house with farm land of just over one hundred and twenty acres.[264]

In 1814 Gitton took out a mortgage of £7,000 to build a new house at Stanmore but before he could enjoy the fruits of his investment, events in Bridgnorth overtook him. On the 10 December 1814, the Bridgnorth Bank, otherwise known as the bank of Macmichael, Gitton & Co., suffered a shortfall in funds caused by the Macmichaels' Bridgnorth Carpet Factory overdrawing at the Bank. The bank was forced to close and although it was hoped this would be temporary, it was not to be.[265] In January 1815, John, William and Joseph Macmichael, Thomas Gitton and Alexander McMath, partners in the Carpet Factory, were all declared bankrupt.[266] As a result, their freehold property had to be sold which included Ludstone Hall and Stanmore Grove belonging to Thomas Gitton, and the Burcote spinning factory which belonged to the Macmichaels.

Gitton was not ready to give up Stanmore Grove and arranged for a relative, George Oldbury, to buy the property at auction. It was described as "all that newly erected capital mansion called Stanmore Grove, a messuage, buildings and land part of which is freehold and the rest leasehold under Thomas Whitmore. All the premises are occupied by William Fletcher."[267] In 1836 the Worfield Rate Book shows Gitton as the owner of Stanmore Grove but in 1837 it was again up for auction as Thomas Gitton's financial affairs were in no better order than previously.[268] [269] Stanmore Grove was heavily mortgaged to George Pritchard who therefore became the next owner. George Pritchard was a member of another family whose fortune had been made from banking and the law. George's father, John Pritchard of Broseley, was initially a solicitor and became a banker in 1799. John's sons, George and John were also solicitors but spent most of their careers in banking.

George Pritchard rented Stanmore to Richard Boycott and his wife; Boycott being a partner in the bank of Pritchard, Boycott and Nicholas of Bridgnorth. On the decease of Richard Boycott in1861, and his wife in 1864, Richard Boycott, their son, remained as the sole

---

263 *The National Archives,* PROB 11/917/366

264 *Shropshire Archives,* 1190/3/350

265 *Oxford University and City Herald,* 10 December 1814, p. 4

266 *Staffordshire Advertiser,* 21 January 1815, p. 2

267 *London Courier and Evening Gazette,* 29 October 1817, p. 4

268 *Shropshire Archives,* Worfield Rate Book, 1836

269 *Chester Courant,* 18 July 1837 p. 1

tenant.[270] [271] John Pritchard took over a somewhat dilapidated Stanmore in 1861 and the house might have descended into terminal decline but for the Bridgnorth, Wolverhampton and Staffordshire Railway.

John Pritchard, as MP for Bridgnorth, was an enthusiastic supporter of the railway until the proposed route took the line close to Stanmore causing Mr. Pritchard to do a complete about-turn. The inhabitants of Bridgnorth and its neighbourhood were outraged at the fact that their MP had put his personal interests before those of his constituents. Furthermore, their trusted MP had also lied, stating that the railway would destroy the beauty of the house, making it "unfit for the petitioner's habitation."[272] In fact, all the locals knew that John Pritchard had never lived at Stanmore Grove. One correspondent to a newspaper, signed himself "Turn Him-Out," and ridiculed the beauty of the house as described by Pritchard saying it was, "a very mean-looking square-built brick house. No-one looking upon the dreary fabric could but conceive of it being an act of charity to remove some little of the perpetual monotony that has characterised 'Gitton's Folly.'"[14]

John Pritchard urgently needed to repair his reputation and thought that living at Stanmore would help in this regard. However it was an indisputable fact that the house as it stood was plain and small; a redesign was clearly necessary. Pritchard chose J. W. Hugall as the architect for the new build, probably on the recommendation of his brother-in-law, The Revd. Osborn Gordon. Stanmore Hall was completed in 1869 at a cost of £40,000 and the result was a very bizarre house indeed.[273] No-one would suspect that somewhere within this building might have been Gitton's Georgian house and probably the pre-Georgian house as well. "Gitton's Folly" had surely become "Pritchard's Folly". The house was furnished with every modern convenience, including central heating in all the main rooms, water and gas piped from Bridgnorth, hot and cold water, a bathroom and toilets. Nor was any expense spared on the interior design, with marble mantlepieces, parquet flooring, elaborate ceilings, and paintings bought with the help of his friend, John Ruskin.[274]

John Pritchard died in 1891 and Stanmore then passed to John Pritchard Gordon. The small farm had grown to an estate of 1300 acres and Pritchard Gordon had no need of another large house as he was already living in one at Danesford.[275] By 1917, some parts of the Estate were being sold and in 1920 the Stanmore Estate was sold in a number of lots including Hoccum Farm, Swancote Farm, Roughton Farm, Roughton House, Old Lodge Farm, as well as other property in Worfield, Quatford and Claverley Parishes. Stanmore Hall was sold and

[270] *Staffordshire Advertiser*, 18 February, 1860, p. 5

[271] *Staffordshire Advertiser*, 9 July 1864, p. 5

[272] *Bridgnorth Journal*, 13 February 1869, p. 4

[273] *Bridgnorth Journal*, 13 February 1869, p. 4

[274] Cynthia Gamble, *John Ruskin, Henry James and the Shropshire Lads: Enduring Friendships*, p. 180, New European Publications, 2008

[275] *Gloucester Echo*, 20 August, 1891, p. 3

rebuilt yet again, replacing most of Hugall's creation with a Georgian style house.[276] [277] It is at this point that I have a gap and assume the Hamilton-Russell family bought part of the Stanmore Estate, including the Hall, in 1920, but I could be wrong. Certainly, in 1939, Stanmore Hall was the home of the Honourable Eustace Scott Hamilton-Russell and, in November of that year, land on the opposite side of the A464 was requisitioned by the government for an RAF camp.[278] All that remains of the Hamilton-Russell connection in the area today is the name of one of the roads in Stanmore; Russell Close.

In 1950 Stanmore Hall was once again altered and reduced in size by the removal of the servants' wings, leaving a three-bay house. Eustace Hamilton Russell died in 1962, his wife, Olive Wolryche Whitmore, having predeceased him, and Stanmore passed to their only child, Rachel Hamilton-Russell. Ten years earlier, in 1952, Geoffrey Wolryche-Whitmore had passed Dudmaston to his niece, Rachel Hamilton-Russell, hence the connection between Dudmaston and Stanmore. Rachel married Sir George Labouchere, a British diplomat, and when he retired they returned to England. Dudmaston was always their intended home but while renovation work was taking place, Sir George and Lady Labouchere lived at Stanmore Hall. The upkeep of Stanmore was felt to be too expensive and was sold by Lady Labouchere in 1965.

It appears that Stanmore Hall is not entirely the Georgian house that some believe, nor does it have a connection with Apley as has also been claimed. The complicated past of Stanmore has taken some unravelling but it is a fascinating story.

Acknowledgment
Thanks are due to Gill Waugh-Pead, Susanne Haines and Ann Walter for providing details of the Thomas Gitton story

[276] *Shropshire Archives,* 5586/5/8/32

[277] *Shropshire Archives,* MI973

[278] *Western Mail,* 5 September 1939, p. 6

WORFIELD'S BLEAK HOUSE

Worfield Rectory from the south side in Sir Oliver & Lady Leese's time

In the seventeenth century, Worfield's own version of Bleak House was playing out. Like Dickens' novel the case probably entertained those who were not involved as much as it caused grief and concern to those who were. Worfield's Bleak House was the Rectory and Vicarage of Worfield and the Wyken Estate, all of which had been owned by the Dean and Chapter of Lichfield. The protagonists of Davenport and Talbott, having failed to resolve matters in the Manor Court of Worfield, fought their corners in the Chancery Court. The issues were some large discrepancies in what Henry Davenport thought he had bought when he purchased the Rectory and Wyken and what George Talbott claimed he had sold.

Before I explain what the case is, let me say that Chancery Court case reports are incredibly difficult to read, which is probably one of the very sensible reasons why historians tend to give them a wide berth. The size of these documents, often more than eighteen inches across, and closely handwritten, makes them very hard to read. It is easy to stray from one line to the next as you move across the page and the flamboyant style makes the sense very hard to follow. I am not trained in law, seventeenth century or any other for that matter; indentures, trusts, bargains and sale, and similar legal terms frankly make my head spin. Dickens managed to cut through all the legalistic jargon and present the human side of the Bleak House case and I will try to do the same for Worfield's case of Davenport versus Talbott and Rydley.[279]

In 1394, the Dean and Chapter of Lichfield Cathedral separated the usage of the Rectory and Vicarage of Worfield. The two buildings butt up against each other and the area which each should have was defined as follows:

"It was agreed with the Dean and Chapter of Lichfield Cathedral that the vicars shall have the chamber and hall, with the garden place as far as the paling which stretches from the entry door of the rectory to the stream running to the lord's mill as his dwelling."[280]

The north side of the rectory showing the adjoining vicarage in 1938

In 1548, Worfield Rectory was leased to Sir John Talbot who was the Lord of the Manor of Albrighton and lived at Pepperhill.[281] He died in 1549, so one supposes he may never have lived at Worfield but the Rectory remained in the Talbot family until George Talbot sold the Worfield holdings over a hundred years later. The sale included the Rectory, the Vicarage, Wyken, Worfield Mill, several other plots of land including a garden adjoining the Rectory, the advowson of the Church, and the rectoral tithes. The purchaser, Henry Davenport, soon found

[279] *The National Archives*, C7/95/51

[280] *Shropshire Archives*, 330/1

[281] *Staffordshire Record Office*, LD/30/4/3/164

that the property had mortgages, loans and annuities attached to it, and was not quite the unencumbered bargain he thought he had bought. Henry took action against George Talbot, bringing a case against him in the Chancery Court in 1696 on the grounds that he believed the estate was free from rent and debt. The court record is as follows:

"And this defendant knoweth not how the fee farm rent became due nor that it was incumbent on the said estate for that the complainant hath never yet delivered him the old deeds relating to the said estate though often requested as also neither hath he delivered the court rolls belonging to the said estate and manor although often demanded of him and his steward nor hath or had this defendant any allowance or abatement for the fee farm rent"[282]

The vicarage in 1938

Not only had Henry Davenport bought property which was mortgaged, and which had been used as security for loans, there were also £1,777 5s 10d of annuities to be paid. George Talbot was vague on the exact figure of these liabilities which suggests that it was probably higher than this. In today's money that would amount to around £350,000, quite a shock no matter how little you had paid for the property or how wealthy one might be. By the time Henry had bought the Rectory and Vicarage, and paid extra for Wyken, he believed he had overpaid by £1400.

Realisation of how bad things were came slowly to Henry Davenport. There wasn't one bombshell but a succession of them. Henry Davenport perhaps smelled a rat when, having paid

[282] *The National Archives,* C7/95/51

for the properties, he received no title deeds. George Talbot searched long and hard, so he said, but failed to find them, in spite of Henry Davenport's repeated requests to be given them, and George proved to be a slippery character to pin down. Living in Ireland made it difficult to contact him and when he came to England he usually stayed in London.

It was during one of George Talbot's visits to London that he offered to hand the deeds over. Henry Davenport must have been relieved but then Talbot said he would only hand them over to his solicitor, Mr. Gattaker, who would have to go to London to collect them. That never happened. Seven years went by and still no deeds appeared nor any court rolls showing when various transfers of property had taken place. At one time, Henry sent George Talbot a letter which George refused to accept so it had to be returned to Henry unread. On another occasion, Henry Davenport asked to see some documents which were indeed presented but had been chewed by rodents. Apparently mice had got into the box in which the documents were stored; or was the mouse deliberately added to the box to make sure little would remain? One document was readable and George Talbot felt he had met his obligations. Henry Davenport must have been tearing his hair out.

Almost every aspect of the purchase was fraught with problems. Wyken, which Henry thought he had bought without any rental obligation, was subject to a rent to be paid to the Dean and Chapter of Lichfield. George Talbott seemed happy to accept the purchase money and then tell Henry Davenport of the conditions of sale. Some of the property was mortgaged, some was subject to trusts, and the tithes which Henry Davenport had thought would bring him a good income were apparently not all his. Some of the townships were not included in the purchase, nor the right to tithe hay and clover. The tithes of Ackleton had been owned by Anne Copley who had been very heavy-handed with the inhabitants, threatening them with eviction if they didn't pay. When Henry did eventually get the rights to the tithes of Ackleton the inhabitants would only pay in kind. Perhaps this is why there was a tithe barn near Rowley which stood on the side of the main road from Ackleton. The location always seemed very odd to me.

Worse news was to come. The Rectory was subject to a 500-year lease to Thomas Kinnersley. Even the garden attached to the Rectory belonged to the poor of the parish. Henry's right to the vicarage was safe as long as Francis Barney, the incumbent, was living but when Francis Barney died, it would revert to Magdalene Talbot and Richard Rydley. Exactly what had Henry Davenport bought? It must have seemed like a very long nightmare.

The loans which Henry had to pay were as follows:

… Sarmon in the County of Gloucester for which there is a mortgage by Thomas Talbot on land in Bagworth, Gloucestershire - £300

Rebecca Batch of Akelton -£106

Thomas Sheppard of Harvington, Worcestershire £60

John Sanders of Claverley £50

John Hickmay of Alveley 320

George Pendrell of Hednesford by bond £30

John Thomason of Roton £21.4s

Thomas Child son of Sir William Child of Kinlet £500

Thomas Kempson of Great Saredon £339 1s 9d

So having considered Henry Davenport's side of things, is there anything to be said on George Talbott's behalf? Why, I wondered, were the Talbotts so short of money? As I read through the list of people to whom money was owed, I noticed a name which you will know, that of George Pendrell. When King Charles II escaped from the Battle of Worcester in 1651, it was the Pendrell brothers who protected him at Whiteladies and saw that the King had safe passage to Moseley Old Hall. It led me to wonder if some of the Talbotts' money problems were due to the Civil War. As staunch Royalists they had probably spent more money in the support of this cause than they could afford. On the other hand this may not have been the whole story. Perhaps, they had spent more on building the Rectory a hundred years earlier than they should have, or was Thomas Talbott (George's father) a spendthrift, as Henry Davenport suggests?[283] Whatever the reasons for the Talbott's poverty it marks a decline in old wealth and the rise of the new in the shape of merchant money.

[283] *The National Archives,* C7/95/51

THE NOEL-HILL CONNECTION

Attingham Hall

One weekend in 2018 I visited Attingham Park. This was my first visit inside the Hall itself, having been put off by a friend who thought the house rather boring and not worth the trouble. Actually I found it fascinating for reasons which will become apparent.

Before Attingham was given to the National Trust it was owned by the Noel-Hill family. Originally from Hodnet, the Hills had made their money in medieval times from the wool trade. Rowland Hill went to London to pursue his business interests, and like many successful merchants he became Mayor of London. As the first Protestant Mayor of London, Hill endeared himself to Henry VIII and lent money to the cash-strapped King. These debts were often repaid in land, as in this case, and the family thus became substantial landowners in Shropshire. When the country returned to Roman Catholicism under Queen Mary, the Hills very sensibly removed themselves from London and retired quietly to their Shropshire home.

The manor of Attingham or Atcham was purchased in 1700 by Richard Hill, a bachelor, who left the property to his nephew Thomas, who took the name Hill. In 1782, on his father's death, Thomas's son, Noel, started ambitious building work. Tern Hall, which had been built by Richard Hill, was replaced by the very grand Attingham Hall, and Noel Hill took the title Baron Berwick, not from the northern town of that name but from Berwick Maviston, a manor adjacent to Attingham. Fifty years after Richard Hill bought Attingham in 1700, Berwick

292

Maviston was still in existence but by 1808 the village had been wiped out by the extension of Attingham Hall and its Park.

So by now you are probably wondering what all this has to do with Worfield. The answer lies in a tantalising piece of information the Attingham guide gave us about how the Barony of Berwick came to an end. The last Lord Berwick to live at Attingham was the eighth Baron, Thomas Henry Noel-Hill. Each of the Barons had taken the Christian name and surname, hyphenated, from the first Baron Berwick. Thomas Henry had no direct heirs so the estate and title should have gone to the next in line, Charles Michael Wentworth Noel-Hill, who was a second cousin. Michael, as he was known, had been made bankrupt in the 1920s and Thomas Noel-Hill felt that he was not a fit person to look after the estate. Michael would take the title, but the Attingham estate was to be handed over to the National Trust on Thomas's death. At this point I remembered that Michael had lived in Worfield. "Oh, I don't think so," the guide said, rather disparagingly, "it must have been another branch of the family". This was enough to send me in search of some facts to prove the Worfield connection.

In old Worfield Parish Magazines I found that Michael's father, the Rector of Stockton, had been to Worfield to preach in 1904. In 1922, Miss K. M. Noel-Hill and her mother were living at the Lowe but when that was sold in 1927 they rented Lower Hall and were joined by Miss Almedingen. Lower Hall proved to be beyond Mrs Noel-Hill's means and the three ladies left Lower Hall in 1938.[284] [285] There was no reference in the magazines to Michael Noel-Hill but at his bankruptcy hearing in 1927, his address was given as The Lowe, Worfield, Shropshire. Prior to the move to the Lowe, Michael had, until 1925, lived in a cottage on the Attingham Estate. There was another sister, Monica, but there is no reference to her having lived at Worfield.

So what on earth had happened to the family that they came to live in Worfield? In 1911, Michael's father, the Rector of Stockton, died, and the family had to find another home. Thomas had offered accommodation at Attingham but it was turned down as unsuitable. I think that the Davenport/Leicester Warren and Noel-Hill families may have been friends, hence how they came to live at Lower Hall and the Lowe. The other link is that Lady Hulton, Tom's mother-in-law, had lived in Chesterton for many years. Lady Hulton died in December 1922 and the Vicar wrote: "It was a great shock to everyone to hear of the sudden death, a fortnight before Christmas, of Lady Hulton, and the cause of much grief to all her friends. During her ten years' residence in the parish, she had endeared herself greatly to all who came to know her. She will long be remembered with affection in Chesterton, where her sympathy and many acts of kindness were always so welcome and deeply appreciated. In a quiet and unostentatious way she was ever ready to take her part in the Church life and business of the parish, and her practical interest in the Worfield Women's Institute was of the greatest assistance. Her V.A.D. work during the war was never done grudgingly. She had the true religious spirit, which aims at living a life consonant with the faith professed."[286]

---

[284] *Shropshire Archives,* 112/22/9/179/1

[285] *Shropshire Archives,* 112/21/4/2/3/52

[286] *Worfield Parish Magazine,* January 1923

And what do we know of Michael, which would have made him an unsuitable custodian of Attingham Park?

In 1911, Michael was fourteen when his father died, and unfortunately for him this made him the perfect age to serve in the First World War. He joined the Rifle Brigade of the KSLI and survived the War although he was wounded twice.[287] In 1919 he was sent to Quetta and served there until 1921 when he returned to England. At this time he was moved from the Rifle Brigade to the Shropshire Regiment. Michael's mother wrote to Tom on the 16 February 1921 about the effect this would have on her son."He is to remain seconded there so that's all right and anything may happen in the next two or three years. But he is ambitious and keen and it is hard luck to be thrown out after seven years' good record." In fact, Michael seems to be more concerned with shooting opportunities than his army position. He wrote to Tom in May 1921 asking if he knew of a good rough shoot within easy distance of Worfield offering two days shooting a fortnight for 20-25 head a day. It must, he said, be something cheap. He wass also looking forward to grouse shooting

Michael secured another post in India as Aide-de-Camp to the Viceroy, Lord Reading, but in returning to India in August 1921, he incurred serious debt.[288] His tailor's bill was £219 and his overdraft over £800. His letters to cousin Tom constantly refer to his shortage of money and in December 1922 Tom settled Michael's inheritance on him. Michael wrote to Tom, "It is a great thing to start on a square basis with a clear and full knowledge of my financial position." Shortly afterwards, Michael lost £300 in the collapse of the Alliance Bank of Simla; the shape of things to come.

Life in India seemed to consist of ceremonial events, dinner parties and the shooting of game. At Tom's expense, Michael's guns were sent out from England, and in 1923 he had a very narrow escape in a hunting accident. With his head resting on a parapet, watching for a tiger he was about to shoot, the whole charge of a rifle entered the parapet nine inches from his head blowing the parapet to pieces. About twenty pieces of stone had to be extracted and one piece of bullet went along his eyelid and lodged in the bone at the side of his eye where it remained.[289]

While Michael had a temporary reprieve from his monetary worries in 1922, his mother, Edith, was facing her own concerns. I don't know what prompted the trustee to take the family's effects, but it cast a pall of sadness over Edith. Just how did a poor widow live without any income, I wonder, especially when she was part of a much wealthier circle of friends? It was in May 1923 that she wrote to Tom as follows.

"Dear Tom,
Dyke the trustee was here as nice as could be on Friday after such an odious piece of work. They have got all the silver. Sir Sam said it would be best to give it up and make no claim but to buy in at valuation or at the sale. The silver frames all go but Kitty and I are taking out the

---

[287] *Shropshire Archives,* 112/21/4/2/4

[288] *Shropshire Archives,* 112/21/4/2/3/8

[289] *Shropshire Archives,* 112/21/4/2/3/14

photographs & packing things today. I said I couldn't let the old silhouettes of C's father go & they have left them. Most of the photos I will burn - anyway none will go to auction."

Edith asked Tom to look at the listing of the silver and see if there was anything she ought to keep. She particularly wanted the pepper and mustard pots with their spoons and asked if Tom would buy them and she would reimburse him.[290]

Michael returned to England when Lord Reading's term of office ended in 1925 and was on half his army pay due to ill-health. At the end of his period in India he received a gratuity of £1,000 and a disablement allowance of £50 but he left India with large debts, for example, he owed the Chief Justice of Bhopal £5,000. Michael thought his wealthy friends would pay his debts but it was not to be. His intention was to work as a land agent for a large estate but, as his mother pointed out, there were hundreds looking for such a post. The country was in an economic depression and opportunities were few and far between.

Unsuited to civilian life, it was in 1925 that Noel-Hill had the misfortune to meet a man named Henry Thomas Hart Spratt who was to lead him into bankruptcy.[291] Spratt was a conman and convinced his victim to part with money supposedly to be invested in a lucrative business in Ireland. It didn't take long for all Michael's money to be swallowed up. By the end of 1926, Noel-Hill was bankrupt, had been in prison, and was forced to resign his commission with the KSLI. On the 11th. January 1927, the Newcastle Journal reported the memorable words of Michael's counsel. "He has been lavish with his uncle's guineas and he bade the son of thrift farewell."[292]

In 1925, Michael began a relationship with Gwendoline Guest. Shropshire Archives describe Gwendoline's genealogy as follows: "She was the illegitimate daughter of the illegitimate daughter of the daughter of a Staffordshire smallholder." One can't imagine the Noel-Hill family were overjoyed at Michael's choice although gradually they saw Gwen as a loyal wife. Nor would they have approved of the fact the couple lived together without being married . The birth of their son Nigel in 1931 was registered in the mother's name and only re-registered to both parents in 1949 after Michael and Gwen had married in 1947. The 8th Baron

[290] *Shropshire Archives,* 112/21/4/2/3/15

[291] *Birmingham Gazette,* 19 October 1928, p. 7. The public examination at the Shrewsbury Bankruptcy Court of Charles Michael Wentworth Noel-Hill revealed that on his return from India he lived extravagantly in England and lost heavily in the promotion of a motor omnibus company in Northern Ireland. Noel-Hill had been associated with a Mr Hart Spratt in this venture to whom he was introduced by a porter at the Princes Hotel. Spratt was constantly sending for cash from the debtor which the latter invariably provided. The messages sent always gave the impression of being on the brink of success but no profits ever materialised. Noel-Hill was also questioned about his betting habit.He said he had a weekly account with a turf commission agent but his betting in 1926 amounted only to £282 of which his losses were £130. In three years from 1924 the debtor had spent £30,000. He estimated he had put just over £11,000 into the Irish scheme whereas Mr Hart Spratt's estimate was £3,000. There was thus considerable discrepancy in the amount invested in Ireland but Noel-Hill also admitted his own gross extravagance. Noel-Hill then increased his liabilities by £5,000 by opposing the bankruptcy petition. So desperate was Noel-Hill for cash that he also used money lenders who happily took even more money out of his pocket.

[292] *Newcastle Journal,* 11 January 1927 p. 7

Berwick died in 1947 and Michael became the 9th Baron but on Michael's death in 1953, the Baronetcy became extinct.

After his bankruptcy, Michael had to find employment, and the family found him work in Scotland in 1934. Michael was lonely here so in 1935 he moved to London and took a job as a private investigator. He stayed there until the beginning of the Second World War and then moved to Tunbridge Wells working first as a fire watcher, and later as a factory worker. Tunbridge Wells would be Michael's home for the rest of his life which was dogged by lack of money. In 1947, after Tom's death, he wrote to Teresa his widow, thanking her for her support. The ever-practical Teresa had sent Michael a suit but he had hoped for money which, he hinted, Tom had promised. "I wrote and told Tom in May that we intended getting married and he said … he would think over what he could do for me." If this had been Tom's intention, he died before any settlement was made. The other aspect of the letter was the inheritance of the title Lord Berwick. Michael explained that he would like to do the title justice as Tom had done and had accepted the presidency of the Noble Order of Foresters, following in Tom's footsteps.[293]

In February 1949 Michael wrote what he says was the most difficult letter he had ever had to write. The circumstances in which his family were living were dire. Michael had been laid up practically the whole of the previous year with arthritis & off work for 26 weeks. Gwen took a job as a cleaner but slipped on ice, broke two fingers, and couldn't work, and the couple just couldn't make ends meet. In February, they had no fire for two weeks and Michael owed money for 10 cwt. of coal. Other household bills were unpaid and Michael needed boots and shoes, underclothes, pyjamas and an overcoat and Gwen similarly needed clothes. Once again he was asking for money and said that he longed for "a cottage and a smallholding which I could turn into a market garden." If he was hoping that a cottage would be offered at Attingham he was to be disappointed.[294]

And then, just two years later, in October 1951, Gwen died, aged just forty-eight. A letter dated 3 October 1951 to Teresa from Chris [Miss Almedingen] suggested that Michael's behaviour may have been a contributory factor. "I do feel that one of the female hyenas may have tracked him down and that the poor Gwen may have collapsed under the shock." Michael was angling for a cottage on the Attingham Estate but that, "Must never happen. To turn this lovely home [Frogmore] …into a drunkard's den, is just unthinkable".[295]

Michael died just two years later, in 1953. His was a tortured life but where did it all go wrong? His father dying when he was so young may have affected him, the First World War certainly, but even more so, perhaps, an army career which never encouraged him to take real responsibility for his life. He never seemed to live a life independently from Attingham, always living in hope that he might be able to get back to a life which he had lost.

And that is the connection between Worfield and Attingham, a sad story which gets no better if I tell you that Katherine, who had been at Worfield with her mother, drowned while in

[293] *Shropshire Archives*, 112/21/4/2/4

[294] Ibid.

[295] *Shropshire Archives*, 12/22/12/5/1/1-4

a psychiatric unit in Herefordshire in 1939. Michael's mother, on leaving Worfield, went back to her home town of Church Stretton, with Miss Almedingen, and died there in 1942.

Further Notes

Extracts from letters in the Attingham Collection, Shropshire Record Office, 112/21/4/2/4 & 112/23/11

Letters from Michael

29/10/16

Dear Cousin Tom, Thank you for the fruit and cigarettes received when I was wounded and at Boulogne. I had hoped to come back to England but the hospital was empty in Boulogne. The doctor on discharge wanted to mark me fit for Base duties only but I asked to be A so I could go back to the battalion. If I can't manage that I will be back on transport duties.

7/1/17

Dear Tom, I expect Mother told you I am practically all right again & got my bandages off about 10 days ago. I have got another Medical Board later this month and hope to go to the reserve battalion in the Isle of Sheppey. I am afraid I shall not get out for some time as my blood is in an awful state. I have had some good shooting here at Acton Reynald & go home tomorrow.

My battalion in France was wiped out about 6 months ago in an attack on Beaucourt. 17 officers & 641 men killed or wounded out of 19 officers and 784 men. 4 of my platoon were killed and 20 wounded. I have seen several of the officers in hospital. They said it was a wonderful show but the Germans were waiting for them. They captured the village, 4 lines of trenches and 1200 prisoners before they were wiped out by Germans. It's awful to think that on 2nd Nov I left them all well.

Letters from Edith

14 Feb 1922

My Dear Tom, I am glad something has been paid in towards the overdraft. The car is entirely out of my money and some people came to look at it yesterday but I gave them time to think it over. She wanted it but I don't think he did. I offered it for £310. It was advertised for £320 & had no answers from the Autocar or the Wellington Journal. The sooner it goes the better I shall be pleased. Micky is getting on so well. It really is rather a joy. The Prince goes to Delhi today & all the ADCs have special tasks. It is rather surprising but he was always adaptive, a very useful quality though not a strong one.

March 18 1922

Dear Tom, I haven't sold the car. They tried to reduce it by another £50 so I am taking a licence for 3 months on the 25th. It would be cheaper than hiring every time. I wish it would sell, my bank book is disgraceful & most depressing. Mrs Davenport has come back from Tabley such a wreck. They have all had bad colds and Margaret has missed several balls

ERIC PLANT'S MEMORIES OF WORFIELD

While John Turnock was carrying out research for his Ph. D. into the history of the Endowed Grammar Schools of Shropshire, he interviewed a number of former pupils of Worfield School.[296] The following is a summary of his conversation with Eric Plant.

Eric Plant was born in 1914 and attended Worfield School in 1919. Frank Turner was then the headmaster and, at the age of 11, Eric won a scholarship to Bridgnorth Grammar School. He recalled that boys in the senior school dug the school garden, did woodwork and kept rabbits, while the girls went to Lower Hall to learn how to cook and do the laundry. When Mr Turner retired, Mr Matthews changed the school completely, and also instituted a series of tests to ensure that those who were intellectually able went to Bridgnorth Grammar School.

We know from many accounts that the school served soup made by Mrs Robinson. Eric went home to lunch as he lived in the village so was not entitled to any soup unless there was some left over. Eric thought the soup was delicious but others have noted that it had 'strings' in it. At the back of the village shop was a big bakehouse and rice pudding was served on the days when there was no soup. It always struck me as odd that you had soup on some days and rice pudding on others.

Some of the pranks the schoolchildren got up to had more than a touch of 'Just William' about them. Take the time Eric Plant and his friends tried to float May Buck down the brook. The idea was that her voluminous skirt would capture the air and May would float happily down the stream. Of course, to the disappointment of the young lads, May sank. One can only hope that it was a warm day but I wonder how May explained her soaking wet clothes to her parents.

Another prank was to smoke out the inhabitants of Rock Cottage. Tommy Williamson was Eric's partner in crime, putting "fir cones and things," on top of the chimney. "Little did we know that poor Mr and Mrs White were sitting happily by the fire.' Of course, the Whites soon realised who the culprits were, and no doubt a severe hiding was meted out by the boys' parents.

This didn't seem to deter young Eric from getting up to other mischief. A favourite playground was the Worfield Mill which at this time was used as a saw mill. Jack Weaver was the miller and time and again he told the children to keep away from the sawmill lest they got hurt. As Eric said, "We ran riot in the mill ... and must have been a blasted nuisance." On this particular day, Jack Weaver went home for his tea leaving the mill open. The children went in to their mill playground but when they were ready to leave, they found the door locked. If Jack Weaver had done this deliberately as a deterrent it certainly did the trick. It wasn't until around 8 o'clock that the children were released and I imagine there were some sore backsides in Worfield that evening.

Acknowledgement. Thanks are due to John Turnock for permitting this interview to be reproduced.

---

[296] John Turnock, *A History Little Known. Four centuries of Education in Shropshire*, J. L. Turnock, 1996

GEORGE & KATE MORRISON

Wyken House - Shropshire.

The Evans family lived at Wyken throughout much of the twentieth century but the Wyken Estate actually came into the family when Robert Cecil Harwood Evans, the son of Hugh Evans of Ely, married Anna Morrison, only daughter of George and Kate Morrison of Wyken, in 1905. According to the Parish Magazine of 1933, Wyken had been bequeathed to George Hampson Morrison and his wife Kate, formerly Kate Turner, but by whom I don't know. The couple were married in 1871 and there were two children; Alfred, born in 1873, and Anna in 1879. The family's wealth came through shipping, particularly in India, and for obvious reasons they lived in Liverpool, at number 10, Abercromby Square. Sadly the Morrisons had only been at Wyken a short time when George Morrison died in Liverpool. His widow, Kate, stayed at Wyken until her death in the 1930s.

Colonel Morrison's obituary in the Parish Magazine of 1901 reads as follows:

"Colonel Morrison (who only recently succeeded to the Wyken estate in this parish, and who, we hoped would have resided amongst at least for a few months in each year) died on January 29th, after an illness of eighteen weeks. He was a most earnest and devout churchman, foremost in all good works ...As a magistrate, as colonel of his regiment, as a member of the Bishop of York's "House of Laymen," as an active member of the Educational Committee, and as a leading spirit in the Temperance cause, he worked with an energy and power which is

George & Kate Morrison

seldom reached and never surpassed. The Bishop of Liverpool ... who ministered to Colonel Morrison, almost daily during his long and trying illness, said that ... he had taught him (the Bishop) lessons which he should never forget."

The Morrisons are forgotten today but they were great benefactors to the parish, building both the Recreation Room, now known as the Village Hall, and the Ackleton Room, at their own expense, for the parish's use.

Rookery Cottages, Wyken, is the oldest house still standing in the village and must have been a very high status house.

MARY LINEKER

In the Summer of 2018 I had the pleasure of speaking to Mary Lineker about how she and Allan came to live in Worfield, with Allan running the butcher's shop at Wyken. While the couple came from Willenhall, Worfield was where they would spend most of their lives.

The story starts just after the end of the Second World War. Allan had been in a tank regiment during the War but was captured early on and was a prisoner of war in Germany and in Italy. After he was demobbed, Allan worked in a pork butcher's shop in Willenhall where he learned his trade which including making pork pies and sausages for which he had quite a reputation. While the work was enjoyable, working for someone else didn't suit Allan, who longed for a business of his own. The retail butchery business at Wyken was advertised for sale around 1950 by H. Flavell, the owner, and the rest, as they say, is history.[297]

The original butcher's shop was part of the farm buildings in Wyken

Mr Flavell had taken over the butcher's shop at Wyken which had previously been run for a number of years by the Wilcox family. The shop itself was not in the current situation it is now, being part of the group of farm buildings to the Wheel side of the current shop. Considerable gloss had been added to the description of the business and Allan soon found that he would have even more work than he imagined to build the business of his dreams.

Mary was born in December 1931 and Allan in 1921 and the couple were married in 1951, making their first home in Worfield. Mary is quite clear what her first impression of Worfield was. "I didn't like it," she said. The prospect of being in a sleepy little village, so different from

---

[297] *Worfield Parish Magzine,* 1950

the hustle and bustle of Willenhall, where both she and Allan were born and grew up, must have been daunting. Even with a car, which she didn't have, of course, Willenhall was a long way away. Without a car, each trip home took two buses. Apart from Allan, Mary knew no-one in Worfield. On the other hand, Mary had no choice but to follow her husband to this inauspicious place which he had chosen for his business.

In the early days Allan worked incredibly hard to get the business going. This can't have been the easiest time to get any business going, let alone a butchery, with meat rationing continuing until 1954. The location of the shop, outside the main village of Worfield was another difficulty, I would imagine. There would be relatively few people walking, cycling, or driving down the road past the Wyken shop. The only solution was to take the shop to the customers. Allan would drive around the parish selling wet fish as well as meat, always with the same courteous service. Sometimes he would stop and have a cup of tea or chat about this and that. Poor Mary never knew when her husband would come home from his rounds but Allan knew that his customers needed time to get to know and trust their new supplier, and Allan needed time to get to understand their needs and circumstances. The foundations of a business

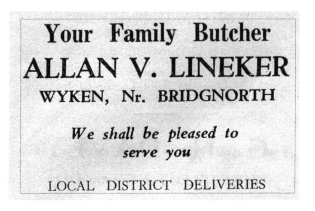

Advertisement from Worfield Parish Magazine 1954

that would last a lifetime were being laid.

The couple's first home was a caravan at the back of Bentley's garage, then a flat at the vicarage recently vacated by Fred Chester and his wife. While Allan ran the business, Mary was busy with making a new home and looking after a baby. China Bank is a steep hill and I can imagine walking up and down there a few times a day would keep you fit, as would trips to Willenhall on the bus with all the paraphernalia which a baby and toddler needs. Fortunately, Mary's mother was a frequent visitor from Willenhall and helped out.

In 1954, the Wyken Estate offered Allan and Mary the cottage which was formerly the garage, with the possibility of building an adjoining shop. The original building which housed Allan's shop was being pulled down for road widening and the potential of having a shop attached to a cottage must have seemed like a really good alternative. There were one or two problems, as you might imagine. The cottage hadn't been lived in for many years and there was

WYKEN
Mary Lineker

a hole in the roof. The garden had also been neglected and was very overgrown. The 'shop' was at this point a wooden building, which wouldn't do at all. Much work was required all round. In the event, the Estate repaired the hole in the roof and made the cottage habitable, and Allan and Mary, with help from Mary's father, did the rest.

By the time Allan and Mary had moved into Wyken they had got to know their neighbours; The Wilcox family, the Nelsons, and Mrs Bishton who lived in the cottage next door. Susanne would be taken to Sunday School by Margaret Wilcox. Church was to be an important part of the Lineker's family life, with Mary joining the Women's Fellowship and Susanne joining the choir.

Eventually sales from the van were replaced by deliveries of orders, and the shop flourished. When I used to go in, it was Doreen who helped to serve. While it was fine to call Doreen by her first name, it was unthinkable to call Mr Lineker by his christian name, and Mary was always Mrs Lineker. One of the things one misses about a local shop is the people you casually see and get chatting to, people you would not otherwise meet. Now, I suppose people bump into each other in Aldi, but it's not the same.

And so life continued until Allan died in 1985. Mary carried on the business for a while and stayed in the cottage at Wyken until 2015.

The following photographs of Wyken have been supplied by Mary.

Anna Evans, wife of the Revd. Robert Evans, died on 7 January 1960.
The cortège sets off from Wyken House

Who was the man standing on the branch, seemingly without being attached
to anything? The man wisely standing on the ground was Charlie Taylor

Bill Stinton in the foreground.

WYKEN
Mary Lineker

Above: Mary Wilcox, born 1931, who lived at what was Wyken Farmhouse, now
called The Grange, Wyken. Below: A car stops at Wyken Garage in the early
1950s, perhaps. Bill Willcox may be the man standing. The cottage on the opposite
side of the road was demolished for road widening

OUTSIDE THE PARISH

AN UNTIMELY DEATH

Murders are always fascinating and none less so than the death, in 1638, of Mrs. Elizabeth Williams, the wife of Richard Williams. Mr. and Mrs. Williams lived in the High Street in Bridgnorth and rented the house next door to John Preene, a vintner. How Mrs. Williams died is not revealed in the inquest record, but the suspicion is that she was killed and the finger of suspicion points to her husband or her tenant, John Preene.[298]

Mrs. Williams was clearly frightened by her neighbour, who threatened and taunted her, and yet she visited him frequently. Living next door to one another only compounded the problem and perhaps Mrs. Williams was attracted to her 'unusual' neighbour.

Matters came to a head on the 16th January when there were several reports of intimidating behaviour by John Preene. A witness who was walking up the High Street described how he came out of his house whilst Mrs. Williams was spinning in her workshop. Preene approached her with a small whip in his hand, and called her a "Welsh whore". Another witness said that he saw Preene in his stall [shop in front of his house] and heard him abusing Mrs. Williams for a quarter of an hour. As a final flourish he bragged that he, "had five beyches and had lost two of them and had but three left and she bade him look after them." On the same day, a baker who was Preene's other neighbour, had just finished pitching faggots [bundles of sticks], when John Preene asked if he could borrow Harley's pikel to shake Mrs. Williams "fare". On a previous occasion, Preene said he could put Mrs. Williams' heart in a kettle.[299] No wonder she was terrified.

Mrs. Williams was in Preene's house between five and six o'clock on the afternoon of the16th January when he was trying to wash the floor. He told his landlady to leave, and when she didn't do so, he threw some very hot water at her. A man who was brewing in Preene's house at this time heard Mrs. Williams say that she was frightened that Preene would set fire to her house while she was in it. She then went to Richard Powell's house at around 7pm where she met Margaret Clarke and repeated her fears that Preene would kill her or set fire to the house with her in it. She showed Mrs. Clarke the marks on her back where Preene had thrown the hot water and Mrs. Clarke urged Mrs. Williams not to provoke him.

Shortly after 7o'clock on the 16th January, Mrs. Williams left Richard Powell's house with a "candlestick upon her arm" and a tankard of ale hidden under her apron. This was the last time she was seen alive. On Friday the 18th January, John Preene said to the wife of a fellow shopkeeper. "What do you say if this woman had made away herself (whereupon this informant asked him what he meant and he answered Mrs. Williams) or else said he, she is dogged for she hath not byn seene since Wednesday night. But my comfort is that the key is upon the inner side of the door." Preene had previously made enquiries from his neighbours

[298] *Shropshire Archives*, BB/F/4/3/1/1

[299] A kettle would have been similar in shape to a jam kettle ie a large open pan which hung over the fire.

whether there was another key to the house and found there was no second key. The body of Mrs. Williams was indeed inside her house which was locked from the inside, with the key in the lock. Perhaps Preene had in all innocence tried Mrs. Williams door and found it locked, but it may be significant that he was interested in the possibility of a second key.

After the death of Mrs. Williams, Preene and her husband were together in a house in Bridgnorth. "Who was the first to discover the body of my wife?" Richard Williams asked, to which Preene replied, "whoever was accessory to the death." Thomas Fennymore was also present and was a witness at the inquest. He asked Preene who was the accessory? To which Preene replied, "The devil was for ought he knew." Although John Preene had previously suggested that Mrs. Williams might have committed suicide, it is obvious from this conversation that he thought she had been murdered although he never admitted any involvement. The jury at the Coroner's Inquest thought there had been foul play and the case was sent to Shrewsbury Assizes to be heard on the 22nd February. Both Richard Williams and John Preene were to be held in gaol until that date.

Unfortunately we know no more of the case than this. Either Preene was innocent and moved away from the town, or he was guilty and executed. Unless I have missed it there is no record of the burial of John Preene in Bridgnorth.

A CHANCERY COURT CASE

In 1558 Thomasine Prene brought the following case in the Chancery Court against her brothers-in-law, Hugh and Jerome Prene. The allegation was that immediately after the decease of her husband, John Prene, they," by force and strong hand entered into the said messuage wherein the said John Prene died as is aforesaid and did then and there by force and strong hand break up all such coffers and chests which then were in the said house and wherein the said money and other the said goods and chattels which were then and there remaining and did by force and strong hand take out of the said house from the said poor oratrix [Thomasine Prene] the same yet do wrongfully detain and keep to the extreme impoverishment and utter undoing [of] the said poor oratrix being a very poor widow who hath 13 small children who have little or nothing towards their educations or living other than the said goods so left unto her and them by her said late husband."300

There was an astonishing amount of money in the house; in gold coins there were sixty angels, six ryals, five crowns and five other coins, six pounds of silver and £11 worth of other goods. There was also "one deed of grant of the next advoydans [vacancy] of the advowson of the vicarage of the Church of Worfeld."301 John Prene had a connection with Worfield as he was curate there in 1558 at the time that Humphrey Barney was the vicar. At the time of his death he was a clerk, a cleric, and had also been a proctor of the Chantry of the Virgin Mary and St. John the Baptist at St. Leonard's in Bridgnorth. The record of an indenture has survived which is a lease by William Swanwyck and John Grene, chaplains of the Chantry of the Glorious Virgin Mary and St. John the Baptist in the church of St Leonard in Bridgnorth, and John Prene and Thomas Heynes proctors of the same chantry, to Fulk Lee and Elizabeth his wife, of a tenement in the High Street in Bridgnorth with half a stable, a small part of garden and a ruinous barn [details given], for the term of 99 years, at the yearly rent of 17s.
Witnesses: Thomas Beturton, John Taylor, bailiff of the vill and liberty of Bridgnorth, George Heyward senior, William Heynes, William Prene, John Lokear, Hugh Whithrok and many others.
Seal of the chantry confraternity. 302

Chantries were abolished under the Chantries Act of 1547 and money distributed to charitable causes and for the "public good," so one wonders if some of the money in John Prene's house was chantry money. Hugh Prene had been involved, with others, in a Court of Requests case brought by John Seymour, concerning the possessions of a Chantry in the

300 *The National Archives,* C 3/136/10, 1558-1579

301 The Advowson is the right of appointment to a living. Sir John Talbot acquired the advowson of Worfield in 1549 so one assumes that he resold this right to John Preene under terms unknown

302 *The National Archives,* WARD 2/30/102/1, 1540

Church of St Leonard.[303] He was also no stranger to violence, having been brought before the Star Chamber together with William Gattacre, on a charge of the false imprisonment of Robert Broke at Bridgnorth.[304] I can find no record of Jerome Prene.

Thomasine begged her brothers-in-law to return the money and the deed of grant, which obviously had a monetary value, but to no avail, and having no recourse in common law she was forced to take her case to the Chancery Court in London. This would have involved more cost since she would have to present her case in person while the accused could remain in Shropshire until they were subpoenaed to attend. As she says in her statement to the court she is, "a poor woman and has now had to live in the city of London being far distant from the County of Salop …And where also the said Hugh Prene and Jerome Prene being of lively wealth do inhabit and dwell and are there greatly friended and allied and the said oratrix is there a mere stranger."

Was Thomasine's money returned to her? As so often happens with these cases we don't know. Chancery cases often drifted on until the complainants ran out of money or died or, as in Thomasine's case, perhaps she remarried.

This is a transcription of the only surviving part of the Chancery Case brought by Thomasine Prene.
Reference: The National Archives, C 3/136/10, 1558-1579

To the right honorable …baron knight lord keeper of the great seale of England

…..[first part is lost]and complayneth unto the honorable lord of the Bayleye,   Oratrix Thomasyn Prene of the cytie of London wif to Jhon Prene of Bridgnorthe in the countie of Salop, clerke, disceased, and administratrix of all suche goods and cattels and of the said Jhon Prene at the tyme of his disceace that whereas the said John Prene in his lyfetyme was lawfully enfeoffed at Bridgnorthe afforesaid as of his owne personal goodes and cattels of and in these severall parcells of current money folowynge that is to say 60 angells, 6 ryolls, 5 crowns of the sone, 5 pisteleys and 6 pounds sylver and of and in divers other goods, & cattels apparel and household stuff such other things to the value of 40 pounds or there about. And also of and in one deade of graunte of the next advoydans of the advowson of the vicarage of the church of Worveld in the said countie of Salop and so being possessed of the said goodes and cattels and of the said deade and writing about one yeare now laste past at Bridgnorthe afforesaid died thereof possessed as is afforesaid understayted after whose deathe the administration of suche goods and cattels as were the said Jhon Prenes, late husband to the said oratrix, were committyd by the comyssarye of lytchefilde ordynary of the same place at lytchfilde afforesaid lawfully commitid to the administration of the said Oratrix as by the said … administration ready to be shewed to this honorable courte now at large and playnely yt dothe and may appear . So yt is right honorable lord that Hugh Prene and Jerome Prene of Bridgnorth aforesaid immediately after the decease of the said John Prene by force and strong hand

---

[303] *The National Archives*, REQ 2/8/127, 1492-1547

[304] *The National Archives*, STAC 2/6, 22 April 1509 - 28 January 1547

entered into the said messuage wherein the said John Prene died as is aforesaid and did then and there by force and strong hand break up all such coffers and chestes which then were in the said house and wherein the said money and other the said goodes and cattals which were then there remayininge and the said money and other the said goodes and cattels did by like force and stronge hand take oute of the said house from the said poore Oratrix and the same yet do wrongfully deteyne and kepe to the extreme impoverishement and utter undoinge of the said poore Oratrix beinge a very poore widow and hath 13 small children who have lyttel or nothinge towardes there education or lyvinge other than the said goodes so lefte unto her and them by her said late husband. And albeit right honorable lorde that the said Oratrix hath at dyverse and sondrey tymes as well by her self as also by diverse other of her ffrendes gentley willed and required the said Hugh Preene and Jerome Preene and eyther of them to have delyvered to the said poore Oratrix the said money and other the said goodes and cattels which were the said Jhon Preenes her said late husband together with the said deade of grannte of the next advoydans of th'advowson of the said vicarage of Worveld offoresaid and peaceablely and privately to permitt and suffer the said Oratrix to enjoye the same without further vexation of sute in the lawe the which do they and eny of them nether respectinge the ffeare of god nor the poore and myserable state of the said poore Oratrix (and her poore children). That to do hitherto always have refused and denyed and yet do refuse and deny contary to all right and good consyens and to the great undoinge of the said poore Oratrix. And for asmoche right honorable lorde as your said poore Oratrix doth not certenly know the certen parcels of the said somes of money and other the said goodes and cattles by them taken as is afforesaid nor the certen date of the said deade of grannt of the next advoydans of the said vicarage of Worveld by reason thereof the said Oratrix is by the order of the commyn lawes of this realme without all remedy to recover all the said goodes or the just value of the same for which cause afforesaid. And if she has any remedy by the comyn lawe as she hath not yet for as much as your said Oratrix ys a very poor woman and doth inhabyte or dwell within the cytie of London beinge farre distante from the countie of Salop where the said money, goodes and other thinges were taken as is afforesaid. And where also the said Hugh Prene and JerromePrene beinge of lyvele wealthe do inhabyte and dwell and are there greatly frinded and alyed and the said Oratrix is there a mere stranger so that the said Oratrix for waynte of indyfferent trial there shulde be without all remedy to recover the premisses and is very lyke to be utterly undone unless your good lordship's favourable goodness and pity be to your said Oratrix herein be directed to the said Hugh Prene and Jerome Prene and to either of them commanding them by the same that they and either of them and personally appear before your good lordship in the Queens Majesty's High Court of Chancery at a then day and under ...by your good lordship to be limited and appointed then and there to answer to your premisses and to abide and stand to such further end and destination therein ... your good lordship shall so to stand ... ... and good conscience and your said oratrix shall daily pray to Almighty god for the preservation of your good lordship's estate long to continue in honour

THE BRIDGNORTH FOOD RIOTS OF 1693/4

In the seventeenth century, just as it is today, Bridgnorth was an important centre for the buying and selling of all kinds of foodstuff. However, in the early 1690s two years of bad harvests caused significant food shortages. This was made worse both by outsiders coming into the town to buy, and by speculators, known as 'badgers', buying and reselling food, thus pushing up the price beyond the reach of ordinary people. A number of violent incidents ensued involving the theft of grain.

On the 22nd April 1693 several agents for Wolverhampton bakers, mainly servants of Compton Mill, came to Bridgnorth to buy grain but there was already a shortage of corn. Henry Pemberton of Perton could only buy enough grain for two of his six clients and he was not alone in being unable to fulfil his orders. Buying the grain was only part of the problem, even if you did manage to buy corn, getting it safely out of Bridgnorth was yet another.

The shortest route from High Town to Low Town, and thence on to Wolverhampton, was down the Cartway, a narrow street in which it was easy to be ambushed. This was also a closely knit community with many neighbours related to each other. Most of the men were employed in jobs associated with the River Severn which ran just at the bottom of the Cartway. There were thirteen watermen, two ships' carpenters, two bricklayers, one gunsmith, and a fisherman. They were young, fit, and poor.

Corn was traded in some of the Bridgnorth Inns, and William Evans, landlord of one of the main trading inns on the High Street, instructed Francis Lacon to transport some grain belonging to William Farmer of Wolverhampton down the Cartway to the Vine Inn. John Lloyd and a man called Head stopped the cart in the Cartway and a crowd unloaded the corn and carried it away. A Wolverhampton chandler was then stopped in the Cartway and his wheat was stolen by a group of people who were never identified.

Two weeks later, also in the Cartway, Thomas Clemson, a Wolverhampton baker, was attacked as he went down the road with his packhorses laden with grain. There was a mob in the street threatening to seize badgers and corn and Rebecca Crudgington, with whom Clemson had just dined, feared for her guest's safety and went to check that he had passed safely on his way. Unfortunately, Clemson and his cargo had been waylaid by a group of women and in spite of Rebecca Crudgington and her daughters' attempts to prevent them, the corn was stolen. One of the women, Margery Minton, tried to take the sacks off the backs of the horses and when she failed to do this, another member of the group, Anne Roe, slit the bags with a knife. The women had no bags to put the corn in so they gathered all they could in their aprons and carried it away.

In June 1693, one of the leaders of an earlier incident, Richard Powell, a gunsmith by trade, approached a baker's shop owned by Humphrey Brayne. Inside was David Evans, servant of Richard Pennall, with some of his master's corn. Powell demanded to see the contents of the sack and called Pennall a badger. Evans said that the sack contained oats, as indeed it did, and Powell went away muttering that the other sacks may have contained corn.

The final incident on the 17 January 1694 was caused by trading outside the market place. Private sales such as these meant that grain passed from grower to wholesaler without the public having an opportunity to purchase. On this occasion, Richard Kynnersley, a farmer from Chetton, had sold a large quantity of barley to John Willmot and John Hay of Worcester, partners in a bakery business. While the grain was being loaded on to Joseph Pinner's barge at Eardington, south of Bridgnorth, a mob approached on both sides of the river, accompanied by the Bridgnorth constables. The presence of the constables caused some confusion. The boatmen thought the constables were there to support the mob's actions, but they were actually there to prevent the grain being exported to France. The bakers' loss was Bridgnorth's gain. The fully-laden barge was towed to Bridgnorth by William Siddal junior, Thomas Bebb, William Perkes, John Pearce, Thomas Baker junior, Richard Gower and a twelve year old boy. At Bridgnorth the men took what they wanted and left the rest to whoever wished to take it.

Another incident which involved theft from a barge took place in October 1693 when buyers from Ironbridge had come to the St. Luke's Fair. Several flitches of bacon and a quantity of cheese were stolen from a barge belonging to Thomas Cope of Broseley which had been moored overnight near the Town Mills. The barge operator complained of the theft to Bridgnorth Corporation and some months later the Corporation offered to replace the cheese and bacon if no further action was taken by him. Had the Corporation been complicit in the theft because of the extreme shortage of food or was it a gesture of goodwill to try to repair the tarnished image of the market town?

The position of the speculators who put personal gain above the survival of their neighbours, was uncomfortable to say the least. In November 1693, Francis Oakes junior had to explain why he was storing twelve tons of cheese in his house at the bottom of the Cartway, after the St Luke's Fair. He claimed that it was the property of a Staffordshire cheesemonger and waiting to be taken by Oakes to Gloucester and thence overland to London but whether that was true we will never know.

The food riots happened for only a few years but throw another light on life in the seventeenth century. Three factors seemed to come together to prompt the riots. Firstly there were the poor harvests, secondly, the increasing demand from Wolverhampton for grain which pushed the price beyond what the poor of Bridgnorth could afford, and thirdly, speculators stockpiled goods in the hope that the price would rise. Faced with the prospect of starvation it is no wonder that Bridgnorth people took matters into their own hands and took the food they needed.

Acknowledgment

Thanks are due to Malcolm Wanklyn for highlighting this fascinating part of Bridgnorth's history. "The Bridgnorth Food Riots of 1693/4," were published in the Transactions of the Shropshire Archaeological Society in 1993, Volume LXVIII, pp. 99-102 and based on the Bridgnorth Quarter Session records held in the Shropshire Archives, Reference 4001/J

HUGH PIGOT OF PATSHULL

Many of us have spent some time over the years in the Pigot Arms in Pattingham without, I suspect, giving much, if any, thought to the family after whom the pub is named. And what, you may ask, has this to do with Worfield? If you need a reason other than that people's lives are never lived wholly within a parish boundary, Robert Pigot owned land in Stanlow and Kingslow and when Kingslow Common was divided and enclosed, Robert Pigot was one of the beneficiaries.

Portrait of Sir George Pigot which hangs in the
National Portrait Gallery

It was at a New Year's Eve party that a friend first mentioned the Pigot family. Knowing my interest in local history, he had a very specific question. Do you know, he asked, if the Pigot Arms was named after Hugh Pigot. I confessed that I knew very little about the Pigot family, and nothing at all about Hugh Pigot. Like all good storytellers, David told me just enough to get my attention. "Hugh Pigot," he said, "was a naval captain in the West Indies in the late eighteenth century who was murdered in the bloodiest mutiny in the history of the Royal Navy. He was reputed to be the most cruel man in the Navy." How could I not want to know more?

PATSHULL

George Pigot, Hugh Pigot's uncle, bought Patshull Park in 1765 from Sir John Astley for a huge amount of money; £100,000.[305] [306]The Pigot money, as with Henry Davenport's fortune, had come from the East India Company. Born in 1719, George Pigot went to India when he was eighteen, to serve with the East India Company. He rose to become Governor of Fort St George (Madras) but his career was not without controversy. In spite of this, Pigot was rewarded with a baronetcy on his return home, and in 1766 he became an Irish peer with the title Lord Pigot of Patshull in the County of Dublin. Again, like Henry Davenport, Pigot returned from India with his spoils, most notably a forty-seven carat diamond valued at £28,000 known as the Pigot Diamond. This was probably only one of the many gifts he had received from Indian rajahs. Pigot sat in Parliament for Bridgnorth but returned to India in 1775 because he was seriously short of money.

Taking up the post of Governor-in-Chief of Madras, Pigot was soon embroiled in another dispute which brought him into conflict with the East India Company and the English government. Both were at a loss to know what to do with the Governor, but in India his colleagues had no doubt; they put him in prison. Back in London, the powers-that-be eventually cobbled together a solution to save face. George Pigot would be returned to office but be forced to resign within a week. Events overtook them when their man died in captivity in 1777. An observer in Madras at this time said of George Pigot, "He appears to me to be a man of shallow abilities, of great spirit, and I believe in general honourable, but of excessive vanity and overbearing despotism."

With five illegitimate children and no legitimate heir, George's estate devolved to his brother Robert who was a soldier. Robert settled in Patshull and bought out his brother Hugh and his sisters, all of whom had a financial interest in the estate. However, Hugh had a local connection to Patshull, having taken Frances Wrottesley as his second wife. The couple were frequent visitors to Patshull and may have lived there for a time. Their son, Hugh, born in 1769, was christened at Patshull Church.

Hugh Pigot, the father, was a captain in the navy but when the Seven Years War ended in 1763, he was surplus to requirements and settled down in England to the life of a country gentleman. Hugh's opportunity to return to the sea came in 1782 when he replaced Admiral Sir George Rodney in charge of the British fleet stationed in the Leeward Islands in the West Indies. This was a promotion which had nothing to do with Pigot's suitability for the job and everything to do with having friends in the right places. The assessment of Pigot's second-in-command was hardly flattering. His judgment was that Pigot was totally inadequate for the job

---

[305] Sir John Astley had also held the following land in Worfield. In 1717 he took from Sir William Myddleton of Chirk Castle and Mary Myddleton, 4 messuages, 3 cottages, 6 gardens, 4 orchards, 150 acres of land, 40 acres of meadow, 80 acres of pasture, 14 acres of wood and 60 acres of heath in Ewdness, Oldington, Hartlebury & Worfield. Mary Myddleton was the daughter and heir of Sir Thomas Whitmore. In 1767 Astley relinquished Ewdness & other Worfield property to Sir Thomas Whitmore (4387/1 Shropshire Archives). The National Library of Wales also holds copies of land transactions in Worfield due to the Myddleton connection.

[306] Astley (1688-1771) had just one child, a son, who predeceased him. The plans for Patshull then seemed to have no purpose without a direct heir and he sold Patshull to Sir George Pigot and moved to Wiltshire.

as he had not been at sea for nineteen years, had no experience in managing a fleet, and precious little in charge of a ship. Admiral Hugh was accompanied on his journey to the West Indies by his son, Hugh, aged twelve, for whom a career in the Royal Navy also beckoned.

Hugh Pigot, the younger, worked his way up (and sometimes down) the naval hierarchy until, in 1794, he was assigned to captain a 32-gun frigate called The Swan, working out of Jamaica. In 1797, Pigot was transferred to another frigate, the Hermione. Such ships were there to protect merchant shipping from the constant threat of French privateers.

The West Indies posting was no easy job. The Hermione had been in the West Indies for five years without a break when Pigot took over and unsurprisingly the crew was disaffected. Few crew members were there for the love of the job, more than half had probably been press ganged and the rest consisted of the desperately poor and foreign mercenaries. Frances Martin, the wife of the bosun, was the only woman on board. Pay was low and working conditions appalling, with the cramped quarters made unbearable by the intense tropical heat. Yellow fever and malaria were endemic and the wait for dead men's shoes was not long. In addition to the duties of accompanying merchant convoys, the Royal Navy ships had to suppress frequent slave insurrections, usually with sickening brutality. It was this tinder box which Captain Hugh Pigot had to manage and, unfortunately for him, he was the fuse which set the whole thing alight.

St Cecilia, formerly Hermione, being cut loose from its moorings by HMS Success (Artist: Thomas Whitcombe)

Pigot's management style was autocratic and tyrannical. Discipline in the navy was maintained by flogging but Pigot took this form of punishment to the extreme. In nine months he ordered 85 floggings and two men died of their injuries. Pigot even had the audacity to flog the master of an American ship which had collided with his own. A diplomatic incident ensued and Pigot was court-martialled but the case was dismissed when he apologised. On board the Hermione, the almost daily public floggings put the crew in a constant state of fear. After just six months, it was time for retribution.

On September 21, 1797, at 10.30pm the mutineers burst into Captain Pigot's cabin. They stabbed him many times but being still alive, an able seaman, Joseph Mansell, ran him through with a bayonet, and pushed the body through the cabin window with the words, "You have shown no mercy yourself, and therefore deserve none." Eight officers and two crewmen were killed, including William Martin, the bosun, but his wife survived. The mutineers sailed the ship to Venezuela and handed it over to the Spanish. The Hermione was renamed the St. Cecilia (as it is named in the picture) but was recaptured by the British and renamed Retaliation. Over thirty mutineers were captured and tried and twenty-four were hanged. The rest of the crew were freed. Frances Martin came home to England via America and in 1803 applied for the widow's pension she was entitled to.

Sometimes the passage of time gives a rosy glow to the past and its people but in reading about Hugh Pigot I didn't find any description of his positive qualities. He was by no means alone in the harsh treatment of his men but he was certainly one of the worst captains the Royal Navy has ever had. Coming back to the original question as to whether the Pigot Arms was named after Hugh Pigot, somehow I doubt it.

Acknowledgment
I am indebted to David Manning who first researched this story and patiently educated me in aspects of naval history of the time.

Reference
Dudley Pope, *The Black Ship*, (Weidenfeld & Nicholson 1963)

A FEW MORE YEARS: A POSTSCRIPT
by Another Hand

Let me be quite straight about the fact that this section has no direct link to Worfield. It was given to me by a Pattingham man who had no idea how he came by it and no desire to keep it. I was handed the unpretentious bundle of foolscap pages held together by a slide binder with the instruction that I could do what I wanted with it. Perhaps my friend was supposed to hand it back after reading it because this was clearly meant to be published. I felt bad that I might have the only copy and it was never going to see the light of day so I put the script on the internet hoping that someone would claim it, but no joy. By some detective work I discovered that the author was Eric Benton. That probably means nothing to you, and certainly meant nothing to me until one day I was in Wolverhampton Archives and a woman sitting opposite was bemoaning the boring nature of some material she was cataloguing. I asked whose they were and the answer was Eric Benton's. I rose to his defence. "No, I said, his work can't be boring. I have the most wonderful description he wrote of life in the 1920s and 1930s." The copy which was in my hands is now in Wolverhampton Archives.[307]

Eric Benton married Grace Agard Evans and worked at Cannon Iron Foundries. He lived in Penn, Wolverhampton, in the 1930s, and was an expert on Bilston and Battersea Enamels. In 1968 he read a paper on Bilston Enamels at the Victoria and Albert Museum.

––––––––––

At the time of our engagement Grace said she hoped I would soon meet her brother Eric. She was the youngest of five children; the others being Eric, Margaret, Burke, and Rodney. Eric and Margaret were born in the reign of Queen Victoria, and Eric was plainly a little sister's ideal of what an elder brother should be. Burke I knew quite well, and I was indebted to him for my first sight of his younger sister. He took me one day, in the autumn of 1921, home to tea, apologising as we walked for the smallness of the house, and the absence of servants. What size house he thought I came from I cannot imagine. He brought me to a very pleasant modern house standing in a garden of some size. His mother and Grace were on the point of leaving. They were going to a performance of "the School For Scandal" at the Church of England Seminary for the Daughters of Gentlemen in Calthorpe Road, Edgbaston. To do this they must walk down to the main road, wait for a tram to take them to Priory Road, and wait again for the rather infrequent inner Circle bus to take them to Edgbaston. Journeys in these days were incredibly tedious but we endured them. To reach my own home after leaving Burke I was to travel three miles by tram into Birmingham, walk across the centre of the city, travel twelve

––––––––––

[307] *Wolverhampton Archives,* L92BENp

miles by train, and finally walk nearly two miles home. I did this journey every day, in term-time twice.

I liked the look of Grace. She was then a school-girl with her hair in two plaits hanging down her back. An oval face, dark eyes, a high forehead, a vivacious, intelligent expression - in fact, quite a beauty. I remember thinking that was the kind of girl I would some day like to marry. I did marry her some seven and a half years later. But that is another story. Grace does not remember this first meeting.

Margaret, her elder sister, I did not meet until some time after Grace and I became engaged. We spent a week-end at Blackheath in the spring, I think, of 1928. She was not unlike Grace in appearance. The same oval face and delicate complexion, the same vivacity and intelligence. Margaret was a wonderful person, imaginative, impulsive, clever and very generous. One could say that life wore her out. But she lives again in her daughters, Margaret and Alison.

Burke's younger brother Rodney I met occasionally. He was not by nature a student. He regarded life with amusement, as something to be continually enjoyed, and manipulated, an idea which seemed to me as rather scandalous. But Grace said he was a very kind brother to her. There is a story in the family that one morning when he was very young he sprang out of bed crying, "Let's go and dwess in gorgeous wobes!" About fifty years later there came a day when he put on a gorgeous robe and his predecessor in the mayoralty of Felixstowe hung a massive gold chain about his neck.

I had still to meet the eldest son. I had heard a lot about him, of his schoolboys and his experiences in the war, and of his adventures in India. In the garage at Selly Park stood a large tin trunk, inscribed in white letters, "Capt. E. A. Evans. 40th Pathans". His mother told me that when he was a member of the School Corps he learned to play the bugle, and was entrusted on some great occasion with blowing a fanfare to welcome a visiting general. Eric may dispute this story. It has possibly undergone some changes. At the critical moment, he raised the bugle to his lips and blew, but no fanfare came out. Emotion prevented his mother from saying any more, so I never heard the end.

But he had no need of a bugle in India. Others blew bugles for him, and his younger sister was his trumpeter at home. I was impressed, and rather apprehensive. The man was obviously a pukka-sahib, and pukka-sahibs or sahibs of any kind, were rather outside my Black Country experience.

A point that certainly distinguished him from other pukka-sahibs was his fondness for English literature. He had even tried his hand at writing poetry. I was shown verses he had written at Cambridge, which seemed to me equal to anything that had come from the pen of the then poet-laureate. Grace admitted that this gift for poesy had shown itself in some curious ways. When he was up at Cambridge his mother was surprised to receive one day a parcel from "Home Chat," addressed to "Miss Angela Evans". It contained an elegant powder puff, the first prize to "Little Angela" in a competition for girls under the age of nine. I felt that with these varied talents, he could not be so inhuman after all.

He, on his part, had been rather perturbed by the news of our engagement. He spoke of "baby-snatching," and expressed a desire to meet the rough Staffordshire lad who had dared to propose to his little sister. His mother, of whom I was very fond, spoke up in defence of her daughter's young man. The fellow had a degree, and a job in London. He might be a bit unpolished, but he would perhaps improve with time.

I think our first meeting was in the autumn of 1927. My work was in laboratories at the back of No. 15, Grosvenor Place. It was arranged that Eric should walk up from Victoria at one o'clock, and I would come out to meet him. He appeared on time. Not very tall, of medium height, slightly built, but walking in a way which one immediately associated with the army. A military bearing? No, not at all; that would be both inaccurate and misleading. But the army does teach a man how to walk properly, how to carry himself, and this I think is invaluable. Boys of my generation, in grammar and public schools, spent a lot of time in the Officers' Training Corps, and went to camp every year. I myself endured three years in the Corps at school, and four at University. I was not good military material, and for a long time I avoided the examination for "Certificate A". But the Army promised on its sacred honour that in the event of another war, every man holding Certificate A would be given a commission. So eventually I made the effort and gained my certificate. One of the first acts of Mr. Chamberlain's government at the outbreak of war in 1939, was to repudiate the undertaking made by the army during the years of peace.

We approached each other. On the one side of the pavement was the soot-stained brick wall, capped by chevaux-de-frise, enclosing the gardens of Buckingham Palace. On the other, the stream of traffic pouring headlong towards Victoria. Innumerable buses, all with open tops, running on solid tyres, racing each other to the next stop. The idea, now obsolete, was to collect as many fares as possible! The most reckless were the "pirate" buses, ancient vehicles which rattled and swayed in a disconcerting fashion. We often boarded buses in motion. I once saw a young man race after a departing bus, catch it up, and swing to and fro by one hand from the back rail for some long, long moments before he found a foothold. The noise in Grosvenor Square was deafening. The hard tyres of the buses gave out a deep and penetrating roar. On the other side of the wall was a Palace garden. One morning I went up the grand staircase of No. 15 to the third floor to see the cashier. From his window I looked across the street and down into the royal pleasance. While I watched, a young man came into sight, clad in white sweater and running shorts. He was plodding along in a conscientious and joyless manner, and in a moment disappeared. After a pause, and some fifty yards behind, came a Sealyham terrier, muddy and tired, but undaunted. He was in attendance on the Prince of Wales, his master.

Both Eric and I were wearing trilby hats, I think, of soft felt, with silk bands. In those days we wore hats on all occasions. How could one salute a lady without a hat? In 1929 I began to wear a black bowler, for business and for church, and this was regulation head-wear until about 1936, when the black Anthony Eden came into favour. I think in 1927 Eric's hat was brown, mine was grey. And I was wearing a grey lounge suit, single-breasted, which had been made to measure by a new firm of tailors in Victoria Street, named Hector Powe. The price was five and a half guineas. They cut the suits very well, and used good worsted cloths. Their sewing and button-work were faultless. It was quite a presentable suit. But Eric's was much better. I think it was of a brown colour, and it had a certain distinction, the hall-mark of a first-class tailor. We wore complete suits, because it was unthinkable that a conventional man's jacket should not match his trousers, except when engaged in some kind of sport. It is true that young men in the city were beginning to turn up to business in wide grey flannel slacks, surmounted by very short navy jackets, double-breasted. And this fashion spread rapidly. But it was strictly controlled. One could not venture on variations of one's own. The London master-tailors told us exactly what we could wear.

And finally, both Eric and I carried gloves. Mine were of cream chamois leather. I never wore them. I think his were of brown kid, a military touch. And probably we both carried rolled umbrellas. I was relieved to see he lacked the special insignia of the hardboiled pukka-sahib, the eye glass and the silver cane. He was a sahib alright, but not, thank God, a pukka-sahib. His complexion was not of the regulation fiery red colour. In Hindustani, "pukka sahib" means "well-cooked boss", not "honourable gentleman", as so many gentlemen have fondly believed. The Sepoy had a sense of humour.

We met in 1927. The clouds of the great depression were already piling up along the horizon. Prices of clothes were to fall dramatically. Hector Powe came down to five guineas, then to four and a half, finally to four guineas. But that was more than many men could afford. A firm appeared calling themselves the "Fifty Shilling Tailors," and was highly successful until another came forward with the slogan, "If you are paying fifty shillings for your Five Guinea Suit you are paying Seven and Sixpence too much!" When Grace and I were married in 1929, goods of all kinds were cheaper than they had ever been before, or ever will be again. One could buy a good house for five hundred pounds, a new car for a hundred and fifty. We bought all our table silver, thirty-four pieces of best quality electro-plate of nickel silver, guaranteed for twenty years, for seven pounds, twelve shillings.

We introduced ourselves. Eric did most of the talking. He was very kind, and gave me no feeling that I was under examination. His voice was educated and quiet, and had no trace of a Birmingham accent. No trace at all? Perhaps that's not quite true. Both he and Grace pronounce "cross" to rhyme with "horse," not "hoss" and this, I think, comes from Birmingham. I had an aunt who lived all her life there and showed a tendency to change some of the vowel sounds in a marked degree. She pronounced "pear" almost like "purr," and "fair" like "fur". On the other hand Eric must have winced when I said "brass," "class," and "pass," to rhyme with "lass"' not "farce". I have changed, of course. Nearly everyone has changed to the long vowels. Sometimes it is ridiculous, as when an advertiser on television speaks of the "garce industry," and praises the "larther" of a detergent. Sir Winston Churchill, let it be remembered to his honour and renown, said "brass" and "bath" to the end of his days. His English was as remarkable as his French

We walked down through Grosvenor Gardens into the maelstrom of Victoria. I pointed out the house of Lord Birkenhead, where one often saw his car standing, an open primrose-yellow

Rolls. I once caught a glimpse of the noble lord being driven down Grosvenor Place. He was lying in the back with his mouth open, and appeared to be drunk.

The choice of a restaurant for lunch was difficult. Usually I went to an A.B.C. in Victoria Street, but I couldn't imagine Eric there. The Pullman Hall at the station would be far too expensive. We went to a respectable eating-place near the station, the name of which I cannot recall. The prices on the menu gave me an unpleasant shock. I usually allowed myself one shilling for lunch, but today was clearly an occasion for extravagance. Eric too seemed a little concerned about the cost, and chose "galantine of chicken". I ordered the same, and it was very good. We drank water with our meal. It would not have occurred to us to drink anything else. Eric had not suggested an aperitif beforehand, nor would I have known what to ask for if he had, In looking back it is astonishing to remember how seldom anyone in our world drank anything alcoholic. An insurance agent about this time recorded my drinking habits as, "a glass of wine at Christmas". And that was an exaggeration.

We talked about all sorts of things and found a common interest in the Arthurian legends. I had recently brought from home, "The High History of the Holy Grail," in Sebastian Evan's translation. It was my father's copy. I was captured by its atmosphere of mystery, beauty, and light-hearted adventure. Imagine a world where people said in parting, "May God give you good adventure!" Some passages remain in the memory. "One morning, early, Percival heard a bell sound loud and clear without the manor toward the sea." Every one of us, at some time in our life, has heard a bell sound loud and clear. (I do not mean the kind of bell that Eric and Freda once heard at Ridley. That ghostly visitant was, I think, caused by mice in the rafters falling on the bell-wires). I had also discovered Bedier's, "Le Roman de Tristan et Iseut". What lyrical possibilities there are in French prose. It was an expedition into another world. Eric talked about Malory, whose prose style he greatly admired.

The meal ended all too soon, and the bill came - eight shillings and sixpence! Eric looked startled. I reached for the few shillings in my pocket. But he said, "No, leave this to me. You can do it next time". I watched him count out this tremendous sum, in good minted coins of solid silver, with a generous tip for the waitress. We walked back up Grosvenor Place, and showed him over the laboratories. He looked at the strange instruments with the amused reverence that disciples of the humanities always betray when brought face to face with the tolls of modern science. And we parted, promising to have another lunch before long. Tiffin, I should have said.

We did meet again, before his marriage, but exactly when I cannot determine. I did not dare to go to the restaurant where we had eaten before. I chose a brash new place, that promised good food at moderate prices. It was a mistake. As we went in, being met with a blast of hot air and an incredible amount of noise, Eric said: "Oh, my God!" I cannot remember what we ate, but it was edible. The bill came to six shillings. I have had a feeling ever since that I owe Eric half-a-crown.

The following year "Eryk" and Freda were married in London. I had been persuaded to accept the new and revolting spelling of his name. The reception was at Caxton Hall. I could not leave work until one o'clock, and by then the festivities were largely over, the speeches

322

made, the toasts drunk, and the bride and bridegroom had departed. Grace, looking very nice, found me some food, and a glass of champagne. What a foul drink that is! I was rather shocked at the tearful hilarity of a number of the old ladies present. But they were all very happy.

At this time, I occasionally sent flowers by post to Grace from London, buying them at a shop in Victoria called Moyses Stevens. It was a very superior place, with the arms of four royal houses emblazoned on the window panes. Once when I was buying some five shillings' worth, hoping that I would be given one of their beautiful gold decorated felt-covered boxes, a young man came in, to whom the whole establishment gave immediate attention. He was rather strikingly and expensively dressed, with a light-coloured felt hat on the side of his head, and he carried a gold-topped cane. He spoke smilingly to the manageress, who called up masses of blooms of superb size and beauty. When the huge bouquet had been put together, he asked casually for the bill. "Thirty-three shillings, sir," "Thank you, please deliver it to this address, this afternoon, with this card." It was, of course, Ivor Novello. Some years later, I saw him at Drury Lane in a show in the course of which an earthquake brought down all the buildings before our eyes. Ivor and the heroine (Dorothy something) were darting about the stage while great masses of masonry fell all around them. They sang delightfully, in sheer enjoyment of life. It was infectious.

I cannot remember when it was that I went with Grace to see Eryk ordained or priested. Probably in the summer of 1928, for I don't think Grace and I were married. After the service Eryk disappeared, to be talked to by the Bishop, and Freda led us out into the country and chose a field where we had a sumptuous lunch. I remember Freda looking very young and beautiful and elegant in a light grey tailor-made, very well cut, with some frilly white stuff at the neck. Her hair was pale gold and shone in the sunshine. It was cut short, like Grace's, bobbed or shingled I suppose we called it, and lay close against her head. Her mother, who was a dear, was helping to pass things around. There were two identical jars, one containing mayonnaise, the other lemon cheese. She unscrewed both and presently started to replace the tops. Freda cried: "No, not that one!" Her mother did not hear. Freda gave a tiny anguished cry: "Now they will be mixed for ever!" A moment later she laughed. Strange that that is all I remember of what must have been a very happy day.

I notice that Eryk was at school with Eric Baker, who later became the Chairman of the Wesleyan Congress (or Union, or whatever they call it). I have met him. About ten years ago the Bishop of Coventry - Cuthbert Bardesley, the nephew of old Bishop Bardesley who ordained Eryk - asked me to speak at a mass meeting of Wesleyans in their huge hall at Coventry. Shortly afterwards there was a great get-together of Anglicans and Wesleyans in the same place. The Bishop was there, with Simon Phipps and Edward Patey, and many others, but the one to whom everyone showed great respect and affection was this nice old boy, Dr. Baker. I remember that a colleague of his was asked to lead us in prayer, and I was startled to hear him begin, in a deep booming voice: "May the God of Abraham, of Isaac, and of Jacob ..." Perhaps it wasn't as archaic as it sounded, for some of the leading tradesmen of Coventry bore those names. But I doubt if they were present.

Two years after the picnic, 1930, Grace and I were now married, and we had acquired a little rough-haired terrier named Benkin. He had many virtues, but no intelligence. Alas, we took him with us to visit Eryk and Freda at Shrewsbury. They had such a nice house called, "Four Winds," with lots of new white paint. I remember that Freda was coaching Eryk in the singing of part of the church service, and I marvelled that anyone could master it, not knowing that one day I would have to do it myself

In the evening, Benkin had been put out of doors, and presently barked to come in. Without waiting for a reply he scrabbled at the beautiful white paint with ferocious violence. Eryke rushed to the door. If I heard him correctly, the curate of St Mary's said, in passing: "That damn dog will have the bloody door down in a minute". The provocation was extreme.

One could write a book about the language of the clergy. It was Eryk who taught Grace the refrain of a famous army marching song:

It's the rich wot gets the pleasure
It's the poor wot gets the blime
It's the sime the wide world over
Ain't it a bleeding shime?

- words which have all the pathos of great poetry. But - and this is the thought that has been nagging at my mind - can Eryk have known the verses that preceded the chorus? And was it he who taught Grace another fragment of English literature?
"The waiter bawled, down through the hall,
You can't have bread, with one fish ba-aw-all!"

 Now I don't know the verses of that one, and I wouldn't want to know.

It was on the advice and urging of Eryk and Freda that we made our first experiment in camping, in 1932. Eryk lent us his own tent, a beautiful one, of pure silk, a real pukka-sahib's tent. He pointed out a repair to the fabric, near to the front, and to some traces of burn. He had been using the Primus, and it appeared to have gone out so he poured methylated spirits over it. Eryk escaped from the conflagration with the loss of part of his eye-brows. Grace says that Eryk advised her to use the khaki blankets, "because they didn't get dirty." A useful hint from the Afghan War.

We enjoyed that first camp, at Porth Ceiriad, enormously. We returned the tent and bought our own. The next year Eryk joined us with Hilary at our camp near Rhiw, on Hell's Mouth. Those were idyllic days. A line of geese appeared every morning from the nearby farm, in military file, perfectly spaced. One evening we had roast goose for supper, cooked in the farmhouse kitchen, and carried across the fields with much shouting to the lamp-lit tents. The next morning the line of geese appeared again, in perfect file, but with a gap. Number 5 had not answered Reveille. We did not ask again for roast goose.

What a holiday that was! In memory, the sun always shone, the sky was blue, the sea inviting and warm. There was no rain, no wind, no storm. Like a sundial, I record only the happiest hours. But it was when we were there that we had news of the death of Janet, Burke and Dorothy's little daughter.

In 1938, Eryk and Freda joined us at Duingt, on the Lake of Annecy. Presently we crossed the lake and stayed at the Abbaye at Talloires. It was high summer. Time seemed to stand still. Barely three months before Munich, we were yet in the carefree world of the Thirties, which we shall never see again. And here I think I should correct Eryk's idea of what I was doing two years later. It is true that I was with the Admiralty, but I didn't invent anything. I worked on the development of ideas which had reached experimental form in peace-time. His Majesty's anti submarine establishment at Portland, called by courtesy, H.M.S. "Osprey", was one of the few Service departments which were ready with new methods and new instruments when war broke out. I went on many sea trials and I was often seasick, but I was fortunate that it never prevented me from doing what we had set out to do. After twenty-four hours, even in the roughest weather, one had the strange experience of losing seasickness altogether. Those whose knowledge of the sea is limited to ocean liners and cross-channel steamers, can have no idea of the violence of the motion of a small ship in an Atlantic storm. It affected even hardened seamen. Picked crews were necessary on the M.L.'s and M.T.B's. But I am digressing.

The holiday at Duingt and Talloires remains as a very bright chapter in our book of memories. A lot of laughter, a great deal of fun. One morning we went down to bathe in the lake, which was very cold. An elderly couple regarded us with some amusement. Eryk turned to them and cried: "Nous sommes les heros!" Now the French aspirate is peculiar, and its elision idiomatic. the good souls looked puzzled. "Comment? Les aviateurs?' they asked. The light dawned. "Ah, bon, les heros."

We ended our stay at Duingt with an adventure. It was Eryk who first put forward the idea that before we left we should row all the way to Annecy, some seven miles, and back, in an afternoon. He persuaded us to do it, and on the hottest day of the summer, we set out in an open boat, after a light lunch, to row to Annecy. The girls sheltered under a large umbrella in the stern, but the air was very still, and the heat was appalling. We reached Annecy, tied up our boat, and found a shady place for tea. It was plain that Grace was suffering severely from the heat. But she insisted on our staying and, with some misgivings, we put her on the bus to Duingt. We walked about the town sharing the feeling that sailors must enjoy when landing on a foreign shore, and finally we adjourned to a good restaurant where we ate a leisurely and excellent dinner, and fortified our spirits for the return with some very good wine. The task in front of us nor seemed ridiculously easy. "Row Back! A bagatelle! Nothing to it."

We should have left earlier. The sun was low when we cast off from Annecy, and half a mile out it suddenly sank behind the mountains and darkness came down with extraordinary swiftness. It was incredible how dark it was on the water. we could see nothing, not even each other, only a far-distant light, the Hotel Pavilion des Fleurs at Menton St. Bernard, on which point we steered. Every now and then a huge shape would loom up out of the blackness and pass close to port or starboard, silently, and with menace. If we had hit one - "quelle marmelade," as Tartarin used to say! But we didn't, and we made good progress on the strength of that good wine, and eventually landed at Menton at the very moment when the last waiter was about to put out the lights. We asked for Cognac. He brought it in a great leather-covered stone jar. "Ah," said Eryk, "Ca suffit!" Immensely refreshed and slightly gay, we made nothing of the last two miles, which involved crossing the lake and passing over the spot where the dark water goes down to more than one hundred feet below. On this last lap, Freda insisted on being one of the two who rowed. She said afterwards that it was eerie sitting in the stern. She could not see us, and she was sure that if she had fallen into the water we would never have noticed. This might have been true because we couldn't see her and we were engaged in reciting, rather loudly, the epic of the "Jabberwock". And so, like Christian, we passed over, and all the lamps were lit to welcome us on the other side. It was very late. The proprietaire himself was on the jetty. There had been some concern for our safety. Grace was in bed, not at all well, and Aunt Jean and Archie had arrived.

There I will end. As Eryk said, "Ca suffit".

INDEX
INDEX

INDEX

INDEX

INDEX

INDEX

Sunbeam Motors 143, 149ff
Sunday School 153, 163, 164, 252, 303
Swancote 6, 29, 70, 76, 82, 235, 285
Swancote, Roger of 25, 30, 31, 32
Swancote, Thomas of 30, 31
Syner, James 77
Tailby, Norman 145
Talbot, George 287ff
Talbot, Gilbert 8
Talbot, John 2, 45, 288, 309
Talbot, Milton 76
Talbot, Thomas 290
Talbot, Sharrington 8
Talbot hunting dog 45
Tarrant, Harry 277
Tarrant, Isaac 69, 277
Taylor, Charlie 304
Taylor, Herbert 140, 141
Taylor, John 309
Taylor, Mary 194
Taylor, Robert 281
Taylor, Widow 175
Taylor, William 13
Taylors of Loughborough 96
Telephone 96, 163, 222
Tennis 71, 88, 120, 195, 216
Tenter's Field 8, 9
Teverell, Richard 8
Thatcher, William 76, 277
The Batch 60, 101, 179, 250, 251, 252, 290
The Hopes 70
The Limbutts 70, 153ff
The Lowe 8, 12, 71, 90, 92, 234, 293
The Tyte 117, 135, 157, 162
The Walls, Hilton 58, 185
Theodore, John Edwin 82
Third Army 220ff
Thomas, Ann 212ff
Thomas, Elizabeth 258
Thomas, John 9
Thomas, Miss 161
Thomas, Samuel 70
Thomas, Stephen 110

Thomas, William 212
Thomason 41, 130, 290
Thompson, Mr & Mrs James 194
Thomson, Doris 104, 196
Thomson, Ida 104
Thomson, Preb. Tom 100ff, 196
Thornett, Ray 113
Thornley, Jennifer 36
Thornley, John 36
Thrashing Box 15, 16, 21
Tildesley, Reginald 145
Timmins, Edward 70
Tithes 2, 185, 270, 288, 290
Titterstone Clee 154, 191
Togge, Richard 186
Togge, Thomas 186
Togge, William 186
Toll Collector 54
Toll Gate 201
Toll House 50, 231, 241, 248
Tomlinson family 212ff
Tomlinson, Geoff 212ff
Tong 191, 279
Torrens, James 147, 148
Totherick, Dr. 261
Toward, Reginald 32
Toward, William 32
Tounsende, Alice at, of Alvescote 32
Townesend, of Allscott 167
Townshend, Turnip 2
Toy 127, 130
Tracey, Eileen 230ff
Tracey, John 231
Tractor 15, 17, 19, 21, 153, 180, 253
Trumper, William 127, 128
Trysell, John 167
Trysull 148, 241, 256
Tub Row 159ff, 192
Tuckley, Percy 55
Turley, Adrian and Neil 220
Turner family of Clee St Margaret 170
Turner, Frank 86, 215, 277, 298
Turner, Jean 88

Printed in Great Britain
by Amazon